# DNS on Windows NT

# DNS on Windows NT

Paul Albitz, Matt Larson, and Cricket Liu

O'REILLY™

Beijing · Cambridge · Köln · Paris · Sebastopol · Taipei · Tokyo

## DNS on Windows NT

by Paul Albitz, Matt Larson, and Cricket Liu

Copyright © 1998 O'Reilly & Associates, Inc. All rights reserved.
Printed in the United States of America.

Portions of this book previously appeared in *DNS and BIND, 3rd Edition*,
Copyright © 1998 O'Reilly & Associates, Inc.

Published by O'Reilly & Associates, Inc., 101 Morris Street, Sebastopol, CA 95472.

**Editor:** Mike Loukides

**Production Editor:** Paula Carroll

**Editorial and Production Services:** Nancy Crumpton

**Printing History:**

        October 1998:     First Edition

ISBN: 1-56592-511-4

# Table of Contents

# *Preface*

You may not know much about the Domain Name System—yet—but whenever you use the Internet, you use DNS. Every time you send electronic mail or surf the World Wide Web, you rely on the Domain Name System.

You see, while you, as a human being, prefer to remember the names of computers, computers like to address each other by number. On an internet, that number is 32 bits long, or between zero and four billion or so.* That's easy for a computer to remember because computers have lots of memory ideal for storing numbers, but it isn't nearly as easy for us humans. Pick ten phone numbers out of the phone book at random, and then try to remember them. Not easy? Now flip to the front of the book, and attach random area codes to the phone numbers. That's about how difficult it would be to remember ten arbitrary internet addresses.

This is part of the reason we need the Domain Name System. DNS handles mapping between host names, which we humans find convenient, and internet addresses, which computers deal with. In fact, DNS is the standard mechanism on the Internet for advertising and accessing all kinds of information about hosts, not just addresses. And DNS is used by virtually all internetworking software, including electronic mail, remote terminal programs such as *telnet*, file transfer programs such as *ftp*, and web browsers such as Netscape's Navigator and Microsoft's Internet Explorer.

Another important feature of DNS is that it makes host information available all over the Internet. Keeping information about hosts in a formatted file on a single computer only helps users on that computer. DNS provides a means of retrieving information remotely, from anywhere on the network.

---

* And, with IP Version 6, it's soon to be a whopping 128 bits long, or between zero and a decimal number with 39 digits.

More than that, DNS lets you distribute the management of host information among many sites and organizations. You don't need to submit your data to some central site or periodically retrieve copies of the "master" database. You simply make sure your section, called a *zone*, is up to date on your name servers. Your name servers make your zone's data available to all the other name servers on the network.

Because the database is distributed, the system also needs the ability to locate the data you're looking for by searching a number of possible locations. The Domain Name System gives name servers the intelligence to navigate through the database and find data in any zone.

Of course, DNS does have a few problems. For example, the system allows more than one name server to store the same data about a zone, for redundancy's sake. But inconsistencies can crop up between copies of the zone data.

But the worst problem with DNS is that despite its widespread use on the Internet, there's really very little documentation about managing and maintaining it. Most administrators on the Internet make do with the documentation their vendors see fit to provide, and with whatever they can glean from following the Internet mailing lists and Usenet newsgroups on the subject.

This lack of documentation means that the understanding of an enormously important internet service—one of the linchpins of today's Internet—is either handed down from administrator to administrator like a closely guarded family recipe, or relearned repeatedly by isolated programmers and engineers. New administrators of domains suffer through the same mistakes made by countless others.

Our aim with this book is to help remedy this situation. We realize that not all of you have the time or the desire to become DNS experts. Most of you, after all, have plenty to do besides managing a domain or a name server: system administration, network engineering, or software development. It takes an awfully big institution to devote a whole person to DNS. We'll try to give you enough information to allow you to do what you need to do, whether that's running a small domain or managing a multinational monstrosity, tending a single name server or shepherding a hundred of them. Read as much as you need to know now, and come back later if you need to know more.

DNS is a big topic—big enough to require two authors, anyway—but we've tried to present it as sensibly and understandably as possible. The first two chapters give you a good theoretical overview and enough practical information to get by, and later chapters fill in the nitty-gritty details. We provide a road map up front, to suggest a path through the book appropriate for your job or interest.

When we talk about actual DNS software, we'll concentrate on the Microsoft DNS Server, which is a popular implementation of the DNS specs included in Windows NT Server 4.0 and later. We've tried to distill our experience in managing and maintaining a domain into this book—a domain, incidentally, that is one of the largest on the Internet. (We don't mean to brag, but we can use the credibility.) Where possible, we've included the real programs that we use in administration, many of them rewritten into Perl for speed and efficiency.

We hope that this book will help you get acquainted with DNS on NT if you're just starting out, let you refine your understanding if you're already familiar with DNS, and provide valuable insight and experience even if you know 'em like the back of your hand.

## *Versions*

This book deals with DNS servers that run on Windows NT Server Version 4.0, particularly the Microsoft DNS Server. Since the version of the Microsoft DNS Server that shipped with NT Server 4.0 had quite a few bugs in it, we concentrate on the version Microsoft released after Service Pack 3, as a hotfix.* We will also occasionally mention other DNS servers that run on NT, especially ports of BIND, a popular implementation of the DNS specifications. However, if you need a book on BIND, we suggest this book's sister edition, *DNS and BIND*. This book is essentially a Windows NT edition of *DNS and BIND*.

We use *nslookup*, a name server utility program, a great deal in our examples. The version of *nslookup* we use is the one shipped with Windows NT Server 4.0. Other versions of *nslookup* provide similar functionality to that in the NT *nslookup*. We have tried to use commands common to most *nslookup*s in our examples; when this was not possible, we tried to note it.

## *Organization*

This book is organized, more or less, to follow the evolution of a domain and a domain administrator. Chapters 1 and 2 discuss Domain Name System theory. Chapters 3 through 6 help you to decide whether to set up your own domain, and then describe how to go about it, should you choose to. The middle chapters, 7 through 10, describe how to maintain your domain, how to configure hosts to use your name server, how to plan for the growth of your domain, and how to create subdomains. The last chapters, 11 through 13, deal with common problems and troubleshooting tools.

---

* For details on how to get this server, see Chapter 3, *Where Do I Start?*

Here's a more detailed, chapter-by-chapter breakdown:

- Chapter 1, *Background*, provides a little historical perspective, discusses the problems that motivated the development of DNS, and then presents an overview of DNS theory.

- Chapter 2, *How Does DNS Work?*, goes over DNS theory in more detail, including the DNS name space, domains, and name servers. We also introduce important concepts like name resolution and caching.

- Chapter 3, *Where Do I Start?*, covers how to choose and acquire your DNS software if you don't already have it, and what to do with it once you've got it: how to figure out what your domain name should be, and how to contact the organization that can delegate your domain to you.

- Chapter 4, *Setting Up the Microsoft DNS Server*, details how to set up your first two name servers, including creating your name server database, starting up your name servers, and checking their operation.

- Chapter 5, *DNS and Electronic Mail*, deals with DNS's MX record, which allows administrators to specify alternate hosts to handle a given destination's mail. The chapter covers mail routing strategies for a wide variety of networks and hosts, including networks with security firewalls and hosts without direct Internet connectivity.

- Chapter 6, *Configuring Hosts*, explains how to configure a Windows resolver.

- Chapter 7, *Maintaining the Microsoft DNS Server*, describes the periodic maintenance administrators must perform to keep their domains running smoothly, like checking name server health and authority.

- Chapter 8, *Growing Your Domain*, covers how to plan for the growth and evolution of your domain, including how to get big and how to plan for moves and outages.

- Chapter 9, *Parenting*, explores the joys of becoming a parent domain. We explain when to become a parent (create subdomains), what to call your children, how to create them (!), and how to watch over them.

- Chapter 10, *Advanced Features and Security*, goes over less often used name server configuration options that can help you tune your name server's operation, secure your name server, and ease administration.

- Chapter 11, *nslookup*, shows the ins and outs of the most popular tool for doing DNS debugging, including techniques for digging obscure information out of remote name servers.

- Chapter 12, *Troubleshooting DNS*, covers many common DNS problems and their solutions and then describes a number of less common, harder-to-diagnose scenarios.

- Chapter 13, *Miscellaneous*, ties up all the loose ends. We cover DNS wildcarding, special configurations for networks that connect to the Internet through firewalls, hosts and networks with intermittent Internet connectivity via dialup, network name encoding, and new, experimental record types.

- Appendix A, *DNS Message Format and Resource Records*, contains a byte-by-byte breakdown of the formats used in DNS queries and responses, as well as a comprehensive list of the currently defined resource record types.

- Appendix B, *Installing the DNS Server from CD-ROM*, describes how to load the Microsoft DNS Server from the Windows NT CD-ROM.

- Appendix C, *Converting from BIND to the Microsoft DNS Server*, covers migrating from an existing BIND 4 name server to the Microsoft DNS Server.

- Appendix D, *Top-Level Domains*, lists the current top-level domains in the Internet's domain name space.

- Appendix E, *Domain Registration Form*, is the Network Information Center's current form for requesting the establishment of a subdomain of an InterNIC-run domain.

- Appendix F, *in-addr.arpa Registration Form*, is the American Registry for Internet Numbers' current form for requesting the establishment of a subdomain of the *in-addr.arpa* domain.

- Appendix G, *Microsoft DNS Server Registry Settings*, describes how to use the Windows NT Registry to customize the DNS Server's operation.

# *Audience*

This book is intended primarily for Windows NT system administrators who manage a domain and one or more name servers, but it also includes material for network engineers, postmasters, and others. Not all of the book's chapters will be equally interesting to a diverse audience, though, and you don't want to wade through thirteen chapters to find the information pertinent to your job. We hope this road map will help you plot your way through the book.

*System administrators setting up their first domain* should read Chapters 1 and 2 for DNS theory, Chapter 3 for information on getting started and selecting a good domain name, and then Chapters 4 and 5 to learn how to set up a domain for the first time. Chapter 6 explains how to configure hosts to use the new name servers. Soon after, they should read Chapter 7, which explains how to "flesh out" their domain implementation by setting up additional name servers and adding data. Then, Chapters 11 and 12 describe troubleshooting tools and techniques.

*Experienced administrators* could benefit from reading Chapter 6 to learn how to configure DNS resolvers on different hosts and Chapter 7 for information on maintaining their domains. Chapter 8 contains instructions on how to plan for a domain's growth and evolution, which should be especially valuable to administrators of large domains. Chapter 9 explains parenting—creating subdomains—which is *de rigueur* reading for those considering the big move. Chapter 10 covers security features of the Microsoft DNS Server, many of which may be very useful for experienced administrators. Chapters 11 and 12 describe tools and techniques for troubleshooting, which even advanced administrators may find worth reading.

*System administrators on networks without full Internet connectivity* should read Chapter 5 to learn how to configure mail on such networks and Chapter 13 to learn how to set up an independent DNS infrastructure.

*Network administrators not directly responsible for a domain* should still read Chapters 1 and 2 for DNS theory, then Chapter 11 to learn how to use *nslookup*, plus Chapter 12 for troubleshooting tactics.

*Postmasters* should read Chapters 1 and 2 for DNS theory and then Chapter 5 to find out how DNS and electronic mail coexist. Chapter 11, which describes *nslookup*, will also help postmasters grub mail routing information out of the domain name space.

*Interested users* can read Chapters 1 and 2 for DNS theory and then whatever else they like!

Note that we assume you're familiar with basic NT system administration and TCP/IP networking. We don't assume you have any other specialized knowledge, though. When we introduce a new term or concept, we'll do our best to define or explain it. Whenever possible, we'll use analogies from NT (and from the real world) to help you understand.

## Obtaining the Example Programs

The example programs in this book are available electronically via *ftp* from the URLs:

> *ftp://ftp.uu.net/published/oreilly/nutshell/dns.nt/dns.zip*
> *ftp://ftp.ora.com/published/oreilly/nutshell/dns.nt/dns.zip*

In either case, extract the files from the archive using WinZip by typing:

```
C:\temp> winzip dns.zip
```

If WinZip is not available on your system, get a copy from *http://www.winzip.com/*.

If you cannot get the examples directly over the Internet but can send and receive email, you can use *ftpmail* to get them. For help using *ftpmail*, send email to *ftp-mail@online.ora.com* with no subject and the single word "help" in the body.

## Conventions Used in This Book

We use the following font and format conventions for NT commands, utilities, and system calls:

- Excerpts from scripts or configuration files are shown in a constant width font:

```
if (-x /winnt/system32/dns.exe )
{
    system( /winnt/system32/dns.exe );
}
```

- Sample interactive sessions, showing command-line input and corresponding output, are shown in a constant width font, with user-supplied input in bold:

```
C\> more <\winnt\system32\drivers\etc\hosts
# Copyright (c) 1993-1995 Microsoft Corp.
#
# This is a sample HOSTS file used by Microsoft TCP/IP for Windows NT.
#
```

- Command lines, when they appear exactly as a user would type them, are printed in italic when they appear in the body of a paragraph. For example: run *dir* to list the files in a directory.

- Domain names are also printed in italic when they appear within a paragraph.

- NT commands (when mentioned in passing and not as part of a command line) appear italicized. For example: to find more information on *nslookup*, a user could consult the Windows help system.

- Filenames and directory paths are printed in italic; for example: the NT DNS Server's boot file is usually *%ServerRoot%\Dns\boot*.

## Quotations

The Lewis Carroll quotations that begin each chapter are from the Millennium Fulcrum Edition 2.9 of the Project Gutenberg electronic text of *Alice's Adventures in Wonderland* and *Through the Looking-Glass*. Quotations in Chapters 1, 2, 5, 6, 8, and 13 are from *Alice's Adventures in Wonderland*, and those in Chapters 3, 4, 7, 9, 11, and 12 are from *Through the Looking-Glass*.

# *Acknowledgments*

The authors would like to thank their technical reviewers, Jon Forrest and David Blank-Edelman, for their invaluable contributions to this book.

Cricket would like to thank his wife, Paige, for her support during the writing of this book. Thanks also to Jim Eagen, Maria Evans, Kirk Johnson, and Heather Walters, whose company makes the trip worthwhile, and to Denver's Imperial Flyers, for providing occasional but much-needed relief from writing.

Matt would like to thank his wife, Sonja, for her support and unflagging patience, and Cricket for asking him to help with this book.

We would also like to thank the folks at O'Reilly & Associates for their hard work and patience. Credit is especially due our editor, Mike Loukides.

# 1

# Background

*The White Rabbit put on his spectacles. "Where shall I begin, please your Majesty?" he asked.*

*"Begin at the beginning," the King said, very gravely, "and go on till you come to the end: then stop."*

It's important to know a little ARPANET history to understand the Domain Name System (DNS). DNS was developed to address particular problems on the ARPANET, and the Internet—a descendant of the ARPANET—remains its main user.

If you've been using the Internet for years, you can probably skip this chapter. If you haven't, we hope it'll give you enough background to understand what motivated the development of DNS.

## A (Very) Brief History of the Internet

In the late 1960s, the U.S. Department of Defense's Advanced Research Projects Agency, ARPA (later DARPA), began funding an experimental wide area computer network, called the ARPANET, that connected important research organizations in the U.S. The original goal of the ARPANET was to allow government contractors to share expensive or scarce computing resources. From the beginning, however, users of the ARPANET also used the network for collaboration. This collaboration ranged from sharing files and software and exchanging electronic mail—now commonplace—to joint development and research using shared remote computers.

The TCP/IP (Transmission Control Protocol/Internet Protocol) protocol suite was developed in the early 1980s and quickly became the standard host networking protocol on the ARPANET. The inclusion of the protocol suite in the University of California at Berkeley's popular BSD UNIX operating system was instrumental in democratizing internetworking. BSD UNIX was virtually free to universities. This meant that internetworking—and ARPANET connectivity—were suddenly available cheaply to many more organizations than were previously attached to the ARPANET. Many of the computers being connected to the ARPANET were being connected to local networks, too, and very shortly the other computers on the local networks were communicating via the ARPANET as well.

The network grew from a handful of hosts to a network of tens of thousands of hosts. The original ARPANET became the backbone of a confederation of local and regional networks based on TCP/IP, called the *Internet*.

In 1988, however, DARPA decided the experiment was over. The Department of Defense began dismantling the ARPANET. Another network, funded by the National Science Foundation and called the *NSFNET*, replaced the ARPANET as the backbone of the Internet.

Even more recently, in the spring of 1995, the Internet made a transition from using the publicly funded NSFNET as a backbone to using multiple commercial backbones, run by long-distance carriers like MCI and Sprint, and long-time commercial internetworking players like PSINet and UUNet.

Today, the Internet connects millions of hosts around the world. In fact, a significant proportion of the non-PC computers in the world is connected to the Internet. Some of the new commercial backbones can carry a volume of 622 megabits per second, over ten thousand times the bandwidth of the original ARPANET. Tens of millions of people use the network daily for communication and collaboration.

# On the Internet and Internets

A word on *the Internet* and on *internets*, in general, is in order. In print, the difference between the two seems slight: one is always capitalized, one isn't. The distinction between their meanings, however, is significant. The *Internet*, with a capital *I*, refers to the network that began its life as the ARPANET and continues today as, roughly, the confederation of all TCP/IP networks directly or indirectly connected to commercial U.S. backbones. Seen close up, it's actually quite a few different networks—commercial TCP/IP backbones, regional TCP/IP networks, corporate and U.S. government TCP/IP networks, and TCP/IP networks in other countries—interconnected by high-speed digital circuits.

A lowercase *internet*, on the other hand, is simply any network made up of multiple smaller networks using the same internetworking protocols. An internet (little *i*) isn't necessarily connected to the Internet (big *I*), nor does it necessarily use TCP/IP as its internetworking protocol. There are isolated corporate internets, and there are Xerox XNS-based internets and DECnet-based internets.

The new term *intranet* is really just a marketing term for a TCP/IP-based little *i* internet, used to emphasize the use of technologies developed and introduced on the Internet within a company's internal corporate network. An *extranet*, on the other hand, is an internet that connects partner companies or a company to its distributors, suppliers and customers.

# The History of the Domain Name System

Through the 1970s, the ARPANET was a small, friendly community of a few hundred hosts. A single file, *HOSTS.TXT*, contained all the information you needed to know about those hosts: it held a name-to-address mapping for every host connected to the ARPANET. The familiar UNIX host table, */etc/hosts*, was compiled from *HOSTS.TXT* (mostly by deleting fields UNIX didn't use).

*HOSTS.TXT* was maintained by SRI's Network Information Center (dubbed "the NIC") and distributed from a single host, SRI-NIC.* ARPANET administrators typically emailed their changes to the NIC and periodically ftp'd to SRI-NIC and grabbed the current *HOSTS.TXT*. Their changes were compiled into a new *HOSTS.TXT* once or twice a week. As the ARPANET grew, however, this scheme became unworkable. The size of *HOSTS.TXT* grew in proportion to the growth in the number of ARPANET hosts. Moreover, the traffic generated by the update process increased even faster: every additional host meant not only another line in *HOSTS.TXT*, but potentially another host updating from SRI-NIC.

And when the ARPANET moved to the TCP/IP protocols, the population of the network exploded. Now there was a host of problems with *HOSTS.TXT*:

*Traffic and load*
> The toll on SRI-NIC, in terms of the network traffic and processor load involved in distributing the file, was becoming unbearable.

*Name collisions*
> No two hosts in *HOSTS.TXT* could have the same name. However, while the NIC could assign addresses in a way that guaranteed uniqueness, it had no authority over host names. There was nothing to prevent someone from adding a host with a conflicting name and breaking the whole scheme. Someone adding a host with the same name as a major mail hub, for example, could disrupt mail service to much of the ARPANET.

*Consistency*
> Maintaining consistency of the file across an expanding network became harder and harder. By the time a new *HOSTS.TXT* could reach the farthest shores of the enlarged ARPANET, a host across the network had changed addresses, or a new host had sprung up that users wanted to reach.

---

* SRI is the Stanford Research Institute in Menlo Park, California. SRI conducts research into many different areas, including computer networking.

The essential problem was that the *HOSTS.TXT* mechanism didn't scale well. Ironically, the success of the ARPANET as an experiment led to the failure and obsolescence of *HOSTS.TXT.*

The ARPANET's governing bodies chartered an investigation into a successor for *HOSTS.TXT.* Their goal was to create a system that solved the problems inherent in a unified host table system. The new system should allow local administration of data, yet make that data globally available. The decentralization of administration would eliminate the single-host bottleneck and relieve the traffic problem. And local management would make the task of keeping data up to date much easier. It should use a hierarchical name space to name hosts. This would ensure the uniqueness of names.

Paul Mockapetris, then of USC's Information Sciences Institute, was responsible for designing the architecture of the new system. In 1984, he released RFCs 882 and 883, which describe the Domain Name System, or DNS. These RFCs were superseded by RFCs 1034 and 1035, the current specifications of the Domain Name System.* RFCs 1034 and 1035 have now been augmented by many other RFCs, which describe potential DNS security problems, implementation problems, administrative gotchas, mechanisms for dynamically updating name servers and for securing domain data, and more.

# *The Domain Name System, in a Nutshell*

The Domain Name System is a distributed database. This allows local control of the segments of the overall database; yet data in each segment are available across the entire network through a client-server scheme. Robustness and adequate performance are achieved through replication and caching.

Programs called *name servers* constitute the server half of DNS's client-server mechanism. Name servers contain information about some segment of the database and make it available to clients, called *resolvers*. Resolvers are often just library routines that create queries and send them across a network to a name server.

The structure of the DNS database, shown in Figure 1-1, is very similar to the structure of the NT filesystem. The whole database (or filesystem) is pictured as an inverted tree, with the root node at the top. Each node in the tree has a text label, which identifies the node relative to its parent. This is roughly analogous to a

---

* RFCs are Request for Comments documents, part of the relatively informal procedure for introducing new technology on the Internet. RFCs are usually freely distributed and contain fairly technical descriptions of the technology, often intended for implementors.

"relative pathname" in a filesystem, like SYSTEM. One label—the null label, or ""—is reserved for the root node. In text, the root node is written as a single dot (.). In the NT filesystem, the root is written as a backslash (\).

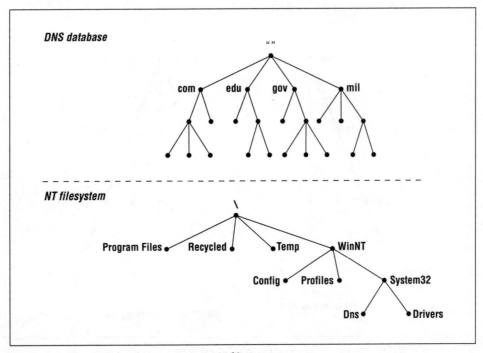

*Figure 1-1. The DNS database versus an NT filesystem*

Each node is also the root of a new subtree of the overall tree. Each of these subtrees represents a partition of the overall database—a "directory" in the NT filesystem or a domain in the Domain Name System. Each domain or directory can be further divided into additional partitions, called *subdomains* in DNS, like a filesystem's "subdirectories." Subdomains, like subdirectories, are drawn as children of their parent domains.

Every domain has a unique name, like every directory. A domain's *domain name* identifies its position in the database, much as a directory's "absolute pathname" specifies its place in the filesystem. In DNS, the domain name is the sequence of labels from the node at the root of the domain to the root of the whole tree, with a single dot (.) separating the labels. In the NT filesystem, a directory's absolute pathname is the list of relative names read from root to leaf (the opposite direction in DNS, as shown in Figure 1-2), using a backslash to separate the names.

In DNS, each domain can be administered by a different organization. Each organization can then break its domain into a number of subdomains and dole out

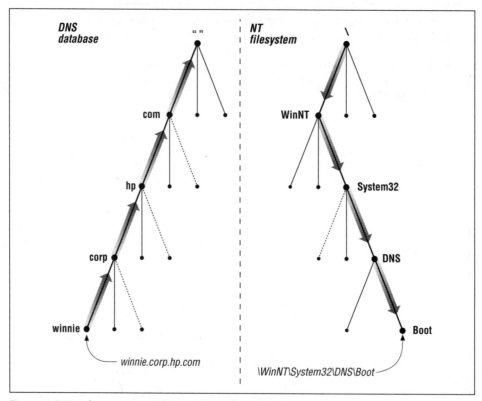

*Figure 1-2. Reading names in DNS and in an NT filesystem*

responsibility for those subdomains to other organizations. For example, the Inter-
NIC runs the *edu* (educational) domain, but assigns UC Berkeley authority over
the *berkeley.edu* subdomain (Figure 1-3).

Domain names are used as indexes into the DNS database. You might think of
data in DNS as "attached" to a domain name. In a filesystem, directories contain
files and subdirectories. Likewise, domains can contain both hosts and subdomains. A domain contains those hosts and subdomains whose domain names are
within the domain.

Each host on a network has a domain name, which points to information about
the host (see Figure 1-4). This information may include IP addresses, information
about mail routing, and so on. Hosts may also have one or more *domain name
aliases*, which are simply pointers from one domain name (the alias) to another
(the official or canonical domain name). In the figure, "*mailhub.nv...*" is an alias
for the canonical name "*rincon.ba.ca...*".

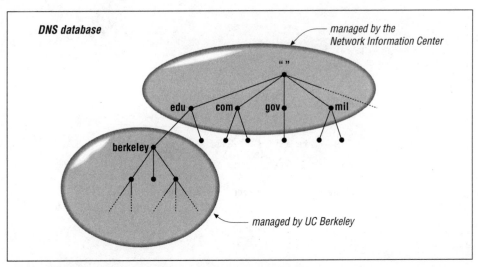

*Figure 1-3. Remote management of subdomains and filesystems*

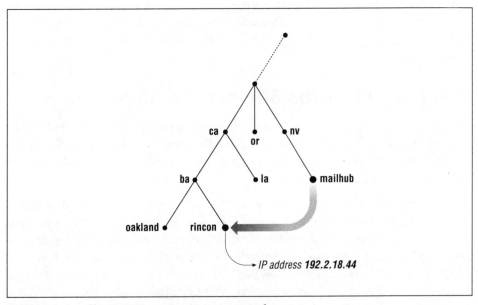

*Figure 1-4. An alias in DNS pointing to a canonical name*

Why all the complicated structure? To solve the problems that *HOSTS.TXT* had. For example, making domain names hierarchical eliminates the pitfall of name collisions. Each domain has a unique domain name, so the organization that runs the domain is free to name hosts and subdomains within its domain. Whatever name

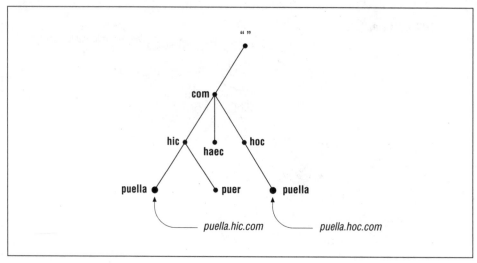

*Figure 1-5. Solving the name collision problem*

they choose for a host or subdomain won't conflict with other organizations' domain names because it will end in their unique domain name. For example, the organization that runs *hic.com* can name a host *puella* (as shown in Figure 1-5), because it knows that the host's domain name will end in *hic.com*, a unique domain name.

# The History of the Microsoft DNS Server

The first implementation of the Domain Name System was called JEEVES, written by Paul Mockapetris himself. A later implementation was BIND,* written for Berkeley's 4.3BSD UNIX operating system by Kevin Dunlap. BIND is now maintained by the Internet Software Consortium.†

Although the Microsoft DNS Server can read BIND's configuration and data files, it is not BIND. Microsoft wrote their server from scratch, according to the DNS specifications. The first version of the Microsoft DNS Server was a beta version that ran on NT 3.51. Microsoft made it available for some time from one of their FTP servers. The first product version of the DNS Server was shipped with Microsoft Windows NT Server 4.0 (but not with NT Workstation 4.0). The server was updated in several NT Service Packs, including the latest (as of this writing), Ser-

---

* BIND is an acronym for Berkeley Internet Name Domain.

† For more information on the Internet Software Consortium and its work on BIND, see *http:// www.isc.org/isc/bind.html.*

vice Pack 3. The most recent version of the Microsoft DNS Server is available as a post-Service Pack 3 hotfix.*

There are many other name servers that run on Windows NT. For example, Software.COM provides a free port of the BIND 4.9.5 server to Windows NT, which runs on NT Server and NT Workstation. MetaInfo offers a commercial version of the BIND 8.1.1 server, ported to Windows NT. It also runs on both NT Server and NT Workstation.

## Must I Use DNS?

Despite the usefulness of the Domain Name System, it doesn't pay to use it in some situations. There are other name resolution mechanisms besides DNS, some of which may come standard with your operating system. Sometimes the overhead involved in managing a domain and its name servers outweighs the benefits. On the other hand, there are circumstances in which you have no other choice but to set up and manage a domain. Here are some guidelines to help you make that decision.

### If you're connected to the Internet . . .

DNS is a must. Think of DNS as the *lingua franca* of the Internet: nearly all of the Internet's network services use DNS. That includes the World Wide Web, electronic mail, remote terminal access, file transfer, and the X Window System.

On the other hand, this doesn't necessarily mean that you have to set up and run a domain by yourself for yourself. If you've only got a handful of hosts, you may be able to find an existing domain to become part of (see Chapter 3, *Where Do I Start?*). Or you may be able to find someone else to run a domain for you. If you pay an Internet service provider for your Internet connectivity, ask if they'll manage a domain for you, too. Even if you aren't already a customer, there are companies who will help out, for a price.

If you have a little more than a handful of hosts, or a lot more, then you'll probably want your own domain. And if you want direct control over your domain and your name servers, then you'll want to manage it yourself. Buy this book, and read on!

### If you have your own TCP/IP-based internet . . .

You probably want DNS. By an *internet*, we don't mean just a single Ethernet of computers using TCP/IP (see the next section if you thought that was what we

---

* See Chapter 3, *Where Do I Start?*, for information on where to get this version of the Microsoft DNS Server.

meant); we mean a fairly complex "network of networks." For example, a multi-site network that uses TCP/IP probably warrants using DNS.

If your internet is basically homogeneous and your hosts don't need DNS (say you just use NetBIOS), you may be able to do without it. But if you've got a variety of hosts, especially if some of those run some variety of UNIX, you'll want DNS. It'll simplify the distribution of host information and rid you of any kludgy host table distribution schemes you may have cooked up.

### *If you have your own local area network or site network . . .*

And that network isn't connected to a larger network, you can probably get away without using DNS. You might consider using Microsoft's Windows Internet Naming Service (WINS) or host tables.

But if you need distributed administration or have trouble maintaining the consistency of data on your network, DNS may be for you. And if your network is likely to be connected to another network soon, like your corporate internet or the Internet, it'd be wise to start up a domain now.

*2*

# How Does DNS Work?

*". . . and what is the use of a book," thought Alice,*
*"without pictures or conversations?"*

The Domain Name System is basically a database of host information. Admittedly, you get a lot with that: funny dotted names, networked name servers, a shadowy name space. But keep in mind that, in the end, the service DNS provides is information about internet hosts.

We've already covered some important aspects of DNS, including its client-server architecture and the structure of the DNS database. However, we haven't gone into much detail, and we haven't explained the nuts and bolts of DNS's operation.

In this chapter, we'll explain and illustrate the mechanisms that make DNS work. We'll also introduce the terms you'll need to know to read the rest of the book (and to converse intelligently with your fellow domain administrators).

First, though, let's take a more detailed look at concepts introduced in the previous chapter. We'll add enough detail to spice it up a little.

## The Domain Name Space

DNS's distributed database is indexed by domain names. Each domain name is essentially just a path in a large inverted tree called the *domain name space*. The tree's hierarchical structure, shown in Figure 2-1, is similar to the structure of the Windows NT filesystem. The tree has a single root at the top.* In the NT filesystem, this is called the *root directory*, represented by a backslash (\). DNS simply calls it *the root*. Like a filesystem, DNS's tree can branch any number of ways at each intersection point, called a *node*. The depth of the tree is limited to 127 levels (a limit you're not likely to reach).

---

* Clearly this is a computer scientist's tree, not a botanist's.

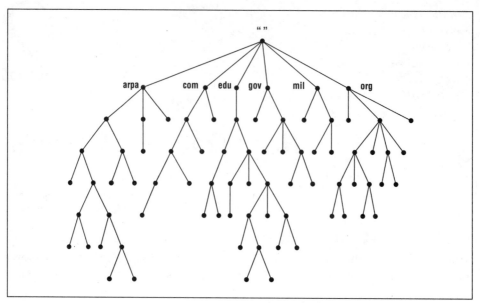

*Figure 2-1. The structure of the DNS name space*

## Domain Names

Each node in the tree has a text label (without dots) that can be up to 63 charac-ters long. A null (zero-length) label is reserved for the root. The full *domain name* of any node in the tree is the sequence of labels on the path from that node to the root. Domain names are always read from the node toward the root ("up" the tree), and with dots separating the names in the path.

If the root node's label actually appears in a node's domain name, the name *looks* as though it ends in a dot, as in *www.oreilly.com.* (It actually ends with a dot—the separator—and the root's null label.) When the root node's label appears by itself, it is written as a single dot (.) for convenience. Consequently, some software inter-prets a trailing dot in a domain name to indicate that the domain name is *abso-lute.* An absolute domain name is written relative to the root and unambiguously specifies a node's location in the hierarchy. An absolute domain name is also referred to as a *fully qualified domain name,* often abbreviated *FQDN.* Names without trailing dots are sometimes interpreted as relative to some domain other than the root, just as directory names without a leading backslash are often inter-preted as relative to the current directory.

DNS requires that sibling nodes—nodes that are children of the same parent—have different labels. This restriction guarantees that a domain name uniquely identifies a single node in the tree. The restriction really isn't a limitation, because the labels only need to be unique among the children, not among all the nodes in the tree. The same restriction applies to the NT filesystem: you can't give two sibling directories the same name. Just as you can't have two *hobbes.pa.ca.us* nodes in the name space, you can't have two *\Temp* directories (Figure 2-2). You can, however, have both a *hobbes.pa.ca.us* node and a *hobbes.lg.ca.us*, as you can have both a *\Temp* directory and a *\WINNT\Temp* directory.

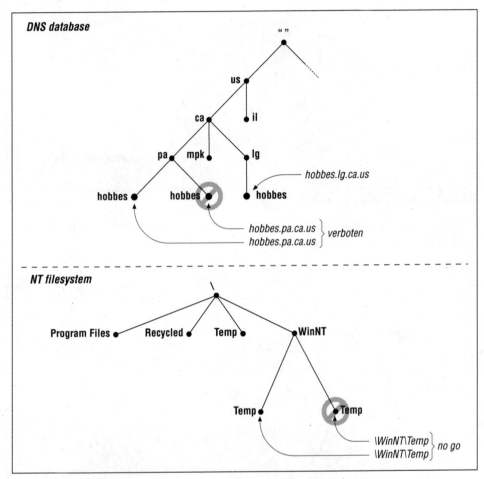

*Figure 2-2. Ensuring uniqueness in domain names and in NT pathnames*

## Domains

A *domain* is simply a subtree of the domain name space. The domain name of a domain is the same as the domain name of the node at the very top of the domain. So, for example, the top of the *purdue.edu* domain is a node named *purdue.edu*, as shown in Figure 2-3.

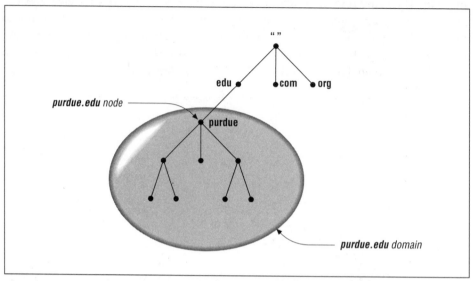

*Figure 2-3. The purdue.edu domain*

Likewise, in a filesystem, at the top of the \\*Program Files* directory, you'd expect to find a node called \\*Program Files*, as shown in Figure 2-4.

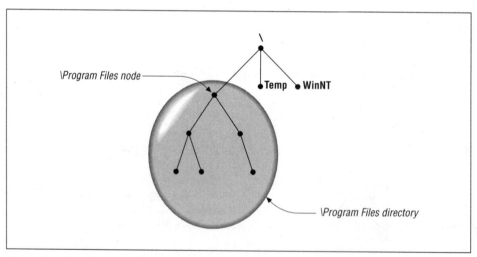

*Figure 2-4. The \\Program Files directory*

Any domain name in the subtree is considered a part of the domain. Because a domain name can be in many subtrees, a domain name can also be in many domains. For example, the domain name *pa.ca.us* is part of the *ca.us* domain and also part of the *us* domain, as shown in Figure 2-5.

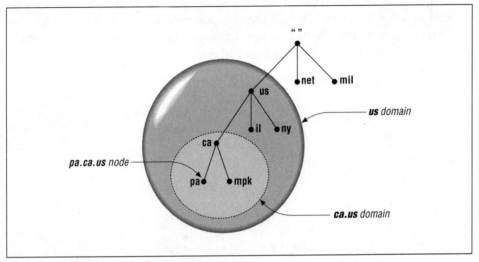

*Figure 2-5. A node in multiple domains*

So in the abstract, a domain is just a subtree of the domain name space. But if a domain is simply made up of domain names and other domains, where are all the hosts? Domains are groups of hosts, right?

The hosts are there, represented by domain names. Remember, domain names are just indexes into the DNS database. The hosts are the domain names that point to information about individual hosts. And a domain contains all the hosts whose domain names are within the domain. The hosts are related *logically*, often by geography or organizational affiliation, and not necessarily by network or address or hardware type. You might have ten different hosts, each of them on a different network and each one perhaps even in a different country, all in the same domain.*

Domain names at the leaves of the tree generally represent individual hosts. They may point to network addresses, hardware information, and mail routing information. Domain names in the interior of the tree can name a host *and* can point to information about the domain. Interior domain names aren't restricted to one or the other. They can represent both the domain they correspond to and a particular host on the network. For example, *hp.com* is both the name of Hewlett-Packard's domain and the domain name of a host that runs HP's main web server.

---

* One note of caution: don't confuse domains in the Domain Name System with NT Domains. Computers in the same NT Domain share account management and security services offered by a Domain Controller. NT Domains don't have any relationship to DNS domains.

The type of information retrieved when you use a domain name depends on the context in which you use it. Sending mail to someone at *hp.com* returns mail routing information, while *telnet*ing to the domain name looks up the host information (in Figure 2-6, for example, *hp.com*'s IP address).

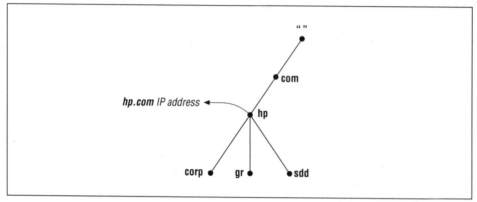

*Figure 2-6. An interior node with both host and domain data*

A domain may have several subtrees of its own, called *subdomains.*[*]

A simple way of deciding whether a domain is a subdomain of another domain is to compare their domain names. A subdomain's domain name ends with the domain name of its parent domain. For example, the domain *la.tyrell.com* must be a subdomain of *tyrell.com* because *la.tyrell.com* ends with *tyrell.com*. Similarly, it's a subdomain of *com*, as is *tyrell.com*.

Besides being referred to in relative terms, as subdomains of other domains, domains are often referred to by *level*. On mailing lists and in Usenet newsgroups, you may see the terms *top-level domain* or *second-level domain* bandied about. These terms simply refer to a domain's position in the domain name space:

- A top-level domain is a child of the root.

- A first-level domain is a child of the root (a top-level domain).

- A second-level domain is a child of a first-level domain, and so on.

## Resource Records

The data associated with domain names are contained in *resource records*, or RRs. Records are divided into classes, each of which pertains to a type of network or

---

[*]  The terms *domain* and *subdomain* are often used interchangeably, or nearly so, in DNS documentation. Here, we use *subdomain* only as a relative term: a domain is a subdomain of another domain if the root of the subdomain is within the domain.

software. Currently, there are classes for internets (any TCP/IP-based internet), networks based on the Chaosnet protocols, and networks that use Hesiod software. (Chaosnet is an old network of largely historic significance.)

The internet class is by far the most popular. (We're not really sure if anyone still uses the Chaosnet class, and use of the Hesiod class is mostly confined to MIT.) We concentrate here on the internet class.

Within a class, records also come in several types, which correspond to the different varieties of data that may be stored in the domain name space. Different classes may define different record types, though some types may be common to more than one class. For example, almost every class defines an *address* type. Each record type in a given class defines a particular record syntax, which all resource records of that class and type must adhere to. (For details on all internet resource record types and their syntaxes, see Appendix A, *DNS Message Format and Resource Records.*)

If this information seems sketchy, don't worry—we'll cover the records in the internet class in more detail later. The common records are described in Chapter 4, *Setting Up the Microsoft DNS Server*, and a comprehensive list is included as part of Appendix A.

## *The Internet Domain Name Space*

So far, we've talked about the theoretical structure of the domain name space and what sorts of data are stored in it, and we've even hinted at the types of names you might find in it with our (sometimes fictional) examples. But this won't help you decode the domain names you see on a daily basis on the Internet.

The Domain Name System doesn't impose many rules on the labels in domain names, and it doesn't attach any *particular* meaning to the labels at a particular level. When you manage a part of the domain name space, you can decide on your own semantics for your domain names. Heck, you could name your subdomains A through Z and no one would stop you (though they might strongly recommend against it).

The existing Internet domain name space, however, has some self-imposed structure to it. Especially in the upper-level domains, the domain names follow certain traditions (not rules, really, as they can be and have been broken). These traditions prevent domain names from appearing totally chaotic. Understanding these traditions is an enormous asset if you're trying to decipher a domain name.

## Top-Level Domains

The original top-level domains divided the Internet domain name space organizationally into seven domains:

*com*

Commercial organizations, such as Hewlett-Packard (*hp.com*), Sun Microsystems (*sun.com*), and IBM (*ibm.com*)

*edu*

Educational organizations, such as UC Berkeley (*berkeley.edu*) and Purdue University (*purdue.edu*)

*gov*

Government organizations, such as NASA (*nasa.gov*) and the National Science Foundation (*nsf.gov*)

*mil*

Military organizations, such as the U.S. Army (*army.mil*) and Navy (*navy.mil*)

*net*

Networking organizations, such as NSFNET (*nsf.net*)

*org*

Noncommercial organizations, such as the Electronic Frontier Foundation (*eff.org*)

*int*

International organizations, such as NATO (*nato.int*)

Another top-level domain called *arpa* was originally used during the ARPANET's transition from host tables to DNS. All ARPANET hosts originally had host names under *arpa*, so they were easy to find. Later, they moved into various subdomains of the organizational top-level domains. However, the *arpa* domain remains in use in a way you'll read about later.

You may notice a certain nationalistic prejudice in the examples: all are primarily U.S. organizations. That's easier to understand—and forgive—when you remember that the Internet began as the ARPANET, a U.S.-funded research project. No one anticipated the success of the ARPANET, or that it would eventually become as international as the Internet is today.

Today, these original domains are called *generic top-level domains,* or gTLDs for short. By the time you read this, we may have quite a few more of these, such as *firm, shop, web,* and *nom,* to accommodate the rapid expansion of the Internet and the need for more domain name "space." For more information on a proposal to create new gTLDs, see *http://www.gtld-mou.org/.*

To accommodate the internationalization of the Internet, the implementers of the Internet name space compromised. Instead of insisting that all top-level domains describe organizational affiliation, they decided to allow geographical designations, too. New top-level domains were reserved (but not necessarily created) to correspond to individual countries. Their domain names followed an existing international standard called ISO 3166.* ISO 3166 establishes official, two-letter abbreviations for every country in the world. We've included the current list of top-level domains in Appendix D, *Top-Level Domains.*

## Further Down

Within these top-level domains, the traditions and the extent to which they are followed vary. Some of the ISO 3166 top-level domains closely follow the U.S.'s original organizational scheme. For example, Australia's top-level domain, *au*, has subdomains such as *edu.au* and *com.au*. Some other ISO 3166 top-level domains follow the *uk* domain's lead and have subdomains such as *co.uk* for corporations and *ac.uk* for the academic community. In most cases, however, even these geographically oriented top-level domains are divided up organizationally.

That's not true of the *us* top-level domain, however. The *us* domain has fifty subdomains that correspond to—guess what?—the fifty U.S. states.† Each is named according to the standard two-letter abbreviation for the state—the same abbreviation standardized by the U.S. Postal Service. Within each state's domain, the organization is still largely geographical: most subdomains correspond to individual cities. Beneath the cities, the subdomains usually correspond to individual hosts.

## Reading Domain Names

Now that you know what most top-level domains represent and how their name spaces are structured, you'll probably find it much easier to make sense of most domain names. Let's dissect a few for practice:

```
lithium.cchem.berkeley.edu
```

You've got a head start on this one, as we've already told you that *berkeley.edu* is UC Berkeley's domain. (Even if you didn't already know that, though, you could have inferred that the name probably belongs to a U.S. university because it's in the top-level *edu* domain.) *cchem* is the College of Chemistry's subdomain of

---

\* Except for Great Britain. According to ISO 3166 and Internet tradition, Great Britain's top-level domain name should be *gb*. Instead, nearly all organizations in Great Britain and Northern Ireland (that is, the United Kingdom) use the top-level domain name *uk*. They drive on the wrong side of the road, too.

† Actually, a few more domains are under *us*: one for Washington, D.C., one for Guam, and so on.

*berkeley.edu.* Finally, *lithium* is the name of a particular host in the domain—and probably one of about a hundred or so, if they've got one for every element.

    winnie.corp.hp.com

This example is a bit harder, but not much. The *hp.com* domain in all likelihood belongs to Hewlett-Packard (in fact, we gave you this earlier, too). Their *corp* sub-domain is undoubtedly their corporate headquarters. And *winnie* is probably just some silly name someone thought up for a host.

    fernwood.mpk.ca.us

Here you'll need to use your understanding of the *us* domain. *ca.us* is obviously California's domain, but *mpk* is anybody's guess. In this case, it would be awfully hard to know that it's Menlo Park's domain unless you knew your San Francisco Bay Area geography. (And no, it's not the same Menlo Park that Edison lived in—that one's in New Jersey.)

    daphne.ch.apollo.hp.com

We've included this example just so you don't start thinking that all domain names have only four labels. *apollo.hp.com* is the former Apollo Computer's subdomain of the *hp.com* domain. (When HP acquired Apollo, it also acquired Apollo's Internet domain, *apollo.com*, which became *apollo.hp.com.*) *ch.apollo.hp.com* is Apollo's Chelmsford, Massachusetts, site. And *daphne* is a host at Chelmsford.

# *Delegation*

Remember that one of the main goals of the design of the Domain Name System was to decentralize administration? This is achieved through *delegation*. Delegating domains works a lot like delegating tasks at work. A manager may break up a large project into smaller tasks and delegate responsibility for each of these tasks to different employees.

Likewise, an organization administering a domain can divide it into subdomains. Each of those subdomains can be *delegated* to other organizations. This means that an organization becomes responsible for maintaining all the data in that sub-domain. It can freely change the data, and even divide its subdomain into more subdomains and delegate those. The parent domain contains only pointers to sources of the subdomain's data so that it can refer queriers there. The domain *stanford.edu*, for example, is delegated to the folks at Stanford who run the university's networks (Figure 2-7).

Not all organizations delegate away their whole domain, just as not all managers delegate all their work. A domain may have several subdomains and may also contain hosts that don't belong in the subdomains. For example, the Acme Corporation (it supplies a certain coyote with most of his gadgets), which has a division

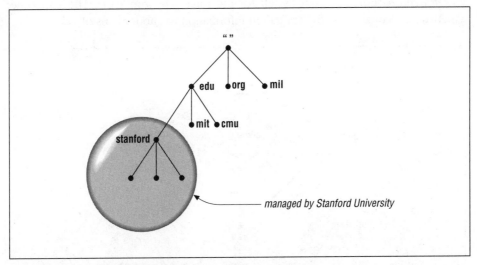

*Figure 2-7. stanford.edu is delegated to Stanford University*

in Rockaway and its headquarters in Kalamazoo, might have a *rock-away.acme.com* subdomain and a *kalamazoo.acme.com* subdomain. However, the few hosts in the Acme sales offices scattered throughout the U.S. would fit better under *acme.com* than under either subdomain.

We'll explain how to create and delegate subdomains later. For now, it's only important that you understand that the term *delegation* refers to assigning responsibility for a subdomain to another organization.

## Name Servers and Zones

The programs that store information about the domain name space are called *name servers*. Name servers generally have complete information about some part of the domain name space, called a *zone,* which it loads from a file or from another name server. The name server is then said to have *authority* for that zone. Name servers can be authoritative for multiple zones, too.

The difference between a zone and a domain is important, but subtle. All top-level domains, and many domains at the second level and lower, like *berkeley.edu* and *hp.com,* are broken into smaller, more manageable units by delegation. These units are called *zones*. The *edu* domain, shown in Figure 2-8, is divided into many zones, including the *berkeley.edu* zone, the *purdue.edu* zone, and the *nwu.edu* zone. At the top of the domain, there's also an *edu* zone. It's natural that the folks who run *edu* would break up the *edu* domain; otherwise, they'd have to manage the *berkeley.edu* subdomain themselves. It makes much more sense to delegate *berkeley.edu* to Berkeley. What's left for the folks who run *edu?* The *edu* zone, which would contain mostly delegation information to subdomains of *edu*.

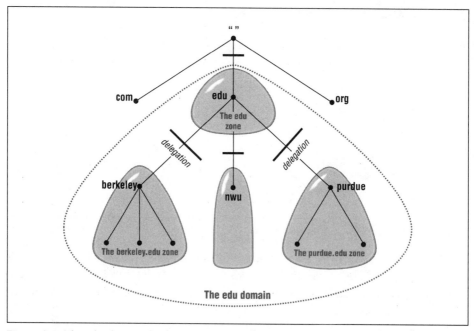

*Figure 2-8. The edu domain broken into zones*

The *berkeley.edu* subdomain is, in turn, broken up into multiple zones by delegation, as shown in Figure 2-9. There are delegated subdomains called *cc, cs, ce, me,* and more. Each of these subdomains is delegated to a set of name servers, some of which are also authoritative for *berkeley.edu*. However, the zones are still separate and may have a totally different group of authoritative name servers.

A zone contains the domain names that the domain with the same domain name contains, except for domain names in delegated subdomains. For example, the top-level domain *ca* (for Canada) may have the subdomains *ab.ca, on.ca,* and *qc.ca,* for the provinces Alberta, Ontario, and Quebec. Authority for the *ab.ca, on.ca,* and *qc.ca* domains may be delegated to name servers in each of the provinces. The *domain ca* contains all the data in *ca* plus all the data in *ab.ca, on.ca,* and *qc.ca*. But the *zone ca* contains only the data in *ca* (see Figure 2-10), which is probably mostly pointers to the delegated subdomains.

If a subdomain of the domain isn't delegated away, however, the zone contains the domain names and data in the subdomain. So the *bc.ca* and *sk.ca* (British Columbia and Saskatchewan) subdomains of the *ca* domain may exist but may not be delegated. (Perhaps the provincial authorities in B.C. and Saskatchewan aren't

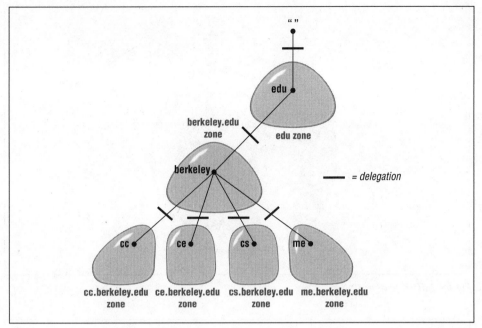

*Figure 2-9. The berkeley.edu domain broken into zones*

yet ready to manage their subdomains, but the authorities running the top-level *ca* domain want to preserve the consistency of the name space and implement subdomains for all the Canadian provinces right away.) In this case, the zone *ca* has a ragged bottom edge, containing *bc.ca* and *sk.ca*, but not the other *ca* subdomains, as shown in Figure 2-11.

Now it's clear why name servers load zones instead of domains: a domain might contain more information than the name server would need.[*] A domain could contain data delegated to other name servers. Since a zone is bounded by delegation, it will never include delegated data.

If you're just starting out, however, your domain probably won't have any subdomains. In this case, because no delegation is involved, your domain and your zone contain the same data.

## Delegating Domains

Even though you may not need to delegate parts of your domain just yet, it's helpful to understand a little more about how the process of delegating a domain

---

[*] Imagine if a root name server loaded the root domain instead of the root zone: it would be loading the entire name space!

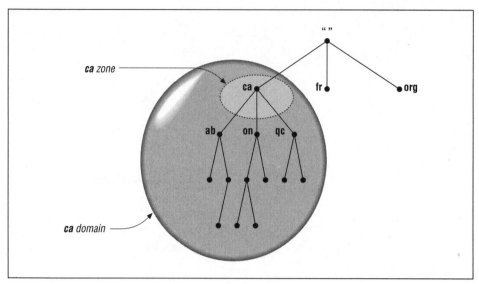

Figure 2-10. The domain ca . . .

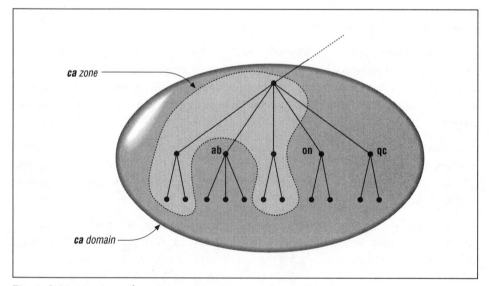

Figure 2-11. . . . versus the zone ca

works. Delegation, in the abstract, involves assigning responsibility for some part of your domain to another organization. What really happens, however, is the assignment of authority for your subdomains to different name servers. (Note that we said "name servers," not just "name server.")

Instead of containing information about the subdomain you've delegated, your data includes pointers to the name servers that are authoritative for that subdomain. Now if one of your name servers is asked for data in the subdomain, it can reply with a list of the right name servers to talk to.

## Types of Name Servers

The DNS specs define two types of name servers: *primary masters* and *secondary masters*. A *primary master* name server for a zone reads the data for the zone from a file on its host. A *secondary master* name server for a zone gets the zone data from another name server that is authoritative for the zone, called its *master server*. Quite often, the master server is the zone's primary master, but that's not required: a secondary master can load zone data from another secondary. When a secondary starts up, it contacts its master name server and, if necessary, pulls the zone data over. This is referred to as a *zone transfer*. Nowadays, the preferred term for a secondary master name server is a *slave,* though many people (and much software, including Microsoft's DNS Manager) still call them *secondaries.*

Both the primary master and slave name servers for a zone are authoritative for that zone. Despite the somewhat disparaging name, slaves aren't second-class name servers. DNS provides these two types of name servers to make administration easier. Once you've created the data for your zone and set up a primary master name server, you don't need to fool with copying that data from host to host to create new name servers for the zone. You simply set up slave name servers that load their data from the primary master for the zone. Once they're set up, the slaves will transfer new zone data when necessary.

Slave name servers are important because it's a good idea to set up more than one name server for any given zone. You'll want more than one for redundancy, to spread the load around, and to make sure that all the hosts in the zone have a name server close by. Using slave name servers makes this administratively workable.

Calling a *particular* name server a primary master name server or a slave name server is a little imprecise, though. We mentioned earlier that a name server can be authoritative for more than one zone. Similarly, a name server can be a primary master for one zone and a slave for another. Most name servers, however, are either primary for most of the zones they load or slave for most of the zones they load. So if we call a particular name server a primary or a slave, we mean that it's the primary master or a slave for *most* of the zones it loads.

## Data Files

The files from which primary master name servers load their zone data are called, simply enough, *zone data files* or just *data files*. We often refer to them as *db files*, short for *database files*. Slave name servers can also load their zone data from data files. Slaves are usually configured to back up the zone data they transfer from a master name server to data files. If the slave is later killed and restarted, it will read the backup data files first, then check to see whether the data are current. This both obviates the need to transfer the zone data if it hasn't changed and provides a source of the data if the master is down.

The data files contain resource records that describe the zone. The resource records describe all the hosts in the zone and mark any delegation of subdomains. The Microsoft DNS Server also allows special directives to include the contents of other data files in a data file, much like the `#include` statement in C programming.

# Resolvers

Resolvers are the clients that access name servers. Programs running on a host that need information from the domain name space use the resolver. The resolver handles:

- Querying a name server

- Interpreting responses (which may be resource records or an error)

- Returning the information to the programs that requested it

In most operating systems, the resolver is just a set of library routines that is linked into programs such as *telnet* and *ftp*. It's not even a separate process. It has the smarts to put together a query, to send it and wait for an answer, and to resend the query if it isn't answered, but that's about all. Most of the burden of finding an answer to the query is placed on the name server. The DNS specs call this kind of resolver a *stub resolver*.

Other implementations of DNS have had smarter resolvers, which could do more sophisticated things such as build up a cache of information already retrieved from name servers.* But these aren't nearly as common as the stub resolver implemented in most operating systems.

---

\* Rob Austein's CHIVES resolver for TOPS-20 could cache, for example.

# Resolution

Name servers are adept at retrieving data from the domain name space. They have to be, given the limited intelligence of some resolvers. Not only can they give you data about zones for which they're authoritative, but they can also search through the domain name space to find data for which they're not authoritative. This process is called *name resolution* or simply *resolution.*

Because the name space is structured as an inverted tree, a name server needs only one piece of information to find its way to any point in the tree: the domain names and addresses of the root name servers (is that more than one piece?). A name server can issue a query to a root name server for any name in the domain name space, and the root name server will start the name server on its way.

## Root Name Servers

The root name servers know the locations of name servers authoritative for all the top-level domains. (In fact, most of the root name servers *are* authoritative for the generic top-level domains.) Given a query about any domain name, the root name servers can at least provide the names and addresses of the name servers that are authoritative for the top-level domain that the domain name is in. And the top-level name servers can provide the list of name servers that are authoritative for the second-level domain the domain name is in. Each name server queried gives the querier information about how to get "closer" to the answer it's seeking or provides the answer itself.

The root name servers are clearly important to resolution. Because they're so important, DNS provides mechanisms—such as caching, which we'll discuss a little later—to help offload the root name servers. But in the absence of other information, resolution has to start at the root name servers. This makes the root name servers crucial to the operation of DNS; if all the Internet root name servers were unreachable for an extended period, all resolution on the Internet would fail. To protect against this, the Internet has thirteen root name servers (as of this writing) spread across different parts of the network. Two are on the MILNET, the U.S. military's portion of the Internet; one is on SPAN, NASA's internet; two are in Europe; and one is in Japan.

Being the focal point for so many queries keeps the roots busy; even with thirteen, the traffic to each root name server is very high. A recent poll of root name server administrators showed some roots receiving thousands of queries per second.

Despite the load placed on root name servers, resolution on the Internet works quite well. Figure 2-12 shows the resolution process for the address of a real host in a real domain, including how the process corresponds to traversing the domain name space tree.

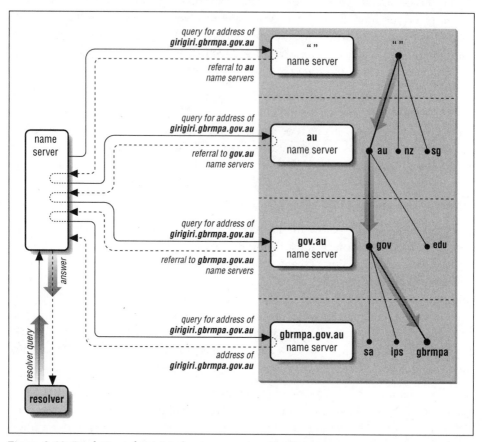

*Figure 2-12. Resolution of girigiri.gbrmpa.gov.au on the Internet*

The local name server queries a root name server for the address of *giri-giri.gbrmpa.gov.au* and is referred to the *au* name servers. The local name server asks an *au* name server the same question and is referred to the *gov.au* name servers. The *gov.au* name server refers the local name server to the *gbrmpa.gov.au* name servers. Finally, the local name server asks a *gbrmpa.gov.au* name server for the address and gets the answer.

## Recursion

You may have noticed a big difference in the amount of work done by the name servers in the previous example. Four of the name servers simply returned the best answer they already had—mostly referrals to other name servers—to the queries they received. They didn't have to send their own queries to find the data requested. But one name server—the one queried by the resolver—had to follow successive referrals until it received an answer.

Why couldn't the local name server simply have referred the resolver to another name server? Because a stub resolver wouldn't have had the intelligence to follow a referral. And how did the name server know not to answer with a referral? Because the resolver issued a *recursive* query.

Queries come in two flavors, *recursive* and *iterative*, also called *nonrecursive*. Recursive queries place most of the burden of resolution on a single name server. *Recursion*, or *recursive resolution*, is just a name for the resolution process used by a name server when it receives recursive queries.

*Iteration* or *iterative resolution*, on the other hand, refers to the resolution process used by a name server when it receives iterative queries.

In recursion a resolver sends a recursive query to a name server for information about a particular domain name. The queried name server is then obliged to respond with the requested data or with an error stating that data of the requested type don't exist or that the domain name specified doesn't exist.* The name server can't just refer the querier to a different name server, because the query was recursive.

If the queried name server isn't authoritative for the data requested, it will have to query other name servers to find the answer. It could send recursive queries to those name servers, thereby obliging them to find the answer and return it (and passing the buck). Or it could send iterative queries and possibly be referred to other name servers closer to the domain name it's looking for. Current implementations are polite and do the latter, following the referrals until an answer is found.†

A name server that receives a recursive query that it can't answer itself will query the "closest known" name servers. The closest known name servers are the servers authoritative for the zone closest to the domain name being looked up. For example, if the name server receives a recursive query for the address of the domain name *girigiri.gbrmpa.gov.au,* it will first check whether it knows the name servers for *girigiri.gbrmpa.gov.au*. If it does, it will send the query to one of them. If not, it will check whether it knows the name servers for *gbrmpa.gov.au,* and after that *gov.au,* and then *au*. The default, where the check is guaranteed to stop,

---

* The Microsoft DNS Server can be configured to refuse recursive queries. See Chapter 10, *Advanced Features and Security,* for how and why you'd want to do this.

† The exception is a name server configured to forward all unresolved queries to a designated name server, called a *forwarder*. See Chapter 10 for more information on using forwarders.

is the root zone, since every name server knows the domain names and addresses of the root name servers.

Using the closest known name servers ensures that the resolution process is as short as possible. A *berkeley.edu* name server receiving a recursive query for the address of *waxwing.ce.berkeley.edu* shouldn't have to consult the root name servers; it can simply follow delegation information directly to the *ce.berkeley.edu* name servers. Likewise, a name server that has just looked up a domain name in *ce.berkeley.edu* shouldn't have to start resolution at the roots to look up another *ce.berkeley.edu* (or *berkeley.edu*) domain name; we'll show how this works in the upcoming section "Caching."

The name server that receives the recursive query always sends the same query that the resolver sends it—for example, for the address of *waxwing.ce.berke-ley.edu*. It never sends explicit queries for the name servers for *ce.berkeley.edu* or *berkeley.edu,* though this information is also stored in the name space. Sending explicit queries could cause problems: there may be no *ce.berkeley.edu* name servers (that is, *ce.berkeley.edu* may be part of the *berkeley.edu* zone). Also, it's always possible that an *edu* or *berkeley.edu* name server would know *waxwing.ce.berke-ley.edu*'s address. An explicit query for the *berkeley.edu* or *ce.berkeley.edu* name servers would miss this information.

## *Iteration*

Iterative resolution, on the other hand, doesn't require nearly as much work on the part of the queried name server. In iterative resolution, a name server simply gives the best answer *it already knows* back to the querier. No additional querying is required. The queried name server consults its local data (including its cache, which we're about to talk about), looking for the data requested. If it doesn't find the data there, it makes its best attempt to give the querier data that will help it continue the resolution process. Usually these are the domain names and addresses of the closest known name servers.

What this amounts to is a resolution process that, taken as a whole, looks like Figure 2-13.

A resolver queries a local name server, which then queries a number of other name servers in pursuit of an answer for the resolver. Each name server it queries refers it to another name server that is authoritative for a zone further down in the name space and closer to the domain name sought. Finally, the local name server queries the authoritative name server, which returns an answer.

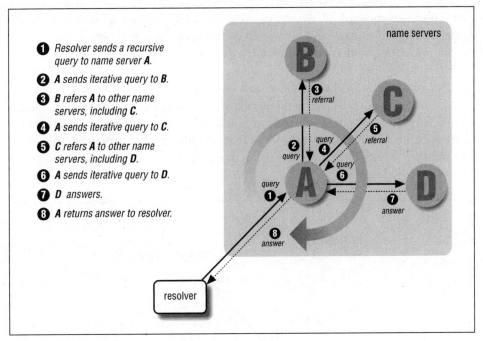

① Resolver sends a recursive query to name server **A**.

② **A** sends iterative query to **B**.

③ **B** refers **A** to other name servers, including **C**.

④ **A** sends iterative query to **C**.

⑤ **C** refers **A** to other name servers, including **D**.

⑥ **A** sends iterative query to **D**.

⑦ **D** answers.

⑧ **A** returns answer to resolver.

*Figure 2-13. The resolution process*

## Mapping Addresses to Names

One major piece of functionality missing from the resolution process as explained so far is how addresses get mapped back to names. Address-to-name mapping is used to produce output (in log files, for instance) that is easier for humans to read and interpret. It's also used in some authorization checks. Some hosts map addresses to domain names to compare against entries in authorization files, for example. When using host tables, address-to-name mapping is trivial. It requires a straightforward sequential search through the host table for an address. The search returns the official host name listed. In DNS, however, address-to-name mapping isn't so simple. Data, including addresses, in the domain name space are indexed by name. Given a domain name, finding an address is relatively easy. But finding the domain name that maps to a given address would seem to require an exhaustive search of the data attached to every domain name in the tree.

Actually, there's a better solution that's both clever and effective. Because it's easy to find data once you're given the domain name that indexes that data, why not create a part of the domain name space that uses addresses as labels? In the Internet's domain name space, this portion of the name space is the *in-addr.arpa* domain.

Nodes in the *in-addr.arpa* domain are labeled after the numbers in the dotted-octet representation of IP addresses. (Dotted-octet representation refers to the common method of expressing 32-bit IP addresses as four numbers in the range 0 to 255, separated by dots.) The *in-addr.arpa* domain, for example, could have up to 256 subdomains, one corresponding to each possible value in the first octet of an IP address. Each of these subdomains could have up to 256 subdomains of its own, corresponding to the possible values of the second octet. Finally, at the fourth level down, resource records are attached to the final octet giving the full domain name of the host or network at that IP address. That makes for an awfully big domain: *in-addr.arpa*, shown in Figure 2-14, is roomy enough for every IP address on the Internet.

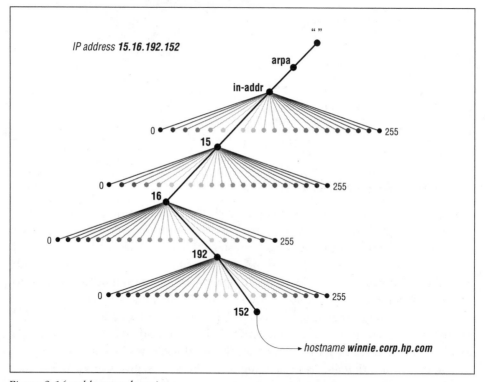

*Figure 2-14. addr.arpa domain*

Note that when read in a domain name, the IP address appears backward because the name is read leaf to root. For example, if *winnie.corp.hp.com* has the IP address 15.16.192.152, the corresponding *in-addr.arpa* subdomain is *152.192.16.15.in-addr.arpa*, which maps back to the domain name *winnie.corp.hp.com*.

IP addresses could have been represented the opposite way in the name space, with the first octet of the IP address at the bottom of the *in-addr.arpa* domain. That way, the IP address would have read correctly (forward) in the domain name.

IP addresses are hierarchical, however, just like domain names. Network numbers are doled out much as domain names are, and administrators can then subnet their address space and further delegate numbering. The difference is that IP addresses get more specific from left to right, while domain names get less specific from left to right. Figure 2-15 shows what we mean.

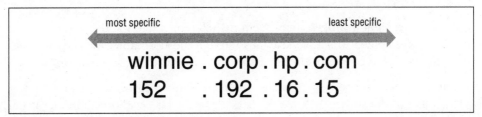

*Figure 2-15. Hierarchical names and addresses*

Making the first octets in the IP address appear highest in the tree gives administrators the ability to delegate authority for *in-addr.arpa* domains along network lines. For example, the *15.in-addr.arpa* domain, which contains the reverse mapping information for all hosts whose IP addresses start with 15, can be delegated to the administrators of network 15.0.0.0. This would be impossible if the octets appeared in the opposite order. If the IP addresses were represented the other way around, *15.in-addr.arpa* would consist of every host whose IP address *ended* with 15—not a practical domain to try to delegate.

## Inverse Queries

The *in-addr.arpa* name space is clearly useful only for IP address-to-domain name mapping. Searching for a domain name that indexes an *arbitrary* piece of data—something besides an address—in the domain name space would require another specialized name space like *in-addr.arpa* or an exhaustive search.

That exhaustive search is to some extent possible, and it's called an *inverse query*. An inverse query is a search for the domain name that indexes a given datum. It's processed solely by the name server receiving the query. That name server searches all of its local data for the item sought and returns the domain name that indexes it, if possible. If it can't find the data, it gives up. No attempt is made to forward the query to another name server.

Because any one name server only knows about part of the overall domain name space, an inverse query is never guaranteed to return an answer. For example, if a name server receives an inverse query for an IP address it knows nothing about, it can't return an answer, but it also doesn't know that the IP address doesn't exist, because it holds only part of the DNS database. What's more, the implementation of inverse queries is optional according to the DNS specification. The Microsoft DNS Server doesn't support inverse queries at all. That's fine with us, because very little software (such as archaic versions of *nslookup*) actually still uses inverse queries.

# Caching

The whole resolution process may seem awfully convoluted and cumbersome to someone accustomed to simple searches through the host table. Actually, it's usually quite fast. One of the features that speeds it up considerably is *caching*.

A name server processing a recursive query may have to send out quite a few queries to find an answer. However, it discovers a lot of information about the domain name space as it does so. Each time it's referred to another list of name servers, it learns that those name servers are authoritative for some zone, and it learns the addresses of those servers. And, at the end of the resolution process, when it finally finds the data the original querier sought, it can store that data for future reference, too. With Microsoft's DNS Server, as well as Versions 4.9 and 8 of BIND, name servers even implement *negative caching:* if an authoritative name server responds to a query with an answer that says that the domain name or data type in the query doesn't exist, the local name server will temporarily cache that information, too. Name servers cache all of this data to help speed successive queries. The next time a resolver queries the name server for data about a domain name the name server knows something about, the process is shortened quite a bit. The name server may have cached the answer, positive or negative, in which case it simply returns the answer to the resolver. Even if it doesn't have the answer cached, it may have learned the identities of the name servers that are authoritative for the zone the domain name is in and be able to query them directly.

For example, say our name server has already looked up the address of *eecs.berkeley.edu*. In the process, it cached the names and addresses of the *eecs.berkeley.edu* and *berkeley.edu* name servers (plus *eecs.berkeley.edu*'s IP address). Now if a resolver were to query our name server for the address of *baobab.cs.berkeley.edu*, our name server could skip querying the root name servers. Recognizing that *berkeley.edu* is the closest ancestor of *baobab.cs.berkeley.edu* that it knows about, our name server would start by querying a *berkeley.edu* name server, as shown in Figure 2-16. On the other hand, if our name server had discovered that there was no address for *eecs.berkeley.edu*, the next time it received a query for the address, it could simply have responded appropriately from its cache.

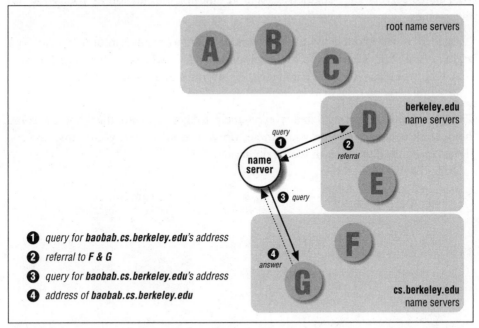

*Figure 2-16. Resolving baobab.cs.berkeley.edu*

In addition to speeding resolution, caching prevents us from having to query the root name servers again. This means that we're not as dependent on the roots, and they won't suffer as much from all our queries.

## Time to Live

Name servers can't cache data forever, of course. If they did, changes to that data on the authoritative name servers would never reach the rest of the network. Remote name servers would just continue to use cached data. Consequently, the administrator of the zone that contains the data decides on a *time to live*, or TTL, for the data. The time to live is the amount of time that any name server is allowed to cache the data. After the time to live expires, the name server must discard the cached data and get new data from the authoritative name servers. This also applies to negatively cached data; a name server must time out a negative answer after a period, too, in case new data has been added on the authoritative name servers.

Deciding on a time to live for your data is essentially deciding on a trade-off between performance and consistency. A small TTL will help ensure that data about your zone is consistent across the network, because remote name servers will time it out more quickly and be forced to query your authoritative name servers more often for new data. On the other hand, this will increase the load on your name servers and lengthen resolution time for information in your zone, on the average.

A large TTL will shorten the average time it takes to resolve information in your zone because the data can be cached longer. The drawback is that your information will be inconsistent for a longer time if you make changes to your data on your name servers.

Enough of this theory—I'll bet you're antsy to get on with this. There's some homework necessary before you can set up your domain and your name servers, though, and we'll assign it in the next chapter.

# 3

# *Where Do I Start?*

*""What do you call yourself?" the Fawn said at last.
Such a soft sweet voice it had!*

*"I wish I knew!" thought poor Alice. She answered,
rather sadly, "Nothing, just now."*

*"Think again," it said: "that won't do."*

*Alice thought, but nothing came of it. Please, would you tell me what you
call yourself?" she said timidly. "I think that might help a little."*

*"I'll tell you, if you come a little further on,"
the Fawn said. "I can't remember here."*

Now that you understand the theory behind the Domain Name System, we can attend to more practical matters. Before you set up a domain, you may need to get name server software. While a name server is included as a standard part of Windows NT Server, you may want to look at alternatives. Even if you do decide to use Microsoft's DNS Server, you should get the newest version, since older versions have quite a few known bugs.

Once you've got the software to run your name server, you need to decide on a domain name—which may not be quite as easy as it sounds, because it entails finding an appropriate parent domain in the Internet name space. That decided, you need to contact the administrators of the parent domain of the domain name you've chosen.

One thing at a time, though. Let's talk about how to decide on name server software and where to get it.

## *Which DNS Server?*

If you plan to set up your own domain and run name servers for it, you'll need DNS server software first. Even if you're planning on having someone else run your domain, it's helpful to have the software around. For example, you can use your local name server to test your data files before giving them to your remote domain administrator.

Microsoft ships a DNS server with Windows NT Server 4.0, although you have to install it separately from your NT CD-ROM. This server, which we call the Microsoft DNS Server, is the server we cover in this book. It's notable because it sports a nice graphical frontend for configuring the server and can query WINS servers for NetBIOS names it can't find in your zones. It only runs on Windows NT Server (that is, it doesn't run on NT Workstation). This isn't the only DNS server available for Windows NT, however. There are several others. Most are ports of BIND, which has traditionally been a UNIX-based name server. If you're more comfortable configuring BIND than learning to configure a new name server (even with a GUI), you might consider these options:

*Meta IP/DNS*

> Meta IP/DNS is a commercial port (that is, you gotta pay for it) of the BIND 8.1.1 server to Windows NT. As such, it supports DNS NOTIFY, dynamic updates, and all of the security features that BIND 8.1.1 offers. Meta IP/DNS is also integrated with WINS and can forward- and reverse-map NetBIOS names with the help of a WINS server. It runs on Windows NT Workstation and Server.

> Meta IP/DNS is actually part of a larger IP management product called Meta IP, but it's available separately, too. For more information, see *http://www.metainfo.com/products/metaip/dns.htm.*

*DrCoffsite's BIND*

> A group of public-spirited programmers ported BIND 4.9.6 to Windows NT. Their port is available free, upon request. Although this isn't the newest version of BIND, it's more than adequate for most uses. It runs on Windows NT Workstation and Server. For access to the FTP site from which you can download the server, send email to *access@drcoffsite.com.*

*Software.COM's BIND*

> Software.COM, the company that produces the Post.Office email software, offers a free version of BIND 4.9.5 for Windows NT for downloading from *http://www.software.com/products/BINDforNT/BINDForNT.html.* Apparently, this is the DrCoffsite port of BIND with an InstallShield frontend for installation. As such, it runs on Windows NT Workstation and Server.

If you decide to use one of these ports of BIND to Windows NT, we suggest you pick up a copy of *DNS and BIND*. That book concentrates on the BIND implementation; this book emphasizes the Microsoft DNS Server.

# Getting the DNS Server

If you've read to this section, we'll assume you've decided to use the Microsoft DNS Server. Before proceeding, you'll need to install the DNS server and its configuration frontend, DNS Manager, from the Windows NT CD-ROM. For detailed instructions on this process, see Appendix B, *Installing the DNS Server from CD-ROM.*

Now that you've installed the Microsoft DNS Server and DNS Manager, we strongly suggest you upgrade to the newest version of the DNS Server.* The DNS Server on your CD-ROM, and even the server in Service Pack 3 (SP3), are known to have quite a few bugs. By downloading the latest, post-SP3 hotfixed version of the server, you'll save yourself a lot of headaches. We can't guarantee that it's bug free, but at least it fixes many of the bugs earlier versions are known to have.

You can download the Intel version of the latest Microsoft DNS Server from *ftp:// ftp.microsoft.com/bussys/winnt/winnt-public/fixes/usa/nt40/hotfixes-postSP3/dns-fix/ dnsfix_i.exe.* The version for Alpha processors running Windows NT is in the same directory, but the file is named *dnsfix_a.exe.* For localized versions of the DNS Server, replace the *usa* in the path with the appropriate three-letter abbreviation for your language. Note that the latest version of the DNS Server may not be available for your language.

Once you've downloaded the file, simply start a **Command Prompt** window or click on **Start → Run**, and type the path to the file:

```
C:\> \temp\dnsfix_i.exe
```

This will extract the updated DNS Server and then prompt you to restart the computer.

## Handy USENet Newsgroups and Web Sites

Now that you've installed your name server, it's important to keep abreast of DNS and name server developments. Two USENet newsgroups are invaluable for this: *microsoft.public.windowsnt.dns* and *comp.protocols.dns.bind. microsoft.public.win-dowsnt.dns* concentrates on the Microsoft DNS Server and is a good place to find out about new bugs. *comp.protocols.dns.bind* is more BIND-centric (as the name indicates) but is an excellent source of information about the art and practice of running domains and name servers. It also arguably has a better signal-to-noise ratio than the Microsoft newsgroup.

Microsoft's online support site, at *http://support.microsoft.com/support/,* is a valuable source of information about known bugs in the DNS Server and updates to the code. Also, be sure to check Andras Salamon's "DNS Resource Directory" at *http://www.dns.net/dnsrd* for pointers to online DNS resources and documentation.

---

\* Why didn't we just have you skip the CD-ROM installation and install the newest version of the server? The self-extracting executable that contains the upgraded server doesn't include the DNS Manager.

A mailing list you might be interested in is the *namedroppers* list. Folks on the *namedroppers* mailing list usually discuss DNS issues, rather than server-specific problems. For example, a discussion of extensions to the DNS protocol or proposed DNS record types would probably take place on *namedroppers*. To join *namedroppers*, send mail to *majordomo@internic.net* with the text **subscribe namedroppers** as the body of the message. The InterNIC also provides a web-based frontend for subscribing at *http://rs.internic.net/cgi-bin/lwgate/NAMEDROPPERS*. To ask a question on *namedroppers*—or on nearly any Internet mailing list—all you need to do is send a message to the mailing list's address. The *namedroppers* mailing list's address is *namedroppers@internic.net* and is gatewayed into the Internet newsgroup *comp.protocols.tcp-ip.domains*. You don't need to subscribe to the list to send a message to it. If you'd like to join the list, however, you have to send a message to the list's maintainer first, requesting him or her to add your electronic mail address to the list. Don't send the request to the list itself—that's considered rude.

## Finding IP Addresses

You'll notice we gave you a number of domain names of hosts that have *ftp*able software, and the mailing lists we mentioned include domain names. That should underscore the importance of DNS: see what valuable software and advice you can get with the help of DNS? Unfortunately, it's also something of a chicken-and-egg problem. You can't send email to an address with a domain name in it unless you've got DNS set up, so how can you ask someone on the list how to set up DNS?

Well, we could give you the IP addresses for all the hosts we mentioned, but since IP addresses change often (in publishing timescales, anyway), we'll show you how you can *temporarily* use someone else's name server to find the information instead. As long as your host has Internet connectivity and the *nslookup* program, you can retrieve information from the Internet name space. To look up the IP address for *ftp.isc.org*, for example, you could use:

```
% nslookup ftp.microsoft.org. 207.69.188.185
```

This instructs *nslookup* to query the name server running on the host at IP address 207.69.188.185 to find the IP address for *ftp.microsoft.com*, and should produce output like:

```
Server:   ns1.mindspring.com
Address:  207.69.188.185


Name:     ftp.microsoft.com
Address:  198.105.232.1
```

Now you can *ftp* to *ftp.microsoft.com*'s IP address, 198.105.232.1.

How did we know that the host at IP address 207.69.188.185 runs a name server? Our ISP, Mindspring, told us—it's one of their name servers. If your ISP provides name servers for its customers' use (and most do), use one of them. If your ISP doesn't provide name servers (shame on them!), you can *temporarily* use one of the name servers listed in this book. As long as you use it to look up only a few IP addresses or other data, the administrators probably won't mind. It's considered very rude, however, to point your resolver or query tool at someone else's name server permanently.

Of course, if you already have access to a host with Internet connectivity *and* DNS configured, you can use it to *ftp* the stuff you need.

Once you've got a working version of the Microsoft DNS Server, you're ready to start thinking about your domain name.

# Choosing a Domain Name

Choosing a domain name is more involved than it may sound because it entails both choosing a name *and* finding a parent. In other words, you need to find out where you fit in the Internet domain name space and decide what you'd like to call your particular corner of that name space.

The first step in picking a domain name is finding where in the existing domain name space you belong. It's easiest to start at the top and work your way down: decide which top-level domain you belong in and then which of that top-level domain's subdomains you fit into.

Note that in order to find out what the Internet domain name space looks like (beyond what we've already told you), you'll need access to the Internet. You don't need access to a host that already has Domain Name System configured, but it would help a little. If you don't have access to a host with DNS configured, you'll have to "borrow" name service from other name servers (as in our previous *ftp.microsoft.com* example) to get you going.

## Where in the World Do I Fit?

If your organization is attached to the Internet outside of the United States, you first need to decide whether you'd rather request a domain under the generic top-level domains, like *com* and *edu*, or under your country's top-level domain. The generic top-level domains, even though some are used largely *by* U.S. organizations, aren't exclusively *for* U.S. organizations. If your company is a multi- or trans-national company, you may wish to join a generic top-level domain, or if you'd simply prefer a generic top level to your country's top-level domain, you're welcome to ask to join one. If you choose this route, skip to the section "Generic top-level domains" later in this chapter.

If you opt for a subdomain under your country's top level, you should check whether your country's top-level domain is registered, and if it is, what kind of structure it has. Consult our list of the current top-level domains (in Appendix D, *Top-Level Domains*) if you're not sure what the domain name of your country's top-level domain would be.

Some countries' top-level domains, like New Zealand's *nz*, Australia's *au*, and the United Kingdom's *uk*, are divided organizationally into second-level domains. The names of their second-level domains, like *co* or *com* for commercial entities, reflect organizational affiliation. Others, like France's *fr* domain and Canada's *ca* domain, are divided into a multitude of subdomains managed by individual universities and companies, like the University of St. Etienne's domain, *univ-st-etienne.fr,* and Bell Northern Research's *bnr.ca.* You'll have to use a tool like *nslookup* to grope around and discover your top-level domain's structure if it isn't well known. (If you're uncomfortable with our rushing headlong into *nslookup* without giving it a proper introduction, you might skim Chapter 11, *nslookup.*) For example, here's how you could list the *au* domain's subdomains using *nslookup*:

```
C:\> nslookup - 207.69.188.185   --Use the name server at 207.69.188.185
Default Server:  ns1.mindspring.com
Address:  207.69.188.185

> set type=ns         --Find the name servers (ns)
> au.                 --for the au domain
Server:  ns1.mindspring.com
Address: 207.69.188.185

au        nameserver = MUNNARI.OZ.AU
au        nameserver = MULGA.CS.MU.OZ.AU
au        nameserver = JATZ.AARNET.EDU.AU
au        nameserver = NS.UU.NET
au        nameserver = NS.EU.NET
au        nameserver = NS1.BERKELEY.EDU
au        nameserver = NS2.BERKELEY.EDU
au        nameserver = VANGOGH.CS.BERKELEY.EDU
MUNNARI.OZ.AU       internet address = 128.250.1.21
MUNNARI.OZ.AU       internet address = 128.250.22.2
MULGA.CS.MU.OZ.AU       internet address = 128.250.1.22
MULGA.CS.MU.OZ.AU       internet address = 128.250.37.150
JATZ.AARNET.EDU.AU       internet address = 139.130.204.4
NS.UU.NET       internet address = 137.39.1.3
NS.EU.NET       internet address = 192.16.202.11
NS1.BERKELEY.EDU   internet address = 128.32.136.9
NS1.BERKELEY.EDU   internet address = 128.32.206.9
NS2.BERKELEY.EDU       internet address = 128.32.136.12
NS2.BERKELEY.EDU       internet address = 128.32.206.12
```

```
> server ns1.berkeley.edu.  --Now query one of the name servers
                            --listed--preferably a close one!
Default Server:  ns1.berkeley.edu
Addresses:  128.32.136.9, 128.32.206.9

> ls -t ns au.  --List all name server records in the domain au
                --(which mark delegation to subdomains and will give
                --you the names of the subdomains)

                --Note that not all name servers will allow you to
                --list domains, for security reasons.  Also, some
                --versions of nslookup don't understand ls -t.
                --If your nslookup doesn't, use ls instead.
                --ls will produce this output and much more.


[ns1.berkeley.edu]
 AU.                          NS      server = munnari.OZ.AU
 AU.                          NS      server = mulga.cs.mu.OZ.AU
 AU.                          NS      server = vangogh.CS.Berkeley.EDU
 AU.                          NS      server = ns1.Berkeley.EDU
 AU.                          NS      server = ns2.Berkeley.EDU
 AU.                          NS      server = ns.UU.NET
 AU.                          NS      server = ns.eu.NET
 ORG.AU.                      NS      server = munnari.OZ.AU
 ORG.AU.                      NS      server = yalumba.connect.COM.AU
 ORG.AU.                      NS      server = mulga.cs.mu.OZ.AU
 ORG.AU.                      NS      server = rip.psg.COM
 INFO.AU.                     NS      server = ns1.telstra.net
 INFO.AU.                     NS      server = munnari.oz.AU
 INFO.AU.                     NS      server = teckla.apnic.net
 INFO.AU.                     NS      server = ns.telstra.net
 OTC.AU.                      NS      server = ns.telstra.com.AU
 OTC.AU.                      NS      server = ns2.telstra.com.AU
 OTC.AU.                      NS      server = munnari.oz.AU
 CSIRO.AU.                    NS      server = steps.its.CSIRO.AU
 CSIRO.AU.                    NS      server = munnari.OZ.AU
 CSIRO.AU.                    NS      server = manta.vic.cmis.CSIRO.AU
 CSIRO.AU.                    NS      server = dmssyd.nsw.cmis.CSIRO.AU
 CSIRO.AU.                    NS      server = zoiks.per.its.CSIRO.AU
 OZ.AU.                       NS      server = munnari.OZ.AU
 OZ.AU.                       NS      server = mulga.cs.mu.OZ.AU
 OZ.AU.                       NS      server = dmssyd.syd.dms.CSIRO.AU
 OZ.AU.                       NS      server = ns.UU.NET
 OZ.AU.                       NS      server = mx.nsi.NASA.GOV
 COM.AU.                      NS      server = munnari.OZ.AU
 COM.AU.                      NS      server = mulga.cs.mu.OZ.AU
 COM.AU.                      NS      server = orb.ISI.EDU
 COM.AU.                      NS      server = mx.nsi.NASA.GOV
 COM.AU.                      NS      server = yalumba.connect.COM.AU
 gov.AU.                      NS      server = ns.telstra.net
 gov.AU.                      NS      server = ns1.telstra.net
 gov.AU.                      NS      server = munnari.oz.AU
 gov.AU.                      NS      server = mulga.cs.mu.oz.AU
 gov.AU.                      NS      server = strul.stupi.se
```

```
www7.conf.AU.                 NS      server = cuscus.cc.uq.OZ.AU
www7.conf.AU.                 NS      server = krefti.cc.uq.OZ.AU
ncyc99.conf.AU.               NS      server = gw.softway.COM.AU
ncyc99.conf.AU.               NS      server = igw.nsw.uca.ORG.AU
ncyc99.conf.AU.               NS      server = ucaweb.vic.uca.ORG.AU
id98.conf.AU.                 NS      server = gateway.omen.COM.AU
id98.conf.AU.                 NS      server = ns1.iinet.NET.AU
id98.conf.AU.                 NS      server = vector.wantree.COM.AU
topgun.conf.AU.               NS      server = steamer.pipeline.COM.AU
topgun.conf.AU.               NS      server = thruster.pipeline.COM.AU
lng12.conf.AU.                NS      server = ns1.telstra.NET
lng12.conf.AU.                NS      server = proxy.tsw.COM.AU
inflate97.conf.AU.            NS      server = black.cat.ORG.AU
inflate97.conf.AU.            NS      server = iggy.triode.NET.AU
ausconfcaban.conf.AU.         NS      server = ns.camtech.NET.AU
ausconfcaban.conf.AU.         NS      server = nstmx.camtech.NET.AU
mahjong.conf.AU.              NS      server = ns1.telstra.NET
mahjong.conf.AU.              NS      server = SYDDNS1.unisys.COM.AU
icss.conf.AU.                 NS      server = dns.zip.COM.AU
icss.conf.AU.                 NS      server = proxy.zip.COM.AU
TELEMEMO.AU.                  NS      server = ns.telstra.com.AU
TELEMEMO.AU.                  NS      server = ns2.telstra.com.AU
TELEMEMO.AU.                  NS      server = munnari.oz.AU
edu.AU.                       NS      server = ns1.telstra.net
edu.AU.                       NS      server = munnari.oz.au
edu.AU.                       NS      server = mulga.cs.mu.oz.au
edu.AU.                       NS      server = ns1.berkeley.edu
edu.AU.                       NS      server = ns2.berkeley.edu
edu.AU.                       NS      server = ns.telstra.net
ID.AU.                        NS      server = munnari.OZ.AU
ID.AU.                        NS      server = mulga.cs.mu.OZ.AU
ID.AU.                        NS      server = rip.psg.COM
ID.AU.                        NS      server = yalumba.connect.COM.AU
asn.AU.                       NS      server = swing.iinet.net.AU
asn.AU.                       NS      server = munnari.oz.AU
asn.AU.                       NS      server = yalumba.connect.com.AU
asn.AU.                       NS      server = rip.psg.com
NET.AU.                       NS      server = mippet.ci.com.AU
NET.AU.                       NS      server = rip.psg.com
NET.AU.                       NS      server = munnari.oz.AU
NET.AU.                       NS      server = yalumba.connect.com.AU
> exit
```

The basic technique we used is straightforward: look up the list of authoritative name servers for the top-level domain—because they're the only ones with complete information about the corresponding zone—then connect to one of those name servers, and list the name servers for the second-level domains.

If you can't tell from the names of the subdomains which one you belong in, you can look up the contact information for the corresponding zone and send email to the technical contact asking, politely, for advice. Similarly, if you think you should be part of an existing subdomain but aren't sure, you can always ask the folks who administer that subdomain to double-check.

To find out who to ask about a subdomain, you'll have to look up the corresponding zone's SOA record. In each zone's start of authority (SOA) record, there's a field that contains the electronic mail address of the zone's technical contact.* (The other fields in the start of authority record provide general information about a zone—we'll discuss them in detail later.) You can look up the zone's SOA record with *nslookup*, too.

If you're curious about the purpose of the *csiro* subdomain, you can find out who runs it by looking up *csiro.au*'s SOA record:

```
C:\> nslookup - 207.69.188.185
Default Server: ns1.mindspring.com
Address:  207.69.188.185

> set type=soa      --Look for start of authority data
> csiro.au.         --for csiro.au
Server:  ns1.mindspring.com
Address: 207.69.188.185

csiro.au
        origin = steps.its.csiro.au
        mail addr = hostmaster.csiro.au
        serial = 1997122201
        refresh = 10800 (3 hours)
        retry   = 3600 (1 hour)
        expire  = 3600000 (41 days 16 hours)
        minimum ttl = 86400 (1 day)
```

The `mail addr` field is the Internet address of *csiro.au*'s contact. To use the address with most UNIX mailers, you'll need to change the first dot (.) in the address into an at sign (@). So *hostmaster.csiro.au* becomes *hostmaster@csiro.au*.†

### whois

The *whois* service can also help you figure out what a given domain is for. A *whois* database contains information about domains, networks, and the people that run them. Although Windows NT doesn't come with a *whois* client, most sites that run *whois* servers now provide web-based frontends for those servers. Many shareware and freeware *whois* clients are also available for Windows NT. See the "Network Information Tools" page at *WinFiles.com* (*http://www.winfiles.com/apps/nt/ net-info.html*) for a large selection.

---

* The subdomain and the zone have the same domain name, but the SOA record really belongs to the zone, not the subdomain. The person at the zone's technical contact email address may not manage the whole subdomain (there may be additional delegated subdomains beneath), but he should certainly know what the purpose of the subdomain is.

† This form of Internet mail address is a vestige of two former DNS records, MB and MG. MB (mail box) and MG (mail group) were to be DNS records specifying Internet mailboxes and mail groups (mailing lists) as subdomains of the appropriate domain. MB and MG never took off, but the address format they would have dictated is used in the SOA record, maybe for sentimental reasons.

As we did with *nslookup,* we'll assume you can beg, borrow, or steal Internet connectivity and access to a name server for long enough to do a few *whois* lookups.

The InterNIC's *whois* web page, at *http://www.internic.net/wp/whois.html,* is a
good starting point. This gives you an HTML forms-based interface for querying
the InterNIC's *whois* database, which includes contacts for top-level country
domains and subdomains of generic top-level domains. You won't find *csiro.au,*
because it's a subdomain of a top-level country domain. Still, you can use it to find
the administrative contact for *au* as shown in Figure 3-1.

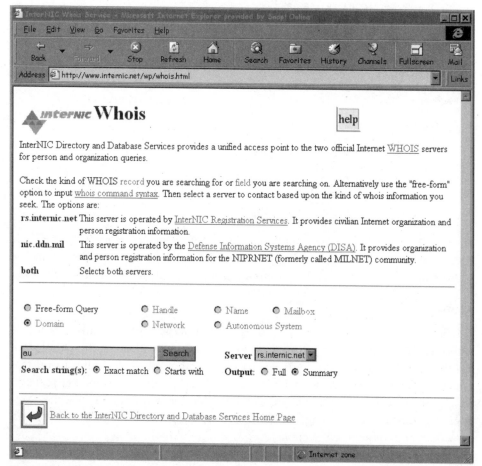

*Figure 3-1. The InterNIC's whois web interface*

Click on **Search**, and you get a ton of results, shown in Figure 3-2.*

---

* Believe it or not, when we did this for the first edition of *DNS and BIND,* there was only one match.

*Figure 3-2. Whois results for "au"*

If we scroll down a little, we find "Australia top-level domain," which is what we're after. If we click on the hypertext link labeled "AU-DOM" on that line, we see the screen shown in Figure 3-3, which tells us to talk to Robert Elz about the top-level *au* domain.

To get *csiro.au* contact information on the Web, you'd need to query the Australian NIC. Is there such a thing? You can check *http://www.allwhois.com/* to find out. Click on "Australia" in the left-hand frame, and Figure 3-4 is what you'll see.

Click on "Whois" to take you to a forms frontend that will let you query the AUNIC's (Australian NIC's) database.

Obviously, this is a very useful web site if you're looking for the contact for a domain outside of the U.S.

*Figure 3-3. Whois information for the top-level AU zone*

## Elsewhere in the World

In true cosmopolitan spirit, we covered international domains first. But what if you're from the good ol' U.S. of A.?

If you're in the U.S., where you belong depends mainly upon how many hosts you have. If you have only one or two, or maybe a handful of, hosts you'd like registered in the Internet's domain name space, you can join the *us* domain. The *us* domain registers individual hosts under third-level domains largely named after cities; the second-level domains correspond to the appropriate U.S. Postal Service two-letter state abbreviation (recall our discussion in the section "The Internet Domain Name Space" in Chapter 2, *How Does DNS Work?*). So, for example, if all you need is to register the two internetworked hosts in your basement in Colorado Springs, Colorado, you can just have them added to the *colospgs.co.us* domain.

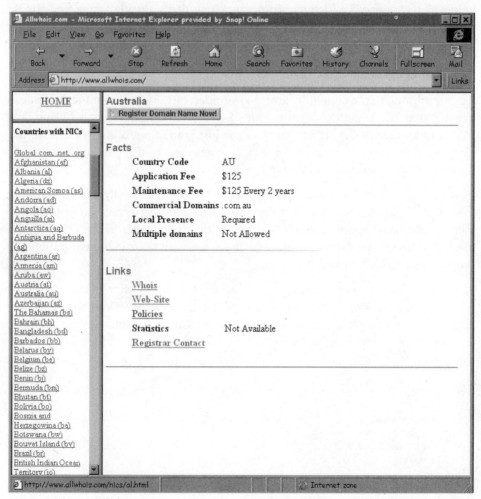

*Figure 3-4. www.allwhois.com*

You can even get your own domain to manage, thanks to a change in policy by the administrators of the *us* domain. Originally, the *us* domain was purely geographical. The *us* domain administrators added address and mail handling information for your host(s) (more on this in the next two chapters—be patient), but not name server information. In other words, they wouldn't delegate a portion of their domain to you. Nowadays, they encourage U.S. schools, governments, and companies to join the *us* domain. If you're interested in the details, check out RFC 1480, available from *ftp://ftp.ds.internic.net/rfc/rfc1480.txt*, or see the information on the *us* domain on ISI's web site, at *http://www.isi.edu/in-notes/usdnr/*.

You can also ask for a subdomain of one of the generic top-level domains, like *edu* and *com*. As long as you don't ask for an overly long subdomain name (the

InterNIC recommends 12 letters or fewer) or one that's already taken, you should get the one you ask for. We'll cover membership under the generic top levels later in this chapter.

### The us domain

Let's go through an example to give you an idea of how to comb the *us* domain name space for the perfect domain name. Say you live in Rockville, Maryland, and you want to register the NT workstation you just bought out of the back of a truck (hey, it could happen). You're not directly connected to the Internet, but you do have a dialup connection to UMD in College Park.

Since you only need to have a single host registered, you really don't need your own domain to manage. You just need to have your host registered in the Internet domain name space somewhere. The *us* top-level domain is the one for you. Letting someone else take care of the name server and domain administration will save you a lot of administrative effort.

Using an account you still have on a host at UMD (from your undergrad days), you can check to see whether a domain for Maryland exists. (If you didn't have an account there, but you did have Internet connectivity, you could still use *nslookup* to query a well-known name server.)

```
C:\> nslookup
Default Server:  noc.umd.edu
Address: 128.8.5.2

> set type=ns            --Look up the name servers
> md.us.                 --for md.us
Server:  noc.umd.edu
Address:  128.8.5.2

md.us    nameserver = NS.UU.NET
md.us    nameserver = ADMII.ARL.MIL
md.us    nameserver = EXCALIBUR.USC.EDU
md.us    nameserver = VGR.ARL.MIL
md.us    nameserver = TRANTOR.UMD.EDU
md.us    nameserver = MX.NSI.NASA.GOV
md.us    nameserver = VENERA.ISI.EDU
md.us    nameserver = NS.ISI.EDU
md.us    nameserver = RS0.INTERNIC.NET
```

Sure enough, there's a domain for Maryland. Now change servers to a *md.us* name server, say *venera.isi.edu,* and check to see if there are any subdomains (you haven't exited out of *nslookup* yet):

```
> server venera.isi.edu.  --Change server to venera.isi.edu
Default Server:  venera.isi.edu
Address:  128.9.0.32
```

```
> ls -t ns md.us.       --List all name server records in the domain md.us
  aa.md.us.                    NS      server = ADMII.ARL.MIL
  aa.md.us.                    NS      server = MX.NSI.NASA.GOV
  aa.md.us.                    NS      server = TRANTOR.UMD.EDU
  aa.md.us.                    NS      server = VGR.ARL.MIL
  adelphi.md.us.               NS      server = primary.southern-domains.com
  adelphi.md.us.               NS      server = top.domainregistry.net
  adelphi.md.us.               NS      server = top2.domainregistry.net
  al.md.us.                    NS      server = ADMII.ARL.MIL
  al.md.us.                    NS      server = MX.NSI.NASA.GOV
  al.md.us.                    NS      server = TRANTOR.UMD.EDU
  al.md.us.                    NS      server = VGR.ARL.MIL
  allegany.md.us.              NS      server = auth00.ns.uu.net
  allegany.md.us.              NS      server = auth50.ns.uu.net
  andrews-afb.md.us.           NS      server = ns2.mci.net
  andrews-afb.md.us.           NS      server = usdns.beltane.com
  andrews-afb.md.us.           NS      server = usdns2.beltane.com
  annapolis.md.us.             NS      server = gaia.nametamer.com
  annapolis.md.us.             NS      server = helicon.nametamer.com
  annapolis.md.us.             NS      server = ns1.sockets.net
  anne-arundel.md.us.          NS      server = ns1.abs.net
  anne-arundel.md.us.          NS      server = ns2.abs.net
  aspen-hill.md.us.            NS      server = ns.manchester.mo.us
  aspen-hill.md.us.            NS      server = ns2.us-domains.com
  aspen-hill.md.us.            NS      server = winnt.i-theta.com
  [...]
```

Aha! So there *is* life in Maryland! There are subdomains called *aa, adelphi, al, allegany,* and many others. But there doesn't seem to be a domain for Rockville. No matter—you may be the first host in Rockville to want to register under the *md.us* domain. Or perhaps this naming scheme is based on county names, and Rockville would fit under its county name. Either way, the administrators of *md.us* can find a home for you. Since your domain name will just be part of the *md.us* zone, it won't require very much work for them—there's no need to set up separate servers.

What to call the new subdomain, if you need a new one? *rockville.md.us? rock.md.us?* Turns out a convention in the *us* domain specifies that city-level domains be named after the appropriate Western Union "City Mnemonic." (Don't worry, the *us* administrators have a copy.) The alternative is to use the full name of the city.

Actually, with any parent domain, it's possible that the administrators of the domain will have strong feelings about the names of their child domains (just as your parents probably had strong feelings about naming you). They may want to preserve the consistency of their name space. We think it's polite to defer to your parent if they feel strongly about naming—after all, they could simply refuse to let you join the domain. You still get to choose the name of your host, after all.

How do you find out how to contact your parent domain's administrator? You can try *whois*, but since *md.us* isn't a top-level country domain or part of a generic top-level domain, you probably won't find much. Your best bet is to use *nslookup* to find the SOA record for the *md.us* zone, just as you did to find out who to ask about *csiro.au*. Though the person or persons who read mail sent to the address in the SOA record may not handle registration themselves (technical and administrative functions for the zone may be divided), it's a good bet they know the folks who do and can direct you to them.

Here's how you'd use *nslookup* to dig up the SOA record for *md.us*:

```
C:\> nslookup
Default Server:  noc.umd.edu
Address:  128.8.5.2

> set type=soa      --Look up SOA record
> md.us.            --for md.us
Server:  noc.umd.edu
Address:  128.8.5.2

md.us
        origin = VENERA.ISI.EDU
        mail addr = us-domain.ISI.EDU
        serial = 971109
        refresh = 43200 (12 hours)
        retry  = 3600 (1 hour)
        expire = 1209600 (14 days)
        minimum ttl = 86400 (1 day)
```

As in the *csiro.au* example, you need to swap the first dot (.) in the `mail addr` field for an at sign (@) before you use it. Thus, *us-domain.ISI.EDU* becomes *us-domain@ISI.EDU*.

### Generic top-level domains

As we said, there are many reasons you might want to ask for a subdomain of one of the generic top-level domains, like *com*, *edu*, and *org:* you work for a multi- or transnational company, you like the fact that they're better known, or you just like the sound of your domain name better with "com" on the end. Let's go through a short example of choosing a domain name under a gTLD.

Imagine you're the student administrator of a small university network in Hopkins, Minnesota. You've just gotten a grant for Internet connectivity and are about to be connected to your regional network, MRNet. Your university has never had so much as a UUCP link, so you're not currently registered in the Internet name space.

Since you're in the United States, you have the choice of joining either *us* or *edu*. You've already got over a dozen computers on your local network, though, and you expect more, so *us* wouldn't be a good choice. A subdomain of *edu* would be best.

Your university is known as the Gizmonics Institute, so you decide *gizmo.edu* might be an appropriate domain name. Now you've got to check if the name *gizmo.edu* has been taken by anyone, so you use an account you have at UMN:

```
C:\> nslookup
Default Server:  ns.unet.umn.edu
Address:  128.101.101.101


> set type=any      --Look for any records
> gizmo.edu.        --for gizmo.edu
Server:  ns.unet.umn.edu
Address:  128.101.101.101


*** ns.unet.umn.edu can't find gizmo.edu.: Non-existent domain
```

Looks like there's no *gizmo.edu* yet (hardly surprising), so you can go on to the next step: finding out who runs your intended parent domain. This time, you use a command-line *whois* client:

```
C:\> whois dom edu
Education top-level domain (EDU-DOM)
    Network Solutions, Inc.
    505 Huntmar Park Dr.
    Herndon, VA  22070

    Domain Name: EDU

    Administrative Contact, Technical Contact, Zone Contact:
        Network Solutions, Inc.  (HOSTMASTER)  HOSTMASTER@INTERNIC.NET
        (703) 742-4777 (FAX) (703) 742-9552

    Record last updated on 17-Jan-97.
        Record created on 01-Jan-85.
        Database last updated on 25-Dec-97 05:33:33 EDT.




    Domain servers in listed order:

    [...]
```

## Checking If Your Network Is Registered

Before proceeding, you should check whether or not your IP network or networks are registered. Many parent domains won't delegate a subdomain to name servers on unregistered networks, and registries won't delegate an *in-addr.arpa* subdomain that corresponds to an unregistered network.

An IP network defines a range of IP addresses. For example, the network 15/8 is made up of all IP addresses in the range 15.0.0.0 to 15.255.255.255. The network 199.10.25/24 starts at 199.10.25.0 and ends at 199.10.25.255.

---

### A Sidebar on CIDR

Once upon a time, the Internet's 32-bit address space was divided up into three main classes of networks: class A, class B, and class C. Class A networks were networks in which the first octet (first eight bits) of the IP address identified the network, and the remaining bits were used by the organization assigned the network to differentiate hosts on the network. Most organizations with class A networks also subdivided their networks into subnetworks, or subnets, adding another level of hierarchy to the addressing scheme. Class B networks devoted two octets to the network identifier and two to the host; class C networks gave three octets to the network identifier and one to the host.

Unfortunately, this small/medium/large system of networks didn't work well for everyone. Many organizations were large enough to require several class C networks, which could accommodate at most 254 hosts, but too small to warrant a class B network, which could serve 65534 hosts. Many of these organizations were allocated class B networks, anyway. Consequently, class B networks quickly became scarce.

To help solve this problem and create networks that were just the right size for all sorts of organizations, Classless Inter-Domain Routing, or CIDR (pronounced "cider") was developed. As the name implies, CIDR does away with the old class A, class B, and class C network designations. Instead of allocating either one, two, or three octets to the network identifier, the allocator could allocate any number of contiguous bits of the IP address to the network identifier. So, for example, if an organization needed an address space roughly four times as large as a class B network, the powers-that-be could assign it a network identifier of 14 bits, leaving 18 bits (four class B's worth) of space to use.

Naturally, the advent of CIDR made the "classful" terminology outdated—although it's still used a good deal in casual conversation. Now, to designate a particular CIDR network, we specify the particular high-order bit value assigned to an organization, expressed in dotted octet notation, and how many bits identify the network. The two terms are separated by a slash. So 15/8 is the old, class A–sized network that begins with the bit pattern 00001111. The old, class B–sized network 128.32.0.0 is now 128.32/16. And the network 192.168.0.128/25 consists of the 128 IP addresses from 192.168.0.128 to 192.168.0.255.

The InterNIC was once the official source of all IP networks; they assigned all IP networks to Internet-connected networks and made sure no two ranges overlapped. Nowadays, the InterNIC's old role has been largely assumed by Internet Service Providers, who allocate space from their own networks for customers to use. If you know your network came from your ISP, the larger network from which your network was carved is probably registered (to your ISP). You may still want to double-check that your ISP took care of registering their network, but you don't (and probably can't) do anything yourself, except nag your ISP if they didn't register their network. Once you've verified their registration, you can skip the rest of this section and move on.

If, however, your network was assigned by the InterNIC, way back when, or you *are* an ISP, you should check to see whether your network is registered. Where do you go to check whether your network is registered? Why, to the same organizations that register networks, of course. These organizations, called (what else?) *registries*, each handle network registration in some part of the world. In the Western Hemisphere, ARIN, the American Registry of Internet Numbers, at *http://www.arin.net/*, hands out IP address space and registers networks. In Asia and the Pacific, APNIC, the Asia Pacific Network Information Center, at *http://www.apnic.net/*, serves the same function. In Europe, it's the RIPE Network Coordination Centre, at *http://www.ripe.net/*. Each registry may also delegate registration authority for a region; for example, ARIN delegates registration authority for Mexico and Brazil to registries in each country. Be sure to check for a registry local to your country.

If you're not sure your network is registered, the best way to find out is to use the *whois* service provided by the various registries and look for your network. Here are the URLs for each registry's *whois* page:

*ARIN*
> *http://www.arin.net/whois/arinwhois.html*

*APNIC*
> *http://www.apnic.net/reg.html*

*RIPE*
> *http://www.ripe.net/db/whois.html*

If you find out your network isn't registered, you'll need to get it registered before setting up your *in-addr.arpa* zones. Each registry has a different process for registering networks, but most involve money changing hands (from your hands to theirs, unfortunately).

You may find out that your network is already assigned to your ISP. If this is the case, you don't need to register independently with the registry.

Once all your Internet-connected hosts are on registered networks, you can give your parent domain a call.

## *Registering with Your Parent*

Different domains have different registration policies. We've included the Inter-NIC's current registration form for second-level domains in Appendix D, *Top-Level Domains.* The form is only valid for registration under the InterNIC-run generic top-level domains like *com* and *edu.* (In other words, don't submit it to the administrators of the *au* or *fr* domain, and expect them to honor it.) It should, however, give you an idea of what to expect in a registration form (especially if you're registering under one of the InterNIC's domains). Other domains often have more informal registration processes. Sometimes simply sending the "registrar" the necessary information in an email message will do.

Since the forms will undoubtedly become obsolete before we update this book again, you should check out the InterNIC's online, HTML forms-based registration process at *http://www.rs.internic.net/rs-internic.html.* Although this process doesn't actually submit the form yet, it does automate the process of creating a properly formatted request that you can then email to the InterNIC. Or you can just retrieve the current forms, print them, and then fill them out by hand.

The basic information that your parent needs is the names and addresses of your domain name servers. If you're not connected to the Internet, give them the addresses of the Internet hosts that will act as your name servers. Some parent domains also require that you already have operational name servers for your domain. (The InterNIC doesn't, but they ask for an estimate of when the domain will be fully operational.) If that's the case with your parent, skip ahead to Chapter 4, *Setting Up the Microsoft DNS Server,* and set up your name servers. Then contact your parent with the requisite information.

If the InterNIC runs your parent domain, they'll also ask for some information about your organization and for an administrative contact and a technical contact for your domain (which can be the same person). If your contacts aren't already registered in the InterNIC's *whois* database, you'll also need to provide information to register them in *whois.* This includes their names, surface mail addresses, phone numbers, and electronic mail addresses. If they are already registered in *whois,* just specify their InterNIC *whois* "handle" (a unique alphanumeric ID) in the registration.

There's one more aspect of registering a new domain with the InterNIC that we should mention: cost. Network Solutions, Inc. (NSI), the contractor that manages the InterNIC, has begun charging to register new top-level domains and domains under the generic top-level domains *com, net,* and *org.* The startup fee is $100

(U.S.). NSI has also instituted an ongoing, annual charge of U.S. $50 for each domain. If you already have a subdomain under *com, net,* or *org* and haven't received a bill from NSI recently, it'd be a good idea to check your contact information with *whois* to make sure they've got a current address and phone number for you. For more information on the billing policy and the current scoop on the InterNIC registration process, see *http://www.rs.internic.net/rs-internic.html.*

If you're directly connected to the Internet, you should also have the *in-addr.arpa* domains corresponding to your IP networks delegated to you. For example, if your company was allocated the network 192.201.44/24, you should manage the *44.201.192.in-addr.arpa* domain. This will let you control the IP address-to-name mappings for hosts on your network. Chapter 4 also explains how to set up your *in-addr.arpa* domains.

In the previous section, "Checking If Your Network Is Registered," we asked you to find the answers to several questions: Is your network a slice of an ISP's network? Is your network, or the ISP's network that your network is part of, registered? In which registry? You'll need these answers to have your *in-addr.arpa* domains delegated to you.

If your network is part of a larger network registered to an ISP, you should contact the ISP to have the appropriate subdomains of *in-addr.arpa* delegated to you. Each ISP uses a different process for setting up *in-addr.arpa* delegation. Your ISP's web page is a good place to research that process. If you can't find the information there, try looking up the SOA record for the *in-addr.arpa* domain that corresponds to your ISP's network. For example, if your network is part of UUNet's 153.35/16 network, you could look up the SOA record of *35.153.in-addr.arpa* to find the email address of the technical contact for the zone.

If your network is registered directly with one of the regional registries, contact them to get your *in-addr.arpa* domain registered. Each registry makes information on their delegation process available on its web site. ARIN's template for requesting *in-addr.arpa* delegation, *inaddrtemplate.txt*, is included in this book as Appendix E, *Domain Registration Form*, and available online at *http://rs.arin.net/templates/inaddrtemplate.txt.*

Now that you've sent your prospective parent word that you'd like to be adopted, you'd better take some time to get your things in order. You've got a domain to set up, and in the next chapter, we'll show you how.

# Setting Up the Microsoft DNS Server

*"It seems very pretty," she said when she had finished it, "but it's rather hard to understand!" (You see she didn't like to confess, even to herself, that she couldn't make it out at all.) "Somehow it seems to fill my head with ideas—only I don't exactly know what they are!"*

If you have been diligently reading each chapter of this book, you're probably anxious to get a name server running. This chapter is for you. Let's set up a couple of name servers. Some of you may have read the table of contents and skipped directly to this chapter. (Shame on you!) If you are one of those people who cuts corners, be aware that we may use concepts from earlier chapters and expect you to understand them.

Several factors influence how you should set up your name servers. The biggest factor is what sort of access you have to the Internet: complete access (that is, you can *ftp* to *ftp.uu.net*), limited access (limited by a security firewall), or no access at all. This chapter assumes you have complete access. We'll discuss the other cases in Chapter 13, *Miscellaneous*.

In this chapter, we'll set up two name servers for a fictitious domain, as an example for you to follow in setting up your own domain. We'll cover the topics in this chapter in enough detail to get your first two name servers running. Subsequent chapters will fill in the holes and go into greater depth. If you already have your name servers running, skim through this chapter to familiarize yourself with the terms we use or just to verify that you didn't miss something when you set up your servers.

# Our Domain

Our fictitious domain is for a college. Movie University studies all aspects of the film industry and researches novel ways to distribute films. One of the most promising projects is research into using Ethernet as the distribution medium. After talking with the folks at the InterNIC, they have decided on the domain name *movie.edu*. A recent grant has enabled them to connect to the Internet.

Movie U. currently has two Ethernets, and they have plans for another network or two. The Ethernets have network numbers 192.249.249.0 and 192.253.253.0. A portion of Movie U.'s host table shows the following entries:

```
127.0.0.1       localhost

# These are our killer machines

192.249.249.2  robocop.movie.edu robocop
192.249.249.3  terminator.movie.edu terminator bigt
192.249.249.4  diehard.movie.edu diehard dh

# These machines are in horror(ible) shape and will be replaced
# soon.

192.253.253.2  misery.movie.edu misery
192.253.253.3  shining.movie.edu shining
192.253.253.4  carrie.movie.edu carrie

# A wormhole is a fictitious phenomenon that instantly transports
# space travelers over long distances and is not known to be
# stable.  The only difference between wormholes and routers is
# that routers don't transport packets as instantly--especially
# ours.

192.249.249.1  wormhole.movie.edu wormhole wh wh249
192.253.253.1  wormhole.movie.edu wormhole wh wh253
```

And the network is pictured in Figure 4-1.

# DNS Manager

To manage a Microsoft DNS Server and maintain your DNS data, you'll use a tool called *DNS Manager.* It has a graphical user interface (surprise) and is capable of managing multiple name servers. DNS Manager is similar in design and operation to WINS Manager and DHCP Manager, if you're already familiar with those tools.

DNS Manager is located on the **Administrative Tools (Common)** menu, provided you've already installed the DNS service. If you don't see DNS Manager on that menu, see Appendix B, *Installing the DNS Server from CD-ROM*, for instructions on installing the DNS service. You can also run DNS Manager on Windows NT

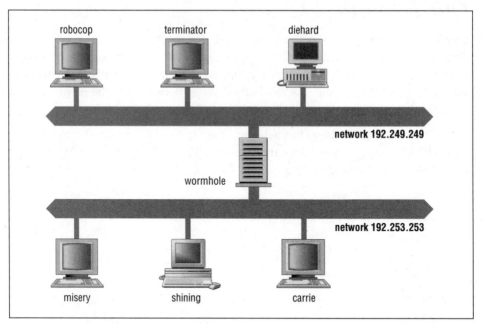

*Figure 4-1. The Movie University network*

Workstation by copying the executable, *%SystemRoot%\system32\dnsadmin.exe*, from a Windows NT Server installation.

DNS Manager communicates with the Microsoft DNS Server using a proprietary management protocol built on Microsoft's RPC (remote procedure call). That means DNS Manager only manages Microsoft's DNS Server and not other name servers, like BIND.

The main DNS Manager window looks like Figure 4-2 (or will look like it, after we've set everything up in the course of this chapter):

The left pane shows name servers, zones, and domains, while the right pane shows either name server statistics or resource records.

This particular DNS Manager knows about only one name server, with IP address 192.249.249.3. That name server is authoritative for three zones: *movie.edu*, *249.249.192.in-addr.arpa*, and *253.253.192.in-addr.arpa*. If any of these zones had subdomains, they would show up as subfolders under the appropriate zone. For example, *comedies.movie.edu* would be represented as a folder called *comedies* under *movie.edu*. Also notice the Cache icon. As you might expect, selecting this icon displays the contents of the name server's cache of resource records from previous queries. If you're familiar with the BIND name server, you probably know that the only way to examine that name server's cache is by dumping it to a file.

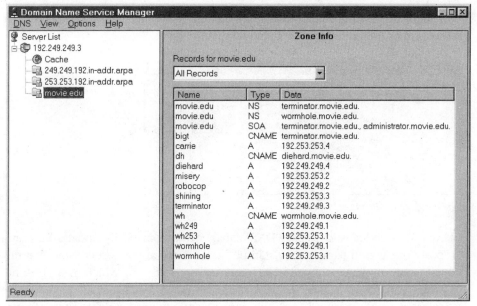

*Figure 4-2. DNS Manager main window*

If a name server is selected in the left pane (instead of a zone, as in Figure 4-2), then the right panel displays usage statistics for that name server. You can see the total number of queries processed by the server and whether the transport was UDP or TCP, the total number of recursive queries, and the total number of look-ups to a WINS server—more on that in Chapter 7, *Maintaining the Microsoft DNS Server.*

Of course, there are pull-down menus:

*DNS*

The really important commands are here: adding new name servers, creating zones and domains, and creating resource records. You can also delete objects and view objects' properties. We'll explain the various commands throughout this chapter.

*View*

Only two commands here: **Split** lets you move the split bar between the two panes (something you can do by just selecting and dragging the bar). **Refresh** causes DNS Manager to query the name server for what's currently selected in the left pane and update its display in the right pane. In other words, DNS Manager's display doesn't track the contents of the name server in real time and is not updated automatically. *We can't overemphasize the importance of the Refresh command:* you should use it all the time to make sure that what you see on the screen is the same information the name server has in memory. Fortunately, the function key F5 is a quick shortcut for **Refresh**.

*Options*

> This menu has only **Preferences,** which opens a window with DNS Manager
> settings as in Figure 4-3.

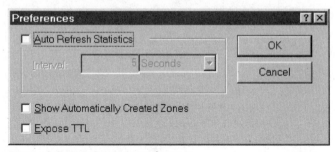

*Figure 4-3. DNS Manager preferences*

> **Auto Refresh Statistics** causes DNS Manager to automatically update the previ-
> ously mentioned name server statistics at the interval you select. Note that this
> automatic update only refreshes name server statistics, which you see only
> when you have a server selected in the left pane. You'll usually have a zone
> selected on the left and view the zone's contents on the right. That informa-
> tion isn't updated automatically no matter what this setting—you'll still need to
> select **View → Refresh** (or hit F5) to see changes.

> **Show Automatically Created Zones** displays three zones that every Microsoft
> name server is authoritative for: *0.in-addr.arpa, 127.in-addr.arpa*, and *255.in-
> addr.arpa.* We'll explain what these zones are for later on in this chapter.

> **Expose TTL** causes DNS to show the time to live (TTL) on every resource
> record it displays. Turning off this option doesn't affect the TTL of any records,
> just whether or not DNS Manager shows you the TTL.

> The default for all three options is off.

# Setting Up DNS Data

Let's configure the first of Movie U.'s name servers. We'll use DNS Manager for
most of this process, so start it up if you haven't already done so. You don't have
to run DNS Manager on the machine running the name server, but for now it's
easier if you do. You'll also need to have Administrator privileges to use DNS
Manager; otherwise, you'll only be able to start the application, not manage any
name servers with it.

## Adding a New Server to DNS Manager

The first step is configuring DNS Manager to manage the *primary master name server* for your zone. The primary master for a zone—also called just the *primary*—stores information about the zone on its disk. You make all changes to your zone on the primary master.

Select **DNS** → **New Server**, and then enter the IP address of your primary master. DNS Manager adds an icon in the left pane for that name server as in Figure 4-4.

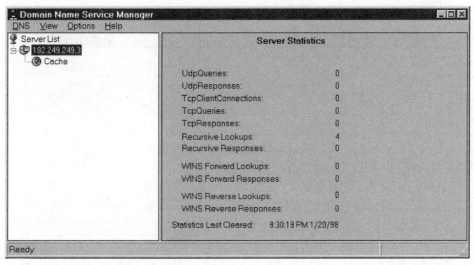

*Figure 4-4. DNS Manager with a new server*

192.249.249.3 is *terminator's* IP addresses in the Movie U. network. This name server is not (yet) authoritative for any zones, so only the Cache icon appears under the IP address. Since the name server itself is selected on the left, its usage statistics appear on the right. This name server hasn't been very busy.

It's important to understand what we just did here. We told DNS Manager about a name server for it to manage. DNS Manager added that name server to its configuration, queried it for a list of zones and statistics, and displayed them. DNS Manager did *not* start the name server on the target machine. If the name server isn't already installed and running, DNS Manager can't manage it and will complain with the rather cryptic error, "There are no more endpoints available from the endpoint mapper." That error, which appears at the bottom of the right pane, means that DNS Manager couldn't contact the name server on the target machine.

Selecting **New Server** just adds that name server to DNS Manager's list of servers it knows about. As you might expect, selecting the server and choosing **DNS** → **Delete** (or just pressing the Delete key) removes the server from DNS Manager's

configuration but doesn't change anything on the name server itself. The server
will still be running—you can use **New Server** to add it, and you'll be right back
where you started.

## Creating a New Zone

Now it's time to create the *movie.edu* zone. Select the name server on the left
where you want to create the zone. (There's only one server now, *terminator,* but
DNS Manager could know about multiple servers.) Choose **DNS → New Zone**.
You'll see a window as in Figure 4-5.

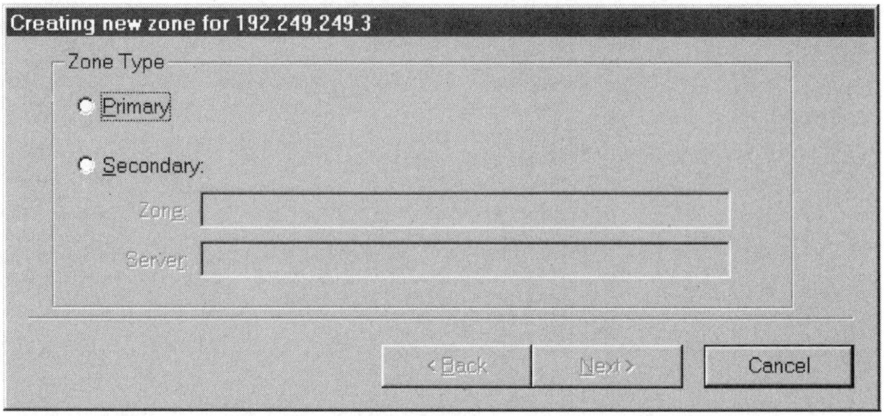

*Figure 4-5. Creating a new zone, first window*

Choose **Primary**, and then click **Next**. In the next window, type the domain name
of the zone in the **Zone Name** field. In our case, it's *movie.edu*. Notice that after
you press Tab, the **Zone File** field is automatically filled in (see Figure 4-6).

*Figure 4-6. Creating a new zone, second window*

The zone file, also called a *zone database file*, is the zone's permanent storage location. It's the file on the name server's disk where all the information about the zone is stored: it contains all the zone's resource records. Other name servers require you to edit the zone database file to make changes to the zone, but DNS Manager allows you to avoid any hand editing. As a result, you probably won't see the zone database files very much. We'll talk about their format later in this chapter.

Even if you won't be looking at it often, you need to specify a zone database file-name when you create a zone. The server expects these files to be in *%System-Root%\System32\DNS*. Microsoft's suggested naming convention uses the domain name of the zone followed by the *.dns* extension. You can name the zone file whatever you want, but as long as DNS Manager fills in the field for you, we recommend sticking with its suggestion. You may be familiar with other naming conventions, such as *db.* followed by a partial domain name, like *db.movie*. In fact, that's the recommendation in our sister book, *DNS and BIND*.

When you've entered a zone name and zone filename, click **Next**, and you'll see a window as in Figure 4-7.

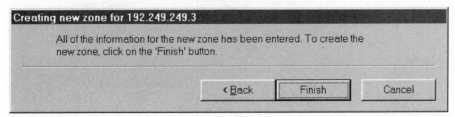

*Figure 4-7. Creating a new zone, third window*

We're not quite sure why this window is necessary, but there it is. Click **Finish** to create the zone. You'll see a window like the one pictured in Figure 4-8.

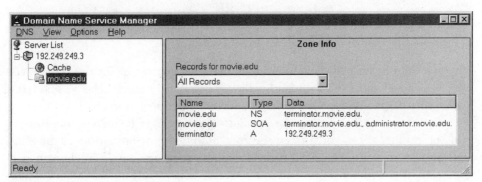

*Figure 4-8. DNS Manager with a new zone*

DNS Manager has created the zone and a few resource records. Let's talk about them one by one.

### The SOA record

We'll start with the second record displayed. It's the SOA (start of authority) resource record. The SOA record indicates that this name server is the best source of information for the data within this zone. Our name server is *authoritative* for the zone *movie.edu* because of the SOA record. (Remember, this SOA record is attached to the domain name of the zone, *movie.edu*.) An SOA record is required in each zone. There can be one, and only one, SOA record in a zone.

Double-click the SOA record to view its details. You'll see a window like the one in Figure 4-9.

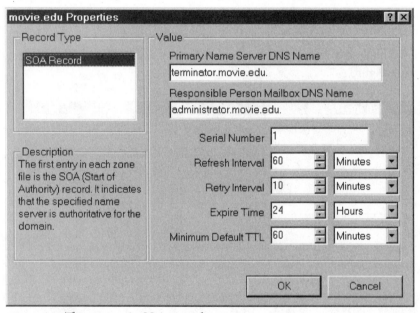

*Figure 4-9. The movie.edu SOA record*

The first field is the name of the primary master name server for this zone. (You may hear it called the MNAME field, which is its official name.) The second name (*administrator.movie.edu.*) is the email address of the person in charge of the data (if you replace the first dot with an at sign). DNS Manager defaults to *administrator*, but in other zones you'll often see *root*, *postmaster*, or *hostmaster* as the email address. Name servers won't use these names—they are meant for human consumption. If you notice a problem in someone's zone, you can send an email message to the listed email address.

Most of the remaining fields are for use by slave name servers and are discussed when we introduce slave name servers, later in this chapter. For now, assume these are reasonable values.

### The NS record

The first record is an NS (name server) resource record. There should be one NS record for each name server for the zone. Like the SOA record, the NS records are attached to the zone's domain name. In our example, the NS records are attached to *movie.edu*. Right now there's only one name server (the primary master), but as we configure slave name servers, we'll add NS records. DNS Manager created an NS record for *terminator* because it's a name server for *movie.edu*.

### The A record

The final automatically created record is an address record or A record. This record type fulfills the main purpose of DNS: it provides a name-to-address mapping. Each A record maps a domain name, like *terminator.movie.edu*, to an IP address, like 192.249.249.3.

When you create a new zone, DNS Manager creates an address record for the primary name server. It uses the host name configured in the primary master's DNS configuration.

Note that some abbreviating is going on in DNS Manager's display. For the SOA and NS records, the fully qualified domain name is shown, *movie.edu*. But for the A record, DNS Manager only displays *terminator* instead of *terminator.movie.edu*. DNS Manager normally displays a relative (that is, abbreviated) domain name on the right, so you have to look at what zone or domain is selected on the left to construct the fully qualified domain name. Only when records are attached to the name of a zone does it display a fully qualified name, as is the case with the *movie.edu* SOA and NS records.

You're probably anxious to add resource records for the rest of your zone, but it's best to create the reverse mapping (*in-addr.arpa*) zones first.

## Creating a New Reverse Mapping Zone

Zones like *movie.edu* handle the mapping of names to addresses using A records. But mapping addresses back to names—reverse mapping—is just as important. As you recall from Chapter 2, *How Does DNS Work?*, a special portion of the name space, the *in-addr.arpa* domain, is designated for reverse mapping. Each domain name in *in-addr.arpa* corresponds to every possible IP address, and PTR records attached to a domain name provide the actual reverse mapping. Just think of a PTR record as the opposite of an A record.

So after we create *movie.edu*, we're not done. Movie U. has two class C networks, 192.249.249.0 and 192.253.253.0. We need to create the corresponding *in-addr.arpa* zones for reverse mapping with DNS Manager: *249.249.192.in-addr.arpa* and *253.253.192.in-addr.arpa*.

Creating an *in-addr.arpa* zone is the same as creating any other zone:

1. Select **DNS → New Zone**.

2. Choose **Primary**, and click **Next**.

3. In the next window, enter the name of the zone (**249.249.192.in-addr.arpa**, in this case), and press **Tab**.

4. We recommend accepting the automatically generated zone filename, but you can change it at this point if you'd like.

5. Click **Next**.

6. In the final window, click **Finish**.

Note that, just as it did with the *movie.edu* zone, DNS Manager automatically creates the SOA record and an NS record.

For Movie U., we'll repeat this process to create the *253.253.192.in-addr.arpa* zone. You would create *in-addr.arpa* zones according to the networks you have. Usually there's one *in-addr.arpa* zone per Class C (or sub-Class C) network. Larger networks, like Class A or Class B, are usually broken into several *in-addr.arpa* zones to make management easier. The zones usually correspond to subnets. This topic is covered in more detail in Chapter 9, *Parenting*.

## Adding Resource Records

Now that we've created Movie U.'s zones, we can add information about all its machines. Each machine requires two resource records: an A record in the *movie.edu* zone to provide name-to-address mapping and a PTR record in the appropriate *in-addr.arpa* zone to provide address-to-name mapping. Adding the A record is intuitive, but it's easy to forget about the PTR record. DNS Manager makes the job easier with the **New Host** command, which creates an A record and a PTR record in one pass.

Select a forward mapping zone (like *movie.edu*), and choose **DNS → New Host**. Enter the name of the host and its IP address. To create the PTR record as well, you also need to check the **Create Associated PTR Record** box. The window looks like the one in Figure 4-10.

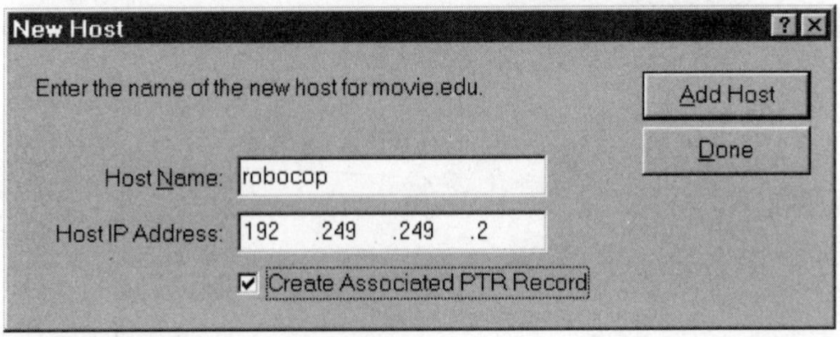

*Figure 4-10. The new host window*

You'll notice that we typed a relative domain name (*robocop*) and not a fully qualified domain name (*robocop.movie.edu.*) DNS Manager requires a relative domain name in this field. It appends the domain name of the zone selected in DNS Manager's left pane to create a fully qualified domain name. Don't worry—if you try to enter a fully qualified domain name, DNS Manager will give you an error message.

### Aliases

Looking back at Movie U.'s host table in the beginning of the chapter, you'll see that some hosts have aliases. (The aliases are any additional names after the first one listed.) For example, *terminator* is also known as *bigt*. There's a special resource record called the CNAME record that's used to make an alias. The name of the record is confusing, because CNAME is short for canonical name, which means the "real" name of the host. But a CNAME record doesn't make a canonical name; it makes an alias. All other types of records make a canonical name. We recommend thinking of it this way: CNAME records *point* to canonical names, while other record types *make* canonical names.

To create an alias, use the **New Record** command. Select the zone you want to add the record to on the left, and choose **DNS → New Record**. Unlike with **New Host**, you can create a record in any zone. The window looks like the one in Figure 4-11.

This window lets you add one of 17 different types of resource records. When you select the record type in the upper-left field, a brief description of the record type appears in the lower left, and the fields on the right change to accommodate the proper kind of data for the record type. Note that you can add A records and PTR records with this window, too.

We've selected CNAME, so fields for the alias name and canonical name (labeled as **For DNS Host Name**) appear on the right. The input in Figure 4-11 will generate an alias from *bigt.movie.edu* to *terminator.movie.edu*. The **Domain** field is just a reminder of the current domain. As was the case with the **New Host** command,

*Figure 4-11. Creating a CNAME record*

you must enter a single-label (that is, no periods) name in the **Alias Name** field: the **Alias Name** field is always relative to the current domain. But there is no such restriction for the canonical name field. You can point an alias anywhere. We could alias *bigt.movie.edu* to *www.whitehouse.gov* if we wanted to. If you leave off the domain in the canonical name field, the zone's domain name will be appended automatically.

It's important to know that the name server handles CNAME records in a different manner than aliases are handled in the host table. When a name server looks up a name and finds a CNAME record, it replaces the alias name with the canonical name and looks up that new name. For example, when the name server looks up *bigt.movie.edu*, it finds a CNAME record pointing to *terminator.movie.edu*. Then it looks up *terminator.movie.edu*, and its address is returned.

One thing you must remember about aliases like *bigt*—they should never appear in the data portion (that is, on the right side) of a resource record. Stated differently: always use the canonical name (*terminator*) in the data portion of the resource record. Notice that the NS records use the canonical name.

Sometimes you can use an A record to get the effect of an alias. Suppose you have a router, like *wormhole*, and you want to check one of the interfaces. One common troubleshooting technique is to *ping* the interface to verify that it is responding. If you *ping* the name *wormhole*, the name server returns the addresses of both interfaces when the name is looked up. *ping* uses the first address in the list. But which address is first?

The solution is to create two A records for *wormhole* with **New Record**. (The first of the two records is shown in Figure 4-12.)

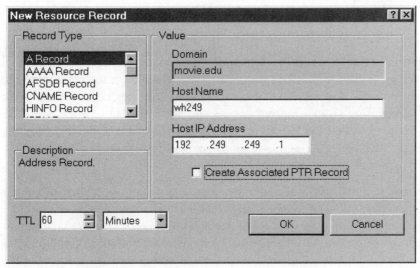

*Figure 4-12. Creating the first of two A records for wormhole*

With the host table, we chose the address we wanted by using either *wh249* or *wh253*—each name referred to *one* of the host's addresses. To provide equivalent capability with DNS, we didn't make *wh249* and *wh253* into aliases (CNAME records). That would result in both addresses for *wormhole* being returned when the alias was looked up. Instead, we used address records. Now, to check the operation of the 192.253.253.1 interface on *wormhole*, we *ping wh253* since it refers to only one address. The same applies to *wh249*.

To state this as a general rule: if a host is multihomed (has more than one network interface), create an address (A) record for each alias unique to one address. Create a CNAME record for each alias common to all the addresses.

### One more note about PTR records

We now have two A records, *wormhole.movie.edu* and *wh249.movie.edu*, pointing to the same address, 192.249.249.1. We also have a PTR record pointing from *1.249.249.192.in-addr.arpa* to *wormhole.movie.edu*. (This record was added automatically to the *249.249.192.in-addr.arpa* zone by the **New Host** command. Remember that addresses are looked up as names: the IP address is reversed, and *in-addr.arpa* is appended.) Thus, 192.249.249.1 maps to *wormhole.movie.edu* and not to *wh249.movie.edu*. Should you create another PTR record that maps 192.249.249.1 to *wh249.movie.edu*? You *can* create two PTR records—it's perfectly legal—but most systems are not prepared to see more than one name for an address. We recommend that you don't bother with multiple PTR records since so few systems can use them.

## Where Is All This Information Stored?

You may be wondering what's been happening to all the resource records we've been entering. Where are they being stored? The answer is: in the memory of the DNS Server process. We mentioned earlier that DNS Manager communicates with the DNS Server using an RPC mechanism. As you add records to a zone with DNS Manager, they are added "on the fly" to the name server's memory. Of course, the name server's memory is transient—when the name server process stops, its memory is lost. Obviously a permanent storage location is needed.

This is where the zone database files we specified when we created the zones come in. The zone database files are the zones' permanent storage location, holding all the zones' resource records. If you use DNS Manager to make a change to a zone, the copy of the zone in the name server's memory is changed, and a flag is set to update that zone's database file. The name server updates the zone database file when it exits, unless you tell it to update it sooner. The command **DNS →** **Update Server Data Files** causes the name server to update the zone database files of all zones it's a primary for, regardless of whether or not they've been modified. To avoid losing data, we recommend using **DNS → Update Server Data Files** after any changes—use it like you use the **Save** command in other applications. Of course, the difference here is that the server will save your data if it exits gracefully. You don't have to use **DNS → Update Server Data Files** after a batch of changes, but it doesn't hurt anything and you can sleep better.

As you've probably guessed, when the name server starts up, it reads the zone database files into memory. When you select **View → Refresh** or press F5, DNS Manager queries the name server and updates its display.

If you've been keeping track, you realize that DNS information exists in three places: zone database files, the name server's memory, and DNS Manager's window. The diagram in Figure 4-13 helps explain how the information flows.

## The Zone Database Files

Let's take a look at the zone database files for Movie U. After inputting the remaining host table entries, we end up with the display shown previously in Figure 4-2. (Of course, this view shows only the contents of *movie.edu*. The *249.249.192.in-addr.arpa* and *253.253.192.in-addr.arpa* zones are populated with PTR records.)

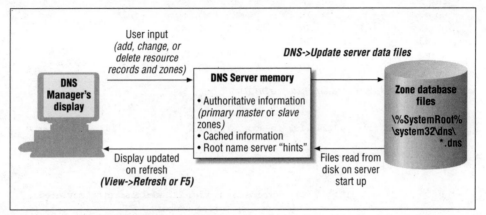

*Figure 4-13. Where everything is stored*

Next we select **DNS → Update Server Data Files**, and the server generates three files in *%SystemRoot%\System32\DNS*: *movie.edu.dns*, *249.249.192.in-addr.arpa.dns*, and *253.253.192.in-addr.arpa.dns*. They look like the following:

Contents of *movie.edu.dns*:

```
;
;  Database file movie.edu.dns for movie.edu zone.
;     Zone version:  41
;

@               IN      SOA terminator.movie.edu.   administrator.movie.edu. (
                        1            ; serial number
                        3600         ; refresh
                        600          ; retry
                        86400        ; expire
                        3600      )  ; minimum TTL


;
;  Zone NS records
;

@               IN      NS   terminator


;
;  Zone records
;

bigt            IN      CNAME    terminator
carrie          IN      A   192.253.253.4
dh              IN      CNAME    diehard
diehard         IN      A   192.249.249.4
misery          IN      A   192.253.253.2
robocop         IN      A   192.249.249.2
shining         IN      A   192.253.253.3
```

```
terminator                  IN      A     192.249.249.3
wh                          IN      CNAME    wormhole
wh249                       IN      A     192.249.249.1
wh253                       IN      A     192.253.253.1
wormhole                    IN      A     192.249.249.1
                            IN      A     192.253.253.1
```

## Contents of *249.249.192.in-addr.arpa.dns*:

```
;
; Database file 249.249.192.in-addr.arpa.dns for 249.249.192.in-addr.arpa
zone.
;      Zone version:  51
;

@                  IN      SOA terminator.movie.edu.administrator.movie.edu.(
                           5               ; serial number
                           3600            ; refresh
                           600             ; retry
                           86400           ; expire
                           3600        )  ; minimum TTL


;
;  Zone NS records
;

@                  IN      NS   terminator.movie.edu.


;
;  Zone records
;

1                          IN      PTR wormhole.movie.edu.
2                          IN      PTR robocop.movie.edu.
3                          IN      PTR terminator.movie.edu.
4                          IN      PTR diehard.movie.edu.
```

## Contents of *253.253.192.in-addr.arpa.dns*:

```
;
; Database file 253.253.192.in-addr.arpa.dns for 253.253.192.in-addr.arpa
zone.
;      Zone version:  41
;

@                  IN      SOA terminator.movie.edu.administrator.movie.edu.(
                           4               ; serial number
                           3600            ; refresh
                           600             ; retry
                           86400           ; expire
                           3600        )  ; minimum TTL


;
```

```
;   Zone NS records
;

@                       IN    NS  terminator.movie.edu.


;
;   Zone records
;

1                       IN        PTR wormhole.movie.edu.
2                       IN        PTR misery.movie.edu.
3                       IN        PTR shining.movie.edu.
4                       IN        PTR carrie.movie.edu.
```

## Zone Database File Format

The format of zone database files is specified in the DNS standards. That means all name servers, whether Microsoft's DNS Server or the BIND name server, can read each other's zone database files.

You've probably already guessed that the semicolon is the comment character. It can appear anywhere on a line, and anything to the right is a comment and is ignored by the name server. Blank lines are okay, too.

Each resource record must start in the first column of the file—no preceding whitespace. (Don't be confused by the examples in this book, which are indented because of the way the book is formatted.) Resource records are case insensitive— you can use uppercase or lowercase. The server doesn't preserve the case, though. It matches the case of the reply to the case of the query. For example, if a record is written as *terminator* in the zone database file but you query for *Terminator*, the server responds with *Terminator*.

Resource records are broken up into fields, with any amount of whitespace (tabs or spaces) separating the fields.

The first field, called the owner, is the domain name of the record. Put another way, it's the node in the name space that the resource record is attached to. You've seen the domain name on the *left* side of the *right* pane of DNS Manager. (Got that?)

The next field in our examples is the class, IN, which stands for Internet. There are other classes, but none of them are currently in widespread use. Our examples use only the IN class.

The field after that is the record type. We've already discussed record types SOA, NS, A, PTR, and CNAME, and you've probably browsed through the list of other record types in DNS Manager's **New Record** window. The type simply specifies what type of data is associated with the domain name on the right: A means IP address, NS means the name of an authoritative name server, and so on.

And that's a good lead in to the final field, the RDATA or resource record data. This field holds the kind of data specified by the record type. This field can be divided into multiple subfields depending on the type. For example, A records may specify only one parameter: an IP address. But the SOA record specifies seven parameters: remember all those fields in Figure 4-9?

Speaking of the SOA record, you'll notice in the examples that it's the only record spanning multiple lines. You can use parentheses to allow a resource record to span multiple lines. This trick works for all record types, not just SOA.

Domain names appear a lot in resource records. The left side of every resource record is a domain name, and the right side (RDATA field) of many record types also contains domain names (for example, NS and SOA records). Using a fully qualified domain name in each case is perfectly legal, but it would be a lot of work: imagine having to type *movie.edu* at the end of every host name if you were entering these files by hand. Fortunately, abbreviations are allowed. You need to understand them to decipher the zone database files in this chapter, because the records generated by the Microsoft DNS Server use these abbreviations.

### Appending domains

Every zone has a domain name: it's just the name of the zone. (This probably strikes you as pretty obvious.) This domain name is the key to the most useful shortcut. This domain name is the *origin* of all the data in the database file. The origin is appended to all names in the file not ending in a dot. The origin is different for each file, because each file is associated with a different zone, each of which has a different name.

Since the origin is appended to names, instead of entering *robocop*'s address in *movie.edu.dns* as this:

```
robocop.movie.edu.    IN A    192.249.249.2
```

the server generated it like this:

```
robocop    IN A    192.249.249.2
```

In *192.249.249.in-addr.arpa.dns,* this is the long way to write this record:

```
2.249.249.192.in-addr.arpa.  IN PTR robocop.movie.edu.
```

But since *249.249.192.in-addr.arpa* is the origin, the server generated:

```
2  IN PTR robocop.movie.edu.
```

Notice that all the fully qualified domain names in the file end in a dot. That tells the server that this domain name is complete and should be left alone. Suppose you forgot the trailing dot. An entry like this:

```
robocop.movie.edu    IN A    192.249.249.2
```

turns into an entry for *robocop.movie.edu.movie.edu,* and you didn't intend that at all.

### @ notation

If the domain name is the *same* as the origin, the name can be specified with an at sign (@). This is most often seen in the SOA record in database files generated by hand, but the Microsoft DNS server also uses the @ notation in the NS records. In the *movie.edu.dns* file in the previous example, the @ stands for *movie.edu.* Of course, in the *249.249.192.in-addr.arpa.dns* file, the @ stands for *249.249.192.in-addr.arpa,* and in the *253.253.192.in-addr.arpa.dns* file . . . well, you get the idea.

### Repeat last name

If a resource record name (that starts in column one) is a space or tab, then the name from the last resource record is used. This shortcut gets used when there are multiple resource records for a name. Here is an example where there are two address records for one name:

```
wormhole    IN A    192.249.249.1
            IN A    192.253.253.1
```

In the second address record, the name *wormhole* is implied. You can use this shortcut even if the resource records are of different types—for example, if *wormhole* also had a TXT (arbitrary text) record.

## The Loopback Address

Those of you familiar with the BIND name server may be wondering if we forgot about the loopback address. If we were setting up a BIND name server, it would need one additional zone database file to cover the *loopback* network: the special address that hosts use to direct traffic to themselves. This network is (almost) always 127.0.0.0, and the host number is (almost) always 127.0.0.1. Therefore, the name of this file would be *0.0.127.in-addr.arpa.dns,* and it would look like the other *in-addr.dns* files.

The following would be the contents of file *0.0.127.in-addr.arpa.dns:*

```
@              IN    SOA terminator.movie.edu.    administrator.movie.edu.(
                     1           ; serial number
                     3600        ; refresh
                     600         ; retry
```

```
                    86400        ; expire
                    3600         ) ; minimum TTL


;
;   Zone NS records
;


@                   IN    NS   terminator.movie.edu.


;
;   Zone records
;


1                         IN         PTR   localhost.
```

Why do name servers need this file? Think about it for a second. No one was given responsibility for network 127.0.0.0, yet systems use it for a loopback address. Since no one has direct responsibility, everyone who uses it is responsible for it individually. If you omit this file on a BIND name server, it will still operate. However, a lookup of 127.0.0.1 might fail: the name server will send the query to a root name server that might not be configured to map 127.0.0.1 to a name.

With the Microsoft DNS Server, you don't have to worry about creating this file and making your name server authoritative for the *in-addr.arpa* zone corresponding to network 127.0.0.0. The server is authoritative for this zone by default. It's called an *automatically created zone* and is visible in DNS Manager only if an option is set. Select **Options → Preferences**, and you'll see the window shown in Figure 4-14.

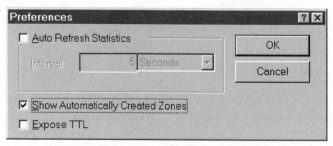

*Figure 4-14. DNS Manager preferences set to show automatically created zones*

Check the **Show Automatically Created Zones** box, and click **OK**. Then select the name server in the left pane, and refresh (**View → Refresh** or F5). You'll see three more zones in your display as shown in Figure 4-15.

We've drilled down into the *127.in-addr.arpa* zone to show that there's a PTR record for *1.0.0.127.in-addr.arpa* pointing to the domain name *localhost*. In other words, a Microsoft DNS Server will reverse-map the IP address 127.0.0.1 to the domain name *localhost* "out of the box" without any work on your part.

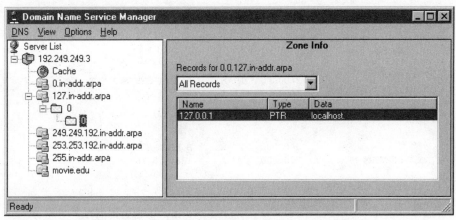

*Figure 4-15. DNS Manager showing automatically created zones*

The *0.in-addr.arpa* and *255.in-addr.arpa* zones are empty, save for NS and A records. Some hosts attempt to reverse-map the IP addresses 0.0.0.0 and 255.255.255.255, and these zones cause the local server to return an immediate NXDOMAIN (name not found) error for those queries, rather then asking a root name server.

## The Root Cache Data

Besides needing to know your local information, the name server also needs to know where the name servers for the root zone are. (Remember the resolution process starts at the root zone, so knowing which name servers are authoritative for the root zone is critical.) This information must be retrieved from the Internet host *ftp.rs.internic.net* (198.41.0.7). Use anonymous *ftp* to retrieve the file *named.root* from the *domain* subdirectory. The file, called the *root name server cache file*, should be named *%SystemRoot%\System32\DNS\cache.dns* on your name server. Here's the version of the file that was current when this book was published:

```
;       This file holds the information on root name servers needed to
;       initialize cache of Internet domain name servers
;       (e.g. reference this file in the "cache  .  <file>"
;       configuration file of BIND domain name servers).
;
;       This file is made available by InterNIC registration services
;       under anonymous FTP as
;           file                /domain/named.root
;           on server           FTP.RS.INTERNIC.NET
;       -OR- under Gopher at    RS.INTERNIC.NET
;           under menu          InterNIC Registration Services (NSI)
;               submenu         InterNIC Registration Archives
;           file                named.root
;
```

```
;       last update:    Aug 22, 1997
;       related version of root zone:    1997082200
;
;
; formerly NS.INTERNIC.NET
;
.                          3600000    IN   NS   A.ROOT-SERVERS.NET.
A.ROOT-SERVERS.NET.        3600000         A    198.41.0.4
;
; formerly NS1.ISI.EDU
;
.                          3600000         NS   B.ROOT-SERVERS.NET.
B.ROOT-SERVERS.NET.        3600000         A    128.9.0.107
;
; formerly C.PSI.NET
;
.                          3600000         NS   C.ROOT-SERVERS.NET.
C.ROOT-SERVERS.NET.        3600000         A    192.33.4.12
;
; formerly TERP.UMD.EDU
;
.                          3600000         NS   D.ROOT-SERVERS.NET.
D.ROOT-SERVERS.NET.        3600000         A    128.8.10.90
;
; formerly NS.NASA.GOV
;
.                          3600000         NS   E.ROOT-SERVERS.NET.
E.ROOT-SERVERS.NET.        3600000         A    192.203.230.10
;
; formerly NS.ISC.ORG
;
.                          3600000         NS   F.ROOT-SERVERS.NET.
F.ROOT-SERVERS.NET.        3600000         A    192.5.5.241
;
; formerly NS.NIC.DDN.MIL
;
.                          3600000         NS   G.ROOT-SERVERS.NET.
G.ROOT-SERVERS.NET.        3600000         A    192.112.36.4
;
; formerly AOS.ARL.ARMY.MIL
;
.                          3600000         NS   H.ROOT-SERVERS.NET.
H.ROOT-SERVERS.NET.        3600000         A    128.63.2.53
;
; formerly NIC.NORDU.NET
;
.                          3600000         NS   I.ROOT-SERVERS.NET.
I.ROOT-SERVERS.NET.        3600000         A    192.36.148.17
;
; temporarily housed at NSI (InterNIC)
;
.                          3600000         NS   J.ROOT-SERVERS.NET.
J.ROOT-SERVERS.NET.        3600000         A    198.41.0.10
;
```

```
; housed in LINX, operated by RIPE NCC
;
.                               3600000    NS    K.ROOT-SERVERS.NET.
K.ROOT-SERVERS.NET.             3600000    A     193.0.14.129
;
; temporarily housed at ISI (IANA)
;
.                               3600000    NS    L.ROOT-SERVERS.NET.
L.ROOT-SERVERS.NET.             3600000    A     198.32.64.12
;
; housed in Japan, operated by WIDE
;
.                               3600000    NS    M.ROOT-SERVERS.NET.
M.ROOT-SERVERS.NET.             3600000    A     202.12.27.33
; End of File
```

The domain name "." refers to the root domain. Since the root domain's name servers change over time, don't assume *this* list is current. Pull a new version of *named.root*.

It's worth noting that the root NS records are not put into the cache and used directly. Rather, upon startup the server queries one of the root servers in the cache file for the list of root servers. The list returned is the one used by the name server to start the resolution process and is the list you see when you double-click the Cache icon. When the name server exits, its list of root name servers is written to the cache file.

The nice thing about this behavior is that if you use an older cache file, as long as at least one of the name servers specified has the correct list of root name servers, your name server will discover the up-to-date list. And because the name server updates *cache.dns* on exit, it'll have the right list to begin with the next time it starts. The whole purpose of this logic is to ensure the name server has the current list of root name servers, which is very important for the resolution process to work properly.

You might be wondering if you can put information other than root name server NS records and their corresponding A records in the cache file. You can, but we don't recommend it. For one thing, the name server only rewrites root NS records (and their A records) to the cache file, so any changes you make will be overwritten eventually. In addition, BIND name servers don't have this feature. If your DNS architecture depends on any preloaded information in the cache, you're locked into using only Microsoft DNS Server as a name server platform. Yet another reason we think this is a bad idea is that you have to remember the information is there and maintain it by hand when it changes. We suggest you let the name server populate its own cache and don't interfere.

You may be wondering what the 3600000s are for. In older versions of this file, this number used to be 99999999. It dates back to the behavior of early versions of BIND, the reference implementation of the name server. The BIND name server used to put the contents of the cache file directly into its cache, and it had to know how long to keep these records active. The **99999999s** meant a *very long time*. The root name server data was to be kept active for as long as the server ran. Since both BIND and the Microsoft DNS Server now store the cache file data in a special place and don't discard it if it times out, the TTL is unnecessary. But it's not harmful to have the **3600000s**, and it makes for interesting DNS folklore when you pass responsibility to the next name server administrator.

One final note about the *cache.dns* file. *To install a new* cache.dns *file, you must first stop the server.* Remember, the server will overwrite the *cache.dns* file when it exits. Let's say you install a new file and then stop and start the server. As soon as the server stopped, your new file was overwritten with the server's list of root name servers. It then restarts, reads that list back in, and queries one of those name servers for the list of root name servers (which will almost certainly be the same list). The solution is to stop the server, replace the *cache.dns* file, and restart the server.

# Running a Primary Master Name Server

Your primary name server is already up and running; you've been talking to it via DNS Manager. You've created a zone and populated it with information. Then you directed the server to write out zone database files with the **DNS → Update Server Data Files** command. To be sure that everything is okay, you should stop and restart the server and then check the Event Log for any messages or errors.

## Starting and Stopping the DNS Server

You start and stop the DNS server just like any other NT service: with the **Services** Control Panel document. Open the Control Panel with **Start → Settings → Control Panel**. Double-click the **Services** icon, and you'll see the **Services** window as shown in Figure 4-16.

Your system should look like this: the server should be running (that is, it should be started). Select the server as we've done by clicking anywhere on the Microsoft DNS Server line. Click **Stop**. You'll be prompted for confirmation; click **Yes**. After the server stops, click **Start**. In a few seconds, the server should be running again.

While you've got this window open, check to make sure that the DNS Server is being started automatically on bootup. You want to see **Automatic** in the **Startup** column (and not **Manual** or **Disabled**). To change the startup behavior, just click the **Startup** button.

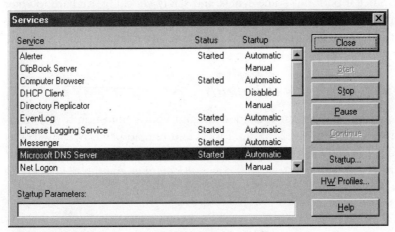

*Figure 4-16. Windows NT services control window*

You can also start and stop the DNS Server from the DOS command line: **net start dns** will start the server, and **net stop dns** stops it.

## Check the Event Log for Messages and Errors

Now you need to check the Event Log. Start the Event Viewer by selecting **Start →
Programs → Administrative Tools (Common) → Event Viewer**. Be sure you're looking at system events: choose **Log → System**. You should see a window like the one
in Figure 4-17.

| Date | Time | Source | Category | Event | User |
|------|------|--------|----------|-------|------|
| 3/22/98 | 4:30:14 PM | Dns | None | 2 | N/A |
| 3/22/98 | 4:30:13 PM | Dns | None | 1 | N/A |
| 3/22/98 | 4:30:07 PM | Dns | None | 3 | N/A |

Event Viewer - System Log on \\TERMINATOR

Log  View  Options  Help

*Figure 4-17. Event Viewer*

DNS Server Event ID 3 is "The DNS Server has shutdown." Event ID 1 is "Starting
Microsoft DNS Server (v4.0 ServicePack3)," and Event ID 2 is "The DNS Server has
started." (More events are listed in Chapter 7.) These three events are just what
you want to see: a normal server shutdown and startup. We're reading from bottom to top since Event Viewer's default view is newest events first. We also
cleared the Event Log before we stopped and started the server—that's why only
DNS events are showing.

If there were any other messages or errors, we'd take steps to correct them now.
To be honest, we didn't expect any problems because we entered all the data via

DNS Manager. Since it performs some syntax and sanity checking, it's hard to enter bad data to make the name server upset enough to complain in the Event Log. Still, it doesn't hurt to check. If you ever start editing zone database files by hand, you definitely need to check the Event Log.

## Testing Your Setup with nslookup

If you have correctly set up your local domain and your connection to the Internet is up, you should be able to look up a local and remote name. We'll step you through the lookups with *nslookup*. This book contains an entire chapter on this topic (Chapter 11, *nslookup*), but we will cover *nslookup* in enough detail here to do basic name server testing.

### Look up a local name

*nslookup* can be used to look up any type of resource record, and it can be directed to query any name server. By default, it looks up A (address) records using the name server on the local system. To look up a host's address with *nslookup*, run *nslookup* with the host's name as the only argument. A lookup of a local name should return almost instantly.

We ran *nslookup* to look up *carrie*:

```
C:\> nslookup carrie
Server:  terminator.movie.edu
Address: 192.249.249.3

Name:    carrie.movie.edu
Address: 192.253.253.4
```

If looking up a local name works, your local name server has been configured properly for your domain. If the lookup fails, you'll see something like this:

```
*** terminator.movie.edu can't find carrie: Non-existent domain
```

This means that either *carrie* is not in your data—check DNS Manager or the zone database file—or some name server error occurred (but you should have caught the error when you checked the Event Log).

### Look up a local address

When *nslookup* is given an address to look up, it knows to make a PTR query instead of an address query. We ran *nslookup* to look up *carrie's* address:

```
C:\> nslookup 192.253.253.4
Server:  terminator.movie.edu
Address: 192.249.249.3

Name:    carrie.movie.edu
Address: 192.253.253.4
```

If looking up an address works, your local name server has been configured properly for your *in-addr.arpa* domain. If the lookup fails, you'll see the same error messages as when you looked up a name.

### Look up a remote name

The next step is to use the local name server to look up a remote name, like *ftp.uu.net,* or another system you know on the Internet. This command may not return as quickly as the last one. If *nslookup* fails to get a response from your name server, it will wait a little longer than a minute before giving up:

```
C:\> nslookup ftp.uu.net.
Server:  terminator.movie.edu
Address:  192.249.249.3

Name:    ftp.uu.net
Address:  192.48.96.9
```

If this works, your name server knows where the root name servers are and how to contact them to find information about domains other than your own. If it fails, either you forgot to initialize the cache file (and a message in the Event Log will show up) or the network is broken somewhere and you can't reach the name servers for the remote domain. Try a different remote domain name.

If these first three lookups succeeded, congratulations! You have a primary master name server up and running. At this point, you are ready to start configuring your slave name server.

### One more test

While you are testing, though, run one more test. Try having a remote name server look up a name in your zone. This is going to work only if your parent name servers have already delegated your zone to the name server you just set up. If your parent required you to have your two name servers running before delegating your zone, skip ahead to the section "Running a Slave Name Server."

To make *nslookup* use a remote name server to look up a local name, give the local host's name as the first argument, and the remote server's name as the second argument. Again, if this doesn't work, it may take a little longer than a minute before *nslookup* gives you an error message. For instance, to have *gatekeeper.dec.com* look up *carrie*:

```
C:\> nslookup carrie gatekeeper.dec.com.
Server:  gatekeeper.dec.com.
Address:  204.123.2.2
```

```
Name:    carrie.movie.edu
Address: 192.253.253.4
```

If the first two lookups worked, but using a remote name server to look up a local name failed, you may not be registered with your parent name server. That is not a problem at first, because systems within your zone can look up the names of other systems within and outside your zone. You'll be able to send email and *ftp* to local and remote systems. Some systems won't allow FTP connections if they can't map your address back to a name. But not being registered will shortly become a problem. Hosts outside of your zone cannot look up names within your zone. You will be able to send email to friends in remote domains, but you won't get their responses. To fix this problem, contact someone responsible for your parent zone and have them check the delegation of your zone.

## Running a Slave Name Server

You need to set up another name server for robustness. You can (and probably will) set up more than two name servers. Two servers are the minimum. If you have only one name server and it goes down, no one can look up names in your zone. A second name server splits the load with the first server or handles the whole load if the first server is down. You *could* set up another primary master name server, but we don't recommend it. Set up a slave name server.

How does a server know if it is a primary master or a slave for a zone? The DNS Server configuration information in the Registry tells the server it is a primary master or a slave on a per zone basis. The NS records don't tell us which servers are primary master for a zone and which servers are slave for a zone—they only say who the servers are. (Globally, DNS doesn't care; as far as the actual name resolution goes, slave servers are as good as primary master servers.)

What is different between a primary master name server and a slave name server? The crucial difference is where the server gets its data. A primary master name server reads its data from files. A slave name server loads its data over the network from another name server. This process is called a *zone transfer*.

A slave name server is not limited to loading zones from a primary master name server; a slave server can load from another slave server.

The big advantage of slave name servers is that you only maintain one set of the DNS database files, the ones on the primary master name server. You don't have to worry about synchronizing the files among name servers; the slaves do that for you.

A slave name server doesn't need to retrieve *all* of its db files over the network; the *cache.dns* is the same as on a primary master, so keep a local copy on the slave.

---

*NOTE*            One point about slaves may become confusing: slaves used to be called *secondary master* name servers. The terminology was changed since DNS Manager came out, and now everyone "in the know" uses the term *slave*. We'll use the term *slave* in this book, but you'll see that DNS Manager still uses the term *secondary*. As we said, the two are synonymous.

---

## Add a New Server to DNS Manager

The first step in configuring a slave server is to add the server to DNS Manager's world view. Just as we did when configuring the primary master, select **DNS →  New Server**, and then enter the IP address of the slave. In this case our slave will be *wormhole* with IP address 192.249.249.1. Of course, the DNS Server has to be installed and running on the slave-to-be for DNS Manager to be able to manage it.

After you've added the slave to DNS Manager's configuration, double-click the IP address of the primary master name server to list the zones it's authoritative for. Having this list of zones visible makes things easier in the next step.

## Create a New Zone

This new server will be a slave for every zone on the primary, so we'll have to go through the new zone process for each zone. Let's start with *movie.edu*. Select **DNS → New Zone**. This time, select **Secondary** (remember, this is synonymous with *slave*) in the resulting window, and you'll see something like Figure 4-18.

In the **Zone** field, enter the domain name of the zone to be a slave for (that is, *movie.edu*). In the **Server** field, enter the IP address of the primary master name server. You could type this information, or you can take advantage of a really slick shortcut offered by DNS Manager. Note the hand pointer in the window: you can specify the zone and server by dragging the hand to the zone on the primary that you want this server to be a slave for. Now you see why we wanted the primary's zones to be visible. Once the hand touches the zone, these fields are filled in. See Figure 4-19.

Whether you enter the zone and server manually or use the hand pointer shortcut, click **Next** to get the next window as shown in Figure 4-20.

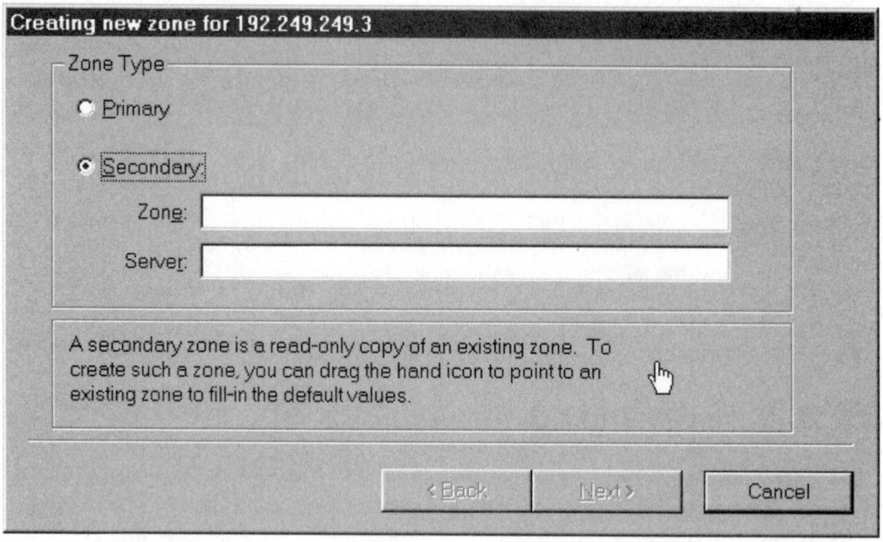

*Figure 4-18. Creating a new secondary zone, first window, with Secondary selected*

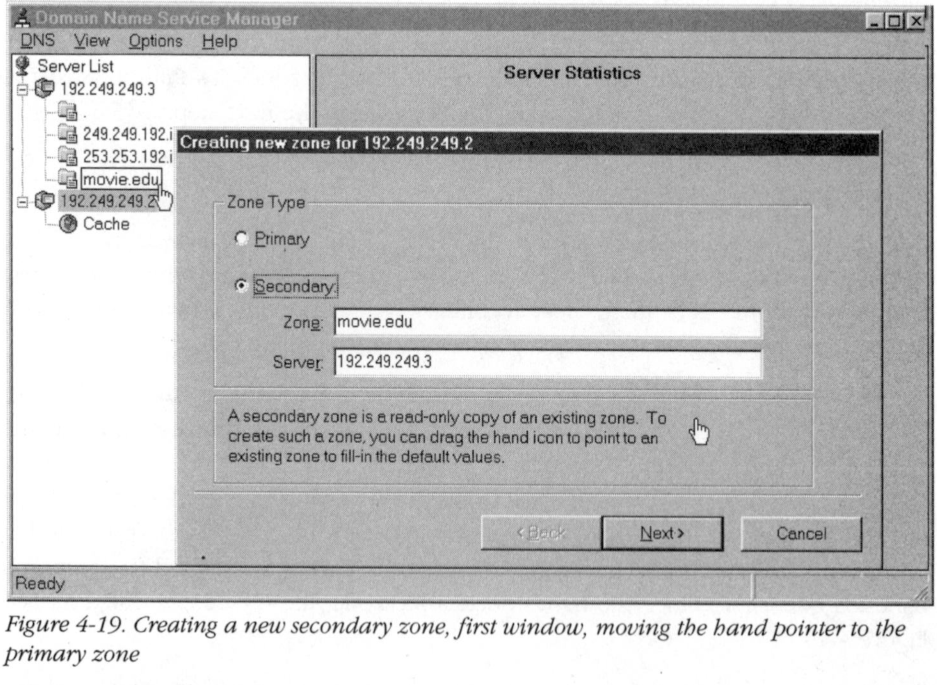

*Figure 4-19. Creating a new secondary zone, first window, moving the hand pointer to the primary zone*

This is the same window you see when creating a primary zone. If you entered the zone and server manually in the previous window, only the zone is filled in here. You can still hit **Tab** to get the automatically generated zone filename

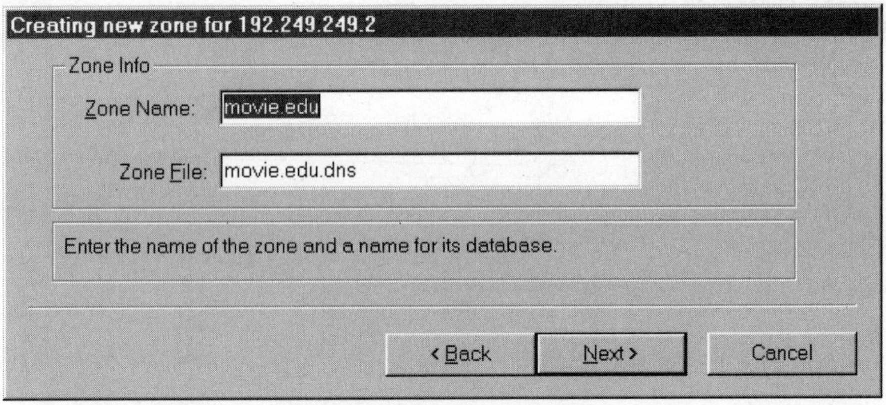

*Figure 4-20. Creating a new secondary zone, second window*

conforming to the *.dns convention. If you used the hand pointer in the previous window, both fields are filled in.

You're probably wondering why we're specifying a zone database file here—after all, this name server will be a slave for the *movie.edu* zone. It will load the zone from the primary, not from a file on its disk. On a slave, the zone file is not the definitive source of information for the zone as it is on the primary. Instead it's treated as a backup copy of the zone. After the slave does a zone transfer, it saves a copy of the zone in the backup file. The slave server reads the backup file on startup and later checks with the primary master server to see if the primary has a newer copy, instead of loading a new copy of the zone immediately. If the primary master server has a newer copy, the slave pulls it over and saves it in the backup file.

The backup file saves time and network bandwidth. When the slave starts up and the zone hasn't changed, it doesn't have to go through the time and expense of performing a zone transfer. Or suppose the primary server is down when the slave starts up. The slave would be unable to transfer the zone and therefore wouldn't function as a server for that zone until the primary server is up. With a backup copy, the slave has some data, although it might be slightly out of date. Since the slave does not rely on the master server always being up, the system is more robust.

The Microsoft DNS server requires slave zones to have a backup file. Those of you familiar with BIND know that backup files are optional, although we don't know anyone who doesn't use them.

When you're finished, click **Next**, and you'll see the window shown in Figure 4-21.

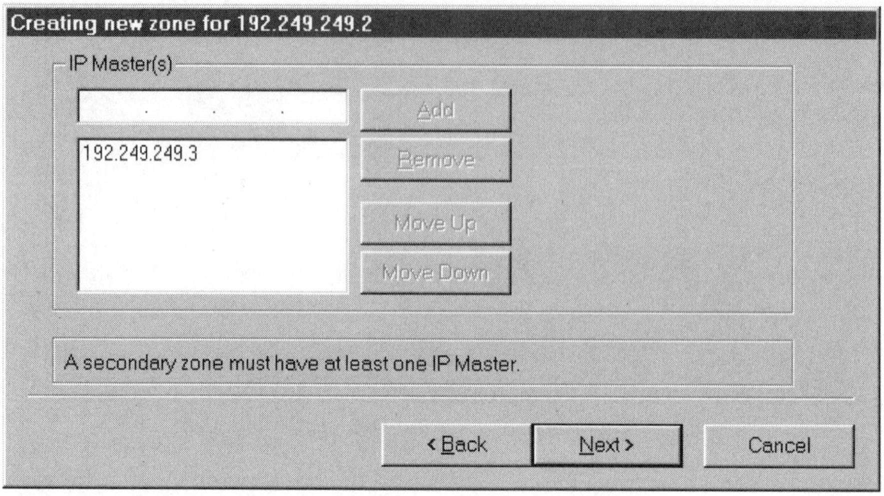

*Figure 4-21. Creating a new secondary zone, third window*

At this point, the process of creating a primary master zone and a slave zone really diverge. This is the screen where you specify where this name server will get the zone data from. In this example, we're making *wormhole* a slave for the *movie.edu* zone. We need to tell *wormhole* to load the zone from *terminator*, the primary master. "But wait," you say, "didn't we already do that two windows ago?" That's a valid question. For whatever reason, DNS Manager requires that you specify the primary's IP address in two places. In fact, on this screen you can specify multiple IP addresses. In advanced (and complicated) configurations, sometimes there are multiple primaries or multiple sources for a slave to get the zone information. DNS Manager supports those configurations. You could also just specify the IP address of another slave after that of the primary: in case the primary is down, this slave can load from another slave. Of course, Movie U. doesn't have another slave (yet).

For now, we just specify *terminator's* IP address, 192.249.249.3. Then click **Next**. The final window in the process is the same as when creating a primary zone: it just tells you that you're done now and asks you to click **Finish**. We'll omit showing it to you.

When you're done, the new slave immediately initiates a zone transfer to the primary to download the zone. Within a few seconds you should be able to double-click the slave's icon for the zone and see the records in the zone.

## Add an NS Record for the New Slave Name Server

Your new slave won't be much good if the rest of the world doesn't know about it. As a general rule, when you add another name server for a zone, you also need to add an NS record for it. (We'll discuss the exceptions to this in Chapter 8, *Growing Your Domain.*)

You need to add an NS record on the zone's primary. (Remember that all changes to a zone are made on the primary and propagate automatically to the slaves. Don't get confused by the fact that DNS Manager lets you see all your name servers—you make the changes only to the zone's primary.) In our case, we need to add an NS record for *wormhole* to the *movie.edu* zone. So we highlight *movie.edu* under *terminator*, and select **DNS** → **New Record** as shown in Figure 4-22.

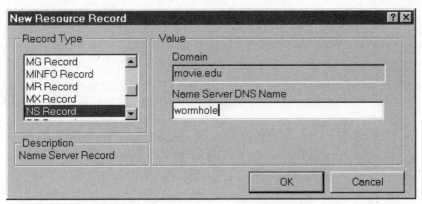

*Figure 4-22. Creating an NS record*

## Don't Forget the in-addr.arpa Zones!

Now repeat this slave zone creation process with the *249.249.192.in-addr.arpa* and *253.253.192.in-addr.arpa* zones.

## SOA Values

Remember this SOA record for the *movie.edu* zone?

```
@    IN     SOA terminator.movie.edu.administrator.movie.edu.(
                       1          ; serial number
                       3600       ; refresh
                       600        ; retry
                       86400      ; expire
                       3600     ) ; minimum TTL
```

We never explained what the values in between the parentheses were for.

The serial number applies to all the data within the zone. We chose to start our serial number at 1, a logical place to start. DNS Manager automatically increments the serial number in a zone's SOA record whenever you make a change to the zone. If you've maintained zone database files by hand, you might have encoded the date in the serial number—like 1997102301. This format is YYYYMMDDNN, where Y is the year, M is the month, D is the day, and NN is a count of how many times the zone data were modified that day. Unforunately, you can't use that convention when also using DNS Manager. It just updates the serial number by one each time a change is made and doesn't understand the date encoding.

When a slave name server contacts a primary master server for zone data, it first asks for the serial number on the data. If the slave's serial number is lower than the primary's, the slave's zone data are out of date. In this case, the slave pulls a new copy of the zone. As you might guess, if you ever modify the zone database files on the primary master by hand, you must increment the serial number, too. Updating zone database files is covered in Chapter 7.

The next four fields specify various time intervals in seconds:

*refresh*

> The refresh interval tells the slave how often to check that its data are up to date. To give you an idea of the system load this feature causes, a slave will make one SOA query per zone per refresh interval. The default value generated by DNS Manager when the zone was created, one hour, is reasonably aggressive. Most users will tolerate a delay of half of a working day for things like name server data to propagate, when they are waiting for their new workstation to be operational. If you provide one-day service for your site, consider raising this value to eight hours. If your data don't change very often, or if all of your slaves are spread over long distances (as the root name servers are), consider a value that is even longer: 24 hours.

*retry*

> If a slave fails to reach the primary name server(s) after the refresh period (the hosts or hosts could be down), then it starts trying to connect every *retry* seconds. The retry interval is usually shorter than the refresh interval, but it doesn't have to be.

*expire*

> If a slave fails to contact the primary server(s) for *expire* seconds, the slave expires its data. Expiring the data means the slave stops giving out answers about the data because the data are too old to be useful. Essentially, this field says: at some point, the data are so old that having *no* data is better than having stale data. We think Microsoft's default expire time of 86400 seconds (24 hours) is awfully short. Expire times on the order of a week are common— longer (up to a month) if you frequently have problems reaching your updating source. The expiration time should always be much larger than the retry and refresh intervals; if the expire time is smaller than the refresh interval, your slaves will expire their data before trying to load new data.

*minimum TTL*

> TTL stands for *time to live*. This value applies to all the resource records in the zone database file. The name server supplies this TTL in query responses, allowing other servers to cache the data for the TTL interval. If your data don't change much, you might consider using a minimum TTL of several days. One week is about the longest value that makes sense. Again, the default value of 3600 seconds (one hour) is very short, which we don't recommend because of the amount of DNS traffic it causes.

What values you choose for your SOA record will depend upon the needs of your site. In general, longer times cause less loading on your systems and lengthen the propagation of changes; shorter times increase the load on your systems and speed up the propagation of changes. We find the following values work well for most sites; they're also a good starting point if you're not sure what values to use:

```
  10800 ;  Refresh      3 hours
   3600 ;  Retry        1 hours
2592000 ;  Expire      30 days
  86400 ;  Minimum TTL  1 day
```

## Adding More Domains

Now that you have your name servers running, you might want to handle more zones. What needs to be done? Nothing special, really. Just use DNS Manager to select the appropriate server in the left pane, and then choose **DNS → New Zone**. Follow the instructions earlier in this chapter according to whether you are creating a primary or a slave (secondary) zone.

At this point, it's useful to repeat something we said in an earlier chapter. Calling a *given* name server a primary master name server or a slave name server is a little silly. Name servers can be authoritative for more than one zone. A name server can be a primary master for one zone and a slave for another. Most name servers, however, are either primary master for most of the zones they load or slave for most of the zones they load. So if we call a particular name server a primary master or a slave, we mean that it's the primary master or a slave for *most* of the zones it loads.

## DNS → Properties

Let's finish this chapter with an explanation of the **DNS → Properties** selection. The **Properties** selection on the DNS menu is context sensitive. When selected, DNS Manager displays the properties of the resource record, zone, or server that is highlighted.

## Resource Record Properties

Select a resource record on the right by single-clicking it. Then choose **DNS →
Properties**. The window should look familiar: it's the same one you used to add
the record. You can get the same effect by simply double-clicking the record, too.

## Zone Properties

The zone properties window is viewed by selecting a zone on the left and choosing **DNS → Properties**. Unlike resource record properties, some zone information
can be changed only from this window. It has four tabs:

*General*

This window shows the name of the zone's database file as well as indicating
if it's a primary or slave (secondary) zone. The type of the zone can be
changed from primary to slave or vice versa. The window for the *movie.edu*
zone is shown in Figure 4-23.

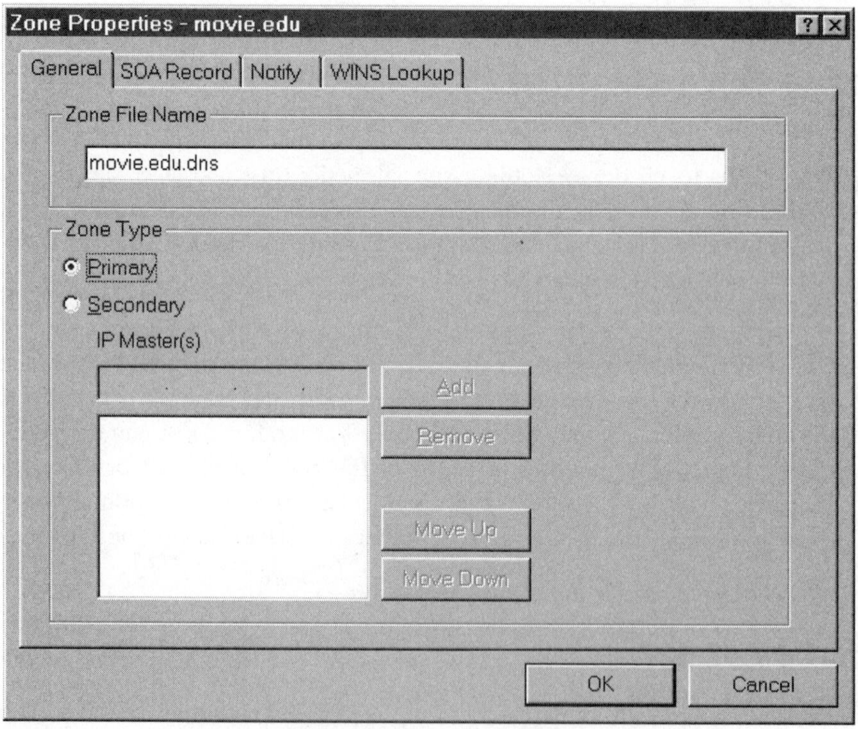

*Figure 4-23. Zone Properties → General*

*SOA Record*

> This window shows the zone's SOA record. The display, shown in Figure 4-24, is no different than if you double-click the SOA record in the right panel.

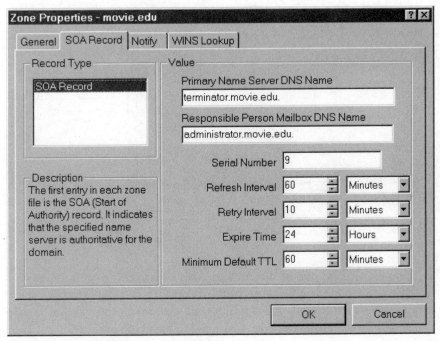

*Figure 4-24. Zone Properties → SOA Record*

*Notify*

> The Notify tab is covered in Chapter 10, *Advanced Features and Security.*

*WINS Lookup*

> The WINS Lookup tab is also covered in Chapter 10.

## Server Properties

You can view the server properties by selecting a server on the left and choosing **DNS → Properties**. It has three tabs:

*Interfaces*

> This window allows you to specify which interfaces the server will listen on for queries. If you have multiple interfaces (like for virtual web hosting), you might not need them all listed here. The default behavior is for the server to listen on all interfaces. The window is shown in Figure 4-25.

*Forwarders*

> This tab is covered in Chapter 10.

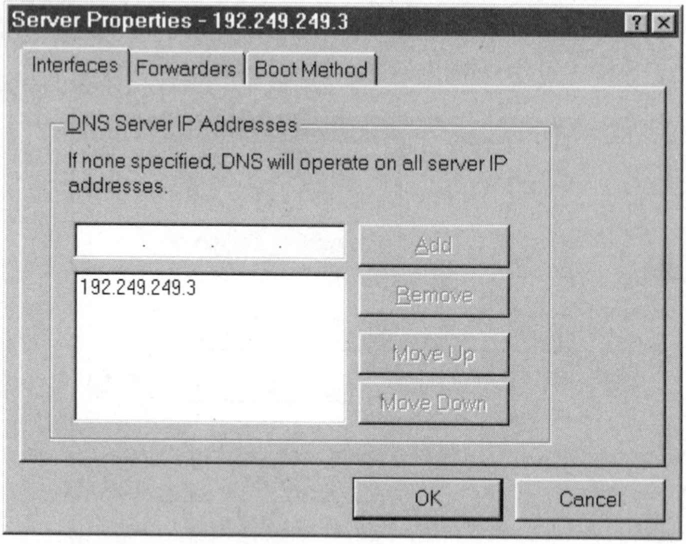

*Figure 4-25. Server Properties → Interfaces*

*Boot Method*

This window displays where the name server is obtaining its configuration information (also referred to as its *boot method*). The default location of the configuration information is the Registry, but the server can also be configured to boot from a BIND Version 4 boot file. This window is "read only" and just displays the current boot method—changing the boot method means changing a Registry setting. More information about this topic is found in Appendix C, *Converting from BIND to the Microsoft DNS Server*.

# What Next?

In this chapter, we showed you how to set up a primary master and a slave name server. There is more work to do to complete setting up your local domain: you need to modify your DNS data for email, configure the other hosts in your domain to use name servers, and you may need to start up more name servers. These topics are covered in the next few chapters.

5

# DNS and Electronic Mail

> *And here Alice began to get rather sleepy, and went on saying to herself, in a dreamy sort of way, "Do cats eat bats? Do cats eat bats?" and sometimes "Do bats eat cats?" for, you see, as she couldn't answer either question, it didn't much matter which way she put it.*

I'll bet you're drowsy, too, after that looong chapter. Thankfully, this next chapter discusses a topic that will probably be very interesting to you system administrators and postmasters: how DNS impacts electronic mail. And even if it isn't interesting to you, at least it's shorter than the last chapter.

One of the advantages of the Domain Name System over host tables is its support of advanced mail routing. When mailers only had *HOSTS.TXT* (and its derivative, *LMHOSTS*) to work with, the best they could do was to attempt delivery to a host's IP address. If that failed, they could either defer delivery of the message and try again later or bounce the message back to the sender.

DNS offers a mechanism for specifying backup hosts for mail delivery. The mechanism also allows hosts to assume mail handling responsibilities for other hosts. This lets diskless hosts that don't run mailers, for example, have mail addressed to them processed by their server. Together, these features give administrators much more flexibility in configuring electronic mail on their networks.

## MX Records

DNS uses a single type of resource record to implement enhanced mail routing, the *MX record*. Originally, this functionality was split between two records, the MD (mail destination) and MF (mail forwarder) records. MD specified the final destination to which a message addressed to a given domain name should be delivered. MF specified a host that would forward mail on to the eventual destination, should that destination be unreachable.

Early experience with DNS on the Internet showed that separating the functionality didn't work very well. A mailer needed both the MD and MF records attached to a domain name (if both existed) to decide where to send the mail—one or the other alone wouldn't do. But an explicit lookup of one type or another (either MD or MF) would cause a name server to cache just that record type. So either mailers had to do two queries, one for MD and one for MF data, or they could no longer accept cached answers. This meant that the overhead of running mail was higher than that of running other services and was eventually deemed unacceptable.

The two records were integrated into a single record type, MX, to solve this problem. Now a mailer just needed all the MX records for a particular domain name destination to make a mail routing decision. Using cached MX records was fine, as long as the TTLs matched.

MX records specify a *mail exchanger* for a domain name: a host that will *either* process *or* forward mail for the domain name (through a firewall, for example). "Processing" the mail means either delivering it to the individual it's addressed to, or gatewaying it to another mail transport, like UUCP, cc:Mail, or Notes Mail. "Forwarding" means sending it to its final destination or to another mail exchanger "closer" to the destination via SMTP, the Internet's Simple Mail Transfer Protocol. Sometimes forwarding the mail involves queuing it for some amount of time, too.

In order to prevent mail routing loops, the MX record has an extra parameter, besides the domain name of the mail exchanger: a preference value. The preference value is an unsigned 16-bit number (between 0 and 65535) that indicates the mail exchanger's priority. For example, the MX record:

```
peets.mpk.ca.us.    IN    MX    10 relay.hp.com.
```

specifies that *relay.hp.com* is a mail exchanger for *peets.mpk.ca.us* at preference value 10.

Taken together, the preference values of a host's mail exchangers determine the order in which a mailer should use them. The preference value itself isn't important, only its relationship to the values of other mail exchangers: is it higher or lower than the values of this host's other mail exchangers? Unless there are other records involved, the following:

```
plange.puntacana.dr. IN  MX  1 listo.puntacana.dr.
plange.puntacana.dr. IN  MX  2 hep.puntacana.dr.
```

does exactly the same thing as:

```
plange.puntacana.dr. IN  MX  50  listo.puntacana.dr.
plange.puntacana.dr. IN  MX  100 hep.puntacana.dr.
```

Mailers should attempt delivery to the mail exchangers with the *lowest* preference values first. This seems a little counterintuitive at first—the *most* preferred mail exchanger has the lowest preference value. But since the preference value is an unsigned quantity, this lets you specify a "best" mail exchanger at preference value 0.

If delivery to the most preferred mail exchanger(s) fails, mailers should attempt delivery to less preferred mail exchangers (those with *higher* preference values), in order of increasing preference value. That is, mailers should try more preferred mail exchangers before they try less preferred mail exchangers. More than one mail exchanger may share the same preference value, too. This gives the mailer its choice of which to send to first. The mailer should try all the mail exchangers at a given preference value before proceeding to the next higher value, though.

For example, the MX records for *ora.com* might be:

```
ora.com.    IN    MX    0 ora.ora.com.
ora.com.    IN    MX    10 ruby.ora.com.
ora.com.    IN    MX    10 opal.ora.com.
```

Interpreted together, these MX records instruct mailers to attempt delivery to *ora.com* by sending to:

1. *ora.ora.com* first

2. Either *ruby.ora.com* or *opal.ora.com* next

3. The remaining preference 10 mail exchanger (the one not used in 2)

Of course, once the mailer successfully delivers the mail to one of *ora.com*'s mail exchangers, it can stop. A mailer successfully delivering *ora.com* mail to *ora.ora.com* doesn't need to try *ruby* or *opal*.

What if a host doesn't have any MX records? Will a mailer simply not deliver mail to that host? Actually, some mailers do just that. Most mailers, however, are more forgiving: if no MX records exist, they'll at least attempt delivery to the host's address. Microsoft Exchange's Internet Mail Connector (IMC) will try the address of a mail destination without MX records. Check your vendor's documentation if you're not sure which variety your mailer is.

Even though nearly all mailers will deliver mail to a host with just an address and no MX records, it's still a good idea to have at least one MX record for each host. Most mailers will request MX records for a host each time they need to deliver mail. If the host doesn't have any MX records, a name server—usually one of your authoritative name servers—still ends up answering that query. If you simply add an MX record for the host pointing to itself, the mailer will have its first query answered, and the mailer's local name server will cache the MX record for future use.

# *Adding MX Records with DNS Manager*

Now that you're familiar with MX records as they appear in zone data files, let's cover how to add them with DNS Manager. First, right-click on the domain name of the zone you'd like to add the MX record to. You'll access the drop-down menu shown in Figure 5-1.

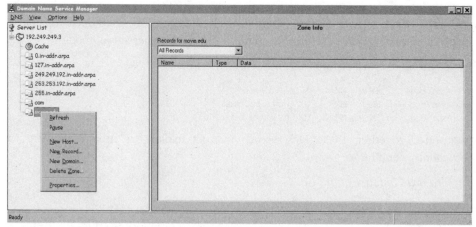

*Figure 5-1. Adding an MX record to a zone*

Choose **New Record** from the pop-up menu. A small window, shown in Figure 5-2, will be displayed.

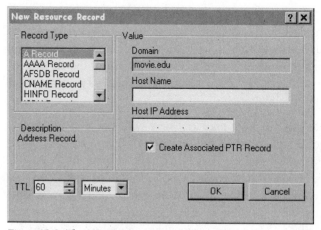

*Figure 5-2. The New Resource Record window*

Choose **MX Record** in the **Record Type** selection box. The fields under **Value** on the right side will change so that you can specify the host in the zone to attach this MX record to, a preference, and the domain name of a mail exchanger (see Figure 5-3).

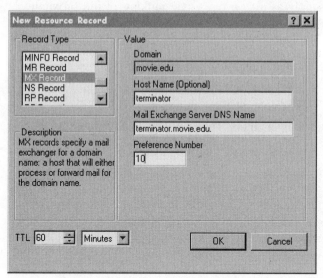

*Figure 5-3. Adding an MX record for terminator.movie.edu*

In Figure 5-3, we're adding an MX record for *terminator.movie.edu* at preference 10, pointing to *terminator.movie.edu* itself. The record that's added to the zone data file looks like this:

```
terminator  3600 IN  MX  10  terminator
```

# What's a Mail Exchanger, Again?

The idea of a mail exchanger is probably new to many of you, so let's go over it in a little more detail. A simple analogy should help here: imagine that a mail exchanger is an airport, and instead of setting up MX records to instruct mailers where to send messages, you're advising your in-laws on which airport to fly into when they come visit you.

Say you live in Los Gatos, California. The closest airport for your in-laws to fly into is San Jose, the second closest is San Francisco, and the third Oakland. (We'll ignore such other factors as price of the ticket, Bay Area traffic, and so on.) Don't see the parallel? Then picture it like this:

```
los-gatos.ca.us.      IN    MX    1 san-jose.ca.us.
los-gatos.ca.us.      IN    MX    2 san-francisco.ca.us.
los-gatos.ca.us.      IN    MX    3 oakland.ca.us.
```

The MX list is just an ordered list of destinations that tells mailers (your in-laws) where to send messages (fly) if they want to reach a given domain name (your house). The preference value tells them how desirable it is to use that destination—you can think of it as a logical "distance" from the eventual destination (in any units you choose) or simply as a "top ten"–style ranking of the proximity of those mail exchangers to the final destination.

With this list, you're saying, "Try to fly into San Jose, and if you can't get there, try San Francisco and Oakland, in that order." It *also* says that if you reach San Francisco, you should take a commuter flight to San Jose. If you wind up in Oakland, you should try to get a commuter to San Jose, or at least to San Francisco.

What makes a good mail exchanger, then? The same qualities that make a good airport:

*Size*

> You wouldn't want to fly into tiny Reid-Hillview Airport to get to Los Gatos, because the airport's not equipped to handle large planes or many people. (You'd probably be better off landing a big jet on Highway 280 than at Reid-Hillview.) Likewise, you don't want to use an emaciated, underpowered host as a mail exchanger; it won't be able to handle the load.

*Uptime*

> You know better than to fly through Denver International Airport in the winter, right? Then you should know better than to use a host that's rarely up or available as a mail exchanger.

*Connectivity*

> If your relatives are flying in from far away, you've got to make sure they can get a direct flight to at least one of the airports in the list you give them. You can't tell them their only choices are San Jose and Oakland if they're flying in from Helsinki. Similarly, you've got to make sure that at least one of your hosts' mail exchangers is reachable to anyone who might conceivably send you mail.

*Management and Administration*

> How well an airport is managed has a bearing on your safety while flying into or just through the airport and on how easy it is to use. Think of these factors when choosing a mail exchanger. The privacy of your mail, the speed of its delivery during normal operations, and how well your mail is treated when your hosts go down all hinge upon the quality of the administrators who manage your mail exchangers.

Keep this example in mind because we'll use it again later.

# *The MX Algorithm*

That's the basic idea behind MX records and mail exchangers, but you should know about a few more wrinkles. To avoid routing loops, mailers need to use a slightly more complicated algorithm than what we've described when they determine where to send mail.*

Imagine what would happen if mailers didn't check for routing loops. Let's say you send mail from your workstation to *nuts@ora.com*, raving (or raging) about the quality of this book. Unfortunately, *ora.ora.com* is down at the moment. No problem! Recall *ora.com*'s MX records:

```
ora.com.    IN    MX    0 ora.ora.com.
ora.com.    IN    MX    10 ruby.ora.com.
ora.com.    IN    MX    10 opal.ora.com.
```

Your mailer falls back and sends your message to *ruby.ora.com*, which is up. *ruby*'s mailer then tries to forward the mail on to *ora.ora.com*, but can't because *ora.ora.com* is down. Now what? Unless *ruby* checks the sanity of what she is doing, she'll try to forward the message to *opal.ora.com*, or maybe even to herself. That's certainly not going to help get the mail delivered. If *ruby* sends the message to herself, we have a mail routing loop. If *ruby* sends the message to *opal*, *opal* will either send it back to *ruby* or send it to herself, and we again have a mail routing loop.

To prevent this from happening, mailers discard certain MX records before they decide where to send a message. A mailer sorts the list of MX records by preference value and looks in the list for the canonical domain name of the host it's running on. If the local host appears as a mail exchanger, the mailer discards that MX record and all MX records in which the preference value is equal or higher (that is, less preferred mail exchangers). That prevents the mailer from sending messages to itself or to mailers "farther" from the eventual destination.

Let's think about this in the context of our airport analogy. This time, imagine you're an airline passenger (a message), and you're trying to get to Greeley, Colorado. You can't get a direct flight to Greeley, but you can fly to either Fort Collins or Denver (the two next highest mail exchangers). Since Fort Collins is closer to Greeley, you opt to fly to Fort Collins.

Now, once you've arrived in Fort Collins, there's no sense in flying to Denver, away from your destination (a lower preference mail exchanger). (And flying from Fort Collins to Fort Collins would be silly, too.) So the only acceptable flight to get you to your destination is now a Fort Collins-Greeley flight. You eliminate flights to less preferred destinations to prevent frequent flyer looping and wasteful travel time.

---

* This algorithm is based on RFC 974, which describes how Internet mail routing works.

One caveat: most mailers will *only* look for their local host's *canonical* domain name in the list of MX records. They don't check for aliases (domain names on the left side of CNAME records). Unless you always use canonical names in your MX records, there's no guarantee a mailer will be able to find itself in the MX list, and you'll run the risk of having your mail loop. If you send mail addressed to a particular domain name to a mailer that isn't configured to accept mail for that domain name, and it finds itself as the most preferred mail exchanger, it may bounce the mail with the error:

```
554 MX list for movie.edu points back to relay.isp.com
554 <root@movie.edu>... Local configuration error
```

This replaces the quainter "I refuse to talk to myself" error in newer versions of *sendmail*. The moral: in an MX record, always use the mail exchanger's canonical name.

One more caveat: the hosts you list as mail exchangers *must* have address records. A mailer needs to find an address for each mail exchanger you name, or else it can't attempt delivery there.

To go back to our *ora.com* example, when *ruby* received the message from your workstation, her mailer would have checked the list of MX records:

```
ora.com.    IN    MX    0  ora.ora.com.
ora.com.    IN    MX    10 ruby.ora.com.
ora.com.    IN    MX    10 opal.ora.com.
```

Finding the local host's domain name in the list at preference value 10, *ruby*'s mailer would discard all the records at preference value 10 or higher (the records in bold):

```
ora.com.                        IN        MX        0 ora.ora.com.
ora.com.                        IN        MX        10 ruby.ora.com.
ora.com.                        IN        MX        10 opal.ora.com.
```

leaving only:

```
ora.com.    IN    MX    0 ora.ora.com.
```

Since *ora.ora.com* is down, *ruby* would defer delivery until later, and queue the message.

What happens if a mailer finds *itself* at the highest preference (lowest preference value) and has to discard the whole MX list? Some mailers attempt delivery directly to the destination host's IP address, as a last-ditch effort. In most mailers, however, it's an error. It may indicate that DNS thinks the mailer should be processing (not just forwarding) mail for the destination, but the mailer hasn't been configured to know that. Or it may indicate that the administrator has ordered the MX records incorrectly by using the wrong preference values.

Say, for example, the folks who run *acme.com* add a mail exchanger record to direct mail addressed to *acme.com* to a mailer at their Internet Service Provider:

```
acme.com.       IN  MX  10  mail.isp.net.
```

Many mailers need to be configured to identify their aliases and the names of other hosts they process mail for. Unless the mailer on *mail.isp.net* is configured to recognize email addressed to *acme.com* as local mail, it will assume it's being asked to relay the mail and attempt to forward the mail to a mail exchanger closer to the final destination.[*] When it looks up the MX records for *acme.com*, it'll find itself as the most preferred mail exchanger and return the mail to the sender. Then it will bounce the mail with the familiar error:

```
554 MX list for acme.com points back to mail.isp.com
554 <root@acme.com>... Local configuration error
```

You may have noticed that we tend to use multiples of ten for our preference values. Ten is convenient because it allows you to insert other MX records temporarily at intermediate values without changing the other weights, but otherwise, there's nothing magical about it.

---

[*] Unless, of course, *mail.isp.net*'s mailer is configured not to relay mail for unknown domains.

# 6

*In this chapter:*
- *The Resolver*
- *Sample Resolver Configurations*
- *Other Naming Services*
- *Differences in Service Behavior*

# Configuring Hosts

*They were indeed a queer-looking party that assembled on the bank—the birds with draggled feathers, the animals with their fur clinging close to them, and all dripping wet, cross, and uncomfortable.*

Now that you or someone else in your organization has set up name servers for your zones, you'll want to configure the hosts on your network to use them. That involves configuring those hosts' resolvers, which you can do by telling the resolvers which name servers to query and which domain names to search. You may also want to add aliases, both for your users' convenience and to minimize the shock of the conversion to DNS.

This chapter covers these topics and also describes the details of configuring the resolver in Microsoft Windows 95 and Windows NT.

## The Resolver

We introduced resolvers way back in Chapter 2, *How Does DNS Work?*, but we didn't say much more about them. The resolver, you'll remember, is the client half of the Domain Name System. It's responsible for translating a program's request for host information into a query to a name server and for translating the response into an answer for the program.

We haven't done any resolver configuration yet because the occasion for it hasn't arisen. When we set up our name servers in Chapter 4, *Setting Up the Microsoft DNS Server*, the resolver's default behavior worked just fine for our purposes. But if we'd needed the resolver to do more than what it does by default, or to behave differently from the default, we would have had to configure the resolver.

There's one thing we should mention up front: what we'll describe in the next few sections is the behavior of the Windows 95 and Windows NT 4.0 resolvers. There are lots of other resolvers, though. Every TCP/IP package for Windows 3.1 has its own resolver, and the configuration of each one is different. UNIX hosts normally use some variant of the BIND resolver, discussed in *DNS and BIND*, but many

UNIX vendors have extended their resolver's functionality. Still, the basic concepts behind the operation of each resolver are quite common. If you don't use one of the resolvers described in this section, read the section, anyway, and then read the vendor's documentation for the details of its configuration. The concepts should translate fairly well.

So, what exactly does the resolver allow you to configure? Most resolvers let you configure at least three aspects of the resolver's behavior: the default domain, the search list, and the name server(s) that the resolver queries. Many newer resolvers will also let you configure the order in which the various naming services supported by the operating system are configured.

Almost all Windows resolver configuration is done though the Network option in the Windows Control Panel. To get there, click **Start** → **Control Panel** → **Network**. You should see a window that looks something like the one in Figure 6-1 (though the options may be different for Windows 95).

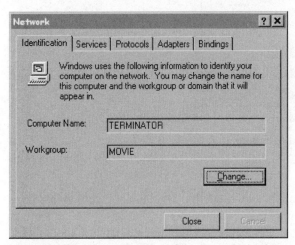

*Figure 6-1. The Network option of the Control Panel*

Now choose **Protocols** → **TCP/IP** → **DNS**. You should see a window that looks like the one in Figure 6-2.

There. Now you're ready to configure the resolver.

But before you go configuring the resolver, you should know what it is you're configuring. Notice that the DNS configuration tab is divided into four areas:

- **Host Name**
- **Domain**
- **Domain Suffix Search Order**
- **DNS Service Search Order**

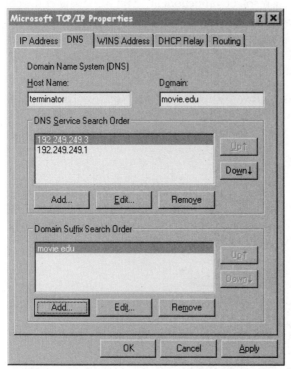

*Figure 6-2. The DNS configuration tab*

The next four sections describe these areas in order.

## Host Name

The **Host Name** field allows you to configure the first label of your host's fully qualified domain name. By default, the host name is the same as your computer name, set in the Network options' **Identification** tab, except dashes replace any characters that are illegal in DNS (anything but alphanumeric characters and dashes). The computer name identifies your computer to NetBIOS, Microsoft's proprietary networking protocol. You can set your host name differently if, for example, your computer is known by one name to NetBIOS networking and by another to DNS. However, if possible, the two should match to avoid confusion.

## Domain

The **Domain** field allows you to configure the domain that your host is a member of. (Remember that this is a DNS domain, not an NT domain.) Together with the **Host Name** field, this determines your host's fully qualified domain name. Also, if you don't set an explicit Domain Suffix Search Order (see the section with that title later in this chapter), the local domain's setting will determine your host's search list.

## Search List

The domain, set in the **Domain** field, also determines the default *search list*. The search list was designed to make users' lives a little easier by saving them some typing. The idea is to search one or more domains for incomplete names—that is, names that might not be fully qualified domain names.

Most Windows networking commands that take a domain name as an argument, like *telnet*, *ftp*, and *ping*, apply the search list to those arguments.

With any Windows resolver, a user can indicate that a domain name is fully qualified by adding a trailing dot to it.* For example, the trailing dot in the command

```
C:\>ftp ftp.ora.com.
```

means "don't bother searching any other domains; this domain name is fully qualified." This is analogous to the leading slash in full pathnames in the Windows filesystem. Pathnames without a leading slash are interpreted as relative to the current working directory, while pathnames with a leading slash are absolute, anchored at the root.

With Windows resolvers, the default search list includes the local domain and each of its parent domains with two or more labels. Therefore, on a host running a Windows resolver and configured with a local domain of *cv.hp.com*, the default search list would contain first *cv.hp.com*, the default domain, then *hp.com*, the default domain's parent, but not *com*, as it only has one label.†

The search list is usually applied *after* the name is tried as is. As long as the argument you type has at least one dot in it, it's looked up exactly as you typed it *before* any element of the search list is appended. If that lookup fails, the search list is applied. Even if the argument has no dots in it (that is, it's a single label name), it's tried as is, after the resolver appends the elements of the search list.

Why is it better to try the argument *literatim* first? From experience, people who wrote resolvers found that, more often than not, if a user bothered to type in a name with even a single dot in it, he was probably typing in a fully qualified domain name without the trailing dot. Better to see right away whether the name was a fully qualified domain name than to create nonsense domain names unnecessarily by appending the elements of the search list to it.

---

\* Note that we said that the resolver can handle a trailing dot. Some programs, particularly mail user agents, don't deal correctly with a trailing dot in email addresses. They cough even before they hand the domain name in the address to the resolver.

† One reason resolvers don't append just the top-level domain is that there are very few hosts at the second level of the Internet's name space, so tacking on just *com* or *edu* to *foo* is unlikely to result in the domain name of a real host. Also, looking up the address of a *foo.com* or *foo.edu* might well require sending a query to a root name server, which taxes the roots and can be time consuming.

Thus, a user typing

```
C:\>telnet pronto.cv.hp.com
```

will cause a lookup of *pronto.cv.hp.com* first, since the name contains three dots, which is certainly more than one. If the resolver doesn't find an address for *pronto.cv.hp.com,* it will then try *pronto.cv.hp.com.cv.hp.com,* and, if necessary, *pronto.cv.hp.com.hp.com.*

A user typing

```
C:\>telnet asap
```

on the same host would cause the resolver to look up first *asap.cv.hp.com,* then *asap.hp.com,* and finally just *asap,* if necessary, since the name typed ("asap") contains no dots.

Note that application of the search list stops as soon as a prospective domain name turns up the data being looked up. In the *asap* example, the search list would never get around to appending *hp.com* if *asap.cv.hp.com* resolved to an address.

## *The Domain Suffix Search Order*

What if you don't like the default search list you get when you set your local domain? Windows will let you set the search list explicitly, domain name by domain name, in the order you want the domains searched. You do this with the Domain Suffix Search Order.

You can add up to six domain names to the Domain Suffix Search Order, in the order in which you want them appended, and this becomes the host's search list. Setting the search list with Domain Suffix Search Order overrides the default search list.

The user interface is simple to use: click **Add** to add a domain name to the list; select a domain name, and click **Remove** to remove it from the list, or click **Edit** to change the domain name. In Windows NT, you can also use the **Up** and **Down** arrow buttons to reorder the list. The basic search algorithm still applies: the resolver will look up domain name arguments as-is if they contain at least one dot.

The settings shown in Figure 6-3, for example, would instruct the resolver to search the *corp.hp.com* domain first, then *paloalto.hp.com,* and then both domains' parent, *hp.com.*

This directive might be useful on a host whose users frequently access hosts in both *corp.hp.com* and *paloalto.hp.com.* On the other hand, the configuration shown in Figure 6-4 would have the resolver skip searching the local domain's parent domain when the search list is applied.

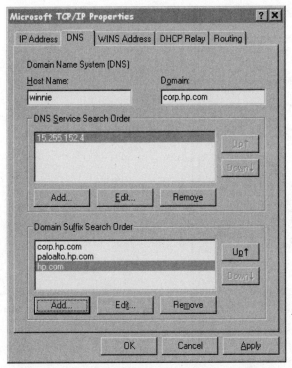

*Figure 6-3. A Domain Suffix Search Order example*

This might be useful if the host's users only access hosts in the local domain, or if connectivity to the parent name servers isn't good (because the configuration minimizes unnecessary queries to the parent name servers).

## The DNS Service Search Order

Back in Chapter 4, we talked about two types of name servers: primary master name servers and slave name servers. But what if you don't want to run a name server on a host, yet still want to use DNS? Or for that matter, what if you *can't* run a name server on a host (because the operating system doesn't support it, for example)? Surely you don't have to run a name server on *every* host, right?

No, of course you don't. By default, the resolver looks for a name server running on the local host—which is why we could use *nslookup* on *terminator* and *wormhole* right after we configured their name servers. You can, however, instruct the resolver to look to another host for name service. This configuration is sometimes called a *DNS client.*

The DNS Service Search Order tells the resolver the IP addresses of the name server to query. For example, the settings in Figure 6-5 instruct the resolver to

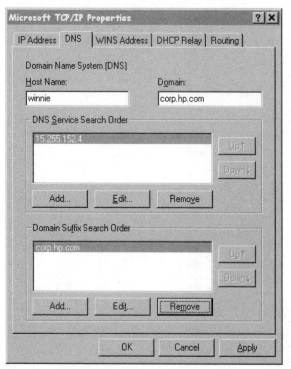

*Figure 6-4. Another Domain Suffix Search Order example*

send queries to the name server running at IP address 192.249.249.3, instead of to the local host. This means that on hosts that don't run name servers, you can use the DNS Service Search Order to point them at a remote name server. Typically, you would configure the resolvers on your hosts to query your own name servers.

However, since Microsoft DNS Servers don't have any notion of access control, you can configure your resolver to query almost anyone's name server. Of course, configuring your host to use someone else's name server without first asking permission is presumptuous, if not downright rude, and using one of your own will usually give you better performance, so we'll consider this only an emergency option.

You can also configure the resolver to query the host's local name server, by using the local host's IP address. Now what if the name server your resolver queries is down? Isn't there any way to specify a backup? Do you just fall back to using the host table?

The resolver will also allow you to specify up to three (count 'em, three) name servers using the DNS Service Search Order. The resolver will query those name servers, in the order listed, until it receives an answer or times out. The number of name servers you configure dictates other aspects of the resolver's behavior, too.

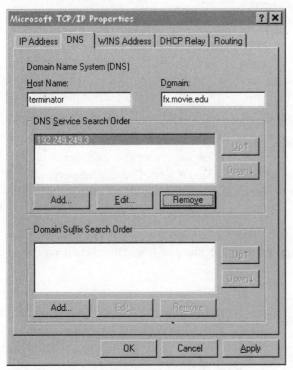

*Figure 6-5. A DNS Service Search Order example*

### One name server configured

If only one name server is configured, the resolver queries that name server with an initial timeout of five seconds. The timeout is the length of time the resolver will wait for a response from the name server before sending another query. If the resolver encounters a network error that indicates the name server is really down or unreachable, or if it times out, it will modify the timeout and query the name server again.

If the domain name or data doesn't exist, the resolver doesn't retry the query. Theoretically, at least, each name server should have an equivalent "view" of the name space; there's no reason to believe one and not another. So if one name server tells you that a given domain name doesn't exist, or that the type of data you're looking for doesn't exist for the domain name you specified, any other name server should give you the same answer.[*]

---

[*] The built-in latency of DNS makes this a small fib—a primary can have authority for a zone and have different data from a slave that also has authority for the zone. The primary may have just loaded new zone data from disk, while the slave may not have had time to transfer the new zone data from the primary. Both name servers return authoritative answers for the zone, but the primary may know about a brand new host that the slave doesn't yet know about.

### More than one name server configured

When more than one name server is configured, the behavior is a little different. Here's what happens: the resolver starts by querying the first name server in the list. If the resolver times out or receives a network error, it will fall back to the next name server, waiting the same timeout for that name server. If the resolver queries all the configured name servers to no avail, it updates the timeouts and cycles through them again.

The Windows resolvers use somewhat, er, unique timeouts for each round of queries. The timeouts start relatively small (about five seconds) and gradually get longer, then peak and get shorter again. After seven sets of retransmissions (a total of eight timeouts for every name server configured), the resolver gives up trying to query name servers.

Based on our experimentation (because we couldn't get official numbers from Microsoft), Table 6-1 shows roughly what the timeouts look like when you have one, two, or three name servers configured.

*Table 6-1. Resolver Timeouts*

| Retry | Name Servers Configured | | |
|-------|----|---------|---------|
|       | 1  | 2       | 3       |
| 0     | 5s | (2x) 5s | (3x) 3s |
| 1     | 10s | (2x) 6s | (3x) 4s |
| 2     | 15s | (2x) 8s | (3x) 5s |
| 3     | 22s | (2x) 6s | (3x) 3s |
| 4     | 10s | (2x) 5s | (3x) 3s |
| 5     | 10s | (2x) 5s | (3x) 3s |
| 6     | 14s | (2x) 7s | (3x) 4s |
| Total | 86s | 84s     | 75s     |

(Note that this is how the Windows NT 4.0 resolver behaves. The behavior of older versions of Windows NT and of Windows 95 is similar but not necessarily identical.)

So if you configure three servers, the resolver queries the first server, with a timeout period of three seconds. If that query times out, the resolver queries the second server with the same timeout, and similarly for the third. If the resolver cycles through all three servers, it updates the timeout to four seconds and queries the first server again.

Do these times seem awfully long? Remember, this describes a worst-case scenario. With properly functioning name servers running on tolerably fast hosts, your resolvers should get their answers back in well under a second. Only if all the configured servers are really busy or they or your network is down will the resolver ever make it all the way through the retransmission cycle and give up.

What does the resolver do after it gives up? It times out and returns an error. Typically this results in an error like:

```
C:\>ping tootsie
Bad IP address tootsie.
```

Of course, it'll take at least 75 seconds of waiting to see this message, so be patient.

# Sample Resolver Configurations

So much for the theory—let's go over what resolver configurations look like on real hosts. Resolver configuration needs vary depending on whether or not a host runs a local name server, so we'll cover both cases: hosts with local name servers and hosts with remote name servers.

## Resolver-Only

We, as the administrators of *movie.edu,* have just been asked to configure a professor's new workstation, which doesn't run a name server. Deciding which domain the workstation belongs in is easy—there's only *movie.edu* to choose from. However, she *is* working with researchers at Pixar on new shading algorithms, so perhaps it'd be wise to put *pixar.com* in her workstation's Domain Suffix Search Order.

The new workstation is on the 192.249.249.0 network, so the closest name servers are *wormhole.movie.edu* (192.249.249.1) and *terminator.movie.edu* (192.249.249.3). As a rule, you should configure hosts to use the closest name server available first. (The closest possible name server is a name server on the local host; the next closest is a name server on the same subnet or network.) In this case, both name servers are equally close, but we know that *wormhole* is bigger (it's a faster host, with more capacity).

Since this particular professor is known to get awfully vocal when she has problems with her computer, we'll also add *terminator.movie.edu* (192.249.249.3) as a backup name server. That way, if *wormhole* is down for any reason, the professor's workstation can still get name service (assuming *terminator* and the rest of the network are up).

Figure 6-6 shows what her workstation's resolver configuration ends up looking like.

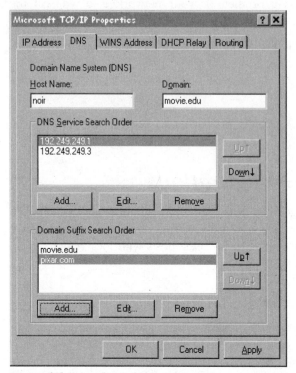

*Figure 6-6. Example resolver configuration*

## Local Name Server

Next, we have to configure the university mail hub, *postmanrings2x*, to use domain name service. *postmanrings2x* is shared by all groups in the *movie.edu* domain. We've recently configured a name server on the host to help cut down the load on the other name servers, so we should make sure the resolver queries the name server on the local host first.

The simplest resolver configuration for this case is to configure the resolver to use the local name server. The Host Name should be set to the first label of the fully qualified domain name of the host, and the Domain should be set to the local domain.

If we decide we need a backup name server—a prudent decision—we can add a name server to the DNS Service Search Order. Whether or not we configure a backup name server depends largely on the reliability of the local name server. A robust name server implementation will keep running for longer than some operating systems, so there may be no need for a backup. If the local name server has a history of problems, though—say it hangs occasionally and stops responding to queries—it's prudent to add a backup name server.

To add a backup name server, we just list the local name server first in the DNS Service Search Order (at the host's IP address)* and then one or two backup name servers. Since we'd rather be safe than sorry, we're going to add two backup name servers. *postmanrings2x* is on the 192.249.249.0 network, too, so *terminator* and *wormhole* are the closest name servers to it (besides its own). We'll reverse the order in which they're tried from the previous resolver-only example, to help balance the load between the two. The final configuration is shown in Figure 6-7.

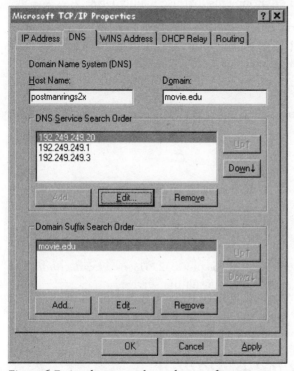

*Figure 6-7. Another example resolver configuration*

## *Other Naming Services*

Native support for DNS in Microsoft's operating systems is a relatively new development. Because DNS is a newcomer, it's just one of the naming services that Windows supports. Left to its own devices, Windows will query the following name services (assuming that both TCP/IP and NetBIOS are configured):

1. The NetBIOS name cache

2. WINS servers

---

* The Microsoft DNS Server doesn't listen on the loopback address, so don't use 127.0.0.1.

3. B-node broadcast

4. The *LMHOSTS* file

5. The *HOSTS* file

6. (Finally) DNS servers

Not all Windows utilities go through this entire pantheon of services. *nslookup*, for example, doesn't bother querying anything but a DNS server. However, this process can slow name resolution in environments that use mainly DNS.

Thankfully, Windows 95 supports reordering the sequence in which the services are searched.* To do this, you'll have to edit your host's Registry. The following Registry entry is the one you're interested in:

> *HKEY_LOCAL_MACHINE\SYSTEM\CurrentControlSet\Services\*

Create a new key under **Services** called **MSTCP**. Then create a new key under **MSTCP** called **ServiceProvider**. Under **ServiceProvider**, create four new binary values:

- DnsPriority

- LocalPriority

- HostsPriority

- NetbtPriority

Each of these takes a value between −32768 and 32767, *in hexadecimal*. The lower the value, the earlier the resolver will consult the service.

Unfortunately, Windows NT 4.0 doesn't support these Registry entries. Microsoft may support them with the next Service Pack (SP4?) of NT 4.0 or with NT 5.0.

# *Differences in Service Behavior*

Now that you've configured your host to use DNS, what's going to change? Will your users be forced to type long domain names? Will they have to change their mail addresses and mailing lists?

Thanks to the search list, much of this will continue working as before. There are some exceptions, though, and there are notable differences in the way that some programs behave when they use DNS.

As you've seen earlier in this chapter, programs like *telnet*, *ftp*, and *ping* apply the search list to domain name arguments that aren't dot terminated. That means that

---

* This method is described in Microsoft Knowledge Base article Q139270, available from *http://support.microsoft.com/support/kb/articles/Q139/2/70.asp*.

if you're in *movie.edu* (that is, your local domain is *movie.edu* and your search list includes *movie.edu*), you can type:

```
C:\>telnet misery
```

or:

```
C:\>telnet misery.movie.edu
```

or even:

```
C:\>telnet misery.movie.edu.
```

and get to the same place (though the second option is slower than the other two because of the way the search list works). The same holds true for the other services, too. You may benefit from one other behavioral difference: because a name server may return more than one IP address when you look up an address, modern versions of *telnet* and *ftp* will try to connect to the first address returned, and if the connection is refused or times out, for example, it will try the next, and so on:

```
C:\>ftp tootsie
-> ftp: connect to address 192.249.249.244:
-> ftp: connect:Connection timed out
-> ftp: connect to address 192.253.253.244:
Connected to tootsie.movie.edu.
220 tootsie.movie.edu FTP server (Version 16.2 Fri Apr 26
    18:20:43 GMT 1991) ready.
Name (tootsie: guest):
```

# 7

In this chapter:
- *What About Signals?*
- *Updating Zone Data*
- *Zone Database File Controls*
- *Keeping Everything Running Smoothly*

# Maintaining the Microsoft DNS Server

*"Well, in our country," said Alice, still panting a little, "you'd generally get to somewhere else—if you ran very fast for a long time as we've been doing."*

*"A slow sort of country!" said the Queen. "Now, here, you see, it takes all the running you can do, to keep in the same place. If you want to get somewhere else, you must run at least twice as fast as that!"*

This chapter discusses a number of related topics pertaining to name server maintenance. We'll talk about commands you can (and can't) send to a running name server, modifying the zone database files, and keeping the root name server cache file up to date. We'll list common Event Log messages and explain the statistics name servers keep.

This chapter doesn't cover troubleshooting problems. Maintenance involves keeping your data current and watching over your name servers as they operate. Troubleshooting involves putting out fires—those little DNS emergencies that flare up periodically. Firefighting is covered in Chapter 12, *Troubleshooting DNS*.

## What About Signals?

Those of you familiar with the BIND name server know that it's possible to signal a running name server to perform certain tasks, such as re-reading its configuration file or turning on debugging information. Unfortunately, the Microsoft DNS Server has no analog—it's more of a "black box" that you can't signal while running. But all hope is not lost: we'll go over the tasks possible using signals with a BIND name server and show how to accomplish the same thing with the Microsoft DNS Server.

*Restart the name server*

You can signal a BIND name server to re-read its configuration file and zone database files. There's no comparable Microsoft DNS Server command. If the server obtains its configuration information from the Registry (the default mode), this command isn't necessary: as you make configuration changes with DNS Manager, they take effect immediately in the running name server. If the server is using a BIND-style boot file, you must stop and restart the server after making a change to the boot file. For more information on the server "boot method," see Appendix C, *Converting from BIND to the Microsoft DNS Server.*

*Dump a copy of the name server's internal database to a file*
A BIND server can dump its entire memory database of authoritative data, cached data, and root name server "hints" to a file. There's no direct Microsoft DNS Server equivalent, but you can come close—all this information is visible in DNS Manager. To see authoritative data, just select the appropriate zone. By selecting the Cache icon, you can see the contents of the name server's cache as well as the list of root name servers it's using.

*Dump name server statistics to a file*
You can't dump the Microsoft DNS Server's usage statistics to a file, but you can view them from DNS Manager. Statistics are covered in detail at the end of this chapter.

*Start/stop writing debugging information to a file*
Unfortunately, no detailed debugging information is available from the Microsoft DNS Server as there is from the BIND server.

*Log all queries*
There's also no way to log individual queries processed as you can with a BIND server.

The only thing you can do to a running Microsoft DNS Server is stop it and start it again. So what does happen when you stop and start the server? Remember that the name server answers queries from its in-memory database. This database includes three kinds of information: authoritative data (zones for which the server is a primary master or slave), cached data (answers from other name servers) and root name server "hints" (the list of root name servers from the root name server cache file, *cache.dns*). When you stop the name server, this data is lost.

When the server is restarted, it reloads the authoritative data from the zone database files on its disk. Zones the server is a primary master for are loaded and not changed for the lifetime of the server process. (Of course, you can make a change to a primary zone with DNS Manager and direct the server to *write* to the zone database file with **DNS → Update Server Data Files**, but the server *reads* the zone database file only at startup.) Zones the server is a slave for are also loaded from the zone database files. But for each zone, the server queries its master (usually the zone's primary master) for the SOA record to compare serial numbers. If the master's serial number is larger than the serial number in the zone just loaded off disk, the server performs a zone transfer.

The server also reads *cache.dns* at startup. In Chapter 4, *Setting Up the Microsoft DNS Server*, we described how root name server information is not used directly, but as a "hint" to find the current list of root name servers: the server queries a root name server from *cache.dns* for the current list of root name servers, and the results are the first records in the cache. Remember, the cache starts empty when the server starts up.

# Updating Zone Data

For most changes to your zones, you'll use DNS Manager. In Chapter 4 we described how to add a name server to DNS Manager, create zones, and create resource records. Deleting these objects is easy: just select the object by left-clicking it, and then press Delete (or select **DNS → Delete**). Modifying objects is also straightforward. Name servers' IP addresses and the zone names cannot be changed but must be deleted and added with the new address or name. For example, if the IP address of a name server you're managing changes, you have to delete the name server within DNS Manager and replace it with the new IP address. The same thing goes if you change the name of a zone, say from *movie.edu* to *movie.net*.

Changing resource record data is easy, too. Just double-click the record in the right pane (or select with a single click, and choose **DNS → Properties**). You'll see the same window as when you added the record. Note that you can change resource record data (also called the *RDATA*), but not the name of the record (the owner). In other words, you can change the right side of the record but not the left side (as viewed in DNS Manager's right pane or in the zone database file). So you can change the IP address of *terminator*'s A record, but you can't change *terminator* to *terminator2*. If you need to change the owner, you'll have to delete the record and replace it with the new owner.

## Adding and Deleting Resource Records by Hand

It's awfully convenient to use DNS Manager to make changes to your zones, but it can't do everything—sometimes you'll need to edit the zone database files by hand. For example, you can't enter CNAME records in an *in-addr.arpa* zone with DNS Manager. You'll need them if you have a network subnetted on a non-octet boundary and split among different organizations as described in Chapter 9, *Parenting*. Adding, deleting, or changing a lot of records at once is tough with DNS Manager but easy with a little Perl code or a good text editor. If you run a name server long enough, you'll eventually need to make a change outside DNS Manager.

Editing by hand is a little complicated because you have to manually perform some steps that DNS Manager does for you automatically. This section describes what to do.

1. Remember that all changes must be made on a zone's primary master name server. This is the case whether you're using DNS Manager or editing by hand. If you make changes to the zone database file on a slave, the next zone transfer from the primary master will overwrite your work.

2. If you've made any changes using DNS Manager since the name server has started (that usually means since the last reboot), stop the name server. Here's why: when you change a zone with DNS Manager, the change takes effect in the primary master name server's memory right away, but the zone database file on disk is not updated immediately. The name server sets an internal "update pending" flag to remind itself that that zone's database file needs updating. If you select **DNS → Update Server Data Files**, *all* the zone database files are updated whether or not the zones have been changed, and any flags are cleared. But if the server stops (halted by you for a system reboot—for whatever reason) and some zones have their update pending flags set, the server updates the corresponding zone database files before terminating. So you can see what happens if you make a change by hand but forget about a recent change made with DNS Manager: when you stop and restart the server to put the manual change into effect, the zone database file gets updated, and your hand editing is lost.

3. Find the zone database file of the zone you want to change. Recall from Chapter 4 that the zone database files are stored in *%SystemRoot%\system32\dns* and the default naming convention is the name of the zone followed by the *dns* extension—for example, *movie.edu.dns*.

4. Bring up the zone database in your favorite text editor. Notepad is a good choice; Microsoft Word isn't. Whatever you use, make sure you eventually save the file in plain text format. That's why we like Notepad—you can't save a file in anything but plain text.

5. Increment the serial number in the SOA record at the top of the file. (See the next section for more information on SOA serial numbers.) Since the SOA record is at the top of the file, it's a good idea to update it first so you won't forget to do it later.

   Make whatever changes you need to make. If you're adding a host, you might need MX records in addition to the A record. For example, we added the following resource records to *movie.edu.dns* when we added the new host *cujo* to our network:

```
cujo  IN  A   192.253.253.5
      IN  MX  10 cujo
      IN  MX  20 terminator
```

When you're done, don't forget to save the file!

6. Don't forget to add PTR records! If you're adding a host, you should add a PTR record to the appropriate *in-addr.arpa* zone for each of its IP addresses. This step is easy to forget because DNS Manager can add PTR records for you automatically. And remember—if you change a zone, don't forget to· increment the serial number in its SOA record. Our new host *cujo* has only one IP address, 192.253.253.5, so we added one PTR record to the *253.253.192.in-addr.arpa.dns* file:

```
5 IN PTR cujo.movie.edu.
```

Your changes won't take effect until you restart the primary master name server: stop it, and then start it again. This is another task handled by DNS Manager. When you make changes with it, the changes take effect immediately in the name server's memory and get written to disk later. Editing by hand reverses the process: you make the changes first on disk and have to restart the name server to get the changes into its memory.

Slave name servers will load the new data some length of time within the time interval defined in the SOA record for refreshing their data. Sometimes your users won't want to wait for the slaves to pick up the new data—they'll want it available right away. (Are you wincing or nodding knowingly as you read this?) Can you force a slave to load the new information right away? If you've enabled zone change notification, the slaves will pick up the new data quickly because the primary master notifies the slave of changes within 15 minutes of the change. (See Chapter 10, *Advanced Features and Security*, for more information on zone change notification.) If you don't have notification set up, you should! But you can get the same effect the hard way by restarting the name server on each of the slaves. When the name server starts up, it does a serial number compare with its master for every zone it's a slave for. If it discovers an out-of-date zone, it immediately performs a zone transfer.

To delete a host, remove all the resource records pertaining to it from the appropriate zone database files. Make sure you remove the A record, any MX records, and the PTR record. Also be sure to increment the serial number in each zone database file you modify and restart your primary master name server.

## SOA Serial Numbers

Every zone database file has a serial number. Every time the data in a file is changed, the serial number must be incremented. If the serial number is not incremented, slave name servers for the zone will not pick up the updated data. The change is simple. If the original database file had the following SOA record:

```
movie.edu. IN SOA terminator.movie.edu. al.robocop.movie.edu. (
                        100      ; Serial
                        10800    ; Refresh
                        3600     ; Retry
                        604800   ; Expire
                        86400 )  ; Minimum TTL
```

the updated database file would have the following SOA record:

```
movie.edu. IN SOA terminator.movie.edu. al.robocop.movie.edu. (
                        101      ; Serial
                        10800    ; Refresh
                        3600     ; Retry
                        604800   ; Expire
                        86400 )  ; Minimum TTL
```

This simple change is the key to distributing the data to all of your slaves. Failing to increment the serial number is the most common mistake made when updating by hand. The first few times you make a change manually, you'll remember to update the serial number because this process is new and you are paying close attention. After modifying zone database files becomes second nature (we bet you can't wait for *that*), you'll make some "quickie" little change, forget to update the serial number . . . and none of the slaves will pick up the new data. Eternal vigilance is the price of modifying zone database files by hand.

The Microsoft DNS Server does allow you to use a decimal serial number, like 1.1, but we highly recommend that you stay with integer values. Here's how it handles decimal serial numbers: if a decimal point is in the serial number, the DNS server multiplies the digits to the left of the decimal by 65536. The digits to the right of the decimal point are then added to that product. Therefore, a number like 1.1 is converted to 65537 internally. 1.10 is converted to 65546. This creates certain anomalies; for example, 1.1 is "greater" than 2. To complicate matters further, BIND name servers interpret decimal serial numbers in a completely different and incompatible manner. Because all this is so counterintuitive, it's best to stick with integer serial numbers.

There are several good ways to manage integer serial numbers. The obvious way is just to use a counter: increment the serial number by one each time the file is modified. That's what DNS Manager does. Every time it updates a zone, it increments the zone's serial number. If you make changes with DNS Manager, you're locked into this method. If you only modify the zone database files by hand, you have other options, such as deriving the serial number from the date. For example, you could use the eight-digit number formed by *<year><month><day>*. Suppose today is March 12, 1998. In this form, your serial number would be 19980312. This scheme only allows one update per day, though, and that may not be enough. Add another two digits to this number to indicate how many times the file has been updated that day. The first number for March 12, 1998, would then be 1998031200. The next modification that day would change the serial number to 1998031201. This scheme allows 100 updates per day. Whatever scheme you choose (or are forced to go along with), the serial number must fit in a 32-bit integer.

## Additional Records

After you've been running a name server for a while, you may want to add data to your name server to help you manage your domain. Have you ever been stumped when someone asked you *where* one of your hosts is? Maybe you don't even remember what kind of host it is. Administrators have to manage larger and larger populations of hosts these days, making it easy to lose track of this information. The name server can help you out. And if one of your hosts is acting up and someone notices remotely, the name server can help them get in touch with you.

So far in the book, we've covered records critical to everyday operation: SOA, NS, A, CNAME, MX, and PTR records. Name servers need these records to operate, and applications look up data of these types. Two other useful resource record types are TXT and RP; these can be used to tell you the machine's location and responsible person. But DNS defines still more data types. For a complete list of the resource records, see Appendix A, *DNS Message Format and Resource Records*.

### General text information

TXT stands for TeXT. These records are simply a list of strings. The Microsoft DNS Server supports one string of up to 255 characters per TXT record. TXT records can be used for anything you want; a common use is to list a host's location. Creating a text record is easy: just highlight the zone or domain in DNS Manager's left pane and select **DNS → New Record**. In the **New Record** window, choose **TXT Record**, and fill in the fields.

The TXT record shown in Figure 7-1 looks like this in a zone database file:

```
cujo  IN  TXT  "Location: machine room dog house"
```

### Responsible Person

Domain administrators will undoubtedly develop a love/hate relationship with the Responsible Person, or RP, record. The RP record can be attached to any domain

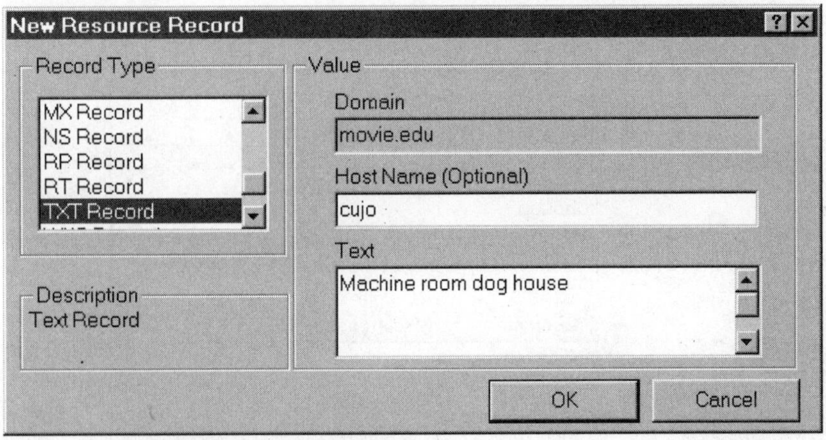

*Figure 7-1. Creating a TXT record*

name, internal or leaf, and indicates who is responsible for that host or domain. This will enable you to locate the miscreant responsible for the host peppering you with DNS queries, for example. But it will also lead people to you when one of your hosts acts up.

The record takes two arguments as its record-specific data: an electronic mail address, in domain name format, and a domain name, which points to additional data about the contact. The electronic mail address is in the same format the SOA record uses: it substitutes a dot (.) for the at sign (@). The next argument is a domain name, which must have a TXT record associated with it. The TXT record then contains free-format information about the contact, like full name and phone number. You can omit either field and specify the root domain (.) as a place-holder instead.

For example, let's say that the Movie U. Network Hotline is responsible for the host *robocop*. It also happens that the Movie U. hotline reads all mail sent to *root@movie.edu*. You'd add the RP record shown in Figure 7-2 with **DNS → New Record**.

And you'd add the TXT record shown in Figure 7-3 for *hotline.movie.edu*.

And here's what these records would look like in a zone database file:

```
robocop     IN  RP   root.movie.edu.  hotline.movie.edu.
hotline     IN  TXT  "Movie U. Network Hotline, (415) 555-4111"
```

Note that a TXT record for *root.movie.edu* isn't necessary, since it's only the domain name encoding of an electronic mail address, not a real domain name.

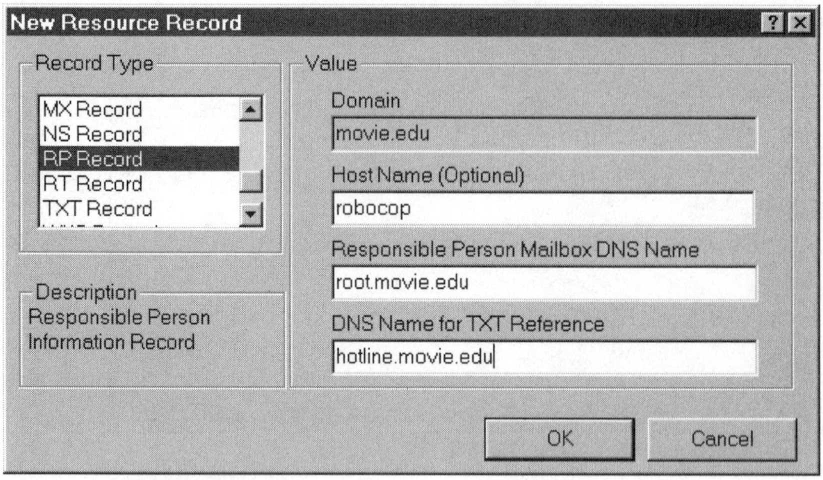

**New Resource Record**                                              **? X**

Record Type                    Value

| MX Record |
| NS Record |
| RP Record |
| RT Record |
| TXT Record |

Domain

movie.edu

Host Name (Optional)

robocop

Responsible Person Mailbox DNS Name

root.movie.edu

Description
Responsible Person
Information Record

DNS Name for TXT Reference

hotline.movie.edu

OK          Cancel

*Figure 7-2. Creating an RP record*

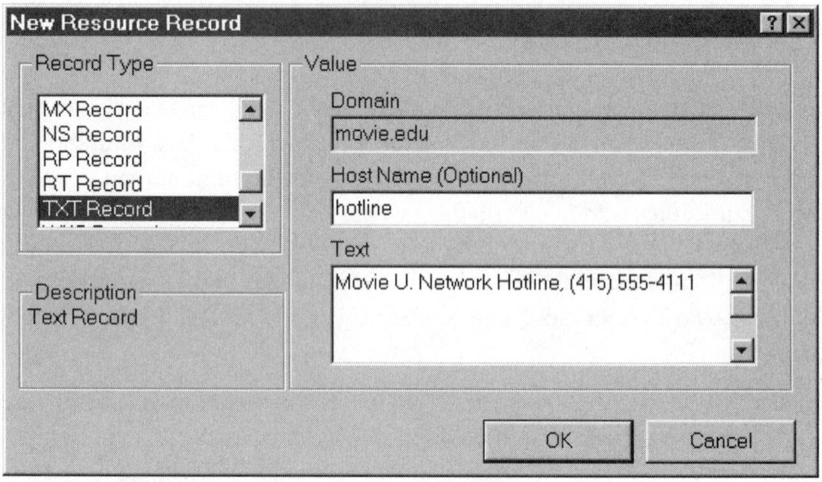

**New Resource Record**                                              **? X**

Record Type                    Value

| MX Record |
| NS Record |
| RP Record |
| RT Record |
| TXT Record |

Domain

movie.edu

Host Name (Optional)

hotline

Text

Movie U. Network Hotline, (415) 555-4111

Description
Text Record

OK          Cancel

*Figure 7-3. Creating an associated TXT record*

## Keeping db.cache Current

As we explained in Chapter 4, the *cache.dns* file tells your server where the servers for the root zone are. We also explained that unlike a BIND name server (which never modifies the cache file), a Microsoft DNS Server updates *cache.dns* with its current notion of the root name servers every time it exits.

The root name servers don't change very often, but they do change. A Microsoft DNS Server that starts with a proper cache file should, in theory, always have the current list of root name servers in its cache file. A good practice and a part of maintaining your name server is to check your *cache.dns* file every month or two. In Chapter 4, we told you to get the current cache file by *ftp*ing to *ftp.rs.inter-nic.net*. And that's probably your best method to keep current. Remember that you must stop the name server before updating *cache.dns*! If you don't, the cache file you install will be overwritten the next time the server does stop.

You can use *dig*, a utility that works a lot like *nslookup*, to retrieve the current list of roots just by running:

```
> dig @a.root-servers.net . ns > cache.dns
```

# Zone Database File Controls

The database files for all name servers, whether Microsoft or BIND, can include two control entries: $ORIGIN and $INCLUDE. $ORIGIN changes the origin, and $INCLUDE inserts a new file into the current file. These database control entries are not resource records; they facilitate the maintenance of DNS data. They were designed back in the "good old days" as a shortcut for humans who had to edit zone database files by hand. But if you make changes to your zones with DNS Manager only, you won't encounter these controls: the Microsoft DNS Server doesn't use them in the zone database files it generates. However, some day you might need to work with zone database files created by hand, so it's important you understand these controls.

## Changing the Origin in a Database File

The default origin for a DNS database file is just the domain name of the zone. The origin is a domain name that is appended automatically to all names not ending in a dot. This origin can be changed within the zone database file using $ORI-GIN, which must be followed by a domain name. (Don't forget the trailing dot if you give the full domain name!) From that point in the file on, all names not ending in a dot have the new origin appended.

If we didn't have DNS Manager to make changes and had to edit files by hand, we'd run into times when $ORIGIN would save us some work. For example, if your name server were responsible for a number of subdomains, you could use the $ORIGIN entry to reset the origin and simplify the files. For example, from the *movie.edu* zone database file):

```
$ORIGIN classics.movie.edu.
maltese        IN  A  192.253.253.100
casablanca     IN  A  192.253.253.101

$ORIGIN comedy.movie.edu.
mash           IN  A  192.253.253.200
twins          IN  A  192.253.253.201
```

We'll cover more on creating subdomains in Chapter 9.

## Including Other Database Files

To continue our example of editing zone database files by hand: once you've sub-divided your domain like this, you might find it more convenient to keep the sub-domain records in separate files. The $INCLUDE statement would let you do this:

```
$ORIGIN classics.movie.edu.
$INCLUDE db.classics

$ORIGIN comedy.movie.edu.
$INCLUDE db.comedy
```

To simplify the file even further, the new origin can be specified on the $INCLUDE line:

```
$INCLUDE db.classics  classics.movie.edu.
$INCLUDE db.comedy     comedy.movie.edu.
```

When you specify the origin on the $INCLUDE line, it only applies to the particular file that you're including. For example, the *comedy.movie.edu* origin applies only to the names in *db.comedy*. After *db.comedy* has been included, the origin returns to what it was before $INCLUDE, even if *db.comedy* contained an $ORIGIN entry.

Remember that, strictly speaking, you don't need to know anything about these directives to create subdomains with DNS Manager, and the Microsoft DNS Server doesn't generate zone database files using these shortcuts. But you do need to know about them to complete your knowledge of zone database files.

# Keeping Everything Running Smoothly

A significant part of maintenance is being aware when something has gone wrong, before it becomes a real problem. If you catch a problem early, chances are it'll be that much easier to fix. As the adage says, an ounce of prevention is worth a pound of cure.

This isn't quite troubleshooting—we'll devote an entire chapter to troubleshooting (Chapter 12)—think of it as "pre-troubleshooting." Troubleshooting (the pound of cure) is what you have to do if you ignore maintenance, after your problem has developed complications, and you need to identify the problem by its symptoms.

The next two sections deal with preventive maintenance: looking periodically at the Event Log and the name server statistics to see whether any problems are developing. Consider this a name server's medical checkup.

## Common Event Log Messages

The Microsoft DNS Server logs events to the System Log. To view the events, use Event Viewer, which you start with **Start** → **Programs** → **Administrative Tools (Common)** → **Event Viewer**. Make sure you're looking at the System Log by selecting **Log** → **System**. To save space, when we describe an event we won't show a screen shot of the complete event. Instead, we'll list just the description from the event detail. (Double-click an event to see its details.) We're not going to list Event ID numbers either, because Microsoft has said these will be changing after the post-SP3 hotfixed server. The SP4 and NT 5.0 DNS Servers will log events with similar descriptions to those listed in this section, but the Event IDs will change completely.

When the server starts up (either at boot time or because you restarted it), you'll see this event:

```
Starting Microsoft DNS Server (NT 4.0 ServicePack3)
```

After the name server has started and is ready to answer queries, there's this event:

```
The DNS Server has started.
```

For a healthy server, you should see these two events after booting. If you stop the server manually, you'll see this event:

```
The DNS Server has shutdown.
```

If a server is a slave for a zone, it will notify you every time it performs a zone transfer:

```
New version 4 of zone movie.edu found at DNS server at 192.249.249.3.  Zone
transfer is in progress.

DNS Server wrote a new version of zone movie.edu, to file movie.edu.dns.  The
data is the new version number.
```

You'll also see that last message on the primary master when you make a change to a zone through DNS Manager and select **DNS** → **Update Server Data Files**. After the server writes the updated file to disk, it logs that event.

If the primary master's serial number for a zone is lower than the slave's—an error condition—the server lets you know:

```
Zone movie.edu version 2086 is newer than version 4 on DNS server at
192.249.249.3.  The zone is not updated.  DNS servers supplying zones for
transfer must have most recent version of zone from primary.  If zone on
remote server 192.249.249.3, is in fact the most recent version of the zone,
stop the DNS server, delete the zone file and restart.  The DNS server will
transfer the new version and rewrite its zone file.
```

If the primary master is not authoritative for the zone—another error condition—you'll see this on the slave:

```
Zone movie.edu failed zone refresh check.  Invalid response from DNS server
at 192.249.249.3.  Check DNS Server at 192.249.249.3 and insure it is
properly authoritative for this zone.
```

Unfortunately, if the name server simply can't reach the primary master (say it has gone down), the DNS server never logs an error.

On the other hand, a server that's a primary master for a zone will notify you when a slave does a zone transfer:

```
DNS Server transfer of zone fx.movie.edu to DNS server at 192.249.249.2,
successfully completed.
```

If you're missing the cache file, *cache.dns*, or a zone database file, the server won't even start. It will log a flurry of messages, though. A missing cache file produces these events:

```
DNS Server could not open the file dns\cache.dns.  The data is the error.

DNS Server could not find or open database file dns\cache.dns

DNS Server could not find or open cache file.
```

A missing zone database file, say *fx.movie.edu.dns*, generates these events:

```
DNS Server could not open the file dns\fx.movie.edu.dns.  The data is the
error.

DNS Server could not find or open database file dns\fx.movie.edu.dns.

DNS Server could not create domain fx.movie.edu.

DNS Server could not parse database file fx.movie.edu.dns for domain
fx.movie.edu.
```

Finally, for both the missing cache file or zone database file errors, you'll also see an event logged by the Service Control Manager complaining that the DNS service didn't start:

```
The Microsoft DNS Server service terminated with the following error:  The
system cannot find the file specified.
```

If *cache.dns* exists but does not contain any data, the server still starts, but you'll see this warning event:

```
DNS Server does not have a cache (or database) entry for root name server.
The cache file MUST have at least one NS records, indicating a root DNS
server and a corresponding A record for that root DNS server.  Otherwise the
DNS server will be unable to contact the root DNS server on startup and will
be unable to answer queries for names outside of its own authoritative zones.
```

How could my *cache.dns* file suddenly contain no data, you ask. The reason is a nasty bug in the server that was fixed in SP3: if you start the server with a missing zone database file, it runs long enough to discover the missing file, log an event, and stop again. But that's not all it does: it also writes out its current notion of the root name servers to *cache.dns*. The server hasn't been running long enough to contact a root name server listed in the cache file and get its working list of root name servers, so it just writes out an empty *cache.dns*. This is reason enough to get SP3, in our opinion.

The server also responds severely to a syntax error in a zone database file. If you always make changes to your zones using DNS Manager, you shouldn't see syntax errors. Editing by hand can get you into trouble, though. Here's what happens when the server encounters a syntax error:

```
DNS Server encountered unknown or unsupported record type asad in database
file fx.movie.edu.dns, line 16.
```

```
DNS Server could not create domain fx.movie.edu.
```

```
DNS Server could not parse database file fx.movie.edu.dns for domain
fx.movie.edu.
```

Just as with a missing file, the server doesn't stay running: you'll need to fix the error before the server will stay up. If the server is pre-SP3, it has also just trashed your *cache.dns* file, by the way.

If you put an invalid IP address (such as 127.0.0.1 or any IP address not corresponding to a network interface on the server) in the DNS Server IP Addresses field of the **Server Properties** → **Interfaces** window, you'll see this:

```
DNS Server listen address list contains IP addresses that are not IP
addresses on the DNS server.  Use the DNS manager server properties,
interfaces dialog, to verify and reset the IP addresses the DNS server should
listen on.
```

Note that the server will *not* receive queries sent to the loopback addresses of 127.0.0.1 or 0.0.0.0.

## Understanding Name Server Statistics

You should periodically look over the statistics on some of your name servers, if only to see how busy they are. Unfortunately, the Microsoft DNS Server lags behind the BIND name server in terms of providing a detailed amount of statistics. But you're not completely blind to what it's doing.

Name server statistics are viewed with DNS Manager. When you select a name server in the left pane, its statistics appear in the right pane. Here are the statistics reported and what they mean:

*UdpQueries*

> The number of queries the name server has received via UDP.

*UdpResponses*

> The number of responses the name server has sent via UDP.

*TcpClientConnections*

> Recall that most DNS queries and responses travel in UDP packets. But a client can open a TCP connection to a server and then exchange a series of queries and responses over that connection. Zone transfers also require a TCP connection. This statistic lists the number of TCP connections the server has received from clients.

*TcpQueries*

> The number of queries the name server has received via TCP.

*TcpResponses*

> The number of responses the name server has sent via TCP.

*Recursive Lookups*

> These next two are a little counterintuitive. This value lists the number of non-recursive queries this name server has sent to other name servers to resolve a recursive query received by this name server. Just think of it as a count of nonrecursive queries sent.

*Recursive Responses*

> This value lists the number of responses to nonrecursive queries sent by this name server. Just think of it as a count of replies to nonrecursive queries sent.

*WINS Forward Lookups*

> The number of queries sent to WINS servers for resolution.

*WINS Forward Responses*

> The number of responses received from WINS servers.

*WINS Reverse Lookups*

> The number of NetBT node status queries sent in response to *in-addr.arpa* queries received.

*WINS Reverse Responses*

> The number of NetBT node status replies received.

# 8

# *Growing Your Domain*

> *"What size do you want to be?" it asked.*
>
> *"Oh, I'm not particular as to size," Alice hastily replied; "only one doesn't like changing so often, you know. . . ."*
>
> *"Are you content now?" said the Caterpillar.*
>
> *"Well, I should like to be a little larger, sir, if you wouldn't mind. . . ."*

## How Many Name Servers?

We set up two name servers in Chapter 4, *Setting Up the Microsoft DNS Server*. Two servers are as few as you'll ever want to run. Depending on the size of your network, you may need to run many more than just two servers. It is not uncommon to run from five to seven servers, with one of them off site. How many name servers are enough? You'll have to decide that based on your network. Here are some guidelines to help out:

- Have at least one name server available directly on each network or subnet you have. This removes routers as points of failure. Make the most of any multihomed hosts you may have, since they're (by definition) attached to more than one network.

- If you have a file server and some diskless nodes, run a name server on the file server to serve this group of machines.

- Run name servers near, but not necessarily on, large time-sharing machines. The users and their processes probably generate a lot of queries, and, as administrators, you will work harder to keep a multiuser host up. But balance their needs against the risk of running a name server—a security critical server—on a system that lots of people have access to.

- Run one name server off site. This makes your data available when your network isn't. You might argue that it's useless to look up an address when you can't reach the host. Then again, the offsite name server may be available if your network is reachable but your other name servers are down. Many ISPs run slave servers for their customers. If you have a close relationship with an organization on the Internet—say another university or a business partner—they may consent to run a slave for you.

Figure 8-1 shows a sample topology and a brief analysis follows to show you how this might work.

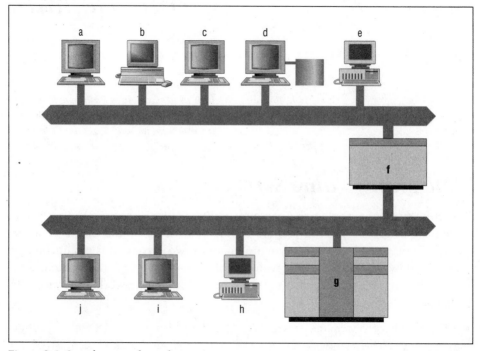

*Figure 8-1. Sample network topology*

Notice that if you follow our guidelines, there are still a number of places you could choose to run a name server. Host *d*, the file server for hosts *a*, *b*, *c*, and *e*, could run a name server. Host *g*, a big, multiuser host, is another good candidate. But probably the best choice is host *f*, the smaller host with interfaces on both networks. You'll need to run only one name server, instead of two, and it'll run on a closely watched host. If you want more than one name server on either network, you can also run one on *d* or *g*.

## *Where Do I Put My Name Servers?*

In addition to giving you a rough idea of how many name servers you'll need, these criteria should also help you decide *where* to run name servers (for example, on file servers, multihomed hosts). But there are other important considerations when choosing the right host.

Other factors to keep in mind are the host's connectivity, the software it runs (the Microsoft DNS Server, BIND, or otherwise), and maintaining the homogeneity of your name servers:

*Connectivity*

It's important that name servers be well connected. Running a name server on the fastest, most reliable host on your network won't do you any good if the host is mired in some backwater subnet of your network behind a slow, flaky serial line. Try to find a host close to your link to the Internet (if you have one), or find a well-connected Internet host to act as a slave for your zone. And on your own network, try to run name servers near the hubs of your network.

It's doubly important that your primary master name server be well connected. The primary needs good connectivity to all the slaves that update from it, for reliable zone transfers. And, like any name server, it'll benefit from fast, reliable networking.

*Software*

Another factor to consider in choosing a host for a name server is the software the host runs. If you bought this book, we'll assume it's because you want to run the Microsoft DNS Server. Keep in mind that you'll be able to manage remote name servers with Microsoft's DNS Manager only if they're running the Microsoft server. That means that your name servers will have to run Windows NT.

If managing servers with DNS Manager isn't important to you (maybe you like the DNS Manager frontend for managing zone data, but you're comfortable editing BIND configuration files by hand), you might consider running some BIND name servers on your network. Newer BIND name servers are fast and robust and can interoperate with Microsoft's DNS Server. If you do decide to implement some BIND name servers, it'd be a good idea to run the most recent version of BIND, BIND 8. BIND 8 servers can use a more efficient zone transfer protocol with Microsoft DNS Servers. (See Chapter 10, *Advanced Features and Security,* and Chapter 12, *Troubleshooting DNS,* for more information on interoperability between the Microsoft DNS Server and BIND.)

*Homogeneity*

Another thing to take into account is the homogeneity of your name servers. Hopping between Windows NT and different versions of UNIX can be frustrating and confusing. Avoid running name servers on lots of different platforms, if you can. You can waste a lot of time porting your scripts (or ours!) from one operating system to another, or looking for the location of *nslookup* on three different operating systems.

*Security*

Since you would undoubtedly prefer that hackers not commandeer your name server to assist them in attacking your own hosts or other networks across the Internet, it's important to run your name server on a secure host. Don't run a name server on a big, multiuser system whose users you can't trust. If you have certain computers that are dedicated to hosting network services but don't permit general logins, those are good candidates for running name servers. If you only have one or a few really secure hosts, consider running the primary master name server on one of those, since its compromise would be more significant than the compromise of the slaves.

Though these are really secondary considerations—it's more important to have a name server on a given subnet than to have it running on the perfect host—do keep these criteria in mind when making a choice.

## Capacity Planning

If you have heavily populated networks, or users who do a lot of name server–intensive work, you may find you need more name servers than we've recommended to handle the load. Or our recommendations may be fine for a little while, but as people add hosts to your nets or install new name server–intensive programs, you may find your name servers bogged down by queries.

Just which tasks are "name server–intensive"? Sending electronic mail, especially to large mailing lists, can be name server–intensive. Programs that make lots of remote procedure calls to different hosts can be name server–intensive. Even running certain graphical user environments can tax your name server. The astute (and precocious) among you may be asking, "But how do I know when my name servers are overloaded? What do I look for?" An excellent question!

Memory utilization is probably the most important aspect of a name server's operation to monitor. *dns.exe,* the name server process, can get very large on a name server authoritative for many zones. If *dns.exe's* size, plus the size of the other processes you run, exceeds your real memory, your host may swap furiously ("thrash") and not get anything done. Another criterion you can use to measure the load on your name server is the load the name server process places on the host's CPU. Correctly configured name servers don't use much CPU time, so high CPU usage is often symptomatic of a configuration error. Windows NT's Performance Monitor can help you characterize your name server's average CPU utilization. To see the name server's CPU utilization, start the Performance Monitor (**Start** → **Programs** → **Administrative Tools (Common)** → **Performance Monitor**), and choose **Edit** → **Add to Chart**. Select **Process** as the **Object**, **% Processor Time** as the **Counter**, and **dns** as the **Instance**. The chart will now show the percentage of processor time the name server is using.

Unfortunately, there are no absolute rules when it comes to acceptable CPU utilization. We offer a rough rule of thumb, though: 5 percent average CPU utilization is probably acceptable; 10 percent is a bit high, unless the host is dedicated to providing name service.

Another statistic to look at is the number of queries the name server receives per minute (or second, if you have a busy name server). Again, there are no absolutes here: a multiprocessor server with oodles of RAM running Windows NT can handle hundreds of queries per second without breaking into a sweat, while a 486-based PC might have problems with more than a few queries a second.

To check the volume of queries your name server is receiving, it's easiest to look at the name server's internal statistics, which are written to the Event Viewer at regular intervals.

Alternatively, you can use DNS Manager to retrieve the name server's statistics. If you click a name server in the Server List, the right panel displays a subset of the statistics for that server, including TCP and UDP queries received. Figure 8-2 provides an example.

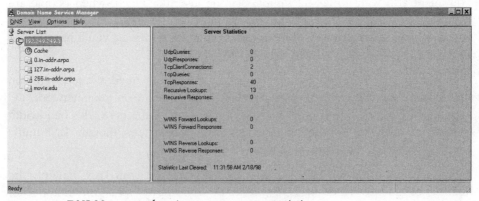

*Figure 8-2. DNS Manager showing name server statistics*

Not much happening on this name server, but you get the idea: *UdpQueries* shows the number of UDP-based queries (the most common kind) received since this server's statistics were reset, and *TcpQueries* shows the number of TCP-based queries received.

If you choose **Options** → **Preferences**, and check **Auto Refresh Server Statistics**, you can tell DNS Manager to refresh the statistics automatically and change the statistics refresh interval to whatever period you'd like to measure statistics over. In Figure 8-3, we've changed it to an hour.

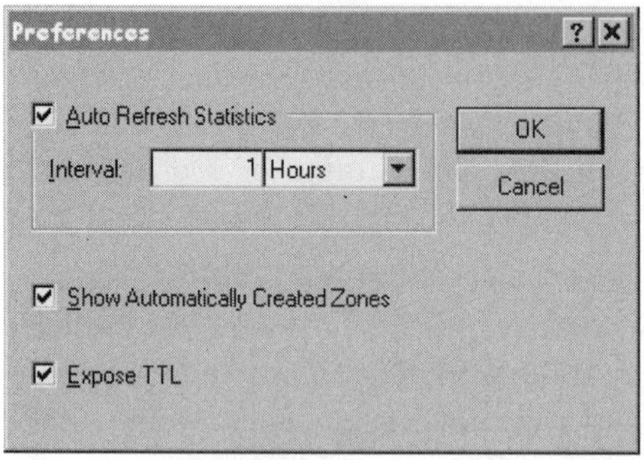

*Figure 8-3. The name server Preferences dialog*

Be sure to take down the statistics you see in the right panel of the **Domain Name Service Manager** window (in Figure 8-2), and then come back after the auto refresh to take down the new statistics.

You should pay special attention to peak periods. Monday mornings are often busy because many people like to respond to mail they've received over the weekend first thing on Mondays.

You might also want to take a sample starting just after lunch, when people are returning to their desks and getting back to work—all at about the same time. Of course, if your organization is spread across several time zones, you'll have to use your own good judgment to determine a busy time.

Even if your host is fast enough to handle the number of queries it receives, you should make sure the DNS traffic isn't placing undue load on your network. On most LANs, DNS traffic will be too small a proportion of the network's bandwidth to worry about. Over slow leased lines or dialup connections, though, DNS traffic could consume enough bandwidth to merit concern.

To get a rough estimate of the volume of DNS traffic on your LAN, multiply the number of queries received (*UdpQueries* + *TcpQueries*) plus the number of answers sent (*UdpResponses* + *TcpResponses*) in an hour by 800 bits (100 bytes, a rough average size for a DNS packet), and divide by 3600 (seconds per hour) to find the bandwidth utilized. This should give you a feeling for how much of your network's bandwidth is being consumed by DNS traffic.

To give you an idea of what's normal, the last NSFNet traffic report (in April, 1995) showed that DNS traffic constituted just over 5 percent of the total traffic volume (in bytes) on their backbone. The NSFNet's figures are based upon actual traffic sampling, not calculations like ours using the name server's statistics.* If you want to get a more accurate idea of the traffic your name server is receiving, you can always do your own traffic sampling with a LAN protocol analyzer.

Once you've found that your name servers are overworked, what then? First, it's a good idea to make sure that your name servers aren't being bombarded with queries by a misbehaving program. To do that, you'll need to find out where all the queries are coming from.

Unfortunately, if you're running the Microsoft DNS Server, the only way to find out which resolvers and name servers are sending all those darned queries is to run Microsoft's Network Monitor, or another program that will capture all the packets that your host receives. While describing how to use Network Monitor is outside of the scope of this book, remember to capture just packets sent to your name server (unidirectionally is fine), and filter out everything but DNS traffic. All you're really interested in is the source IP addresses of the queries your name server is receiving. When poring over the Network Monitor output, look for hosts sending repeated queries, especially for the same or similar information. That may indicate a misconfigured or buggy program running on the host, or a foreign name server pelting your name server with queries.

If all the queries appear to be legitimate, add a new name server. Don't put the name server just anywhere, though; use the information from the Network Monitor output to help you decide where best to run one. In cases where DNS traffic is gobbling up your Ethernet, it won't help to choose a host at random and create a name server there. You need to consider which hosts are sending all the queries, and then figure out how to best provide them name service. Here are some hints to help you decide:

- Look for queries from resolvers on hosts that share the same file server. You could run a name server on the file server.

- Look for queries from resolvers on large, multiuser hosts. You could run a name server there.

- Look for queries from resolvers on another subnet. Those resolvers should be configured to query a name server on their local subnet. If there isn't one on that subnet, create one.

---

* We're not sure how representative of the current state of the Internet these numbers are, but it's extremely difficult to wheedle equivalent numbers out of the commercial backbone providers that succeeded the NSFNet.

- Look for queries from resolvers on the same bridged segment (assuming you use bridging). If you run a name server on the bridged segment, the traffic won't need to be bridged to the rest of the network.

- Look for queries from hosts connected to each other via another, lightly loaded network. You could run a name server on the other network.

# Adding More Name Servers

When you need to create new name servers for your domain, the simplest recourse is to add slaves. You already know how—we went over it in Chapter 4—and once you've set one slave up, cloning it is a piece of cake. But you can run into trouble by indiscriminately adding slaves.

If you run a large number of slave servers for a zone, the primary master name server can take quite a beating just keeping up with the slaves' polling to check that their data are current. There are a number of courses of action to take for this problem:

- Make more primary master name servers.

- Increase the refresh interval so that the slaves don't check so often.

- Direct some of the slave name servers to load from other slave name servers.

- Create caching-only name servers (described later).

- Create "partial-slave" name servers (also described later).

## Primary Master and Slave Servers

Creating more primaries will mean extra work for you, since you have to keep the db files synchronized manually. Whether or not this is preferable to your other alternatives is your call. You can use tools like *xcopy* and *sc* (the Windows NT service control manager from the Windows NT Resource Kit) to simplify the process of distributing the files. A batch file to synchronize files between primaries might be as simple as:[*]

```
# stop the name server before copying files

sc \\wormhole stop  Microsoft DNS Server

# copy zone data files to dup'd primary

xcopy C:\WinNT\System32\DNS\*.dns \\wormhole\c$\WinNT\System32\DNS\ /Q /Z
```

---

[*] This assumes that your name servers have Windows NT installed on their C: drives.

```
# restart server

sc \\wormhole start  Microsoft DNS Server
```

or for multiple primaries:

```
FOR %%i IN (wormhole carrie) DO sc \\%i stop  Microsoft DNS Server

FOR %%i IN (wormhole carrie) DO xcopy C:\\WinNT\System32\DNS \\%%I\c$\WinNT\
System32\DNS\ /Q /Z

FOR %%i IN (wormhole carrie) DO sc \\%%i start  Microsoft DNS Server
```

This stops the name server on the duplicate primary master name servers with *sc*, copies the zone data files over, and then restarts the servers. Increasing your name servers' refresh interval is another option. This slows down the propagation of new information, however, which in some cases, is not a problem. If you rebuild your DNS data only once each day at 1 a.m. (run from the NT *at* command) and then allow six hours for the data to distribute, all the slaves will be current by 7 a.m.* That may be acceptable to your user population. See the section "Changing Other SOA Values," later in this chapter, for more detail.

You can even have some of your slaves load from other slaves. Slave name servers *can* load zone data from another slave name server, instead of loading from a primary name server. The slave name server can't tell if it is loading from a primary or another slave. It's only important that the name server serving the zone transfer is authoritative for the zone. There's no trick to configuring this. Instead of specifying the IP address of the primary in the slave's configuration, you simply specify the IP address of another slave, as shown in Figure 8-4.

When you go to this "second level" of distribution, though, it can take up to twice as long for the data to percolate from the primary name server to all the slaves. Remember that the refresh interval is the period after which the slave servers will check to make sure that their zone data are still current. Therefore, it can take the first-level slave servers the entire refresh interval before they get their copy of the zone files from the primary master server. Similarly, it can take the second-level slave servers the entire refresh interval to get their copy of the files from the first-level slave servers. The propagation time from the primary master server to all of the slave servers can therefore be twice the refresh interval.

One way to avoid this is to use the DNS NOTIFY feature, described in Chapter 10. This is on by default and will trigger zone transfers soon after the zone is updated on the primary master. Unfortunately, it works only on Microsoft DNS Server and Version 8 BIND slaves.

---

\* And, of course, if you're using DNS NOTIFY, described in Chapter 10, they'll catch up much sooner than that.

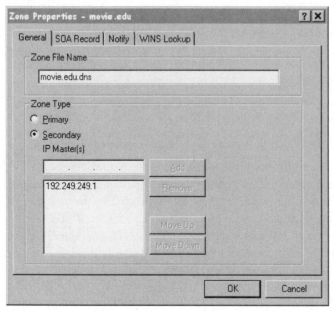

*Figure 8-4. Second-tier slave*

If you decide to configure your network with two (or more) tiers of slave servers, be careful to avoid updating loops. If we were to configure *wormhole* to update from *diehard*, and then we accidentally configured *diehard* to update from *wormhole,* neither would ever get data from the primary. They would merely check their out-of-date serial numbers against each other and perpetually decide that they were both up to date.

## Caching-Only Servers

Creating caching-only name servers is another alternative when you need more servers. Caching-only name servers are name servers not authoritative for any zones (except *0.0.127.in-addr.arpa*). The name doesn't imply that primary and slave name servers don't cache—they do. The name means that the *only* function this server performs is looking up data and caching them. As with primary and slave name servers, a caching-only name server needs a *cache.dns* file and the  zones that DNS Manager automatically creates, *0.in-0.addr.arpa, 127.in-addr.arpa,* and *255.in-addr.arpa*. The configuration of a caching-only server looks like Figure 8-5.

A caching-only name server can look up names inside and outside your zone, as can primary and slave name servers. The difference is that when a caching-only name server initially looks up a name within your zone, it ends up asking one of the primary or slave name servers for your zone for the answer. A primary or slave

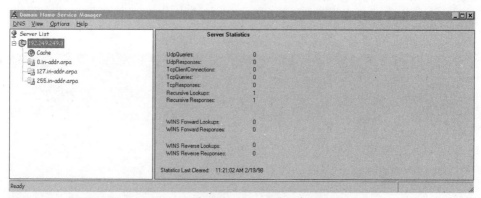

*Figure 8-5. DNS Manager on a caching-only name server*

would answer the same question out of its authoritative data. Which primary or slave does the caching-only server ask? As with name servers outside of your domain, it finds out which name servers serve your zone from one of the name servers for your parent zone. Is there any way to prime a caching-only name server's cache so it knows which hosts run primary and slave name servers for your zone? No, there isn't. You can't use *cache.dns*—the *cache.dns* file is only for *root* name server hints.

A caching-only name server's real value comes after it builds up its cache. Each time it queries an authoritative name server and receives an answer, it caches the records in the answer. Over time, the cache will grow to include the information most often requested by the resolvers querying the caching-only name server. And you avoid the overhead of zone transfers—a caching-only name server doesn't need to do them.

## Partial-Slave Servers

In between a caching-only name server and a slave name server is another variation: a name server that is a slave for only a few of the local zones. We call this a *partial-slave name server* (and probably nobody else does). Suppose *movie.edu* had twenty class C networks (and a corresponding twenty *in-addr.arpa* zones). Instead of creating a slave server for all 21 zones (all the *in-addr.arpa* subdomains plus *movie.edu*), we could create a partial-slave server for *movie.edu* and only those *in-addr.arpa* zones the host itself is in. If the host had two network interfaces, then its name server would be a slave for three zones: *movie.edu* and the two *in-addr.arpa* zones.

Let's say we scare up the hardware for another name server. We'll call the new host *zardoz.movie.edu,* with IP addresses 192.249.249.9 and 192.253.253.9. We'll create a partial-slave name server on *zardoz*, with the configuration shown in Figure 8-6.

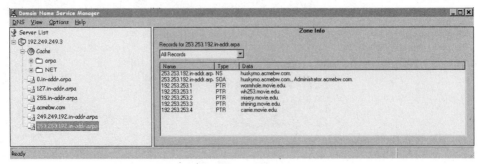

*Figure 8-6. DNS Manager on a partial-slave server*

This server is a slave for *movie.edu* and only two of the 20 *in-addr.arpa* zones.

What's so useful about a partial-slave name server? They're not much work to administer, because their configuration doesn't change much. On a server authoritative for all the *in-addr.arpa* zones, we'd need to add and delete *in-addr.arpa* zones as our network changed. That can be a surprising amount of work on a large network.

A partial-slave can still answer most of the queries it receives, though. Most of these queries will be for data in the *movie.edu* and the two *in-addr.arpa* zones. Why? Because most of the hosts querying the name server are on the two networks it's connected to, 192.249.249 and 192.253.253. And those hosts probably communicate primarily with other hosts on their own network. This generates queries for data within the *in-addr.arpa* zone that corresponds to the local network.

# Registering Name Servers

When you get around to setting up more and more name servers, a question may strike you—must I register *all* of my primary and slave name servers with my parent zone? No, only those servers you want to make available to servers outside of your zone need to be registered with the parent. For instance, if you run nine name servers for your zone, you may choose to tell the parent zone about only four of them. Within your zone, all nine servers are used. Five of those nine servers, however, are only queried by resolvers on hosts that are configured to query them. Their parent name servers don't delegate to them, so they're not registered in the domain name space. Only the four servers registered with your parent zone are queried by other name servers, including caching-only and partial-slave name servers within your domain. This setup is shown in Figure 8-7.

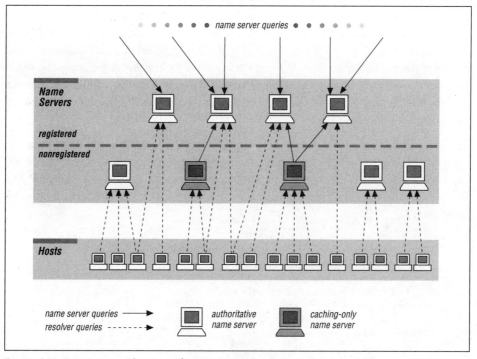

*Figure 8-7. Registering only some of your name servers*

Besides being able to pick and choose which of your name servers are hammered by outside queries, there's a technical motivation for registering only some of your zone's name servers: there is a limit to how many servers will fit in a UDP response packet. In practice, around ten name server records should fit. Depending on the data (how many servers are in the same domain), you could get more or fewer.* There's not much point in registering more than ten servers, anyway—if none of the ten servers can be reached, it's unlikely the destination host can be reached.

If you've set up a new authoritative name server and you decide it should be registered, make a list of the parents of the zones it's authoritative for. You'll need to contact the administrators for each of these parent zones. For example, let's say we want to register the name server we set up on *zardoz* earlier. In order to get this slave registered in all the right zones, we'll need to contact the administrators of *edu* and *in-addr.arpa*. (For help determining who runs your parent zones, turn back to Chapter 3, *Where Do I Start?*)

---

* The domain names of the Internet's root name servers were changed because of this. All of the roots were moved into the same domain, *root-servers.net*, to take the most advantage of domain name compression and store as many roots as possible in a single UDP packet.

When you contact the administrators of a parent zone, be sure to fill out the form they specify (if any) on their web site. If there's no standard form, give them the domain name of the zone the new name server is authoritative for. If the new name server is in the new zone, you'll also need to give them the IP address(es) of the new name server. In fact, *if there's no official format for submitting the information,* it's often best just to send your parent the complete list of registered name servers for the zone, plus any addresses necessary, in data file format. That avoids any potential confusion.

Since our networks were originally assigned by the InterNIC, we submitted the form at *http://www.arin.net/templates/inaddrtemplate.txt* to *hostmaster@arin.net,* per their web site, to change our registration. If they hadn't had a template for us to use, our message to the administrator of *in-addr.arpa* might have read something like:

```
Howdy!

I've just set up a new slave name server on
zardoz.movie.edu for the 249.249.192.in-addr.arpa
and 253.253.192.in-addr.arpa zones.  Would you
please add NS records for this name server to the
in-addr.arpa zone?  That would make our delegation
information look like:

253.253.192.in-addr.arpa. 86400 IN NS terminator.movie.edu.
253.253.192.in-addr.arpa. 86400 IN NS wormhole.movie.edu.
253.253.192.in-addr.arpa. 86400 IN NS zardoz.movie.edu.

249.249.192.in-addr.arpa. 86400 IN NS terminator.movie.edu.
249.249.192.in-addr.arpa. 86400 IN NS wormhole.movie.edu.
249.249.192.in-addr.arpa. 86400 IN NS zardoz.movie.edu.

Thanks!

Albert LeDomaine
al@robocop.movie.edu
```

Notice we specified explicit TTLs on the NS and A records. That's because our parent name servers aren't authoritative for those records; *our* name servers are. By including them, we're indicating our choice of a TTL for our zone's delegation. Of course, our parent may have other ideas about what the TTL should be.

In this case, glue data—A records for each of the name servers—aren't necessary, since the domain names of the name servers aren't within the *in-addr.arpa* zones. They're within *movie.edu,* so a name server that was referred to *terminator* or *wormhole* could still find their addresses by following delegation to the *movie.edu* name servers.

Is a partial-slave name server a good name server to register with your parent zone? Actually, it's not *ideal*, because it's only authoritative for *some* of your *in-addr.arpa* zones. Administratively, it may be easier to register only servers backing up *all* the local zones; that way, you don't need to keep track of which name servers are authoritative for which zones. All of your parent zones can delegate to the same set of name servers: your primary and your "full" slaves.

If you don't have many name servers, though, or if you're good at remembering which name servers are authoritative for what, go ahead and register a partial-slave.

Caching-only name servers, on the other hand, must *never* be registered. A caching-only name server rarely has complete information for any given zone, just the bits and pieces of it that it has looked up recently. If a parent name server were mistakenly to refer a foreign name server to a caching-only name server, the foreign name server would send the caching-only name server a nonrecursive query. The caching-only name server might have the data cached, but then again, might not. If it didn't have the data, it would refer the querier to the best name servers it knew (those closest to the domain name in the query)—which might include the caching-only name server itself! The poor foreign name server might never get an answer. This kind of misconfiguration—actually, delegating a zone to any name server not authoritative for that zone—is known as *lame delegation*.

## Changing TTLs

An experienced domain administrator needs to know how to set the time to live on his zone's data to his best advantage. The TTL on a resource record, remember, is the time in seconds any server can cache that record. So if the TTL for a particular resource record is 3600 (seconds), and a server outside your domain caches that record, it will have to remove the entry from its cache after an hour. If it needs the same data after the hour is up, it'll have to query your name servers again.

When we introduced TTLs, we emphasized that your choice of a TTL would dictate how current you'd keep copies of your data, at the cost of increased load on your name servers. A low TTL would mean that name servers outside your domain would have to get data from your name servers often and would therefore keep current. On the other hand, your name servers would be peppered by their queries.

You don't *have* to choose a TTL once and for all, though. You can—and experienced administrators do—change TTLs periodically to suit your needs.

Suppose we know that one of our hosts is about to be moved to another net-work. This host is the *movie.edu* film library. It houses a large collection of files our site makes available to hosts on the Internet. During normal operation, out-side name servers cache the address of our host according to the minimum TTL in the SOA record. (We set the *movie.edu* TTL to be one day in our sample files.) A name server caching the old address record just before the change could have the wrong address for as long as a day. A loss of connectivity for a day is unaccept-able, though. What can we do to minimize the loss of connectivity? We can lower the TTL, so that outside servers cache the address record for a shorter period. By reducing the TTL, we force the outside servers to update their data more fre-quently, which means that any changes we make when we actually move the sys-tem will be propagated to the outside world quickly. How long can we make the TTL? Unfortunately, we can't use a TTL of zero, which should mean "don't cache this record at all." Some older BIND 4 name servers can't return records with a TTL of zero, instead returning null answers or SERVFAIL errors. Short TTLs, like 30 seconds, are okay, though. The easiest change is to lower the TTL in the *movie.edu* SOA record. If you don't place an explicit TTL on resource records, the name server applies this minimum TTL from the SOA record to each resource record. If you lower the minimum TTL field, though, the new, lower TTL applies to all zone data, not just the address of the host being moved. The drawback to this approach is that your name server will be answering a lot more queries, since the querying servers will cache *all* the data in your zone for a shorter period. A better alternative is to put a different TTL only on the affected address record.

To add an explicit TTL on an individual resource record, first you'll need to change DNS Manager's preferences to actually *show* you TTLs. Choose **Options →
Preferences**, and click the **Expose TTL** box in the **Preferences** dialog, which is shown in Figure 8-8.

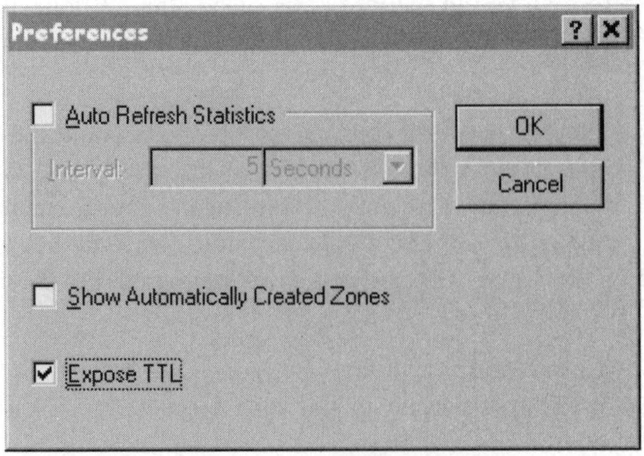

*Figure 8-8. The Options → Preferences dialog*

Click on the domain name of the zone in the left panel, and then double-click the record when it appears in the right panel. The **Properties** window is displayed, and you can type or dial in the TTL in units from seconds to years.

Figure 8-9 provides an example of an explicit TTL from *movie.edu.*

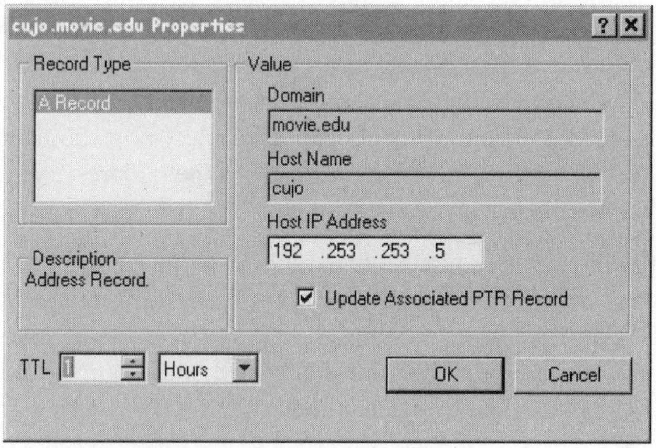

*Figure 8-9. An explcit TTL on cujo.movie.edu*

The record that DNS Manager adds to the *movie.edu* zone data file looks like this:

```
cujo  3600  IN  A  192.253.253.5
```

Note the explicit TTL of 3600 seconds (one hour) in the optional TTL field, over-riding the TTL in the zone's SOA record.

If you're observant, you may have noticed a potential problem: the explicit TTL on *cujo*'s address is an hour, but the TTL field in the SOA record—ostensibly the *minimum* TTL for the zone—is *higher.* Which takes precedence?

If the Microsoft DNS Server followed the DNS RFCs, the TTL field in the SOA record would really define the minimum TTL value for all resource records in the zone. Thus, you could only specify explicit TTLs larger than this minimum. Neither Microsoft nor BIND name servers work this way, though. In other words, in real life, "minimum" is not really minimum. Instead, the name server implements the minimum TTL field in the SOA record as a "default" TTL. If there is no TTL on a record, the minimum applies. If there is a TTL on the resource record, the name server allows it even if it is smaller than the minimum. That one record is sent out in responses with the smaller TTL, while all other records are sent out with the "minimum" TTL from the SOA record.

You should also know that when giving out answers, a slave supplies the same TTL a primary does—that is, if a primary gives out a TTL of 86400 for a particular record, a slave will, too. The slave doesn't decrement the TTL according to how long it has been since it loaded the zone. So, if the TTL of a single resource record is set smaller than the SOA minimum, both the primary and slave name servers give out the resource record with the same, smaller TTL. If the slave name server has reached the expiration time for the zone, it expires the whole zone. It will never expire an individual resource record within a zone.

So the Microsoft DNS Server does allow you to put a small TTL on an individual resource record if you know that the data is going to change shortly. Thus, any server caching that data caches it only for a brief time. Unfortunately, while the name server makes tagging records with a small TTL possible, most domain administrators don't spend the time to do it. When a host changes address, you often lose connectivity to it for a while.

More often than not, the host having its address changed is not one of the main hubs on the site, so the outage impacts few people. If one of the mail hubs or a major *ftp* repository—like the film library—is moving, though, a day's loss of connectivity may be unacceptable. In cases like this, the domain administrator should plan ahead and reduce the TTL on the data to be changed.

Remember that the TTL on the affected data will need to be lowered *before* the change takes place. Reducing the TTL on a workstation's address record and changing the workstation's address simultaneously may do you little or no good; the address record may have been cached minutes before you made the change and may linger until the old TTL times out. *And* be sure to factor in the time it'll take your slaves to load from your primary. For example, if your minimum TTL is 12 hours and your refresh interval is three hours, be sure to lower the TTLs at least 15 hours ahead of time, so that by the time you move the host, all the long TTL records will have timed out. Of course, if all of your slaves are using NOTIFY, the slaves shouldn't take the full refresh interval to synchronize.

## *Changing Other SOA Values*

We briefly mentioned increasing the refresh interval as a way of offloading your primary name server. Let's discuss refresh in a little more detail and go over the remaining SOA values, too.

The *refresh* value, you'll remember, controls how often a slave checks whether its data is up to date. The *retry* value then becomes the refresh time after the first failure to reach a master name server. The *expire* value determines how long data can be held before it's discarded, when a master is unreachable. Finally, the *minimum TTL* sets how long zone information may be cached.

Suppose we've decided we want the slaves to pick up new information every hour instead of every three hours. We change the refresh value to an hour in each of the zones. Since the retry is related to refresh, we should probably reduce retry, too—to every 15 minutes or so. Typically, the retry is less than the refresh, but that's not required. Although lowering the refresh value will speed the distribution of data, it will also increase the load on the server being loaded from since the slaves will check more often. The added load isn't much, though; each slave makes a single SOA query during each zone's refresh interval to check its master's copy of the zone. So with two slave name servers, changing the refresh time from three hours to one hour will generate only four more queries (per zone) to the primary in any three-hour span.

If all of your slaves use NOTIFY, of course, refresh doesn't mean as much. But if you have even one BIND 4 slave, your zone data will take up to the refresh interval to reach it.

Some older versions of BIND slaves stopped answering queries during a zone load. As a result, BIND was modified to spread out the zone loads, reducing the periods of unavailability. So, even if you set a low refresh interval, your slaves may not check exactly as often as you request. BIND name servers attempt a certain number of zone loads and then wait 15 minutes before trying another batch. On the other hand, BIND 4.9.3 and later may also refresh *more often* than the refresh interval. These newer BINDs will wait a random number of seconds between one-half the refresh interval and the full refresh interval to check serial numbers.

Expiration times on the order of a week are common—longer if you frequently have problems reaching your updating source. The expiration time should always be much larger than the retry and refresh interval; if the expire time is smaller than the refresh interval, your slaves will expire their data before trying to load new data. If your data don't change much, you might consider raising the minimum TTL. The SOA's minimum TTL value is typically one day (86400 seconds), but you can make it longer. One week is about the longest value that makes sense for a TTL. Longer than that and you may find yourself unable to change bad, cached data in a reasonable amount of time.

# Planning for Disasters

It's a fact of life on a network that things go wrong. Hardware fails, software has bugs, and people very occasionally make mistakes. Sometimes this results in minor inconvenience, like having a few users lose connections. Sometimes the results are catastrophic and involve the loss of important data and valuable jobs.

Because the Domain Name System relies so heavily on the network, it is vulnerable to network outages. Thankfully, the design of DNS takes into account the imperfection of networks: it allows for multiple, redundant name servers, retransmission of queries, retrying zone transfers, and so on.

The Domain Name System doesn't protect itself from every conceivable calamity, though. There are types of network failure—some of them quite common—that DNS doesn't or can't protect against. But with a small investment of time and money, you can minimize the threat of these failures.

## Outages

Power outages, for example, are relatively common in many parts of the world. In some parts of the U.S., thunderstorms or tornadoes may cause a site to lose power, or to have only intermittent power, for an extended period. Elsewhere, typhoons, volcanoes, or construction work may interrupt electrical service.

If all your hosts are down, of course, you don't need name service. Quite often, however, sites have problems when power is *restored*. Following our recommendations, they run their name servers on file servers and big multiuser machines. And when the power comes up, those machines are naturally the last to boot—because all those disks need to be checked and fixed first! Which means that all the hosts onsite that are quick to boot do so without the benefit of name service.

This can cause all sorts of wonderful problems, depending on what services your hosts access when they boot. For example, your PCs may mount (via *net use*) your servers' drives when they boot. If they do, they almost certainly specify the servers' domain names or NetBIOS names.

Using host names in commands is admirable because it allows administrators to change the servers' IP addresses without changing all the startup files on site. However, if name service isn't available when your PCs boot, the *net use* command will fail, which may cause successive commands to fail, too. This will certainly not help your users' productivity.

## Recommendations

Our recommendation is to add the names and IP addresses of critical hosts to your PCs' *HOSTS* files. Any host whose name is referenced during the boot process should appear in the file. You can synchronize the file by copying it from share to share.

On Windows NT, the default location for the file is *%ServerRoot%\System32\Drivers\Etc,* often *C:\WinNT\System32\Drivers\Etc.* On Windows 95, the default location for the file is *%ServerRoot%,* usually *C:\Windows.* The format of the file is just like the format of the UNIX */etc/hosts* file: each line consists of an IP address, in dotted-octet notation, which starts in the first column, followed by whitespace and the canonical name of the host. Optionally, one or more aliases may follow the canonical name, for example:

```
192.249.249.1 wormhole.movie.edu wormhole
192.249.249.3 terminator.movie.edu terminator
```

Now, if your PC needs to look up *wormhole* or *wormhole.movie.edu* when it boots, it will be able to resolve the name.

However, there's some danger in using *HOSTS* files: unless you take care to keep the files up to date, the information in them may become stale. And since both Windows 95's and Windows NT's resolvers use *HOSTS* before querying a name server, a stale entry can cause resolution failures that are hard to diagnose.

We certainly recommend that you keep your *HOSTS* files current since they contain information about critical hosts. But there's something else you can do: you can reconfigure the Windows 95 resolver to use the *HOSTS* file only *after* querying a name server. We described how to do that in Chapter 6, *Configuring Hosts*. With this configuration, a stale *HOSTS* entry won't affect normal operation, since the resolver will use DNS for name resolution. Unfortunately, there's no way to configure this on NT—yet.

Even if you do set up *HOSTS* files on your PCs, it's always a good idea to run a name server on a host with uninterruptible power, if you can afford it. If you rarely experience extended power loss, battery backup might be enough. If your outages are longer and name service is critical, you should consider an uninterruptible power system (UPS) with a generator of some kind.

If you can't afford luxuries like these, you might just try to track down the fastest booting host around and run a name server on it. Hosts with small filesystems should boot quickly, since they don't have many disks to check.

Once you've located the right host, you'll need to make sure the host's IP address appears in the resolver configurations of all your hosts that need full-time name service. You'll probably want to list the backed-up name server last, since during normal operation, hosts should use the name server closest to them. Then, after a power failure, your critical applications will still have name service, albeit at a small sacrifice in performance.

## Coping with Disaster

When disaster strikes, it really helps to know what to do. Knowing to duck under a sturdy table or desk during an earthquake can save you from being pinned under a toppling monitor. Knowing how to turn off your gas can save your house from conflagration.

Likewise, knowing what to do in a network disaster (or even just a minor mishap) can help you keep your network running. Living out in California, as we do, we have some experience and some suggestions.

## Short Outages (Hours)

If your network is cut off from the outside world (whether "the outside world" is the rest of the Internet or the rest of your company), your name servers may start to have trouble resolving names. For example, if your domain, *corp.acme.com*, is cut off from the rest of the Acme Internet, you may not have access to your parent (*acme.com*) name servers or to the root name servers.

You'd think this wouldn't impact communication between hosts in your local domain, but it can. For example, if you type:

```
C:\>telnet selma.corp.acme.com
```

on a host running a resolver configured with *corp.acme.com* as its local domain, the first domain name the resolver looks up will be *selma.corp.acme.com.corp.acme.com* (assuming your host is using the default search list—remember this from Chapter 6?). The local domain name server, if it's authoritative for *corp.acme.com*, can tell that's not a kosher domain name. The following lookup, however, is for *selma.corp.acme.com.acme.com*. This prospective domain name is no longer in the *corp.acme.com* domain, so the query is sent to the *acme.com* name servers. Or rather your local name server *tries* to send the query there and keeps retransmitting until it times out.

You can avoid this problem by making sure the first domain name the resolver looks up is the right one. Don't type:

```
C:\>telnet selma.corp.acme.com
```

Instead, type:

```
C:\>telnet selma
```

or:

```
C:\>telnet selma.corp.acme.com.
```

(Note the trailing dot.) Either of these commands will result in a lookup of *selma.corp.acme.com* first.

You can also avoid querying offsite name servers by taking advantage of the definable search list. You can use the Windows resolvers' Domain Suffix Search Order to define a search list that doesn't include your parent zone's domain name. For example, to work around the problem *corp.acme.com* is having, you could temporarily set your hosts' search lists to just *corp.acme.com*.

Now, when a user types:

```
C:\>telnet selma.corp.acme.com
```

the resolver looks up *selma.corp.acme.com.corp.acme.com* first (which the local name server can answer) and then *selma.corp.acme.com*, the correct domain name. And:

```
C:\>telnet selma
```

works fine, too.

## Longer Outages (Days)

If you lose network connectivity for a long time, your name servers may have other problems. If they lose connectivity to the root name servers for an extended period, they'll stop resolving queries outside their authoritative data. If the slaves can't reach their master, sooner or later they'll expire the zone.

In case your name service really goes haywire because of the connectivity loss, it's a good idea to keep a sitewide or workgroup *HOSTS* file around, as we recommended earlier in this chapter. If your name servers all go down, your hosts will still be able to resolve the names of hosts in the *HOSTS* file.

As for slaves, you can reconfigure a slave that can't reach its master to run as a primary master. Just right-click on the zone's domain name in DNS Manager, select **Properties**, and change the **Zone Type** from **Secondary** to **Primary**. If more than one slave for the same zone are cut off, you can configure one of them as a primary master temporarily and reconfigure the other to load from the temporary primary.

## Really Long Outages (Weeks)

If an extended outage cuts you off from the Internet—say for a week or more— you may need to restore connectivity to root name servers artificially to get things working again. Every name server needs to talk to a root name server occasionally. It's a bit like therapy: the name server needs to contact the root to regain its perspective on the world.

To provide root name service during a long outage, you can set up your own root name servers, *but only temporarily*. Once you're reconnected to the Internet, you *must* shut off your temporary root servers. The most obnoxious vermin on the Internet are name servers that believe they're root name servers but don't know anything about most top-level domains. A close second is the Internet name server configured to query—and report—a false set of root name servers.

That said, and our alibis in place, here's what you have to do to configure your own root name server. First, you need to create the root zone. The root zone will delegate to the highest-level zones in your isolated network. For example, if *movie.edu* were to be isolated from the Internet, we might create a root zone data file, *root.dns*, for *terminator*:

```
. IN SOA terminator.movie.edu. al.robocop.movie.edu. (
                    1        ; Serial
                    10800    ; Refresh after 3 hours
                    3600     ; Retry after 1 hour
                    604800   ; Expire after 1 week
                    86400 )  ; Minimum TTL of 1 day

; Refresh, retry and expire really don't matter, since all
; roots are primaries.  Minimum TTL could be longer, since
; the data are likely to be stable.

  IN NS terminator.movie.edu. ; terminator is the temp. root

; Our root only knows about movie.edu and our two
; in-addr.arpa domains

movie.edu. 86400 IN NS terminator.movie.edu.
           86400 IN NS wormhole.movie.edu.

249.249.192.in-addr.arpa. 86400 IN NS terminator.movie.edu.
                          86400 IN NS wormhole.movie.edu.

253.253.192.in-addr.arpa. 86400 IN NS terminator.movie.edu.
                          86400 IN NS wormhole.movie.edu.

terminator.movie.edu. 86400 IN A 192.249.249.3
wormhole.movie.edu.   86400 IN A 192.249.249.1
                      86400 IN A 192.253.253.1
```

Then we need to add the zone with DNS Manager and update all of our name servers (except the new, temporary root) with a *cache.dns* file that includes just the temporary root (best to move the old cache file aside—we'll need it later, once connectivity is restored):

```
. 99999999 IN NS terminator.movie.edu.

terminator.movie.edu. IN A 192.249.249.3
```

That will keep *movie.edu* name resolution going during the outage. Once Internet connectivity is restored, we can then delete the root zone on *terminator* and restore the original cache files on all our other name servers.

# 9

# Parenting

*The way Dinah washed her children's faces was this: first she held the poor thing down by its ear with one paw, and then with the other paw she rubbed its face all over, the wrong way, beginning at the nose: and just now, as I said, she was hard at work on the white kitten, which was lying quite still and trying to purr—no doubt feeling that it was all meant for its good.*

Once your domain reaches a certain size, or you decide you need to distribute the management of parts of your domain to various entities within your organization, you'll want to divide the domain into subdomains. These subdomains will be the children of your current domain on the domain tree; your domain will be the parent. If you delegate responsibility for your subdomains to another organization, each becomes its own zone, separate from its parent zone. We like to call the management of your subdomains—your children—*parenting*.

Good parenting starts with carving up your domain sensibly, choosing appropriate names for your child domains, and then delegating the subdomains to create new zones. Responsible parents also work hard at maintaining the relationship between the name servers authoritative for their zone and its children; they ensure that delegation from parent to child is current and correct.

Good parenting is vital to the success of your network, especially as name service becomes critical to navigating between sites. Incorrect delegation to a child zone's name servers can render a site effectively unreachable, while the loss of connectivity to the parent zone's name servers can leave a site unable to reach any hosts outside the local zone.

In this chapter we present our views on when to create subdomains, and we go over how to create and delegate them in some detail. We also discuss management of the parent-child relationship and, finally, how to manage the process of carving up a large domain into smaller subdomains with a minimum of disruption and inconvenience.

# When to Become a Parent

Far be it from us to *tell* you when you should become a parent, but we will be so bold as to offer you some guidelines. You may find some compelling reason to implement subdomains that isn't on our list, but some of the most common reasons are:

- A need to delegate or distribute management of the domain to a number of organizations

- The large size of your domain—dividing it would make it easier to manage and offload the name servers for the domain

- A need to distinguish hosts' organizational affiliation by including them in particular subdomains

Once you've decided to have children, the next question to ask yourself is, naturally, how many children to have.

# How Many Children?

Of course, you won't simply say, "I want to create four subdomains." Deciding how many child domains to implement is really choosing the organizational affiliation of your subdomains. For example, if your company has four branch offices, you might decide to create four subdomains, each of which corresponds to a branch office.

Should you create subdomains for each site, for each division, or even for each department? You have a lot of latitude in your choice because of DNS's scalability. You can create a few large subdomains or many small subdomains. There are trade-offs whichever you choose, though.

Delegating to a few large subdomains isn't much work for the parent zone, because there's not much delegation to keep track of. However, you wind up with larger subdomains, which require more memory and faster name servers, and administration isn't as distributed. If you implement site-level subdomains, for example, you may force autonomous or unrelated groups at a site to share a single name space and a single point of administration.

Delegating to many smaller subdomains can be a headache for the administrator of the parent. Keeping delegation data current involves keeping track of which hosts run name servers and which zones they're authoritative for. The data change each time a subdomain adds a new name server, or when the address of a name server for the subdomain changes. If the subdomains are all administered by different people, that means more administrators to train, more relationships for the parent administrator to maintain, and more overhead for the organization overall.

On the other hand, the subdomains are smaller and easier to manage, and the administration is more widely distributed, allowing closer management of subdomain data.

Given the advantages and disadvantages of either alternative, it may seem difficult to make a choice. Actually, there's probably a natural division in your organization. Some companies manage computers and networks at the site level; others have decentralized, relatively autonomous workgroups that manage everything themselves. Here are a few basic rules to help you find the right way to carve up your name space:

- Don't shoehorn your organization into a weird or uncomfortable domain structure. Trying to fit 50 independent, unrelated U.S. divisions into four regional subdomains may save you work (as the administrator of the parent zone), but it won't help your reputation. Decentralized, autonomous operations demand different zones—that's the *raison d'être* of the Domain Name System.

- The structure of your domain should mirror the structure of your organization, especially your organization's *support* structure. If departments run networks, assign IP addresses, and manage hosts, then departments should manage the subdomains.

- If you're not sure or can't agree about how the namespace should be organized, try to come up with guidelines for when a group within your organization can carve off their own subdomain (for example, how many hosts do you need to create a new subdomain, what level of support must the group provide) and grow the namespace organically, only as needed.

## What to Name Your Children

Once you've decided how many subdomains you'd like to create and what they correspond to, you should choose good names for them. Rather than unilaterally deciding on your subdomains' names, it's considered polite to involve your future subdomain administrators and their constituencies in the decision. In fact, you can leave the decision entirely to them if you like.

This can lead to problems, though. It's nice to use a relatively consistent naming scheme across your subdomains. It makes it easier for users in one subdomain, or outside your domain entirely, to guess or remember your subdomain names and to figure out in which domain a particular host or user lives.

Leaving the decision to the locals can result in naming chaos. Some will want to use geographical names, and others will insist on organizational names. Some will want to abbreviate; others will want to use full names.

Therefore, it's often best to establish a naming convention before choosing subdomain names. Here are some suggestions from our experience:

- In a dynamic company, the names of organizations can change frequently. Naming subdomains organizationally in a climate like this can be disastrous. One month the Relatively Advanced Technology (RAT) group seems stable enough, the next month they've been merged into the Questionable Computer Systems organization, and the following quarter they're all sold to a German conglomerate. Meanwhile, you're stuck with well-known hosts in a subdomain whose name no longer has any meaning.

- Geographical names are more stable than organizational names but sometimes not as well known. You may know that your famous Software Evangelism Business Unit is in Poughkeepsie or Waukegan, but people outside your company may have no idea where it is (and might have trouble spelling either name).

- Don't sacrifice readability for convenience. Two-letter subdomain names may be easy to type, but impossible to recognize. Why abbreviate "Italy" to "it" and have it confused with your Information Technology organization, when for a paltry three more letters you can use the full name and eliminate ambiguity?

- Too many companies use cryptic, inconvenient domain names. The general rule seems to be: the larger the company, the more indecipherable the domain names. Buck the trend: make the names of your subdomains obvious!

- Don't use existing or reserved top-level domain names as subdomain names. It might seem sensible to use two-letter country abbreviations for your international subdomains, or to use organizational top-level domain names like *net* for your networking organization, but it can cause nasty problems. For example, naming your Communications department's subdomain *com* might impede your ability to communicate with hosts under the top-level *com* domain. Imagine the administrators of your *com* subdomain naming their new Sun workstation *sun* and their new HP 9000 *hp* (they aren't the most imaginative folks): users anywhere within your domain sending mail to friends at *sun.com* or *hp.com* could have their letters end up in your *com* subdomain, since the name of your parent zone may be in some of your hosts' search lists.

# How to Become a Parent: Creating Subdomains

Once you've decided on names, creating child domains is easy. But first, you've got to decide how much autonomy you're going to give your subdomains. It's odd that you have to decide that before you actually create them.

Thus far, we've assumed that if you create a subdomain, you'll want to delegate it to another organization, thereby making it a separate zone from the parent. Is this always true, though? Not necessarily.

Think carefully about how the computers and networks within a subdomain are managed when choosing whether or not to delegate it. It doesn't make sense to delegate a subdomain to an entity that doesn't manage its own hosts or nets. For example, in a large corporation, the Personnel department probably doesn't run its own computers: the MIS (Management Information Systems) or IT (Information Technology—same animal as MIS) department manages them. So while you may want to create a subdomain for Personnel, delegating management for that subdomain to them is probably wasted effort.

## Creating a Subdomain in the Parent's Zone

You can create a subdomain without delegating it, however. How? By creating resource records that refer to the subdomain within the parent's zone.

Say one day a group of students approaches us, asking for a DNS entry for a web server for student home pages. The name they'd like is *www.students.movie.edu.* You might think that we'd need to create a new zone, *students.movie.edu*, and delegate to it from the *movie.edu* zone. Well, that's one way to do it, but there's an easier way: just create an A record for *www.students.movie.edu* in the *movie.edu* zone. We find that few people realize this is perfectly legal. You don't need a new zone for each new level in the name space. A new zone would make sense if the students were going to run *students.movie.edu* by themselves and wanted to administer their own name servers. But they just want one A record, so creating a whole new zone is more work than necessary.

How do you add this record with DNS Manager? It's easy. First create a *students.movie.edu* subdomain in the *movie.edu* zone, and then add the *www.students.movie.edu* A record. To create the subdomain, first select the zone in the left pane. Then select **DNS** → **New Domain**, and you'll see the window shown in Figure 9-1.

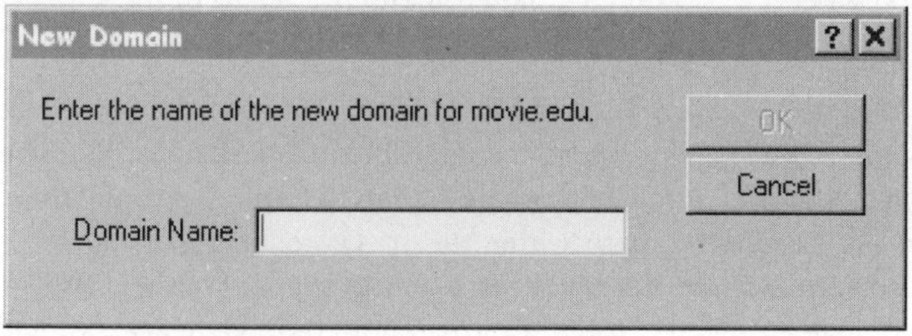

*Figure 9-1. Creating a subdomain in a zone*

Enter the name of the new subdomain. You don't need to append *movie.edu*—
DNS Manager knows what you mean. You'll then see a folder icon for the new
domain in DNS Manager, as shown in Figure 9-2.

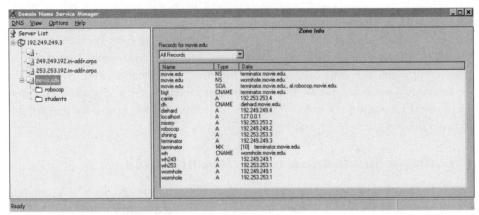

*Figure 9-2. The students.movie.edu subdomain in the movie.edu zone*

To enter the *www.students.movie.edu* A record, just select the *students* folder, and
follow the procedures described previously to add a new host.

Now users can access *www.students.movie.edu* to get to the students' home pages.
We could make this setup especially convenient for students by adding *stu-
dents.movie.edu* to their PCs' or workstations' search lists; they'd need to type only
*www* as the URL to get to the right host.

Did you notice there's no SOA record for *students.movie.edu?* There's no need for
one, since the *movie.edu* SOA record indicates the start of authority for the entire
*movie.edu* zone. Since there's no delegation to *students.movie.edu*, it's part of the
*movie.edu* zone.

## Creating and Delegating a Subdomain

If you decide to delegate your subdomains, to send your children out into the
world, as it were, you'll need to do things a little differently. We're in the process
of doing it now, so you can follow along with us.

We need to create a new subdomain of *movie.edu* for our special effects lab.
We've chosen the name *fx.movie.edu*—short, recognizable, unambiguous. Because
we're delegating *fx.movie.edu* to administrators in the lab, it'll be a separate zone.
The hosts *bladerunner* and *outland*, both within the special effects lab, will serve
as the zone's name servers (*bladerunner* will serve as the primary master). We've
chosen to run two name servers for the zone for redundancy—a single

*fx.movie.edu* name server would be a single point of failure that could effectively isolate the entire special effects lab. Since not many hosts are in the lab, though, we feel two name servers should be enough.

The special effects lab is on *movie.edu*'s new 192.253.254 subnet. Here's the partial contents of *HOSTS*:

```
192.253.254.1 movie-gw.movie.edu movie-gw
# fx primary
192.253.254.2 bladerunner.fx.movie.edu bladerunner br
# fx secondary
192.253.254.3 outland.fx.movie.edu outland
192.253.254.4 starwars.fx.movie.edu starwars
192.253.254.5 empire.fx.movie.edu empire
192.253.254.6 jedi.fx.movie.edu jedi
```

First, we create a new server on *bladerunner*. Then we create the new zone *fx.movie.edu* on *bladerunner* using the process described in Chapter 4, *Setting Up the Microsoft DNS Server*, in the section "Creating a New Zone." We also create the corresponding *in-addr.arpa* zone, *254.253.192.in-addr.arpa*. Then we populate the zone with all of the hosts from our snippet of *HOSTS*, making sure DNS Manager automatically adds the PTR records that correspond to our A records. We add MX records for all of our hosts, pointing to *starwars.fx.movie.edu* and *wormhole.movie.edu*, at preferences 10 and 100, respectively.

The zone data file we end up with, called *fx.movie.edu.dns*, looks like this:

```
;
;   Database file fx.movie.edu.dns for fx.movie.edu zone.
;       Zone version:  41
;
@                       IN      SOA bladerunner.fx.movie.edu.
hostmaster.fx.movie.edu.(                   3           ; serial number
                        3600          ; refresh
                        600           ; retry
                        86400         ; expire
                        3600       ) ; minimum TTL


;
;  Zone NS records
;


@                       IN      NS  bladerunner
@                       IN      NS  outland


;
;  Zone records
;


@                       IN      MX  10    starwars
@                       IN      MX  100   wormhole.movie.edu.
```

```
bladerunner             IN      A    192.253.254.2
                        IN      MX   10    starwars
                        IN      MX   100   wormhole.movie.edu.
br                      IN      CNAME     bladerunner
empire                  IN      A    192.253.254.5
                        IN      MX   10    starwars
                        IN      MX   100   wormhole.movie.edu.
jedi                    IN      A    192.253.254.6
                        IN      MX   10    starwars
                        IN      MX   100   wormhole.movie.edu.
outland                 IN      A    192.253.254.3
                        IN      MX   10    starwars
                        IN      MX   100   wormhole.movie.edu.
starwars                IN      A    192.253.254.4
                        IN      MX   10    starwars
                        IN      MX   100   wormhole.movie.edu.
```

The *254.253.192.in-addr.arpa.dns* file ends up looking like this:

```
;
;   Database file 254.253.192.in-addr.arpa.dns for 254.253.192.in-addr.arpa
;   zone.
;       Zone version:  31
;
@                   IN      SOA bladerunner.fx.movie.edu.hostmaster.fx.movie.edu.
(
                        3           ; serial number
                        3600        ; refresh
                        600         ; retry
                        86400       ; expire
                        3600     )  ; minimum TTL


;
;   Zone NS records
;

@  IN  NS   outland.fx.movie.edu.
@  IN  NS   bladerunner.fx.movie.edu.


;
;   Zone records
;

1  IN  PTR  movie-gw.movie.edu.
2  IN  PTR  bladerunner.fx.movie.edu.
3  IN  PTR  outland.fx.movie.edu.
4  IN  PTR  starwars.fx.movie.edu.
5  IN  PTR  empire.fx.movie.edu.
6  IN  PTR  jedi.fx.movie.edu.
```

Notice that the PTR record for *1.254.253.192.in-addr.arpa* points to *movie-gw.movie.edu*. That's intentional. The router connects to the other *movie.edu* networks, so it really doesn't belong in the *fx.movie.edu* domain, and there's no requirement that all the PTR records in *254.253.192.in-addr.arpa* map into a single zone—though they should correspond to the canonical names for those hosts. Although DNS Manager added PTR records for all of the *fx.movie.edu* hosts automatically when we added their A records, we had to add the PTR record for *movie-gw.movie.edu* explicitly with DNS Manager.

Now we need to configure *bladerunner*'s resolver. Following the directions in Chapter 6, *Configuring Hosts,* we add *bladerunner*'s IP address to the DNS Service Search Order. Then we set *bladerunner*'s domain to *fx.movie.edu*.

Next we'll use *nslookup* to look up a few hosts in *fx.movie.edu* and in *254.253.192.in-addr.arpa*:

```
Default Server:  bladerunner.fx.movie.edu
Address:  192.253.254.2


> jedi
Server:  bladerunner.fx.movie.edu
Address:  192.253.254.2
Name:    jedi.fx.movie.edu
Address:  192.253.253.6


> set type=mx
> empire
Server:  bladerunner.fx.movie.edu
Address:  192.253.254.2

empire.fx.movie.edu       preference = 10,
                          mail exchanger = starwars.fx.movie.edu
empire.fx.movie.edu       preference = 100,
                          mail exchanger = wormhole.movie.edu
starwars.fx.movie.edu     internet address = 192.253.254.4
 > ls fx.movie.edu
[bladerunner.fx.movie.edu]
 fx.movie.edu.                    server = bladerunner.fx.movie.edu
 bladerunner                      192.253.254.2
 fx.movie.edu.                    server = outland.fx.movie.edu
 outland                          192.253.254.3
 jedi                             192.253.254.6
 starwars                         192.253.254.4
 bladerunner                      192.253.254.2
 empire                           192.253.254.5
 > set type=ptr
 > 192.253.254.3
Server:  bladerunner.fx.movie.edu
Address:  192.253.254.2

3.254.253.192.in-addr.arpa       name = outland.fx.movie.edu

> ls 254.253.192.in-addr.arpa.
[bladerunner.fx.movie.edu]
 254.253.192.IN-ADDR.ARPA.        server = bladerunner.fx.movie.edu
```

```
bladerunner.fx.movie.edu.        192.253.254.2
254.253.192.IN-ADDR.ARPA.        server = outland.fx.movie.edu
outland.fx.movie.edu.            192.253.254.3
6                                host = jedi.fx.movie.edu
1                                host = movie-gw.movie.edu
2                                host = bladerunner.fx.movie.edu
3                                host = outland.fx.movie.edu
4                                host = starwars.fx.movie.edu
5                                host = empire.fx.movie.edu
> ^D
```

The output looks reasonable, so it's safe to set up a slave name server for *fx.movie.edu* and to delegate *fx.movie.edu* from *movie.edu*.

## An fx.movie.edu Slave

Setting up the slave name server for *fx.movie.edu* is simple: use DNS Manager to add *outland* as a new server, and then add two slave (secondary) zones, according to the instructions in Chapter 4.

Like *bladerunner*, *outland's* resolver will point to the local name server in the **DNS Server Search Order**, and we'll configure the **Domain** to *fx.movie.edu*.

## On the movie.edu Primary Master

All that's left now is to delegate the *fx.movie.edu* subdomain to the new *fx.movie.edu* name servers on *bladerunner* and *outland*. We need to add the delegation information manually by adding the appropriate NS records to *movie.edu*. If the *movie.edu* primary master name server, *terminator*, had been configured as authoritative for *fx.movie.edu* (as a slave, for example), the delegation information for *fx.movie.edu* would have been added automatically to *movie.edu*. This would save us the step of manually adding the delegation information.

To add the delegation manually, we first create a new *fx.movie.edu* domain under *movie.edu*, as in the *students.movie.edu* example. Then we add two NS records to the *fx.movie.edu* subdomain, one pointing to *bladerunner.fx.movie.edu* and one pointing to *outland.fx.movie.edu*.

According to RFC 1034, the domain names in the resource record–specific portion of these two records (*bladerunner.fx.movie.edu* and *outland.fx.movie.edu*) must be the canonical domain names for the name servers. A remote name server following delegation expects to find one or more address records attached to that domain name, not an alias (CNAME) record. Actually, the RFC extends this restriction to any type of resource record that includes a domain name as its value—all must specify the canonical domain name.

These two records alone aren't enough, though. Do you see the problem? How can a name server outside of *fx.movie.edu* look up information within *fx.movie.edu*? Well, a *movie.edu* name server would refer it to the name servers authoritative for *fx.movie.edu*, right? That's true, but the NS records in *movie.edu* give only the *names* of the *fx.movie.edu* name servers. The foreign name server needs the IP addresses of the *fx.movie.edu* name servers in order to send queries to them. Who can give it those addresses? Only the *fx.movie.edu* name servers. A real chicken-and-egg problem!

The solution is to include the addresses of the *fx.movie.edu* name servers in *movie.edu*. While these aren't strictly part of the *movie.edu* zone, they're necessary for delegation to *fx.movie.edu* to work. Of course, if the name servers for *fx.movie.edu* weren't within *fx.movie.edu*, these addresses—called *glue records*—wouldn't be necessary. A foreign name server would be able to find the address it needed by querying other name servers.

As with the NS records, if the primary master name server for *movie.edu* had been authoritative for *fx.movie.edu,* too, the glue records would have automatically been added to *movie.edu*. If you've added the NS records delegating the subdomain manually, however, you'll have to add any necessary glue by hand, too.

To add the glue records manually, just right-click the subdomain's name in the left pane, and use **Add Host** to add an address to the name server's domain name.

Note that DNS Manager won't let you include unnecessary glue records in the zone. If you try to add a record other than an NS record or a necessary glue record to the subdomain in the parent's zone, you'll get an "Unable to register record" error.

Remember to keep the glue up to date, too. If *bladerunner* gets a new network interface, and hence another IP address, then you should add another A record to the glue data.

We might also want to include aliases for any hosts moving into *fx.movie.edu* from *movie.edu*. For example, if we were to move *plan9.movie.edu*, a server with an important library of public domain special effects algorithms, into *fx.movie.edu*, we should create an alias under *movie.edu* pointing the old name to the new one. In the zone data file, the record would look like this:

```
plan9          IN     CNAME   plan9.fx.movie.edu.
```

This will allow people outside of *movie.edu* to reach *plan9* even though they're using its old domain name, *plan9.movie.edu.*

Don't get confused about which zone this alias belongs in. The *plan9* alias record is actually in the *movie.edu* zone, so it belongs in *movie.edu.dns*. An alias pointing *p9.fx.movie.edu* to *plan9.fx.movie.edu*, on the other hand, is in the *fx.movie.edu* zone and belongs in *fx.movie.edu.dns*.

## Delegating an in-addr.arpa Zone

We almost forgot to delegate the *254.253.192.in-addr.arpa* zone! This is a little trickier than delegating *fx.movie.edu*, because we don't manage the parent zone.

First, we need to figure out what *254.253.192.in-addr.arpa*'s parent zone is and who runs it. Figuring this out may take some sleuthing; we covered how to do this in Chapter 3, *Where Do I Start?*

As it turns out, the *in-addr.arpa* zone is *254.253.192.in-addr.arpa*'s parent zone. And, if you think about it, that makes some sense. There's no reason for the administrators of *in-addr.arpa* to delegate *253.192.in-addr.arpa* or *192.in-addr.arpa* to a separate authority, because unless 192.0.0.0 or 192.253.0.0 is all one big CIDR block, networks like 192.253.253 and 192.253.254 don't have anything in common with each other. They may be managed by totally unrelated organizations.

You might have remembered (from Chapter 3, *Where Do I Start?*) that the *in-addr.arpa* zone is managed by ARIN, the American Registry of Internet Numbers. (Of course, if you didn't remember, you could always use *nslookup* to find the contact address in *in-addr.arpa*'s SOA record, like we showed you in Chapter 3.) All that's left is for us to fill out *inaddrtemplate.txt* (there's a copy in Appendix F, *in-addr.arpa Registration Form,* or you can find it online at *http://www.arin.net/templates/inaddrtemplate.txt*) and send it to the email address *hostmaster@arin.net*.

## Adding a movie.edu Slave

If the special effects lab gets big enough, it may make sense to put a *movie.edu* slave somewhere on the 192.253.254 network. That way, a larger proportion of DNS queries from *fx.movie.edu* hosts can be answered locally. It seems logical to make one of the existing *fx.movie.edu* name servers into a *movie.edu* slave, too—that way, we can make better use of an existing name server, instead of setting up a brand new name server.

We've decided to make *bladerunner* a slave for *movie.edu*. This won't interfere with *bladerunner*'s primary mission: the primary master for *fx.movie.edu*, that is. A single name server, given enough memory, can be authoritative for literally thousands of zones. One name server can load some zones as a primary master and others as a slave.*

The configuration change is simple: we use DNS Manager to add a slave (secondary) zone to *bladerunner,* and tell *bladerunner* to get the *movie.edu* zone data from *terminator*'s IP address, per the instructions in Chapter 4.

# Subdomains of in-addr.arpa Domains

Forward mapping domains aren't the only domains you can divide into subdomains and delegate. If your *in-addr.arpa* name space is large enough, you may need to divide it, too. Typically, you divide the domain that corresponds to your network number into subdomains to correspond to your subnets. How that works depends on the type of network you have and on your network's subnet mask.

## Subnetting on an Octet Boundary

Since Movie U. just has three /24 (class C–sized) networks, one per segment, there's no particular need to subnet those networks. However, our sister university, Altered State, has a class B–sized network, 172.20/16. Their network is subnetted between the third and fourth octet of the IP address; that is, their subnet mask is 255.255.255.0. They've already created a number of subdomains of their domain, *altered.edu,* including *fx.altered.edu* (okay, we copied them), *makeup.altered.edu,* and *foley.altered.edu.* Since each of these departments also runs its own subnet (their Special Effects department runs subnet 172.20.2.0, Makeup runs 172.20.15.0, and Foley runs 172.20.25.0), they'd like to divvy up their *in-addr.arpa* namespace appropriately, too.

Delegating *in-addr.arpa* subdomains is no different from delegating subdomains of forward-mapping domains. First, they or their departments create three new zones, *2.20.172.in-addr.arpa, 15.20.172.in-addr.arpa,* and *25.20.172.in-addr.arpa.* If the primary master name server for *20.172.in-addr.arpa* is also authoritative for these subdomains, the NS records delegating the subdomains to the right server will be added automatically. Otherwise, the *20.172.in-addr.arpa* administrators will need to add the NS records manually, just as we described in the *fx.movie.edu* example earlier in this chapter.

---

* Clearly, though, a name server can't be both the primary master and a slave for a single zone. Either the name server gets the data for a given zone from a local file (and is a primary master for the zone) or from another name server (and is a slave for the zone).

After adding the delegation—either manually or by DNS Manager—the NS records in *20.172.in-addr.arpa.dns* would look something like the following, which lists the partial contents of file *20.172.in-addr.arpa.dns*:

```
;
; Delegated sub-zone:  15.20.172.in-addr.arpa.
;
15                      IN      NS   prettywoman.makeup.altered.edu.
15                      IN      NS   priscilla.makeup.altered.edu.
; End delegation


;
; Delegated sub-zone:  2.20.172.in-addr.arpa.
;
2                       IN      NS   gump.fx.altered.edu.
2                       IN      NS   toystory.fx.altered.edu.
; End delegation


;
; Delegated sub-zone:  25.20.172.in-addr.arpa.
;
25                      IN      NS   blowup.foley.altered.edu.
25                      IN      NS   muppetshow.foley.altered.edu.
; End delegation
```

Two important reminders: the Altered State admins needed to use the fully quali-fied domain names of the name servers in the NS records. That's because the default origin in this file is *20.172.in-addr.arpa*, and they *didn't* need glue address records since the names of the name servers they delegated the zone to weren't in the delegated zones.

## Subnetting on a Non-Octet Boundary

What do you do about networks that aren't subnetted neatly on octet boundaries, like subnetted /24 (class C–sized) networks? In these cases, you can't delegate along lines that match the subnets. This forces you into one of two situations: you have multiple subnets per *in-addr.arpa* subdomain, or you have multiple *in-addr.arpa* subdomains per subnet. Neither is particularly pleasing.

### Class A and B networks

Let's take the case of the /8 (class A–sized) network 15.0.0.0, subnetted with the subnet mask 255.255.248.0 (a 13-bit subnet field and an 11-bit host field, or 8192 subnets of 2048 hosts). In this case, the subnet 15.1.200.0, for example, extends from 15.1.200.0 to 15.1.207.255, which corresponds to eight different *in-addr.arpa* subdomains. Therefore, the delegation for that single subdomain in *15.in-*

*addr.arpa.dns*, the zone database file for *15.in-addr.arpa*, looks like the following, which lists the partial contents of file *15.in-addr.arpa.dns*:

```
200.1.15.in-addr.arpa.     86400     IN     NS     ns-1.cns.hp.com.
200.1.15.in-addr.arpa.     86400     IN     NS     ns-2.cns.hp.com.
201.1.15.in-addr.arpa.     86400     IN     NS     ns-1.cns.hp.com.
201.1.15.in-addr.arpa.     86400     IN     NS     ns-2.cns.hp.com.
202.1.15.in-addr.arpa.     86400     IN     NS     ns-1.cns.hp.com.
202.1.15.in-addr.arpa.     86400     IN     NS     ns-2.cns.hp.com.
203.1.15.in-addr.arpa.     86400     IN     NS     ns-1.cns.hp.com.
203.1.15.in-addr.arpa.     86400     IN     NS     ns-2.cns.hp.com.
204.1.15.in-addr.arpa.     86400     IN     NS     ns-1.cns.hp.com.
204.1.15.in-addr.arpa.     86400     IN     NS     ns-2.cns.hp.com.
205.1.15.in-addr.arpa.     86400     IN     NS     ns-1.cns.hp.com.
205.1.15.in-addr.arpa.     86400     IN     NS     ns-2.cns.hp.com.
206.1.15.in-addr.arpa.     86400     IN     NS     ns-1.cns.hp.com.
206.1.15.in-addr.arpa.     86400     IN     NS     ns-2.cns.hp.com.
207.1.15.in-addr.arpa.     86400     IN     NS     ns-1.cns.hp.com.
207.1.15.in-addr.arpa.     86400     IN     NS     ns-2.cns.hp.com.
```

That's a lot of delegation for one subnet!

You'd set this up with DNS Manager by adding two levels of subdomains under *15.in-addr.arpa* and then adding two NS records at the second level.

### /24 (class C-sized) networks

In the case of a subnetted /24 (class C–sized) network, say 192.253.254.0, subnetted with the mask 255.255.255.192, you have a single *in-addr.arpa* zone, *254.253.192.in-addr.arpa*, that corresponds to subnets 192.253.254.0/26, 192.253.254.64/26, 192.253.254.128/26, and 192.253.254.192/26. You can solve this one of three ways, none of which is pretty.

**Solution 1.** The first solution is to administer the *254.253.192.in-addr.arpa* zone as a single entity and not even try to delegate. This requires either cooperation between the administrators of the four subnets involved or the use of a tool like DNS Manager to allow each of the four admins to take care of their own data.

**Solution 2.** The second solution is to delegate at the *fourth* octet. That's even nastier than the /8 delegation we just showed. You'll need at least a couple of NS records per IP address. To set this up with DNS Manager, you'd need to create the *254.253.192.in-addr.arpa* zone, create new subdomains under the zone for all values of the fourth octet, and then manually add NS records for each subdomain pointing to the correct servers. Here's how the *254.253.192.in-addr.arpa.dns* file might end up looking:

```
;
;   Delegated sub-zone:   1.254.253.192.in-addr.arpa.
;
1        IN       NS      ns1.foo.com.
1        IN       NS      ns2.foo.com.
```

```
;   End delegation


;
;  Delegated sub-zone:  2.254.253.192.in-addr.arpa.
;
2        IN      NS       ns1.foo.com.
2        IN      NS       ns2.foo.com.
;   End delegation


...


;  Delegated sub-zone:  65.254.253.192.in-addr.arpa.
;
65       IN     ·NS       gw.bar.com.
65       IN      NS       relay.bar.com.
;   End delegation


;  Delegated sub-zone:  66.254.253.192.in-addr.arpa.
;
66       IN      NS       gw.bar.com.
66       IN      NS       relay.bar.com.
;   End delegation


...


;
;  Delegated sub-zone:  129.254.253.192.in-addr.arpa.
;
129      IN      NS       mail.baz.com.
129      IN      NS       www.baz.com
;   End delegation


;.
;  Delegated sub-zone:  193.254.253.192.in-addr.arpa.
;
193      IN      NS       mail.baz.com.
192      IN      NS       www.baz.com
;   End delegation
```

and so on, all the way down to *254.254.253.192.in-addr.arpa*. Of course, on *ns1.foo.com*, you'd also expect the name server to be authoritative for *1.254.253.192.in-addr.arpa*, and in the zone data file for *1.254.253.192.in-addr.arpa*, you'd find just the one PTR record (plus an SOA and two NS records):

```
@    IN    SOA    ns1.foo.com.    root.ns1.foo.com.    (
                          1          ; Serial
                          10800      ; Refresh
                          3600       ; Retry
                          608400     ; Expire
                          86400      ; Default TTL
```

```
          IN    NS    ns1.foo.com.
          IN    NS    ns2.foo.com.

          IN    PTR   thereitis.foo.com.
```

Note that the PTR record is attached to the zone's domain name, since the zone's domain name corresponds to just one IP address. Now, when a *254.253.192.in-addr.arpa* name server receives a query for the PTR record for *1.254.253.192.in-addr.arpa,* it will refer the querier to *ns1.foo.com* and *ns2.foo.com,* which will respond with the one PTR record in the zone.

*Solution 3.* Finally, there's a clever technique that obviates the need to maintain a separate zone data file for each IP address.* The organization responsible for the overall /24 network creates CNAME records for each of the domain names in the zone, pointing to domain names in new subdomains, called *0-63, 64-127, 128-191* and *192-255,* which are then delegated to the proper servers. Each subdomain will contain only the PTR records in the range the subdomain is named for.

Here's the partial contents of file *254.253.192.in-addr.arpa.dns:*

```
1.254.253.192.in-addr.arpa.    IN   CNAME   1.0-63.254.253.192.in-addr.arpa.
2.254.253.192.in-addr.arpa.    IN   CNAME   2.0-63.254.253.192.in-addr.arpa.

...

0-63.254.253.192.in-addr.arpa.    86400   IN   NS   ns1.foo.com.
0-63.254.253.192.in-addr.arpa.    86400   IN   NS   ns2.foo.com.

65.254.253.192.in-addr.arpa.  IN   CNAME 65.64-127.254.253.192.in-addr.arpa.
66.254.253.192.in-addr.arpa.  IN   CNAME 66.64-127.254.253.192.in-addr.arpa.

...

64-127.254.253.192.in-addr.arpa.    86400   IN   NS   relay.bar.com.
64-127.254.253.192.in-addr.arpa.    86400   IN   NS   gw.bar.com.

129.254.253.192.in-addr.arpa. IN CNAME  129.128-191.254.253.192.in-addr.arpa.
130.254.253.192.in-addr.arpa. IN CNAME  130.128-191.254.253.192.in-addr.arpa.

...

128-191.254.253.192.in-addr.arpa.    86400   IN   NS   mail.baz.com.
128-191.254.253.192.in-addr.arpa.    86400   IN   NS   www.baz.com.
```

The zone data file for *0-63.254.253.192.in-addr.arpa, 0-63.254.253.192.in-addr.arpa.dns,* can contain just PTR records for IP addresses 192.253.254.1 through 192.253.254.63.

---

* We first saw this explained by Glen Herrmansfeldt at Cal Tech in the newsgroup *comp.protocols.tcp-ip.domains.* It's now codified as RFC 2317.

Here's the partial contents of file *0-63.254.253.192.in-addr.arpa:*

```
@    IN    soa    ns1.foo.com.     root.ns1.foo.com.    (
                              1        ; Serial
                              10800    ; Refresh
                              3600     ; Retry
                              608400   ; Expire
                              86400 )  ; Default TTL

          in    NS     ns1.foo.com.
          in    NS     ns2.foo.com.

     1    IN    PTR    thereitis.foo.com.
     2    IN    PTR    setter.foo.com.
     3    IN    PTR    mouse.foo.com.
     ...
```

When a resolver requests the PTR record for *1.254.253.192.in-addr.arpa*, a *254.253.192.in-addr.arpa* name server will transparently (to the resolver) map this to a request for the PTR record for *1.0-63.254.253.192.in-addr.arpa*. This request will wind up at one of the *0-63.254.253.192.in-addr.arpa* name servers, run by the organization that runs the low (addresses 0–63) subnet.

The tricky part about the delegation is that you can't use DNS Manager to set it up. The current version of DNS Manager won't let you add CNAME records to an *in-addr.arpa* zone. However, it will *accept* CNAMEs in an *in-addr.arpa* zone data file that you write yourself. So, if you're the delegator (the administrator of *254.253.192.in-addr.arpa*, in this case), you can either create the zone data file by hand or you can use a tool like *gencidrzone\** to generate the CNAMEs, and then use **New Zone** to create the new zone, giving DNS Manager the filename of the file you created for the zone file.

## Good Parenting

Now that the delegation to the *fx.movie.edu* name servers is in place, we—responsible parents that we are—should check that delegation using *host*. What? We haven't given you *host* yet? A version of *host* for Windows NT is available via anonymous *ftp* from *ftp://ftp.nikhef.nl/pub/network/host_970908.exe.Z*. To uncompress *host,* you'll need WinZip or a similar Windows utility. WinZip is available from *http://www.winzip.com/*.

Once you have *host_970908.exe* uncompressed, install it as *host* somewhere on your computer. (We install it in the same directory as *nslookup.exe.*) Next, you'll have to set up a *resolv.conf* file in your *%windir%* directory. (If you're not sure

---

\* A Perl script that automates the process of creating the CNAME and NS records in a CIDR delegation, available from *ftp://ftp.is.co.za/networking/ip/dns/gencidrzone/gencidrzone.*

where *%windir%* is, right-click **My Computer** → **Properties**, and select the **Environment** tab. Scroll the **System Variables** window down to *windir*.)

*host* makes it easy to check delegation. With *host*, you can look up the NS records for your zone on your parent name servers. If those look good, you can use *host* to query each name server listed for the zone's SOA record. The query is nonrecursive, so the name server queried doesn't query other name servers to find the SOA record. If the name server replies, *host* checks the reply to see whether the *aa*—authoritative answer—bit in the reply packet is set. If it is, the name server checks to make sure that the packet contains an answer. If both these criteria are met, the name server is flagged as authoritative for the zone. Otherwise, the name server is not authoritative, and *host* reports an error.

Why all the fuss over bad delegation? Incorrect delegation can cause the propagation of old and erroneous root name server information. When a name server is queried for data in a zone it isn't authoritative for, it does its best to provide useful information to the querier. This "useful information" comes in the form of NS records for the closest ancestor domain the name server knows. (We mentioned this briefly in Chapter 8, *Growing Your Domain*, when we discussed why you shouldn't register a caching-only name server.)

For example, say one of the *fx.movie.edu* name servers mistakenly receives an iterative query for the address of *carrie.horror.movie.edu*. It knows nothing about the *horror.movie.edu* zone (except for what it might have cached), but it likely has NS records for *movie.edu* cached, since those are its parent name servers. So it would return those records to the querier.

In that scenario, the NS records may help the querying name server get an answer. However, it's a fact of life on the Internet that not all administrators keep their cache files up to date. If one of your name servers follows a bad delegation and queries a remote name server for records it doesn't have, look what can happen:

```
% nslookup
Default Server:  terminator.movie.edu
Address:  192.249.249.3
> set type=ns
> .
Server:  terminator.movie.edu
Address:  192.249.249.3

Non-authoritative answer:
(root)    nameserver = D.ROOT-SERVERS.NET
(root)    nameserver = E.ROOT-SERVERS.NET
(root)    nameserver = I.ROOT-SERVERS.NET
(root)    nameserver = F.ROOT-SERVERS.NET
(root)    nameserver = G.ROOT-SERVERS.NET
(root)    nameserver = A.ROOT-SERVERS.NET
(root)    nameserver = H.ROOT-SERVERS.NETNIC.NORDU.NET
```

```
(root)   nameserver = B.ROOT-SERVERS.NET
(root)   nameserver = C.ROOT-SERVERS.NET
(root)   nameserver = A.ISI.EDU          --These three name
(root)   nameserver = SRI-NIC.ARPA       --servers are no longer
(root)   nameserver = GUNTER-ADAM.ARPA   --roots
```

A remote name server tried to "help out" our local name server by sending it the current list of roots. Unfortunately, the remote name server was corrupt and returned NS records that were incorrect. And our local name server, not knowing any better, cached that data.

Queries to misconfigured *in-addr.arpa* name servers often result in bad root NS records, because the *in-addr.arpa* and *arpa* domains are the closest ancestors of most *in-addr.arpa* subdomains, and name servers very seldom cache either *in-addr.arpa* or *arpa*'s NS records. (The roots seldom give them out, since they delegate directly to lower-level subdomains.) Once your name server has cached bad root NS records, your name resolution may suffer.

Those root NS records may have your name server querying a root name server that is no longer at that IP address, or a root name server that no longer exists at all. If you're having an especially bad day, the bad root NS records may point to a real, nonroot name server that is close to your network. Even though it won't return authoritative root data, your name server will favor it because it will have a low RTT (Round Trip Time) due to its proximity to your network.

## *Using host*

If our little lecture has convinced you of the importance of maintaining correct delegation, you'll be eager to learn how to use *host* to ensure that you don't join the ranks of the miscreants.

The first step is to use *host* to look up your zone's NS records on a name server for your parent zone and make sure they're correct. Here's how we'd check the *fx.movie.edu* NS records on one of the *movie.edu* name servers:

```
% host -Ct ns movie.edu. terminator.movie.edu.
```

If everything's okay with the NS records, we'll simply see the NS records in the output:

```
fx.movie.edu   NS   bladerunner.fx.movie.edu
fx.movie.edu   NS   outland.fx.movie.edu
```

This tells us that all the NS records delegating *fx.movie.edu* from *terminator.movie.edu* are correct.

If one of the *fx.movie.edu* name servers—say *outland*—were misconfigured, we might see this:

```
fx.movie.edu    NS    bladerunner.fx.movie.edu
fx.movie.edu    NS    outland.fx.movie.edu
fx.movie.edu SOA record currently not present at outland.fx.movie.edu
fx.movie.edu has lame delegation to outland.fx.movie.edu
```

This indicates that the name server on *outland* is running, but it's authoritative for *fx.movie.edu*.

If one of the *fx.movie.edu* name servers weren't running at all, we'd see:

```
fx.movie.edu    NS    bladerunner.fx.movie.edu
fx.movie.edu    NS    outland.fx.movie.edu
fx.movie.edu SOA record not found at outland.fx.movie.edu, try again
```

In this case, the "try again" message indicates that *host* sent *outland* a query and didn't get a response back in an acceptable amount of time.

While we could have checked the *fx.movie.edu* delegation using *nslookup*, *host*'s powerful command-line options make the task especially easy.

## Managing Delegation

If the special effects lab gets bigger, we may find that we need additional name servers. We dealt with setting up new name servers in Chapter 8 and even went over what information to send to the parent zone's administrator. But we never explained what the parent needed to do.

It turns out that the parent's job is relatively easy, especially if the administrators of the subdomain send complete information. Imagine that the special effects lab expands to a new network, 192.254.20. They have a passel of new, high-powered graphics workstations. One of them, *alien.fx.movie.edu*, will act as the network's name server.

The administrators of *fx.movie.edu* (we delegated it to the folks in the lab) send their parent zones' administrators (that's us) a short note:

```
Hi!

We've just set up alien.fx.movie.edu (192.254.20.3) as a name
server for fx.movie.edu.  Would you please update your
delegation information?  I've attached the NS records you'll
need to add.

Thanks,

Arty Segue
ajs@fx.movie.edu
```

```
----- cut here -----

fx.movie.edu.   86400   IN   NS   bladerunner.fx.movie.edu.
fx.movie.edu.   86400   IN   NS   outland.fx.movie.edu.
fx.movie.edu.   86400   IN   NS   alien.fx.movie.edu.

bladerunner.fx.movie.edu.   86400   IN   A   192.253.254.2
outland.fx.movie.edu.       86400   IN   A   192.253.254.3
alien.fx.movie.edu.         86400   IN   A   192.254.20.3
```

Our job as the *movie.edu* administrator is straightforward: add the NS and A records to *movie.edu*. This is as simple as adding an NS record and the corresponding glue address record to the *fx.movie.edu* subdomain using DNS Manager.

The final step for the *fx.movie.edu* administrator is to send a similar message to *hostmaster@arin.net* (administrator for *in-addr.arpa*), requesting that the *20.254.192.in-addr.arpa* subdomain be delegated to *alien.fx.movie.edu*, *bladerunner.fx.movie.edu*, and *outland.fx.movie.edu*.

# Managing the Transition to Subdomains

We won't lie to you—the *fx.movie.edu* example we showed you was unrealistic for several reasons. The main one is the magical appearance of the special effects lab's hosts. In the real world, the lab would have started out with a few hosts, probably in the *movie.edu* zone. After a generous endowment, an NSF grant, or a corporate gift, they might expand the lab a little and buy a few more computers. Sooner or later, the lab would have enough hosts to warrant the creation of a new subdomain. By that point, however, many of the original hosts would be well known by their names under *movie.edu*.

We briefly touched on using CNAME records under the parent zone (in our *plan9.movie.edu* example) to help people adjust to a host's change of domain. But what happens when you move a whole network or subnet into a new subdomain?

The strategy we recommend uses CNAME records in much the same way but on a larger scale. Using DNS Manager, you can create CNAMEs for hosts. This allows users to continue using the old domain names for any of the hosts that have moved. When they *telnet* or *ftp* (or whatever) to those hosts, however, the command will report that they're connected to a host in *fx.movie.edu*:

```
C:\> ftp plan9
Connected to plan9.fx.movie.edu.
220 plan9.fx.movie.edu FTP server (Version wu-2.4.2-academ[BETA-13](2) Wed
Jul 9 00:0
9:24 EDT 1997) ready.
User (plan9.fx.movie.edu:(none)):
```

Some users, of course, don't notice subtle changes like this, so you should also do some public relations work and notify folks of the change.

How do you create all these aliases? Well, you could do it manually using DNS Manager, CNAME record by CNAME record. Or you could use Perl to create CNAME records for every host it finds in *fx.movie.edu.dns:*

```
#
# Simple Perl script to create aliases
# Run with <script> <domain name of child zone>
#
die "Usage: $0 <child zone>\n" if $#ARGV!=0;

open(ZDF, "$ARGV[0].dns") || die "Couldn't open $ARGV[0]: $!\n";

($label, $parent) = split(/\./, $ARGV[0], 2);
$parent .= ".dns";

open(PZDF, ">>$parent") || die "Couldn't open $parent: $!\n";

while (<ZDF>) {
        if (/\s+IN\s+A\s+/) {
            ($host, $rest) = split(/[\s\.]/, $_, 2);
            printf PZDF "%s IN  CNAME%s.%s.\n", $host, $host, $ARGV[0];
        }
};
```

## Removing Parent Aliases

Although parent-level aliases are useful for minimizing the impact of moving your hosts, they're also a crutch of sorts. Like a crutch, they'll restrict your freedom. They'll clutter your parent name space, when one of your motivations for implementing a subdomain may have been making the parent zone smaller. And they'll prevent you from using the names of hosts in the subdomain as names for hosts in the parent zone.

After a grace period—which should be well advertised to users—you should remove all the aliases, with the possible exception of aliases for extremely well-known Internet hosts. During the grace period, users can adjust to the new domain names and modify scripts, files, and the like. But don't get suckered into leaving all those aliases in the parent zone; they defeat part of the purpose of the DNS, because they prevent you and your subdomain administrator from naming hosts autonomously.

You might want to leave CNAME records for well-known Internet hosts or central network resources intact, because of the potential impact of a loss of connectivity. On the other hand, rather than moving the well-known host or central resource into a subdomain at all, it might be better to leave it at the parent zone level.

# The Life of a Parent

That's a lot of parental advice to digest in one sitting, so let's recap the highlights. The life cycle of a typical parent goes something like this:

1. You have a single zone, with all of your hosts in that zone.

2. You break your zone into a number of subdomains, some of them in the same zone as the parent, if necessary. You provide CNAME records in the parent zone for well-known hosts that have moved into subdomains.

3. After a grace period, you delete any remaining CNAME records.

4. You handle subdomain delegation updates, either manually or by using stubs, and periodically check delegation.

Okay, now that you know all there is to parenting, let's go on to talk about more advanced name server features. You may need some of these tools to keep those kids in line.

# 10

# *Advanced Features and Security*

*"What's the use of their having names," the Gnat said, "if they won't answer to them?"*

In this chapter, we'll cover some of the Microsoft DNS Server's more advanced features and suggest how they might come in handy in your DNS infrastructure. (We do save some of the hard-core firewall material 'till the last chapter, though.)

## *DNS NOTIFY (Zone Change Notification)*

Traditionally, slaves have used a polling scheme to determine when they need a zone transfer. The polling interval is called the *refresh time*. Other parameters in the zone's SOA record govern other aspects of the polling mechanism.

Wouldn't it be nice if the primary master name server could *tell* its slave servers when the information in a zone changed? After all, the primary master name server *knows* the data has changed: every time a zone is changed with DNS Manager, DNS Manager notifies the server, which immediately changes the zone in its memory. The primary's notification could come soon after the actual modification, instead of waiting for the refresh interval to expire.

RFC 1996 proposed a mechanism that would allow primary master servers to notify their slaves of changes to a zone's data. The Microsoft DNS Server implements this scheme, called DNS NOTIFY for short.

DNS NOTIFY works like this: when a primary master name server notices a change to data in a zone, it sends a special notification message to all of the slave servers for that zone. It uses the list of NS records in the zone to build the list of slave servers for the zone. The primary master removes the NS record corresponding to the name server listed in the first field in the zone's SOA record (which by convention lists the name of the primary master name server for the zone), as well as the local host. Removing those name servers prevents the primary master from sending a notification message to itself.

The special NOTIFY request is identified by its opcode in the query header. The opcode for most queries is QUERY. NOTIFY messages have a special opcode, NOTIFY. Other than that, the request looks very much like a query for the SOA record for the zone: it specifies the zone's domain name, class, and a type of SOA.

When a slave receives a NOTIFY request for a zone from one of its configured master name servers, it sends a NOTIFY response. The response tells the master that the slave received the NOTIFY request, so that it can stop sending NOTIFY messages for the zone. Then the slave proceeds just as if the refresh timer had expired: it queries the master server for the SOA record for the zone that the master claimed had changed. If the serial number is higher, the slave transfers the zone.

Why doesn't the slave simply take the master's word that the zone has changed? It's possible that a miscreant could forge NOTIFY requests to our slaves, causing lots of unnecessary zone transfers, amounting to a denial of service attack against our master server.

If the slave actually transfers the zone, RFC 1996 says that it should issue its own NOTIFY requests to the other authoritative name servers for the zone. The idea is that the primary master may not be able to notify all of the slave servers for the zone itself, since it's possible some slaves can't communicate directly with the primary master and so use another slave as their master. However, the Microsoft DNS Server doesn't implement this, and Microsoft DNS Server slaves don't send NOTIFY messages unless explicitly configured to do so.

Here's how that works in practice: on our network, *terminator.movie.edu* is the primary master for *movie.edu*, and *wormhole.movie.edu* and *zardoz.movie.edu* are slaves. See Figure 10-1.

When we update *movie.edu* on *terminator*, *terminator* sends NOTIFY messages to *wormhole* and *zardoz*. Both slaves check to see whether *movie.edu*'s serial number has been incremented and, when they find it has, perform a zone transfer.

Let's also look at a more complicated zone transfer scheme. In Figure 10-2, *a* is the primary master name server for the zone and *b*'s master server, but *b* is *c*'s master server. Moreover, *b* has two network interfaces.

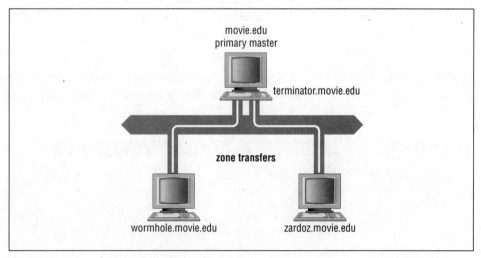

*Figure 10-1. movie.edu zone transfer example*

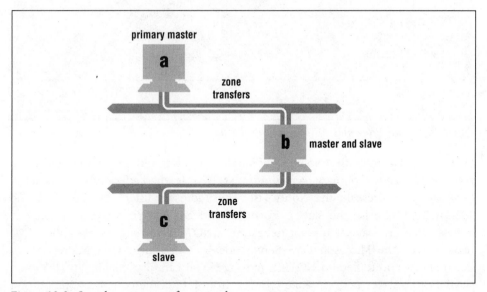

*Figure 10-2. Complex zone transfer example*

In this scenario, *a* notifies both *b* and *c* after the zone is updated. *b* checks to see whether the zone's serial number has been incremented and initiates a zone transfer. However, *c* ignores *a*'s NOTIFY message, because *a* is not *c*'s configured master name server (*b* is). If *b* is explicitly configured to notify *c*, then after *b*'s zone transfer completes, it sends *c* a NOTIFY message, which prompts *c* to check the serial number *b* holds for the zone.

Older BIND slave name servers, and other name servers that don't support NOTIFY, will respond with a "Not Implemented" (NOTIMP) error, wait until their refresh timers expire, and transfer the zone then. The Microsoft DNS Server just ignores the NOTIMP error.

NOTIFY is turned off by default and has to be enabled on a zone-by-zone basis. The controls for NOTIFY are accessed via the **Notify** tab on the **Zone Properties** window.

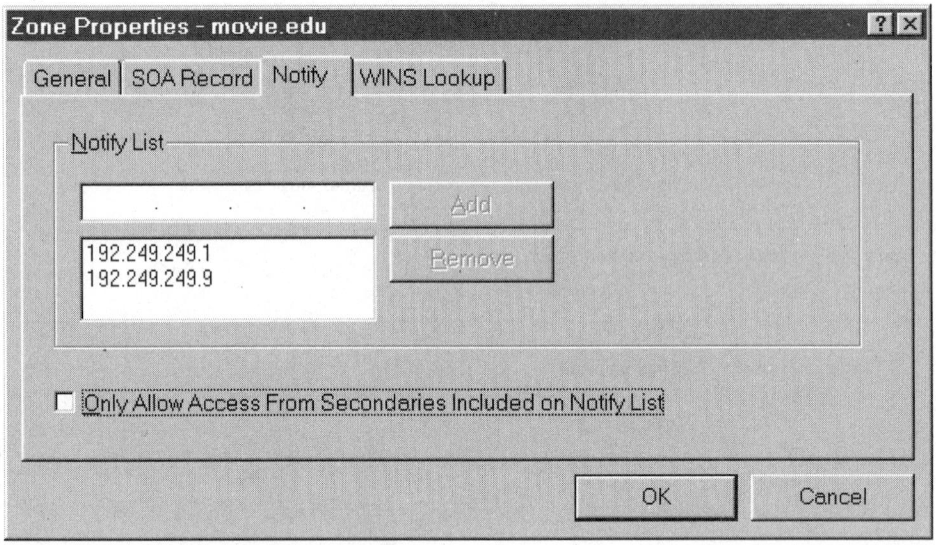

*Figure 10-3. Zone Properties → Notify for movie.edu*

Figure 10-3 illustrates the Notify configuration for our old friend the *movie.edu* zone on the zone's primary, *terminator*. NOTIFY is enabled simply by listing at least one IP address in the **Notify List**. The addresses listed, 192.249.249.1 and 192.249.249.9, are for the slaves, *wormhole* and *zardoz*. You have to list the IP address of every slave you want to receive a NOTIFY message. Unlike the BIND name server, the Microsoft DNS Server does not use the zone's NS records to determine whom to send a NOTIFY message. You can also enable NOTIFY on a slave if other slaves perform zone transfers from it (a la the complex zone transfer scheme described previously).

We'll talk about the **Only Allow Access** checkbox in the "Securing Your Name Server" section, later in this chapter.

# WINS Linkage

Our next topic requires a short detour into the world of Microsoft networking. Networks based on NetBT (NetBIOS over TCP) need to perform name resolution, too: hosts need a way to map NetBIOS names* to IP addresses. The way this name resolution works has evolved over time. In the early days, hosts would broadcast a query on the LAN to resolve a NetBIOS name. This forced all hosts to listen to every broadcast. Since broadcasts don't leave the local LAN, this method didn't allow name resolution beyond the local subnet. The next evolutionary step was the *LMHOSTS* file, which is just a list of NetBIOS names and IP addresses. Every host needed an *LMHOSTS* file to resolve names beyond the local subnet. This model didn't scale very well, either: it was tough to keep the *LMHOSTS* files up to date and distribute them. The introduction of DHCP essentially made basing a network's NetBIOS name resolution on *LMHOSTS* files impossible.

DHCP stands for Dynamic Host Configuration Protocol. A detailed description is beyond the scope of this book,† but suffice it to say that DHCP eliminates the requirement of configuring a static IP address on every one of your hosts. If those hosts support DHCP, they can contact a DHCP server when they boot to obtain an IP address and other configuration parameters, like the IP addresses of the default router, name servers, and WINS servers.

WINS, which stands for Windows Internet Naming Service, is a Microsoft invention introduced in Windows NT 3.5. The server component of WINS is an implementation of a NetBIOS Name Server as described in RFCs 1001 and 1002. The idea is nothing new—the RFCs date from early 1987. The function of a NetBIOS Name Server is simple: it maps NetBIOS names to IP addresses.

The name and IP address information in a WINS server comes from the various hosts on the network. Once a host sets its IP address using the value sent by a DHCP server, the host registers its name with the WINS server the DHCP server told it about. Actually, any modern NetBT host registers its name with a WINS server, regardless of how it obtained its IP address (dynamically from a DHCP server or statically from a user-input configuration). Modern NetBT hosts also know to contact a WINS server for NetBIOS name resolution, rather than relying on broadcasting or an *LMHOSTS* file.

---

* A host's NetBIOS name is simply the name it's known by for NetBT networking purposes. NetBIOS names are limited to one label of up to 15 characters (that is, no multiple label names like DNS domain names). On NT systems the NetBIOS name is set on the **Network Control Panel** window, **Identification** tab. A host's NetBIOS name need not be the same as the host name portion of its fully qualified domain name in DNS.

† But see another book from O'Reilly & Associates, *TCP/IP Network Administration* by Craig Hunt.

So where does DNS fit in to all this? The new name-to-IP address mappings generated when the DHCP server makes IP address assignments aren't visible to DNS. (The traditional DNS update model isn't suited to making incremental changes to zones on the fly, anyway, so it would be difficult to get this information into DNS.) Microsoft realized there would be some value to enabling a DNS Server to query a WINS server, which does know about names for dynamically assigned IP addresses. After all, a NetBIOS name in the WINS server is usually the same as a machine's host name (the first label of its fully qualified domain name in DNS), which is what would be in the DNS Server if there were an easy way to get it there. So a Microsoft DNS Server can be configured to ask a WINS server when it receives a query for a domain name that's not in its zone database.

You may be thinking that a name server contacting a WINS server is kind of silly—isn't there a way for name servers to know what the DHCP servers are doing directly? Yes, and it's coming in NT Version 5. DHCP servers will update name servers after every assignment using the new DNS dynamic update protocol. The importance of WINS in NT 5 is greatly reduced, too. NT 5 hosts will resolve NetBIOS names with DNS rather than WINS. WINS will still be required for a while to support older, legacy clients. But we digress.

## Configuring WINS Lookup

WINS Lookup, as it's called, is enabled on a zone-by-zone basis using the **WINS Lookup** tab of the **Zone Properties** window. The DNS Server will forward queries for names it doesn't know about to a WINS server for those zones with WINS Lookup enabled. The WINS Lookup configuration for the *movie.edu* zone on the zone's primary, *terminator*, is shown in Figure 10-4.

WINS Lookup is enabled by checking the **Use WINS Resolution** box. The IP addresses of up to five WINS servers go in the **WINS Servers** field. The DNS Server will try them in the order listed.

By default, the WINS Lookup configuration you establish on the primary master takes effect on the slaves as well. The primary master inserts a special WINS record that gets transferred with the rest of the zone to the slaves. If the slaves are Microsoft DNS Servers, they understand the WINS record and perform WINS lookups accordingly. If the slaves are BIND name servers, they complain about the unknown WINS record. You can suppress sending this WINS record to the slaves by checking **Settings only affect local server**.

The WINS Lookup window looks slightly different on the slave, as shown in Figure 10-5.

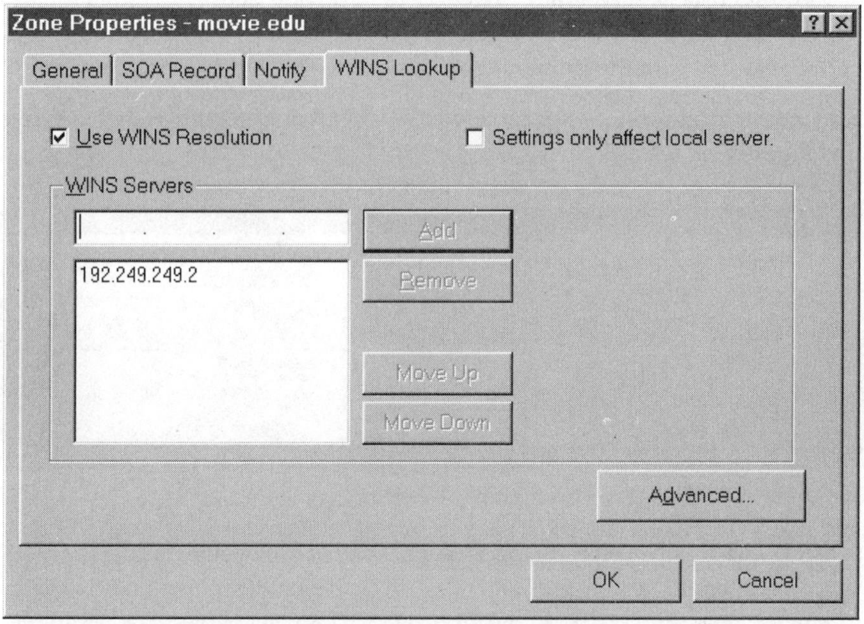

Figure 10-4. Zone Properties → WINS Lookup for movie.edu

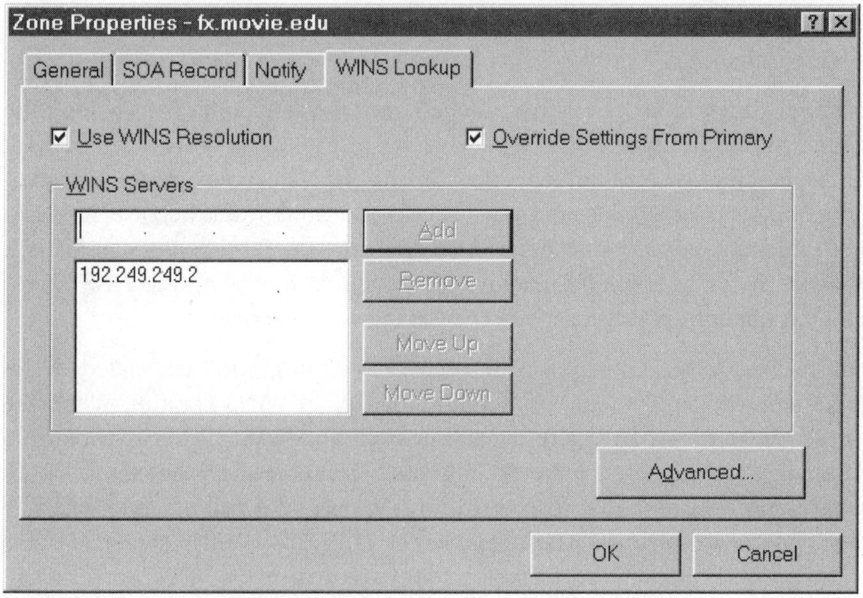

Figure 10-5. Zone Properties → WINS Lookup for movie.edu on a slave

**Settings only affect local server** has changed to **Override Settings From Primary**. Checking this box does just what you'd think: if the slave has received WINS lookup configuration from the primary, you can override it by checking this box.

The **Advanced** button produces the same window, shown in Figure 10-6, for either the primary master or a slave.

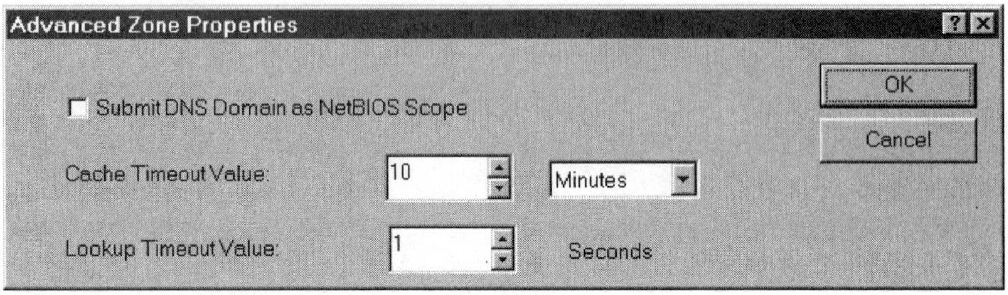

*Figure 10-6. Zone Properties → WINS Lookup → Advanced*

**Submit DNS Domain as NetBIOS Scope** is applicable only if you're using NetBIOS scope in your network. If you are, and if your scope names correspond to DNS domain names, you can pass along the DNS domain name (for example, *movie.edu*) along with the host name to the WINS server. Your NetBIOS scope names have to be consistent across your network for this to work. Another potential pitfall is that NetBIOS scope names are case sensitive, but DNS domain names are case insensitive.

The next two values control timeouts. **Cache Timeout Value** controls how long the DNS Server will cache information it receives from the WINS server. The default value is 10 minutes. That value may seem small, but it's a good choice: information in the WINS server is transient by nature, so you don't want the DNS Server to hold on to it for a long time. If it needs a name again, the DNS Server can just ask the WINS server for it. **Lookup Timeout Value** controls how long the DNS Server will wait after querying a WINS server. The default is one second.

You can enable WINS Lookup on *in-addr.arpa* zones, too. It's called WINS Reverse Lookup. It's implemented differently than plain WINS Lookup. When the name server receives a PTR query it can't answer and WINS Reverse Lookup is enabled for the zone, it sends a NetBIOS Adapter Status request directly to the IP address referenced by the PTR record. In other words, the name server asks the host directly what its name is. The name server can't ask a WINS server because lookups based on IP address aren't supported: you can't give a WINS server an IP address and get the corresponding NetBIOS name back. WINS servers have obviously never heard of *Jeopardy!* ("The host with IP address 192.249.249.3." "What is *terminator?*")

WINS Reverse Lookup is configured similarly to WINS Lookup—select the **WINS Reverse Lookup** tab of the **Zone Properties** window of any *in-addr.arpa* zone. The WINS Reverse Lookup configuration for the *249.249.192.in-addr.arpa* zone on the zone's primary, *terminator,* is shown in Figure 10-7.

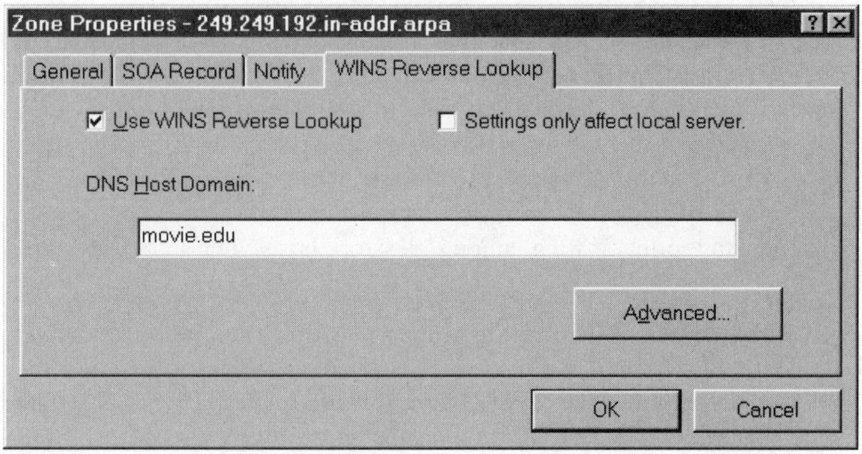

*Figure 10-7. Zone Properties → WINS Reverse Lookup for 249.249.192.in-addr.arpa*

**Use WINS Reverse Lookup** enables the NetBIOS Adapter Status requests for unknown PTR records in this zone. **Settings only affect local server** has the same effect as its WINS Lookup counterpart. If you look in an *in-addr.arpa* zone database file, though, you'll see a WINS-R record instead of a WINS record. The **DNS Host Domain** field takes a DNS domain name that will be appended to the Net-BIOS name returned by the host to form a fully qualified domain name. The **Advanced** button is very similar to the one for WINS Lookup (see Figure 10-8).

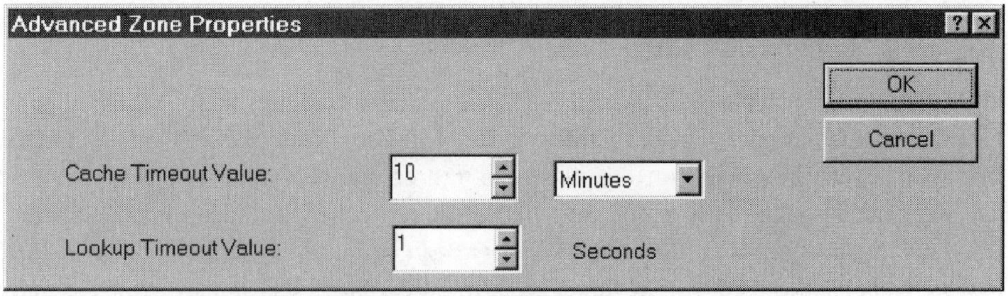

*Figure 10-8. Zone Properties → WINS Reverse Lookup → Advanced*

There's no reference to NetBIOS scope since it's not applicable here. **Cache Timeout Value** controls how long the DNS Server will cache the name received from the host. The default value is 10 minutes, just like WINS Lookup. **Lookup Timeout**

**Value** controls how long the DNS Server will wait on the NetBIOS Adapter Status request. The default is one second.

## Using WINS Lookup and WINS Reverse Lookup

What's WINS Lookup good for? In most networks, not a lot. The names that get resolved the most are the servers, and they usually have fixed IP addresses and thus static DNS entries. They're resolved directly in DNS, not via the WINS Lookup detour. Most networks don't have much peer-to-peer networking—your average desktop host usually doesn't offer network services, like a web server, name server, and so on. It's the need to reach those kind of network services that requires DNS name resolution to work for every host. (Sure, there's a lot of Net-BIOS-based file and print sharing among desktop hosts, but that uses WINS natively.)

If you do need to support WINS Lookup in your network, a big problem with it is that the standard BIND name server doesn't support it.* Many people find they need WINS Lookup after they have a DNS infrastructure in place using BIND name servers. One option is to replace all those name servers with the Microsoft DNS Server and enable WINS Lookup. That's not realistic for most people. A better, but not perfect, option is to create a new subdomain for DHCP clients resolvable via WINS Lookup and delegate the subdomain to a set of Microsoft DNS Servers.

For example, let's say the folks running the domain *acmebw.com* suddenly find themselves with dozens of PCs doing peer-to-peer networking with DHCP-assigned IP addresses. Since they've already got a BIND infrastructure in place, they decide to create the domain *pcs.acmebw.com* for these PCs. (The domain name could be anything: *dhcp.acmebw.com, wins.acmebw.com, projectx.acmebw.com*, whatever.) They configure a couple Microsoft DNS Servers for this zone and enable WINS Lookup. Finally, they delegate to the *pcs.acmebw.com* zone from the *acmebw.com* zone.

In practice, we find WINS Reverse Lookup is much more useful. It's really nice to have complete reverse mapping information for your network in DNS. Network management applications can report names rather than IP addresses. Web servers can log usage statistics by name and make named-based authorization decisions, like only giving access to hosts in the *movie.edu* domain. Troubleshooting is easier, as well. Without WINS Reverse Lookup, the name server can't reverse-map dynamically assigned IP addresses. Of course, to use WINS Reverse Lookup, all the name servers for your *in-addr.arpa* zones need to support WINS Reverse Lookup.

---

* MetaInfo has ported BIND to NT and added WINS Lookup and WINS Reverse Lookup. See *http://www.metainfo.com.*

# System Tuning

While the default configuration values will work fine for most sites, yours may be one of the rare sites that needs some further tuning. The following tuning requires changes to the Registry. All DNS parameters referenced in this section are values of this Registry key:

> *HKEY_LOCAL_MACHINE\SYSTEM\CurrentControlSet\Services\DNS\*
> *Parameters*

A complete listing of Registry settings for the DNS Server can be found in Appendix G, *Microsoft DNS Server Registry Settings.*

## More Efficient Zone Transfers

A zone transfer, we said earlier, comprises many DNS messages sent end to end over a TCP connection. Traditional zone transfers put only a single resource record in each DNS message. That's a waste of space: you need a full header on each DNS message, even though you're only carrying a single record. It's like being the only person in a Chevy Suburban. A DNS message could carry many more records.

The Microsoft DNS Server understands a new zone transfer format that puts as many records as possible into a single DNS message. The resulting "many answers" zone transfer takes less bandwidth, because there's less overhead, and less CPU time, because less time is spent unmarshaling DNS messages.

The DNS Server uses the "many answers" format by default, which is fine if all your slaves can understand it. Older BIND name servers (prior to Version 4.9.4) can't cope with this format and require the traditional one. Fortunately, you can tell the DNS Server to use the traditional method by changing the *BindSecondaries* Registry value. When set to one, the server sends traditional zone transfers to satisfy older BIND servers. The default value is one, but that doesn't affect zone transfers between two Microsoft DNS Servers. They recognize each other, and the master uses the "many answers" format to the slave.

You should change this value only if you have no BIND slaves, or if all your BIND slaves are running Version 4.9.4 or later.

## Cleaning Up the Database

The Registry value *CleanupInterval* controls how often the DNS Server performs housekeeping on its memory database of cached records. The default value is 900 seconds (15 minutes), and valid values range from 600 seconds (10 minutes) to 86,400 seconds (24 hours). At every cleanup interval, the name server examines its cache for expired records and removes them. (Expired records are simply ones that have been kept longer than the time to live value set by the name server they came from.) It also verifies that the root name servers are reachable at this interval. If it can't reach any, it reloads the cache file and follows the usual algorithm to obtain a list of root name servers.

We recommend leaving this value at the default. You might want to increase it, though, if your name server is especially busy and running the cleanup interval too often bogs it down. You might also raise it if you want records to persist in the cache longer than their original TTL. Remember, though, that the DNS administrators set the TTL according to their local circumstances, so there might be a very good reason not to keep data longer than the TTL.

One more note about *CleanupInterval*: if the server receives a response containing an NS record (or its corresponding A record) that's already in the cache, it checks the TTL of the cached record. If the TTL is less than CleanupInterval, the server updates the cached record's TTL with the TTL from the record it just received, essentially refreshing the cached record.

## *Name Server Address Sorting*

When you are contacting a host that has multiple network interfaces, using a particular interface may give you better performance. If the multihomed host is local and shares a network (or subnet) with your host, one of the multihomed host's addresses is "closer."

Suppose you have an FTP server on two networks, cleverly called network A and network B, and hosts on both networks access the server often. Hosts on network A will experience better performance if they use the server host's interface to network A. Likewise, hosts on network B would benefit from using the server host's interface to network B as the address for their FTP client.

In Chapter 4, *Setting Up The Microsoft DNS Server*, we mentioned that the Microsoft DNS Server returns all the addresses for a multihomed host. There was no guarantee of the order in which a DNS server would return the addresses, so we assigned aliases (*wb249* and *wb253* for *wormhole*) to the individual interfaces. If one interface was preferable, you (or more realistically, a DNS client) could use an appropriate alias to get the correct address. You *can* use aliases to choose the "closer" interface, but because of address sorting, they are not always necessary.

The post-Service Pack 3 hotfixed version of the Microsoft DNS Server supports address sorting; earlier versions do not. The server sorts addresses, by default, if one condition holds: if the host that sent the query to the name server *shares* a network with the name server host (for example, both are on network A), then the

DNS Server sorts the addresses in the response. How does the DNS Server know when it shares a network with the querier? When it starts up, it finds all the interface addresses of the host it is running on. The DNS Server extracts the network numbers from these addresses to create the default sort list. When a query is received, the DNS Server checks if the sender's address is on a network in the default sort list. If it is, then the query is local, and it sorts the addresses in the response.

In Figure 10-9, assume that a Microsoft DNS Server is on *notorious*. The name server's default sort list would contain network A and network B. When *spellbound* sends a query to *notorious* looking up the addresses of *notorious*, it will get an answer back with *notorious*'s network A address first. That's because *notorious* and *spellbound* share network A. When *charade* looks up the addresses of *notorious*, it will get an answer back with *notorious*'s network B address first. Both hosts are on network B. In both of these cases, the name server sorts the addresses in the response because the hosts share a network with the name server host. The sorted address list has the "closer" interface first.

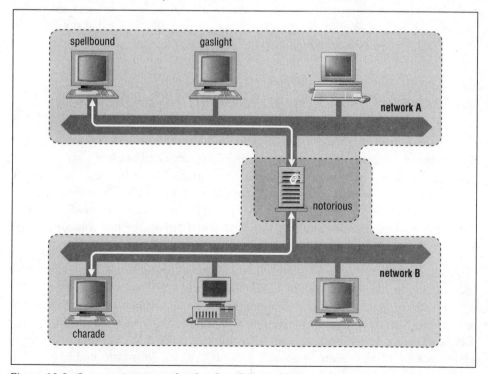

*Figure 10-9. Communicating with a local multihomed host*

Let's change the situation slightly. Suppose the name server is running on *gaslight*. When *spellbound* queries *gaslight* for *notorious*'s address, *spellbound* will see the same response as in the last case because *spellbound* and *gaslight* share network A, which means that the name server will sort the response. However, *charade* may see a differently ordered response, since it does not share a network with *gaslight*. The closer address for *notorious* may still be first in the response to *charade*, but only because of luck, not name server address sorting. In this case, you'd have to run an additional name server on network B for *charade* to benefit from the DNS Server's default address sorting.

As you can see, you benefit by running a name server on each network; not only is your name server available if your router goes down, it also sorts addresses of multihomed hosts. Because the name server sorts addresses, you do not need to specify aliases to get the best response.

There's a small catch with the DNS Server's address sorting: it disables round robin. (Round robin is explained in the section "Load Sharing Between Mirrored Servers," later in this chapter.) In the post-SP3 hotfixed server, address sorting is enabled by default and round robin is disabled. If you want round robin and can live without address sorting (unfortunately they're mutually exclusive), you can disable address sorting with the *LocalNetPriority* value. Set it to zero to disable address sorting and enable round robin. Note, though, that this value doesn't exist in the Registry by default. You'll need to add it before you can change its value to zero.

# Building Up a Large Sitewide Cache with Forwarders

Certain network connections discourage sending large volumes of traffic off site, either because the network connection is pay-per-packet or because the network connection is a slow link with a high delay, like a remote office's satellite connection to the company's network. In these situations, you'll want to limit the offsite DNS traffic to the bare minimum. The Microsoft DNS Server has a feature to do this called *forwarding*.

If you designate one or more servers at your site as forwarders, all the offsite queries are sent to the forwarders first. The idea is that the forwarders handle all the offsite queries generated at the site, building up a rich cache of information. For any given query in a remote domain, there is a high probability that the forwarder can answer the query from its cache, avoiding the need for the other servers to send packets off site. Nothing special is done to these servers to make them forwarders; you modify all the *other servers* at your site to direct their queries through the forwarders.

A primary master or slave name server's mode of operation changes slightly when it is directed to use a forwarder. If the requested information is already in its database of authoritative data and cache data, it answers with this information; this part of the operation hasn't changed. However, if the information is not in its database, the name server will send the query to a forwarder and wait a short period for an answer before resuming normal operation and contacting the remote servers itself. What the name server is doing that's different is sending a *recursive* query to the forwarder, expecting it to find the answer. At all other times, the name server sends out *nonrecursive* queries to other name servers and deals with responses that only refer to other name servers.

Forwarding is serverwide, not zone specific: a server is either forwarding or it isn't. It's configured by selecting the **Forwarders** tab on the **Server Properties** window. Figure 10-10 shows how a *movie.edu* name server would be configured to use forwarders, assuming *wormhole* and *terminator* are the site forwarders. (Remember, forwarding is configured on every name server *except* the forwarders themselves— *wormhole* and *terminator* in this case.)

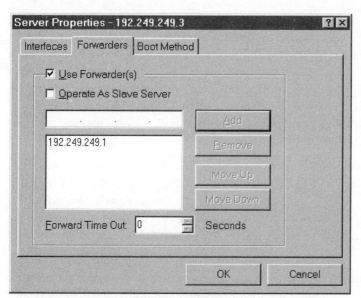

*Figure 10-10. Server Properties → Forwarders*

**Use Forwarder(s)** enables forwarding on this name server. You can specify up to five forwarders. This name server will forward to them in the order they're listed, using a default timeout of five seconds per forwarder—that is, if the first forwarder doesn't respond within five seconds, try the next, wait five more seconds, try the next, and so on. The forwarding timeout can be changed with—surprise!— the **Forward Time Out** field. This value is stored in a Registry value, *Forwarding-*

*Timeout*, which you can also change. (The list of forwarders is stored in the *Forwarders* value.) We'll talk about **Operate As Slave Server** in the next section.

When you use forwarders, try to keep your site configuration simple. You *can* end up with configurations that are really twisted.

- Avoid having "mid-level" servers forward packets (that is, avoid configuring forwarding on your mid-level name servers). Mid-level servers mostly refer name servers to subdomain name servers. If they have been configured to forward packets, do they refer to subdomain name servers, or do they contact the subdomain name server to find out the answer? Whichever way it works, you're probably making your site configuration too hard for mere mortals (and subdomain administrators) to understand.

- Avoid chaining your forwarders. Don't configure server *a* to forward to server *b*, and configure server *b* to forward to server *c* (or worse yet, back to server *a*).

## A More Restricted Name Server

You may want to restrict your name servers even further—stopping them from even *trying* to contact an offsite server if their forwarder is down or doesn't respond. You can do this by making the server a *forwarding server in slave mode* or just *slave server* for short. The terminology gets really confusing, unfortunately: this slave has nothing to do with zone transfers and primary master servers. A name server can be a primary master, slave, or caching-only server and still be forwarding in slave mode. Later versions of the BIND name server eliminate the confusion by calling this a *forward only* server.

A slave server is a variation on a server that forwards. It still answers queries from its authoritative data and cache data. However, it relies *completely* on its forwarders; it *doesn't* try to contact other servers to find out information if the forwarders don't give it an answer. You can turn a forwarding server into a slave server by checking the **Operate As Slave Server** box in the **Forwarders** configuration window (see Figure 10-10).

The slave server contacts each forwarder only once, and it waits a short time for the forwarder to respond. Listing the forwarders multiple times directs the forward-only server to *retransmit* queries to the forwarders, and increases the overall length of time that the forward-only name server will wait for an answer from forwarders. With a slave server, you might want to consider listing the forwarders' IP addresses more than once for redundancy: If the first query to a forwarder is lost, the second might still get through and get answered.

However, you must ask yourself if it *ever* makes sense to use a slave server. A slave server is completely dependent on the forwarders. You can achieve much the same configuration (and dependence) by not running a slave server at all; instead, configure your hosts' resolvers to point to the forwarders you were using. Thus, you are still relying on the forwarders, but now your applications are querying the forwarders directly instead of having a slave name server query them for the applications. You lose the local caching that the forward only server would have done, and the address sorting, but you reduce the overall complexity of your site configuration by running fewer "restricted" name servers.

# A Nonrecursive Name Server

By default, resolvers send recursive queries, and name servers do the work required to answer recursive queries. (If you don't remember how recursion works, refer to Chapter 2, *How Does DNS Work?*) In the process of finding the answer to recursive queries, the name server builds up a cache of nonauthoritative information about other zones.

In some circumstances, it is *undesirable* for name servers to do the extra work required to answer a recursive query or to build up a cache of data. The root name servers are an example of these circumstances. The root name servers are so busy that they should not be spending the extra effort to recursively find the answer to a request. Instead, they send a response based only on the authoritative data they have. The response may contain the answer, but it is more likely that the response contains a referral to other name servers. And since the root servers do not support recursive queries, they do not build up a cache of nonauthoritative data, which is good because their cache would be huge.*

You can induce the Microsoft DNS Server to run as a nonrecursive name server by setting the *RecursionNo* Registry value to true. By default the name server supports recursion, and this value is false.

If you choose to make one of your servers nonrecursive, do not configure any of your hosts' resolvers to use it. While you can make your name server nonrecursive, there is no corresponding option to make your resolver work with a nonrecursive name server.†

You can list a nonrecursive name server as one of the servers authoritative for your zone data (that is, you can tell a parent name server to refer queries about

---

\* Note that a root name server wouldn't normally receive recursive queries, unless a name server's administrator configured it to use a root server as a forwarder, or a host's administrator configured its resolver to use the root server as a name server, or a user pointed *nslookup* at the root server.

† In general. Clearly, programs designed to send nonrecursive queries, or ones that can be configured to send nonrecursive queries, like *nslookup*, would still work.

your zone to this server). This works because name servers send nonrecursive queries between themselves.

Do not list a nonrecursive name server as a forwarder. When a name server is using another server as a forwarder, it sends the query to the forwarder as a recursive query instead of a nonrecursive query.

# Securing Your Name Server

Compared to a modern BIND name server, the Microsoft DNS Server is short on security features, but you do have some options. We'll discuss how to prevent unauthorized zone transfers from your servers and how to "lock down" a name server directly connected to the Internet.

## Preventing Unauthorized Zone Transfers

It's important to ensure that only your real slave name servers can transfer zones from your name server. Users on remote hosts that can query your name server's zone data can only look up data (for example, addresses) for hosts whose domain names they already know, one at a time. Users who can start zone transfers from your server can list all of the hosts in your zones. It's the difference between letting random folks call your company's switchboard and ask for John Q. Cubicle's phone number and sending them a copy of your corporate phone directory.

Remember that list of name servers on the **Notify** window of the **Zone Properties** window (Figure 10-3)? It has two uses. The first tells the name server which slaves to send NOTIFY messages to. The second is security related. If you check the **Only Allow Access From Secondaries Included on Notify List** box, the server limits which servers can perform zone transfers: only authorized slaves on the Notify List can initiate a zone transfer.

For a primary master name server accessible from the Internet, you definitely want to limit zone transfers to just your slave name servers. You probably don't need to restrict zone transfers on name servers inside your firewall, unless you're worried about your own employees listing your zone data.

## Delegated Name Server Configuration

Some of your name servers answer nonrecursive queries from other name servers on the Internet because your name servers appear in NS records delegating your zones to them. We'll call these name servers *delegated* name servers.

You can take special measures to secure your delegated name servers. But first, you should make sure that these servers don't receive any recursive queries (that is, you don't have any resolvers configured to use these servers, and no name servers use them as forwarders). Some of the precautions we'll take—like disabling recursive queries—preclude your resolvers from using these servers.

Once you know your name server only answers queries from other name servers, you can turn off recursion. This eliminates a major vector of attack: the most common spoofing attacks involve inducing the target name server to query name servers under the hacker's control by sending the target a recursive query for a domain name in a zone served by the hacker's servers. Disabling recursion is described in the section "A Nonrecursive Name Server," earlier in this chapter. You should also restrict zone transfers of your zones to known slave servers, as described in the previous section "Preventing Unauthorized Zone Transfers."

## Load Sharing Between Mirrored Servers

The Microsoft DNS Server has a feature called *round robin*, named after the equivalent feature in the BIND name server. The server rotates address records for the same domain name between responses. For example, if the domain name *foo.bar.baz* has three address records for IP addresses 192.1.1.1, 192.1.1.2, and 192.1.1.3, the round robin feature causes the name server to give them out first in the order

```
192.1.1.1 192.1.1.2 192.1.1.3
```

then in the order

```
192.1.1.2 192.1.1.3 192.1.1.1
```

and then in the order

```
192.1.1.3 192.1.1.1 192.1.1.2
```

before starting over again with the first order, and repeating the rotation *ad infinitum.*

The functionality is enormously useful if you have a number of equivalent network resources, like mirrored FTP servers, web servers, or terminal servers, and you'd like to spread the load among them. You establish one domain name that refers to the group of resources, configure clients to access that domain name, and the name server inverse-multiplexes the accesses between the IP addresses you list.

It's a good idea to reduce the records' time to live, too. This ensures that, if the addresses are cached on an intermediate name server that doesn't support round robin, they'll time out of the cache quickly. If the intermediate name server looks up the name again, your authoritative name server can round robin the addresses again.

Note that this is really load sharing, not load balancing, since the name server gives out the addresses in a completely deterministic way, without regard to the actual load or capacity of the servers servicing the requests. In our example, the server at address 192.1.1.3 could be a 486DX33 running Linux, and the other two servers HP9000 K420s, and the Linux box would still get a third of the queries.

# 11

# *nslookup*

*"Don't stand chattering to yourself like that," Humpty Dumpty said, looking at her for the first time, "but tell me your name and your business."*

*"My name is Alice, but—"*

*"It's a stupid name enough!" Humpty Dumpty interrupted impatiently. "What does it mean?"*

*"Must a name mean something?" Alice asked doubtfully.*

*"Of course it must," Humpty Dumpty said with a short laugh....*

To be proficient at troubleshooting name server problems, you'll need a special tool to make DNS queries, one that gives you complete control. We'll cover *nslookup* in this chapter because it's distributed with Windows NT and with many other operating systems. If you're the explorer type, you might also check out *dig*; it provides similar functionality, and some people like its user interface better.

Note that this chapter isn't comprehensive; there are aspects of *nslookup*—mostly obscure and seldom used—that we won't cover. You can always consult the manual pages for information on those aspects.

## *Is nslookup a Good Tool?*

Much of the time you'll use *nslookup* to make queries, in the same way the resolver makes them. Sometimes, though, you'll use *nslookup* to query other name servers as a name server would. Which one you emulate will depend on the problem you're trying to debug. You might wonder, "How accurately does *nslookup* emulate a resolver or a name server? Does *nslookup* actually use the Windows resolver library routines?" No, *nslookup* uses its own routines for querying name servers, but those routines are based on the resolver routines. Consequently, *nslookup*'s behavior is very similar to the resolver's behavior, but it does differ slightly. We'll point out some of those differences. As for emulating name server behavior, *nslookup* allows us to query another server with the same query packet that a name server would use, but the retransmission scheme is quite different. Like a name server, though, *nslookup* can pull a copy of the zone data. So *nslookup* does not exactly emulate either the resolver or the name server, but it does emulate them well enough to make a good troubleshooting tool. Let's delve into those differences we alluded to.

## Multiple Servers

*nslookup* talks to only one name server at a time. This is the major difference between *nslookup*'s behavior and the resolver's behavior. The resolver makes use of all the name servers listed in the Windows resolver configuration window.* If two name servers are listed, the resolver tries the first name server, then the second, then the first, then the second, until it receives a response or it gives up. The resolver does this for every query. On the other hand, *nslookup* tries the first name server listed and keeps retrying until it finally gives up on the first name server and tries the second. Once it gets a response, it locks onto that server and doesn't try the other. But, you *want* your troubleshooting tool to talk with only one name server, so you can reduce the number of variables when analyzing a problem. If *nslookup* used more than one name server, you wouldn't have as much control over your troubleshooting session. So talking to only one server is the right thing for a troubleshooting tool to do.

## Timeouts

The *nslookup* timeouts are similar to the resolver timeouts when the resolver is querying only one name server. A name server's timeouts, however, are based on how quickly the remote server answered the last query, a dynamic measure. *nslookup* will never match name server timeouts, but that's not a problem either. When you're querying remote name servers with *nslookup*, you probably care only *what* the response was, not how long it took.

## Domain Searches

*nslookup* implements the search list just as the resolver code does. Name servers don't implement search lists, so, to act like a name server, the *nslookup* search function must be turned off—more on that later.

---

* In Windows NT, the resolver configuration window is accesseed by choosing **Start** → **Settings** → **Control Panel** → **Network** → **Protocols** → **TCP/IP** → **DNS**.

## Zone Transfers

*nslookup* will do zone transfers just like a name server. Unlike the name server, *nslookup* does not check SOA serial numbers before pulling the zone data; you'll have to do that manually, if you want to.

## Using NetBIOS Names

This last point doesn't compare *nslookup* to the resolver or name server, but to ways of looking up names in general. *nslookup*, as distributed by Microsoft, only uses DNS; you can't use it to look up NetBIOS names via broadcast, *LMHOSTS*, or WINS. Before using *nslookup* to help you find your lookup problem, you need to determine if your problem is really with DNS. For example, if an application is using a different IP address than you expect, perhaps it's treating a value as a Net-BIOS name and not a DNS domain name. To diagnose this kind of problem, you need to understand how the Windows resolver works, which we discussed in Chapter 6, *Configuring Hosts*. Just remember that *nslookup* talks only to name servers.

# Interactive versus Noninteractive

Let's start our tutorial on *nslookup* by looking at how to start it and how to exit from it. *nslookup* can be run either interactively or noninteractively. If you want to look up only one piece of data, use the noninteractive form. If you plan on doing something more extensive, like changing servers or options, then use an interactive session.

To start an interactive session, just type **nslookup**:

```
C:\> nslookup
Default Server:  terminator.movie.edu
Address:  192.249.249.3

> ^Z
```

If you need help, type **?** or **help**. When you want to exit, type **^Z** (CTRL-Z) followed by Enter. You can also exit from *nslookup* with ^C or ^Break (CTRL-Break). This behavior is different than *nslookup*'s operation on a UNIX host, where if you send *nslookup* an interrupt, it catches it, stops whatever it is doing (like a zone transfer), and gives you the > prompt. There's no way to just interrupt the Microsoft *nslookup*: you just have to stop *nslookup* completely and restart it.

For a noninteractive lookup, include the name you are looking up on the command line:

```
C:\> nslookup carrie
Server:  terminator.movie.edu
```

```
Address:  192.249.249.3

Name:    carrie.movie.edu
Address:  192.253.253.4
```

# Option Settings

*nslookup* has its own set of dials and knobs, called *option settings*. All of the option settings can be changed. We'll discuss here what each of the options means. We'll use the rest of the chapter to show you how to use them.

```
C:\> nslookup
Default Server:  terminator.movie.edu
Address:  192.249.249.3

> set all
Default Server:  terminator.movie.edu
Address:  192.249.249.3

Set options:
  nodebug        defname        search        recurse
  nod2          novc           noignoretc      port=53
  querytype=A   class=IN       timeout=2   retry=3
  root=ns.nic.ddn.mil.     domain=movie.edu
  srchlist=movie.edu


> ^Z
```

Before we get into the options, we need to cover the introductory lines. The default name server is *terminator.movie.edu*. This means that every query sent by *nslookup* is going to be sent to *terminator*.

The options come in two flavors: *Boolean* and *value*. The options that do not have an equal sign after them are Boolean options. They have the interesting property of being either "on" or "off." The value options can take on different, well, values. How can we tell which Boolean options are on and which are off? The option is *off* when a "no" precedes the option's name. **nodebug** means that debugging is off. As you might guess, the option **search** is on.

How you change Boolean or value options depends on whether or not you are using *nslookup* interactively. In an interactive session, you change an option with the *set* command, as in **set debug** or **set domain=classics.movie.edu**. From the command line, you omit the word *set* and precede the option with a hyphen, as in **nslookup -debug** or **nslookup -domain=classics.movie.edu**. The options can be abbreviated to their shortest unique string—for example, *nodeb* for *nodebug*. In addition to its abbreviation, the *querytype* option can also be entered simply **type**.

Let's go through each of the options:

*[no]debug*

> Debugging is turned off by default. If it is turned on, *nslookup* displays the complete contents of the response packets from the name server. See *[no]d2* for a discussion of debug level 2.

*[no]defname*

> This option reflects *nslookup's* BIND heritage. By default, *nslookup* adds the default domain name to names without a dot in them. Before search lists existed, the BIND resolver code would only add the default domain to names without *any* dots in them; this option reflects that behavior. *nslookup* can implement the presearch list behavior (with *search* off and *defname* on), or it can implement the search list behavior (with *search* on).

*[no]search*

> The search option "overshadows" the default domain name (*defname*) option. That is, *defname* only applies if *search* is turned off. By default, *nslookup* appends the domains in the search list (*srchlist*) to names that don't end in a dot. *nslookup's* search list is constructed from the **Domain Suffix Search Order** field of the Windows resolver configuration window.

*[no]recurse*

> *nslookup* requests recursive service by default. This turns on the recursion-desired bit in query packets. The Windows resolver sends recursive queries in the same way. Name servers, however, send nonrecursive queries to other name servers.

*[no]d2*

> Debugging at level 2 is turned off by default. If it is turned on, you see the query packets sent to the name server in addition to the regular debugging output. Turning on *d2* also turns on *debug*. Turning off *d2* turns off *d2* only; *debug* is left on. Turning off *debug* turns off both *debug* and *d2*.

*[no]vc*

> By default, *nslookup* makes queries using UDP packets instead of over a TCP connection (*virtual circuit*). Most Windows resolver queries are made with UDP, so the default *nslookup* behavior matches the resolver.

*[no]ignoretc*

> By default, *nslookup doesn't* ignore truncated packets. If a packet is received that has the "truncated" bit set—indicating that the name server couldn't fit all the important information in the UDP response packet—*nslookup* doesn't ignore it; it retries the query using a TCP connection instead of UDP.

*port=53*

The DNS service is on port 53. You can start a name server on another port—for debugging purposes, for example—and *nslookup* can be directed to use that port.

*querytype=A*

By default, *nslookup* looks up A (address) resource record types. In addition, if you type in an IP address (and the *nslookup* query type is address or pointer), then *nslookup* will invert the address, append *in-addr.arpa*, and look up PTR (pointer) data instead.

*class=IN*

The only class that matters is *Internet*. Well, there is the *Hesiod* (HS) class, too, if you are an MITer or run Ultrix.

*timeout=2*

If the name server doesn't respond within two seconds, *nslookup* resends the query and doubles the timeout (to four and then eight seconds). The Windows resolver uses different timeouts when querying a single name server—see Chapter 6.

*retry=3*

Sends the query three times before giving up. After each retry, the timeout value is doubled. Again, the Windows resolver behaves slightly different as discussed in Chapter 6.

*root=ns.nic.ddn.mil.*

A convenience command called *root* switches your default server to the server named here. Executing the *root* command from *nslookup*'s prompt is equivalent to executing *server ns.nic.ddn.mil*. That host actually is a root name server, but Microsoft's *nslookup* is (unfortunately) hardcoded with its old name—you may know it as *g.root-servers.net*. You can change the default "root" server with *set root=server*.

*domain=movie.edu*

This is the default domain appended if the *defname* option is on.

*srchlist=movie.edu*

If *search* is on, these are the domains appended to names that do not end in a dot. The domains are listed in the order that they are tried, separated by a slash.

## Avoiding the Search List

*nslookup* implements the search list, as the resolver does. When you are debugging, the search list can get in your way. You need to either turn the search list off completely (*set nosearch*), or add a trailing dot to the fully qualified domain name you are looking up. We prefer the latter, as you'll see in our examples.

# Common Tasks

You'll come to use *nslookup* for little chores almost every day: finding out the IP address or MX records for a given domain name, or querying a particular name server for data. We'll cover these first, before moving on to the more occasional stuff.

## Looking Up Different Data Types

By default, *nslookup* looks up the address for a name, or the name for an address. You can look up any data type by changing the *querytype*, as we show in this example:

```
C:\> nslookup
Default Server:  terminator.movie.edu
Address:  192.249.249.3

> misery               --Look up address
Server:  terminator.movie.edu
Address:  192.249.249.3

Name:    misery.movie.edu
Address:  192.253.253.2

> 192.253.253.2        --Look up name
Server:  terminator.movie.edu
Address:  192.249.249.3

Name:    misery.movie.edu
Address:  192.253.253.2

> set q=mx             --Look up MX data
> wormhole
Server:  terminator.movie.edu
Address:  192.249.249.3
wormhole.movie.edu     MX preference = 10, mail exchanger = wormhole.movie.edu
wormhole.movie.edu      internet address = 192.249.249.1
wormhole.movie.edu      internet address = 192.253.253.1

> set q=any            --Look up data of any type
> diehard
Server:  terminator.movie.edu
Address:  192.249.249.3

diehard.movie.edu      internet address = 192.249.249.4
diehard.movie.edu      MX preference = 10, mail exchanger = diehard.movie.edu
diehard.movie.edu      internet address = 192.249.249.4
```

These are only a few of the valid DNS data types, of course. For the complete list, see Appendix A, *DNS Message Format and Resource Records.*

## Authoritative versus Nonauthoritative Answers

If you've used *nslookup* before, you might have noticed that it sometimes precedes its answers with the phrase "Non-authoritative answer":

```
C:\> nslookup
Default Server:  relay.hp.com
Address:  15.255.152.2

> slate.mines.colorado.edu.
Server:  relay.hp.com
Address:  15.255.152.2

Non-authoritative answer:
Name:    slate.mines.colorado.edu
Address:  138.67.1.3
```

"Nonauthoritative" is *nslookup*'s way of telling you that the name server is not authoritative for the data in the answer. (Recall that a name server is authoritative for data when it's a primary master or slave for the zone containing the data.) There are two reasons why you'll see a nonauthoritative response. The first is that the name server you queried didn't have the data you were looking for and had to query a remote name server to get it. The remote name server is authoritative for the data (that's the reason it was queried!) and returns it with the "authoritative answer" bit set in the DNS message header. The Microsoft DNS Server you queried puts this data in its cache and returns it to you marked nonauthoritative. If you ask for the same data again, this time the name server can answer from its cache and will mark the data nonauthoritative: that's the second reason you'll see a nonauthoritative answer. Authoritative answers, on the other hand, aren't announced by *nslookup*: the absence of the nonauthoritative message means the answer is authoritative.

This brings up a significant difference between the Microsoft DNS Server and the BIND name server. When you send a query to a BIND name server and it has to contact an authoritative name server to find the answer, the BIND name server returns the answer to you marked authoritative (unlike the Microsoft DNS Server). The BIND name server, in effect, passes the authoritative response directly back to you. Then, like the Microsoft DNS Server, it caches the response, and subsequent queries for the data result in a nonauthoritative answer.

Notice that we ended the domain name with a trailing dot each time we looked it up. The response would have been the same had we left the trailing dot off. Sometimes it is critical that you use the trailing dot while debugging, and at times it is not. Rather than stopping to decide if *this* name needs a trailing dot, we always add one if we know the name is fully qualified, except, of course, for the example where we turn off the search list.

## Switching Servers

Sometimes you want to query another name server directly—you may think it is misbehaving, for example. You can switch servers with *nslookup* by using the *server* or *lserver* commands. The difference between *server* and *lserver* is that *lserver* queries your "local" server—the one you started out with—to get the address of the server you want to switch to; *server* uses the default server instead of the local server. This difference is important to know because the server you just switched to may not be responding, as we'll show in this example:

```
C:\> nslookup
Default Server:  relay.hp.com
Address:  15.255.152.2
```

When we start up, our first server, *relay.hp.com*, becomes our *lserver*. This will matter later on in this session.

```
> server galt.cs.purdue.edu.
Default Server:  galt.cs.purdue.edu
Address:  128.10.2.39

> cs.purdue.edu.
Server:  galt.cs.purdue.edu
Address:  128.10.2.39

DNS request timed out.
    timeout was 2 seconds.
DNS request timed out.
    timeout was 4 seconds.
DNS request timed out.
    timeout was 8 seconds.
*** Request to galt.cs.purdue.edu timed-out
>
```

At this point we try to switch back to our original name server. But there is no name server running on *galt* to look up *relay*'s address.

```
> server relay.hp.com.
DNS request timed out.
    timeout was 2 seconds.
DNS request timed out.
    timeout was 4 seconds.
DNS request timed out.
    timeout was 8 seconds.
*** Can't find address for server relay.hp.com.: Timed out
```

Instead of being stuck, though, we use the *lserver* command to have our local
server look up *relay*'s address.

```
> lserver relay.hp.com.
Default Server:  relay.hp.com
Address:  15.255.152.2

>
```

Since the server on *galt* did not respond—it's not even running a name server—it
wasn't possible to look up the address of *relay* to switch back to using *relay*'s
name server. Here's where *lserver* comes to the rescue: the local name server,
*relay*, was still responding, so we used it. Instead of using *lserver*, we could have
recovered by using *relay*'s IP address directly—server 15.255.152.2.

You can even change servers on a per-query basis. To specify that you'd like
*nslookup* to query a particular server for information about a given domain name,
you can specify the server as the second argument on the line, after the domain
name to look up—like so:

```
C:\> nslookup
Default Server:  relay.hp.com
Address:  15.255.152.2

> saturn.sun.com. ns.sun.com.
Server:  ns.sun.com
Address:  192.9.9.3

Name:     saturn.sun.com
Address:  192.9.25.2

> ^Z
```

And, of course, you can change servers from the command line. You can specify
the server to query as the argument after the domain name to look up, like this:

```
C:\> nslookup -type=mx fisherking.movie.edu. terminator.movie.edu.
```

This instructs *nslookup* to query *terminator.movie.edu* for MX records for *fisher-
king.movie.edu*.

To specify an alternate default server and enter interactive mode, you can use a
hyphen in place of the domain name to look up:

```
C:\> nslookup - terminator.movie.edu.
```

One final note about switching servers: those of you who are familiar with using
*nslookup* to talk to BIND name servers have probably entered an address of
0.0.0.0 or 127.0.0.1 to mean "this host." The Microsoft DNS Server never responds
to queries sent to the loopback address—you need to use the IP address of one of
the host's network interfaces.

# *Less Common Tasks*

These are tricks you'll probably have to use less often but are very handy to have in your repertoire. Most of these will be helpful when you're trying to trouble-shoot a DNS problem; they'll enable you to grub around in the packets the resolver sees, and mimic a name server querying another name server or transfer-ring zone data.

## *Seeing the Query and Response Packets*

If you need to, you can direct *nslookup* to show you the queries it sends out and the responses it receives. Turning on *debug* shows you the responses. Turning on *d2* shows you the queries as well. When you want to turn off debugging com-pletely, you have to use *set nodebug*, since *set nod2* only turns off level 2 debug-ging. After the following trace, we'll explain some parts of the packet output. If you want, you can pull out your copy of RFC 1035, turn to page 25, and read along with our explanation.

```
C:\> nslookup
Default Server:  terminator.movie.edu
Address:  192.249.249.3

> set q=mx
> acmebw.com.
Server:  terminator.movie.edu
Address:  192.249.249.3

------------
Got answer:
    HEADER:
          opcode = QUERY, id = 9, rcode = NOERROR
          header flags:  response, want recursion, recursion avail.
          questions = 1,  answers = 2,  authority records = 0,  additional = 2

    QUESTIONS:
          acmebw.com, type = MX, class = IN
    ANSWERS:
    ->  acmebw.com
          type = MX, class = IN, dlen = 29
          MX preference = 10, mail exchanger = store-forward.MSPRING.NET
          ttl = 86400 (1 day)
    ->  acmebw.com
          type = MX, class = IN, dlen = 17
          MX preference = 0, mail exchanger = domain-relay.MSPRING.NET
          ttl = 86400 (1 day)
    ADDITIONAL RECORDS:
    ->  store-forward.MSPRING.NET
          type = A, class = IN, dlen = 4
          internet address = 207.69.231.6
          ttl = 3600 (1 hour)
```

```
    -> domain-relay.MSPRING.NET
         type = A, class = IN, dlen = 4
         internet address = 207.69.231.10
         ttl = 3600 (1 hour)


    ------------
Non-authoritative answer:
acmebw.com
         type = MX, class = IN, dlen = 29
         MX preference = 10, mail exchanger = store-forward.MSPRING.NET
         ttl = 86400 (1 day)
acmebw.com
         type = MX, class = IN, dlen = 17
         MX preference = 0, mail exchanger = domain-relay.MSPRING.NET
         ttl = 86400 (1 day)

store-forward.MSPRING.NET
         type = A, class = IN, dlen = 4
         internet address = 207.69.231.6
         ttl = 3600 (1 hour)
domain-relay.MSPRING.NET
         type = A, class = IN, dlen = 4
         internet address = 207.69.231.10
         ttl = 3600 (1 hour)


>
> set d2
> acmebw.com.
Server:  terminator.movie.edu
Address:  192.249.249.3
```

This time the query is also shown.

```
    ------------
SendRequest(), len 28
    HEADER:
         opcode = QUERY, id = 9, rcode = NOERROR
         header flags:  query, want recursion
         questions = 1,  answers = 0,  authority records = 0,  additional = 0

    QUESTIONS:
         acmebw.com, type = MX, class = IN


    ------------
    ------------
Got answer (130 bytes):
```

The answer is the same as in the previous example.

The text between the dashes is the query and response packets. As promised, we will go through the packet contents. DNS packets are composed of five sections:

- Header section
- Question section

- Answer section

- Authority section

- Additional section

*Header section*

The Header section is present in every query and response. The operation code is always QUERY. The only other opcodes are inverse query (IQUERY) and status (STATUS), but those aren't used. The ID is used to associate a response with a query and to detect duplicate queries or responses. You have to look in the header flags to see which packets are queries and which are responses. The string want recursion means that the querier wants the name server to do all the work. The flag is parroted in the response. The string auth. answer, when present, means that the response is authoritative—in other words, a response from the name server's authoritative data, not from its cache data. (This response isn't authoritative, so the string is absent.) The response code, rcode, can be one of no error, server failure, name error (also known as "NXDOMAIN" or "nonexistent domain"), not implemented, or refused. The server failure, name error, not implemented, and refused response codes cause the *nslookup* "Server failed," "Nonexistent domain," "Not implemented," and "Query refused" errors, respectively. The last four entries in the Header section are counters—they indicate how many resource records there are in each of the next four sections.

*Question section*

There is always *one* question in a DNS packet; it includes the name and the requested data type and class. There is never more than one question in a DNS packet. The capability of handling more than one question in a DNS packet would require a redesign of the packet format. For one thing, the single authority bit would have to be changed, because the Answer section could contain a mix of authoritative answers and nonauthoritative answers. In the present design, setting the authoritative answer bit means that the name server is an authority for the domain name in the Question section.

*Answer section*

This section contains the resource records that answer the question. There can be more than one resource record in the response. For example, if the host is multihomed, there will be more than one address resource record.

*Authority section*

The Authority section is where name server records are returned. When a response refers the querier to some other name servers, those name servers are listed here.

*Additional section*

The Additional records section adds information that may complete information included in other sections. For instance, if a name server is listed in the Authority section, the name server's address is added to the Additional records section. After all, to contact the name server, you need to have its address.

For you sticklers for detail, there *is* a time when the number of questions in a query packet isn't one: in an inverse query, when it's zero. In an inverse query, there is one answer in the query packet, and the Question section is empty. The name server fills in the question. But, as we said, inverse queries are almost nonexistent. The Microsoft DNS Server doesn't even support them.

## Querying Like a Name Server

You can make *nslookup* send out the same query packet a name server would. Name server query packets are not much different from resolver packets. The primary difference in the query packets is that resolvers request recursion and name servers seldom do. Recursion is the default with *nslookup*, so you have to explicitly turn it off. The difference in *operation* between a resolver and a name server is that the resolver implements the search list, and the name server doesn't. By default, *nslookup* implements the search list, so that, too, has to be turned off. Of course, judicious use of the trailing dot will have the same effect.

In raw *nslookup* terms, this means that to query like a resolver, you use *nslookup*'s default settings. To query like a name server, use *set norecurse* and *set nosearch*. On the command line, that's **nslookup -norecurse -nosearch**.

When a name server gets a query, it looks for the answer in its cache. If it doesn't have the answer, and it is authoritative for the zone, the name server responds that the name doesn't exist or that there is no data for that type. If the name server doesn't have the answer, and it is *not* authoritative for the zone, it starts walking up the name space looking for NS records. There will always be NS records somewhere higher in the domain tree. As a last resort, it will use the NS records at the root domain, the highest level.

If the name server received a nonrecursive query, it would respond to the querier by giving the NS records that it had found. On the other hand, if the original query was a recursive query, the name server would then query the remote name servers in the NS records that it found. When the name server receives a response from one of the remote name servers, it caches the response, and repeats this process, if necessary. The remote server's response will either have the answer to the question, or contain a list of name servers lower in the name space and closer to the answer.

Let's assume for our example that we are trying to satisfy a recursive query and that we didn't find any NS records until we checked the *gov* domain. That is, in fact, the case when we ask the name server on *relay.hp.com* about *www.white-house.gov*—it doesn't find any NS records until the *gov* domain. From there we switch servers to a *gov* name server and ask the same question. It directs us to the *whitehouse.gov* servers. We then switch to a *whitehouse.gov* name server and ask the same question.

```
C:\> nslookup
Default Server:  relay.hp.com
Address:  15.255.152.2

> set norec           --Query like a name server: turn off recursion
> set nosearch        --turn off the search list
> www.whitehouse.gov  --We don't need to dot-terminate since we've turned
                      --search off
Server:  relay.hp.com
Address:  15.255.152.2

Name: www.whitehouse.gov
Served by:
- H.ROOT-SERVERS.NET
  128.63.2.53
  gov
- B.ROOT-SERVERS.NET
  128.9.0.107
  gov
- C.ROOT-SERVERS.NET
  192.33.4.12
  gov
- D.ROOT-SERVERS.NET
  128.8.10.90
  gov
- E.ROOT-SERVERS.NET
  192.203.230.10
  gov
- I.ROOT-SERVERS.NET
  192.36.148.17
  gov
- F.ROOT-SERVERS.NET
  192.5.5.241
  gov
- G.ROOT-SERVERS.NET
  192.112.36.4
  gov
- A.ROOT-SERVERS.NET
  198.41.0.4
  gov
```

*Switch to a gov name server. You may have to turn recursion back on temporarily, if the name server doesn't have the address already cached.*

```
> server e.root-servers.net
Default Server:  e.root-servers.net
Address: 192.203.230.10
```

*Ask the same question of the* gov *name server. It will refer us to name servers closer to our desired answer.*

```
> www.whitehouse.gov.
Server:  e.root-servers.net
Address:  192.203.230.10

Name:    www.whitehouse.gov
Served by:
- SEC1.DNS.PSI.NET
         38.8.92.2
         WHITEHOUSE.GOV
- SEC2.DNS.PSI.NET
         38.8.93.2
         WHITEHOUSE.GOV
```

*Switch to a* whitehouse.gov *name server—either of them will do.*
```
> server sec1.dns.psi.net.
Default Server:  sec1.dns.psi.net
Address:  38.8.92.2
```

```
> www.whitehouse.gov.
Server:  sec1.dns.psi.net
Address:  38.8.92.2

Name:    www.whitehouse.gov
Addresses:  198.137.240.91, 198.137.240.92
```

We hope this example gives you a feeling for how name servers look up names. If you need to refresh your understanding of what this looks like graphically, flip back to Figure 2-13.

Before we move on, notice that we asked each of the servers the very same question: "What's the address for *www.whitehouse.gov?*" What do you think would happen if the *gov* name server itself had already cached *www.whitehouse.gov's* address? The *gov* name server would have answered the question out of its cache instead of referring you to the *whitehouse.gov* name servers. Why is this significant? Suppose you messed up a particular host's address in your zone. Someone points it out to you, and you clean up the problem. Even though your name server now has the correct data, some remote sites find the old, messed-up data when they look up the name. One of the name servers higher up in the domain tree has cached the incorrect data; when it receives a query for that host's address, it returns the incorrect data instead of referring the querier to your name servers. What makes this problem hard to track down is that only one of the "higher up" name servers has cached the incorrect data, so only some of the remote lookups get the wrong answer—the ones that use this server. Fun, huh? Eventually, though, the "higher up" name server will time out the old record. If you're pressed for time, you can contact the administrators of the remote name server and ask them to kill and restart their name servers to flush the cache. Of course, if the remote name server is an important, much-used name server, they may tell you where to go with that suggestion.

## Zone Transfers

*nslookup* can be used to transfer a whole zone using the *ls* command. This feature is useful for troubleshooting, for figuring out how to spell a remote host's name, or just for counting how many hosts are in some remote zone. Since the output can be substantial, *nslookup* allows you to redirect the output to a file.

Beware: a lot of hosts won't let you pull a copy of their zone, either for security reasons or to limit the load on their name server host. The Internet is a friendly place, but administrators have to defend their turf.

*nslookup* filters zone transfer data: it shows you only some of the zone unless you tell it otherwise. By default, you see only address and name server data. You will see all of the zone data if you tell *nslookup* to display data of *any* type. The *nslookup* help (available in the main Windows NT help) or command summary (shown by typing **help** at the *nslookup* prompt) tells you all the parameters to the *ls* command. We are going to show only the *–t* parameter, since the others can be emulated with *–t*. The *–t* option takes one argument: the data type to filter on. So, to pull a copy of a zone and see all the MX data, use **ls -t mx**. Let's do some zone transfers.

```
C:\> nslookup
Default Server:  terminator.movie.edu
Address:  192.249.249.3

> ls movie.edu.      --List NS and A records for movie.edu
[terminator.movie.edu]
 movie.edu.                  NS       server = terminator.movie.edu
 movie.edu.                  NS       server = wormhole.movie.edu
 carrie                      A        192.253.253.4
 diehard                     A        192.249.249.4
 misery                      A        192.253.253.2
 robocop                     A        192.249.249.2
 shining                     A        192.253.253.3
 terminator                  A        192.249.249.3
 wh249                       A        192.249.249.1
 wh253                       A        192.253.253.1
 wormhole                    A        192.253.253.1
 wormhole                    A        192.249.249.1
> ls -t any movie.edu  > /temp/movie.edu.txt    --List all data into \temp\
                                                --movie.edu.txt
```

```
[terminator.movie.edu]
Received 25 records.
```

Those forward slashes in the *ls* command above aren't a misprint—*nslookup* was originally written for UNIX as part of the BIND distribution. Microsoft must have missed the slashes when porting *nslookup* to Windows NT.

# Troubleshooting nslookup Problems

The last thing you want is to have problems with your troubleshooting tool. Unfortunately, some types of failures render the troubleshooting tool mostly useless. Other types of *nslookup* failures are, at best, confusing because they don't give you any direct information to work with. While there may be a few problems with *nslookup* itself, most of the problems you encounter will be with name server configuration and operation. We'll cover a few odd problems here.

## Looking Up the Right Data

This isn't really a problem, *per se*, but it can be awfully confusing. If you use *nslookup* to look up a type of data for a domain name, and the domain name exists, but no data of the type you're looking for exists, you'll get an error like this:

```
C:\> nslookup
Default Server:  terminator.movie.edu
Address:  192.249.249.3

> movie.edu.

*** No address (A) records available for movie.edu.
```

So what types of records *do* exist? Just *set type=any* to find out:

```
> set type=any
> movie.edu.
Server:  terminator.movie.edu
Address:  192.249.249.3

movie.edu        nameserver = terminator.movie.edu
movie.edu        nameserver = wormhole.movie.edu
movie.edu
        primary name server = terminator.movie.edu
        responsible mail addr = administrator.movie.edu
        serial  = 6
        refresh = 3600 (1 hour)
        retry   = 600 (10 mins)
        expire  = 86400 (1 day)
        default TTL = 3600 (1 hour)
movie.edu        MX preference = 10, mail exchanger = wormhole.movie.edu
terminator.movie.edu    internet address = 192.249.249.3
wormhole.movie.edu      internet address = 192.253.253.1
```

```
wormhole.movie.edu          internet address = 192.249.249.1
wormhole.movie.edu          internet address = 192.249.249.1
wormhole.movie.edu          internet address = 192.253.253.1
```

Why the IP addresses for *terminator* and *wormhole*? If you receive the NS records for *movie.edu* listing these two hosts as that zone's name servers, chances are the next thing you'll want are those hosts' IP addresses. The name server anticipates that and sends along address records in the Additional section. The same thing goes for the *movie.edu* MX record pointing to *wormhole*: if you get that record, you'll want *wormhole*'s IP address next. That explains why *wormhole*'s show up twice, but this is arguably a bug in the Microsoft DNS Server.

## No PTR Data for Name Server's Address

Here's a cryptic message:

```
C:\> nslookup
*** Can't find server name for address 192.249.249.3: Non-existent domain
*** Can't find server name for address 192.249.249.3: Non-existent domain
*** Default servers are not available
Default Server:  UnKnown
Address:  192.249.249.3

>
```

The "non-existent domain" means that there's no PTR record for *3.249.249.192.in-addr.arpa.* In other words, *nslookup* couldn't find the name for 192.249.249.3, which is the first name server the resolver's configured to query. The only reason *nslookup* looks up this address is to print the "Default Server" startup message. Obviously, this name server's data is messed up, at least for the *249.249.192.in-addr.arpa* zone, so *nslookup* prints "UnKnown."

At least we've got the *nslookup* prompt: even if the server "doesn't know its own name," it might still be able to answer other queries. This behavior is a vast improvement over the standard version of *nslookup* in the BIND distribution, the one found shipped with most UNIXes. That version of *nslookup* refuses even to run unless it can successfully reverse map the default server's IP address.

Still, the "default servers are not available" message in the example is misleading. After all, a name server is there to say the address doesn't exist. More often, you'll see the error "timed out" if the name server isn't running on the host or the host can't be reached. Only then does the "default servers are not available" message make sense.

## Timeouts

What if your resolver is pointing to a name server that isn't running or a host that can't be reached? We kinda gave the answer away in the previous section, but here's what happens:

```
C:\> nslookup
DNS request timed out.
    timeout was 2 seconds.
DNS request timed out.
    timeout was 4 seconds.
DNS request timed out.
    timeout was 8 seconds.
*** Can't find server name for address 192.249.249.4: Timed out
DNS request timed out.
    timeout was 2 seconds.
DNS request timed out.
    timeout was 4 seconds.
DNS request timed out.
    timeout was 8 seconds.
*** Can't find server name for address 192.249.249.4: Timed out
*** Default servers are not available
Default Server:  UnKnown
Address:  192.249.249.4

>
```

The resolver is configured to use the name server 192.249.249.4 (and only that name server). *nslookup* tries valiantly to contact it—it goes through its timeout sequence twice in attempt to get the name server to reverse-map its own IP address. Finally *nslookup* gives up, prints "UnKnown" for the default server, and gives you a prompt. You can't really do anything productive without changing servers at this point—after all, no server is running at that IP address—but at least you've got a prompt. Again, this is a better than the standard *nslookup*, which would have dumped us back to the command line.

Note that if your resolver is configured to send queries to more than one name server, *nslookup* tries the servers in order until it finds one that responds:

```
C:\> nslookup
DNS request timed out.
    timeout was 2 seconds.
DNS request timed out.
    timeout was 4 seconds.
DNS request timed out.
    timeout was 8 seconds.
*** Can't find server name for address 192.249.249.1: Timed out
Default Server:  terminator.movie.edu
Address:  192.249.249.3

>
```

Occasionally you'll see timeouts during the course of an *nslookup* session. If you are looking up some remote information, the name server could fail to respond because it is still trying to look up the item and *nslookup* gave up waiting. How can you tell the difference between a name server that isn't running and a name server that is running but didn't respond? Use the *ls* command to point out the difference. In this case, no name server is running, or the host couldn't be reached:

```
C:\> nslookup
Default Server:  terminator.movie.edu
Address:  192.249.249.3

> ls foo.
ls: connect: No error
*** Can't list domain foo.: Unspecified error
```

If a name server is running, you'll see the following error message:

```
C:\> nslookup
Default Server:  terminator.movie.edu
Address:  192.249.249.3

> ls foo.
[terminator.movie.edu]
*** Can't list domain foo.: Non-existent domain
```

That is, unless there's a top-level *foo* domain in your world.

## Query Refused

You generally see a "query refused" error message under two conditions. The first is when you attempt a zone transfer and the server refuses for security reasons. (For example, because you checked **Only Allow Access From Secondaries Included on Notify List** in the zone properties **Notify** window.)  This is what you'll see:

```
C:\> nslookup
Default Server:  terminator.movie.edu
Address:  192.249.249.3

> ls movie.edu                    --This attempts a zone transfer
[terminator.movie.edu]
*** Can't list domain movie.edu: Query refused
>
```

You might also see a "query refused" error from recent BIND name server, which has the ability to restrict queries to different zones based on the querier's source IP address.

## Unspecified Error

You can run into a rather unsettling problem called "unspecified error." We have an example of this error here:

```
C:/> nslookup
Default Server:  terminator.movie.edu
Address:  192.249.249.3

> set type=ns
> .
Server:  terminator.movie.edu
Address:  192.249.249.3

Non-authoritative answer:
(root)   nameserver = NS.NIC.DDN.MIL
(root)   nameserver = B.ROOT-SERVERS.NET
(root)   nameserver = E.ROOT-SERVERS.NET
(root)   nameserver = D.ROOT-SERVERS.NET
(root)   nameserver = F.ROOT-SERVERS.NET
(root)   nameserver = C.ROOT-SERVERS.NET
(root)   nameserver = G.ROOT-SERVERS.NET
(root)   nameserver = hpfcsx.fc.hp.com
(root)   nameserver = hp-pcd.cv.hp.com
(root)   nameserver = hp-ses.sde.hp.com
(root)   nameserver = hpsatc1.gva.hp.com
(root)   nameserver = named_master.ch.apollo.hp.com
(root)   nameserver = A.ISI.EDU
(root)   nameserver = SRI-NIC.ARPA
(root)   nameserver = GUNTER-ADAM.ARPA

Authoritative answers can be found from:
(root)   nameserver = NS.NIC.DDN.MIL
(root)   nameserver = B.ROOT-SERVERS.NET
(root)   nameserver = E.ROOT-SERVERS.NET
(root)   nameserver = D.ROOT-SERVERS.NET
(root)   nameserver = F.ROOT-SERVERS.NET
(root)   nameserver = C.ROOT-SERVERS.NET
(root)   nameserver =

*** Error: record size incorrect (1050690 != 65519)

*** terminator.movie.edu can't find .: Unspecified error
```

What happened here is that there was too much data to fit into a UDP datagram.[*] The name server stopped filling in the response when it ran out of room. The name server *didn't* set the truncation bit in the response packet, or *nslookup* would have retried the query over a TCP connection; the name server must have

---

[*] What are all those *hp.com* name servers doing in there? This example illustrates a problem besides just filling a UDP datagram: under some conditions, older BIND name servers could easily be contaminated with "bogus" root name servers. This output shows a query to such a name server.

decided that enough of the "important" information fit. You won't see this kind of error very often. You'll see it if you create too many NS records for a zone, so don't create too many. (Advice like this makes you wonder why you bought this book, right?) How many is too many depends upon how well the names can be "compressed" in the packet, which, in turn, depends upon how many name servers share the same domain in their domain name. The root name servers were renamed to all be in the *root-servers.net* domain for this very reason—more names fit in DNS packets if they share a common domain, which allows more root name servers to support the Internet. As a rule of thumb, don't go over ten NS records.

# Best of the Net

System admins have a thankless job. They are asked certain questions, usually quite simple ones, over and over again. And sometimes, in a creative mood, they come up with a clever way to help their users. When the rest of us find out about their ingenuity, we can only sit back, smile admiringly, and wish we had thought of it ourselves. Here is one such case, where a system admin found a way to communicate the solution to the sometimes perplexing puzzle of how to end an *nslookup* session:

```
C:\> nslookup
Default Server:  envy.ugcs.caltech.edu
Address:   131.215.134.135

> quit
Server:   envy.ugcs.caltech.edu
Addresses:   131.215.134.135, 131.215.128.135

Name:     ugcs.caltech.edu
Addresses:   131.215.128.135, 131.215.134.135
Aliases:   quit.ugcs.caltech.edu
           use.exit.to.leave.nslookup.-.-.-.ugcs.caltech.edu

> exit
C:\>
```

# 12

# Troubleshooting DNS

*"Of course not," said the Mock Turtle. "Why, if a fish came to me, and told me he was going on a journey, I should say, 'With what porpoise?'"*

*"Don't you mean 'purpose'?" said Alice.*

*"I mean what I say," the Mock Turtle replied, in an offended tone. And the Gryphon added, "Come, let's hear some of your adventures."*

In the last chapter, we demonstrated how to use *nslookup*. In this chapter, we'll show you how to use *nslookup*—plus traditional TCP/IP networking tools like trusty ol' *ping*—to troubleshoot real-life problems with DNS.

Troubleshooting, by its nature, is a tough subject to teach. You start with any of a world of symptoms and try to work your way back to the cause. We can't cover the whole gamut of problems you may encounter on the Internet, but we will certainly do our best to show you how to diagnose the most common of them. And along the way, we hope to teach you troubleshooting techniques that will be valuable in tracking down more obscure problems that we don't document.

## Is DNS Really Your Problem?

Before we launch into a discussion of how to troubleshoot a DNS problem, we should make sure you know how to tell whether a problem is caused by DNS, not by another naming service. On Windows hosts, figuring out whether the culprit is actually DNS can be difficult. Windows supports a whole panoply of naming services: DNS, WINS, *HOSTS*, *LMHOSTS*, and more. The stock Windows NT *nslookup*, for example, doesn't pay any attention to these other naming services. You can run *nslookup* on an NT box and query the name server 'till the cows come home, while the service with the problem is using a different naming service.

How do you know where to put the blame? First, you need to consider what kind of program is having the problem. If it's a TCP/IP client, like *telnet* or *ftp*, then the possible culprits are DNS and the *HOSTS* file. If it's a NetBIOS utility, like *net* (as in *net use*), then the likely suspects are WINS and the *LMHOSTS* file. A few clients, like *ping,* can take either a DNS name or a NetBIOS name as an argument; they can use any of these naming services.

Next, consider the order in which Windows uses the naming services. See the section "Other Naming Services" in Chapter 6, *Configuring Hosts,* for details. Unless you've modified the order manually, by editing the Registry, you should look through the various services in this order, too, when troubleshooting the problem.

These hints should help you identify the guilty party or at least exonerate one suspect. If you narrow down the suspects, and DNS is still implicated, you'll just have to read this chapter.

## Checking the Cache

As we've said earlier, you can check the contents of your name server's cache with DNS Manager. This can come in handy if you suspect that your name server has cached bad or out-of-date data from another server. To inspect a server's cache, double-click the IP address of the server in DNS Manager's left pane. You should see an icon of the globe (showing the Eastern Hemisphere, if you look closely) and the label "Cache" to the right of it. Double-click either the icon or the label to expand the next level. This shows you the top-level domains for which your name server has cached data. Double-click your way to the domain name to which the cached data you're looking for is attached. In Figure 12-1, we've clicked our way down to *acmebw.com* to look for cached data.

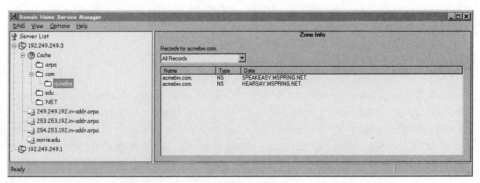

*Figure 12-1. NS records for acmebw.com in the cache*

As you can see in the right pane, our name server has cached the NS records for *acmebw.com.* If we double-clicked NET, and then MSPRING, we could find the cached addresses of these name servers, too.

If you'd like to see the TTL on the cached data, select **Expose TTL** under **Options** →
**Preferences**. Then double-click (or right-click and choose **Properties**) the record
whose TTL you're interested in (in the right pane). For example, in Figure 12-2
we've double-clicked the *acmebw.com* NS record pointing to *HEAR-
SAY.MSPRING.NET*.

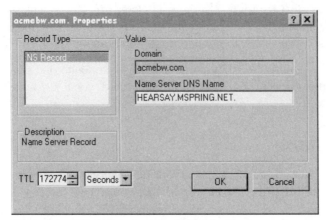

*Figure 12-2. The TTL on a cached record*

Be sure to refresh DNS Manager with **View** → **Refresh** or F5 before checking the
TTL, or the TTL you see may be bigger than the current TTL.

If you right-clicked the record, you may have noticed a **Delete Record** selection.
Now there's something you can't do in BIND. Using the DNS Manager, you can
actually delete cached data record by record! If you know that some records in
your name server's cache are out of date, you can delete them and let your name
server pick up updated records from an authoritative name server.

# Potential Problem List

Let's go through some common real-world DNS problems. Many of these problems are easy to recognize and correct. We cover these problems as a matter of
course—they're some of the most common problems because they're caused by
some of the most common mistakes. Here are the contestants, in no particular
order. We call 'em our "Unlucky Thirteen."

## 1. DNS Manager Reports Endpoint Error

If you're just setting up your name server and, in your rush to get going, forget to
start the Microsoft DNS Server service before starting, you may see the error,
"There are no more endpoints available from the endpoint mapper." Usually, this
just means that you need to go to **Control Panel** → **Services**, and start the Microsoft

DNS Manager service. Sometimes, the server will die again shortly after you try to start it, and you'll see the same error again. In that case, look at the next problem in the list.

## 2. DNS Server Keeps Dying

DNS Manager does a good job of checking the syntax of records it adds to name servers; the same may not be true of you, however. If you make a mistake when editing a zone data file by hand, you may add or modify a record and inadvertently introduce a syntax error. If this happens, you'll probably see an error message like the following:

```
Could not start the Microsoft DNS Server service on \\terminator.
Error 0013: The data is invalid.
```

appear in a pop-up window. If you check the Event Viewer, you'll see a more detailed description of the error:

```
DNS Server encountered unknown or unsupported record type B in database file
movie.edu.dns, line 58.
```

followed by:

```
DNS Server could not create domain movie.edu.
```

and

```
DNS Server could not parse database file movie.edu.dns for domain movie.edu.
```

In this case, the DNS server choked on a B in the type field of the record at line 58 of *movie.edu.dns*.

## 3. Event Viewer Can't Find Event ID Descriptions

If you mess around (er, experiment) with other vendor's DNS servers on Windows NT, and eventually decide to use the Microsoft DNS Server, you may find that the Event Viewer can no longer decode the server's events. Instead, you see garbage like:

```
The description for Event ID (1) in Source (DNS) could not be found.  It
contains the following insertion string(s): .
```

in the Event Viewer. Now that's not very helpful at all (unless you happen to have the source code in front of you, and I'll bet you don't).

What has happened is that the other DNS servers have changed an important Registry entry that tells the Event Viewer where to look to decode the server's events. That Registry key lives at:

*HKEY_LOCAL_MACHINE\SYSTEM\CurrentControlSet\Services\EventLog\*
*Application\DNS\EventMessageFile*

Use your favorite Registry editor to change the key's value to the full path to *DNS.EXE* (for example, *C:\WINNT\SYSTEM32\DNS.EXE*), restart the Event Viewer, and you'll see that that impenetrable gobbledygook actually means:

```
Starting Microsoft DNS Server (v4.0).
```

## 4. Forget to Increment Serial Number

This particular problem would only occur if you make changes to your zone data file by hand, without using DNS Manager. DNS Manager remembers to increment the serial number in the SOA record each time it changes zone data, so you don't have to worry about it. However, this also means that you probably won't be in the habit of updating the serial number, so you may forget when making that one-off manual modification.

The main symptom of this problem is that slave name servers don't pick up any changes you make to the zone on the primary server. The slaves think the zone data hasn't changed, since the serial number is still the same.

How do you check whether or not you remembered to increment the serial number? Unfortunately, that's not so easy. If you don't remember what the old serial number was, and your serial number gives you no indication of when it was updated, there's no direct way to tell whether it's changed.* When you start the primary, it will load the updated zone data file regardless of whether you've changed the serial number. About the best you can do is to use *nslookup* to compare the data returned by the primary and by a slave. If they return different data, you probably forgot to increment the serial number. If you can remember a recent change you made, you can look for that data. If you can't remember a recent change, you could try transferring the zone from a primary and from a slave, sorting the results, and using a file comparison tool to compare them.

The good news is that, although determining whether the zone was transferred is tricky, making sure the zone is transferred is simple. Just increment the serial number on the primary's copy of the zone by double-clicking the SOA record in DNS Manager and manually editing the serial number field. The slaves should pick up the new data within their refresh interval, or sooner if they use NOTIFY.

## 5. Forget to Restart Primary Master Server

Like the last problem, you'd only see this problem if you make changes to your zone data files by hand. DNS Manager adds and deletes data on the fly, so there's no need to restart your primary master name server.

---

\* On the other hand, if you encode the date into the serial number, as many people do (for example, 1998010500 is the first rev of data on January 5, 1998), you may be able to tell at a glance whether you last updated the serial number when you made the change. However, DNS Manager makes this almost impossible, since it just increments by one for each change.

If you're not using DNS Manager, though, you may forget to restart your primary master name server after making a change to a zone data file. The name server won't know to load the new data—it doesn't automatically check the file and notice that it changed. Consequently, any changes you've made won't be reflected in the name server's data: new zones won't be loaded, and new records won't percolate out to the slaves.

To check when you last restarted the name server, scan the Event Viewer output for the last entries like this:

```
Starting Microsoft DNS Server (NT4.0 ServicePack3).
```

And

```
The DNS Server has started.
```

The date and time on these events will tell you the last time you restarted the name server.

If the time of the restart doesn't correlate with the time you made the last change, use **Control Panel → Services** to stop and restart the name server and reload its data. And check that you incremented the serial numbers on zone data files you changed, too.

## 6. The DNS Server Loses Manual Changes

One final, but important note about making manual changes: remember that the DNS server periodically updates its zone data files. Each time you make changes to a zone's data using DNS Manager, a write is pending: before the DNS server exits, it must rewrite the zone's data file, or it will lose the changes you made. Think of this as a dirty page in memory: the operating system must write it to disk before exiting.

If you make a manual change to a zone data file while a write is pending, you'll mysteriously lose the change when the name server exits. Say you add delegation to a new subdomain of *movie.edu* while the server is running and a write is pending. After you've made the change, you have to stop the server and start it again to get it to read the zone data again. But as the server exits, it rewrites the *movie.edu* zone data file, and your delegation disappears. If you're watching the Event Viewer carefully (like you should be), you'll see this message before the server stops:

```
DNS Server wrote new version of zone movie.edu, to file movie.edu.dns. The
data is the new version number.
```

Once you force the server to rewrite its zone data files with **DNS → Update Server Data Files**, the server is in sync with the zone data files and doesn't have to rewrite them on exit. So, if you're going to make manual changes to the zone data files, you should either stop the server first (although that means your server won't answer queries while you make the change), or use DNS Manager to sync the server to the zone data files, and then make the change.

## 7. Slave Server Can't Load Zone Data

If a slave name server can't get the current serial number for a zone server, you won't be warned about it initially. However, if the problem persists, and the slave can't determine within the expire interval whether or not its data is up to date, it will expire the zone. On a Microsoft DNS Server, you'd see a message like this in the Event Viewer:

```
Zone movie.edu expired before successful zone transfer from zone master(s).
Zone has been shutdown.
```

Once the zone has expired, you'll start getting SERVFAIL errors when you query the name server for data in the zone:

```
% nslookup robocop wormhole.movie.edu.
Server:  wormhole.movie.edu
Addresses:  192.249.249.1, 192.253.253.1

*** wormhole.movie.edu can't find robocop.movie.edu: Server failed
```

There are three leading causes of this problem: a loss in connectivity to the master server due to network failure, an incorrect IP address configured for the master server, and a syntax error in the zone data file on the master server. First, use DNS Manager to check the address of the master server(s) the slave is attempting to load from. Right-click the domain name of the zone in the left pane, choose **Properties**, and look on the **General** tab as shown in Figure 12-3.

Make sure that's really the IP address of the master name server. If it is, check connectivity to that IP address:

```
C:\> ping 192.249.249.3
Pinging 192.249.249.3 with 32 bytes of data:

Request timed out.
Request timed out.
Request timed out.
Request timed out.
```

If the master server isn't reachable, make sure that the server's host is really running (for example, is powered on, and so on), or look for a network problem.

You may also want to check that the master server is returning authoritative responses to queries for data in the zone. If the master server is responding as not authoritative for the zone, the slave won't transfer the zone from it. Here's how you could use *nslookup* to check for an authoritative response for the zone's SOA record from the master server:

```
C:\> nslookup —norec —type=SOA movie.edu. 192.249.249.3
```

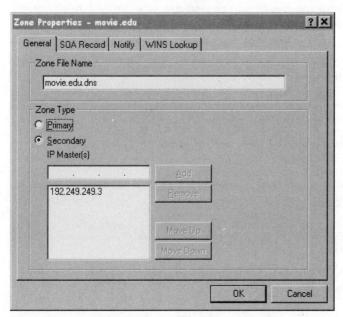

*Figure 12-3. Zone Properties showing master server(s)*

This sends a nonrecursive query for the SOA record for *movie.edu* to the name server at 192.249.249.3. We need to send a nonrecursive query so that the name server at 192.249.249.3 doesn't try to forward the query to another server.

If this master server is correctly configured, the answer to this query should be authoritative. (Remember that unless *nslookup* reports "Non-authoritative answer," the answer is authoritative.) If the answer isn't authoritative, this may indicate that the master server had a problem loading the zone, usually because of a syntax error in the zone data file. Contact the administrator of the master server, and have him check his Event Viewer or syslog output for indications of a syntax error (see problem 2, earlier in this chapter).

If the answer to the query is authoritative, but the slave server still can't transfer the zone successfully, you can use *nslookup*'s *ls* command to try to transfer the zone manually (*ls,* as we said in Chapter 11, *nslookup,* performs a zone transfer). If you see an error like this, it's a good bet that the master server restricts zone transfers:

```
C:\>nslookup - 192.249.249.3
Default Server:  terminator.movie.edu
Address:  192.249.249.3
> ls movie.edu
[terminator.movie.edu]
*** Can't list domain movie.edu: Query refused
>
```

Contact the administrator of the master server, and ask whether she has the **Only Allow Access From Secondaries on Notify List** option checked on the **Notify** tab of the **Zone Properties** window for the zone you're trying to transfer (assuming she's running the Microsoft DNS Server), or is using the BIND *xfernets* or *allow-transfer* features to restrict zone transfers.

Once the problem has been cleared up and your server successfully transfers the zone, you'll see messages like these in the Event Viewer:

```
New version 3 of zone acmebw.com found at DNS server at 192.249.249.1. Zone
transfer is in progress.

DNS Server wrote new version of zone acmebw.com, to file acmebw.com.dns. The
data is the new version number.

DNS Server transfer of zone movie.edu to DNS server at 192.249.249.1,
successfully completed.
```

## *8.Add Address to Zone, but Forget to Add Corresponding PTR Record*

Because the mappings from host names to IP addresses are disjointed from the mappings from IP addresses to host names in DNS, it's easy to forget to add a PTR record for a new host. Adding the A record is intuitive, but many people who are used to host tables assume that adding an address record takes care of the reverse mapping, too. That's not true—you need to add a PTR record for the host to the appropriate *in-addr.arpa* zone. Thankfully, DNS Manager makes that easy by providing a checkbox to **Create Associated PTR Record** when you choose **New Host** or **New Record**.

Neglecting to add the PTR record for a host usually causes that host to fail authentication checks. For example, users on the host won't be able to *rsh* or *rcp* to other hosts. The servers these programs talk to need to be able to map the connection's IP address to a domain name to check authorization files.

In addition, many large *ftp* archives, including *ftp.uu.net*, refuse anonymous *ftp* access to hosts whose IP addresses don't map back to domain names. *ftp.uu.net*'s FTP server emits a message that reads, in part:

```
530- Sorry, we're unable to map your IP address 140.186.66.1 to a hostname
530- in the DNS.  This is probably because your nameserver does not have a
530- PTR record for your address in its tables, or because your reverse
530- nameservers are not registered.  We refuse service to hosts whose
530- names we cannot resolve.
```

That makes the reason you can't use anonymous *ftp* pretty evident. Other FTP sites, however, don't bother printing informative messages; they simply deny service.

*nslookup* is handy for checking whether or not you've forgotten the PTR record:

```
% nslookup
Default Server: terminator.movie.edu
Address: 192.249.249.3

> beetlejuice        --Check for a host name-to-address mapping
Server: terminator.movie.edu
Address: 192.249.249.3

Name:    beetlejuice.movie.edu
Address: 192.249.249.23

> 192.249.249.23   --Now check for a corresponding address-to-host name mapping
Server: terminator.movie.edu
Address: 192.249.249.3

*** terminator.movie.edu can't find 192.249.249.23: Non-existent domain
```

On the primary for *249.249.192.in-addr.arpa*, a quick check of DNS Manager or the *249.249.192.in-addr.arpa.dns* file will tell you if the PTR record hasn't been added to the zone yet.

## 9. Wrong Domain Name in RDATA of Record

When you add CNAME, MX, and NS records with DNS Manager, remember to specify the fully qualified domain name of the host for the resource record-specific data. DNS Manager assumes that the name you type as the RDATA field is fully qualfied. So if you try to create an NS record as shown in Figure 12-4, the NS looks like this in the zone data file:

```
@        IN  NS  terminator.
```

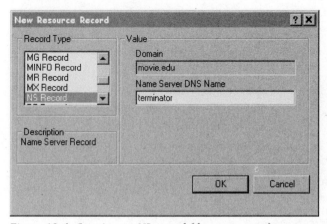

*Figure 12-4. Creating an NS record (the wrong way)*

This is probably not what you intended, since there's no top-level *terminator* domain. You probably assumed DNS Manager would append the name of the zone to the name if you left off the dot. Nope.

These mistakes are easy to discover if you simply examine the zone data file (after a **DNS → Update Server Data Files**) or use *nslookup*:

```
C:\> nslookup -type=ns movie.edu.
Server:  terminator.movie.edu
Address:  192.249.249.3


movie.edu          nameserver = wormhole.movie.edu
movie.edu          nameserver = terminator
wormhole.movie.edu      internet address = 192.253.253.1
wormhole.movie.edu      internet address = 192.249.249.1
```

## 10. Loss of Network Connectivity

Though the Internet is more reliable today than it was back in the wild and woolly days of the ARPANET, network outages are still relatively common. Without "lifting the hood" and poking around in debugging output, these failures usually look like poor performance:

```
C:\> nslookup nisc.sri.com.
Server:  terminator.movie.edu
Address:  192.249.249.3

DNS request timed out.
    timeout was 2 seconds.
DNS request timed out.
    timeout was 4 seconds.
DNS request timed out.
    timeout was 8 seconds.
*** Request to terminator.movie.edu timed-out
```

Using *nslookup,* you can look up the names and addresses of the name servers your name server needs to talk to in order to resolve the name:

```
C:\>nslookup
Default Server:  terminator.movie.edu
Address:  192.249.249.3


> set type=ns
> sri.com.
Server:  terminator.movie.edu
Address:  192.249.249.3


Non-authoritative answer:
sri.com nameserver = NS.sri.com
sri.com nameserver = NS.CSL.sri.com
sri.com nameserver = TURTLE.MCC.COM
sri.com nameserver = NS1.sri.com
```

```
NS.sri.com        internet address = 128.18.30.66
NS.CSL.sri.com    internet address = 130.107.4.94
NS.CSL.sri.com    internet address = 192.12.33.94
TURTLE.MCC.COM    internet address = 128.62.1.215
NS1.sri.com       internet address = 128.18.30.65
> com.
Server: terminator.movie.edu
Address:  192.249.249.3

Non-authoritative answer:
com       nameserver = C.ROOT-SERVERS.NET
com       nameserver = D.ROOT-SERVERS.NET
com       nameserver = E.ROOT-SERVERS.NET
com       nameserver = I.ROOT-SERVERS.NET
com       nameserver = F.ROOT-SERVERS.NET
com       nameserver = G.ROOT-SERVERS.NET
com       nameserver = J.GTLD-SERVERS.INTERNIC.NET
com       nameserver = A.ROOT-SERVERS.NET
com       nameserver = H.ROOT-SERVERS.NET
com       nameserver = B.ROOT-SERVERS.NET

C.ROOT-SERVERS.NET        internet address = 192.33.4.12
D.ROOT-SERVERS.NET        internet address = 128.8.10.90
E.ROOT-SERVERS.NET        internet address = 192.203.230.10
I.ROOT-SERVERS.NET        internet address = 192.36.148.17
F.ROOT-SERVERS.NET        internet address = 192.5.5.241
G.ROOT-SERVERS.NET        internet address = 192.112.36.4
J.GTLD-SERVERS.INTERNIC.NET     internet address = 198.41.0.21
A.ROOT-SERVERS.NET        internet address = 198.41.0.4
H.ROOT-SERVERS.NET        internet address = 128.63.2.53
B.ROOT-SERVERS.NET        internet address = 128.9.0.107
```

Then you can check your host's connectivity to those servers. Odds are, *ping* won't have much better luck than your name server did. If it does, you should check that the remote name servers are really running.

```
% ping 128.18.30.66     --ping first sri.com name server
Pinging 128.18.30.66 with 32 bytes of data:

Request timed out.
Request timed out.
Request timed out.
Request timed out.
% ping 130.107.4.94      --ping second sri.com name server
Pinging 130.107.4.94 with 32 bytes of data:

Request timed out.
Request timed out.
Request timed out.
Request timed out.
```

Now all that's left to do is to locate the break in the network. Utilities like *tracert* can be very helpful in determining whether the problem is on your network, the destination network, or somewhere in the middle.

You should also use your own common sense when tracking down the break. If, for example, your *ping* testing showed that you couldn't reach any of the Internet's root name servers, it's not very likely that each root's local network went down, nor is it likely that the Internet's commercial backbone networks collapsed entirely. Occam's razor says that the simplest condition that could cause this behavior—namely, the loss of *your* network's link to the Internet—is the most likely cause.

## 11. Missing Subdomain Delegation

Even though the InterNIC does its best to process your requests as quickly as possible, it may take a week or two for your subdomain's delegation to appear in the root name servers. If the InterNIC doesn't manage your parent zone, your mileage may vary. Some parents are quick and responsible; others are slow and inconsistent. Just like in real life, though, you're stuck with them.*

Until your delegation data appear in your parent zone's name servers, your name servers will be able to look up data in the Internet domain name space, but no one else on the Internet (outside of your domain) will know how to look up data in *your* name space.

That means that even though you can send mail outside of your domain, the recipients won't be able to reply to it. Furthermore, no one will be able to *telnet* to, *ftp* to, or even *ping* your hosts by name.

Remember that this applies equally to any *in-addr.arpa* subdomains you may run. Until the parent delegates those subdomains to your servers, name servers on the Internet won't be able to reverse-map addresses on your networks.

To determine whether or not your zone's delegation has made it into your parent zone's name servers, query a parent name server for the NS records for your zone. If the parent name server has the data, any name server on the Internet can find it:

```
% nslookup
Default Server:  terminator.movie.edu
Address:  192.249.249.3

> server a.root-servers.net.      --Query a root name server
Default Server:  a.root-servers.net
Address:  198.41.0.4

> set norecurse                   --Instruct the server to answer out of
> set type=ns                     --its own data and to look for NS records
> 249.249.192.in-addr.arpa.       --for 249.249.192.in-addr.arpa
Server:  a.root-servers.net
```

---

* Until the "GTLD Memorandum of Understanding" is adopted, that is. See *http://www.gtld-mou.org/*.

```
Address:  198.41.0.4

*** a.root-servers.net can't find 249.249.192.in-addr.arpa.: Non-existent
domain
```

Here, the delegation clearly hasn't been added yet. You can either wait patiently, or if an unreasonable amount of time has passed since you requested delegation from your parent, contact your parent and ask what's up.

## 12. Incorrect Subdomain Delegation

Incorrect subdomain delegation is another familiar problem on the Internet. Keeping delegation up to date requires human intervention—informing your parent zone's administrator of changes to your set of authoritative name servers. Consequently, delegation information often becomes inaccurate as administrators make changes without letting their parents know. Far too many administrators believe that setting up delegation is a one-shot deal: they let their parents know which name servers are authoritative once, when they set up their zone, and then they never talk to them again. They don't even call on Mother's Day.

An administrator may add a new name server, decommission another, and change the IP address of a third, all without telling the parent zone's administrator. Gradually, the number of name servers correctly delegated to by the parent zone dwindles. In the best case, this leads to long resolution times, as querying name servers struggle to find an authoritative name server for the zone. If the delegation information becomes badly out of date, and the last authoritative name server host is brought down for maintenance, the information within the zone will be inaccessible.

If you suspect bad delegation, from your parent to your zone, from your zone to one of your children, or from a remote zone to one of its children, you can check with *nslookup*:

```
% nslookup
Default Server:  terminator.movie.edu
Address:  192.249.249.3

> server a.root-servers.net.   --Set server to the parent name
                               -- server you suspect has bad delegation
Default Server:  a.root-servers.net
Address:  198.41.0.4

> set type=ns       --Look for NS records
> hp.com.           --for the zone in question
Server:  a.root-servers.net
Address:  198.41.0.4

Non-authoritative answer:
hp.com          nameserver = RELAY.HP.COM
```

```
hp.com            nameserver = HPLABS.HPL.HP.COM
hp.com            nameserver = NNSC.NSF.NET
hp.com            nameserver = HPSDLO.SDD.HP.COM

Authoritative answers can be found from:
hp.com            nameserver = RELAY.HP.COM
hp.com            nameserver = HPLABS.HPL.HP.COM
hp.com            nameserver = NNSC.NSF.NET
hp.com            nameserver = HPSDLO.SDD.HP.COM
RELAY.HP.COM        internet address = 15.255.152.2
HPLABS.HPL.HP.COM      internet address = 15.255.176.47
NNSC.NSF.NET        internet address = 128.89.1.178
HPSDLO.SDD.HP.COM      internet address = 15.255.160.64
HPSDLO.SDD.HP.COM      internet address = 15.26.112.11
```

Let's say you suspect that the delegation to *hpsdlo.sdd.hp.com* is incorrect. You now query *hpsdlo* for data in the *hp.com* zone, and check the answer:

```
> server hpsdlo.sdd.hp.com.
Default Server:  hpsdlo.sdd.hp.com
Addresses:  15.255.160.64, 15.26.112.11

> set norecurse
> set type=soa
> hp.com.
Server:  hpsdlo.sdd.hp.com
Addresses:  15.255.160.64, 15.26.112.11

Non-authoritative answer:
hp.com
        origin = relay.hp.com
        mail addr = hostmaster.hp.com
        serial = 1001462
        refresh = 21600 (6 hours)
        retry   = 3600 (1 hour)
        expire  = 604800 (7 days)
        minimum ttl = 86400 (1 day)

Authoritative answers can be found from:
hp.com            nameserver = RELAY.HP.COM
hp.com            nameserver = HPLABS.HPL.HP.COM
hp.com            nameserver = NNSC.NSF.NET
RELAY.HP.COM        internet address = 15.255.152.2
HPLABS.HPL.HP.COM        internet address = 15.255.176.47
NNSC.NSF.NET        internet address = 128.89.1.178
```

If *hpsdlo* really were authoritative, it would have responded with an authoritative answer. The administrator of the *hp.com* zone can tell you whether *hpsdlo* should be an authoritative name server for *hp.com*, so that's who you should contact.

## 13. Default Domain Not Set

Failing to set your host's domain is another old standby gaffe. You set it in the **Network** Control Panel, as described in Chapter 6. The characteristics of an unset domain are straightforward: folks who use single-label names (or abbreviated domain names) in commands get no joy:

```
C\:>ftp br
br: Unknown host.
C\:>ftp br.fx
br.fx: Unknown host.
C\:>ftp br.fx.movie.edu
Connected to bladerunner.fx.movie.edu.
220 bladerunner.fx.movie.edu FTP server (Version wu-2.4.2-academ[BETA-13](2)
Wed Jul 9 00:0
9:24 EDT 1997) ready.
User (bladerunner.fx.movie.edu:(none)):
```

You can use *nslookup* to check this one, much as you do when you suspect a syntax error in *resolv.conf*:

```
% nslookup
Default Server:  terminator.movie.edu
Address:  192.249.249.3

> set all
Default Server:  terminator.movie.edu
Address:  192.249.249.3

Set options:
  nodebug         defname        search          recurse
  nod2            novc           noignoretc      port=53
  querytype=A     class=IN       timeout=5       retry=4
  root=ns.nic.ddn.mil.
  domain=
  srchlist=
```

Notice that neither the domain \\*CW* (**domain=**) nor the searchlist \\*CW* (**srchlist=**) is set.

## Interoperability Problems

With the relatively recent introductions of the Microsoft DNS Server and BIND version 8, more interoperability problems are cropping up between name servers. Since you're running the Microsoft DNS Server—the "new kid on the block," if you will—you should be aware of these pitfalls because you'll quite likely run afoul of at least one of them.

## Zone Transfer Fails Because of Proprietary WINS Record

When a Microsoft Windows DNS Server is configured to consult a WINS server for names it can't find in a given zone, it inserts a special record into the zone data file. The record looks like this:

```
@       IN  WINS     <IP address of WINS server>
```

Unfortunately, WINS is not a standard record type in the IN class. Consequently, if there are BIND slaves that transfer this zone, they'll choke on the WINS record and refuse to load the zone. Here's the message the administrator of the BIND server would see in his syslog output:

```
May 23 15:58:43 terminator named-xfer[386]: "fx.movie.edu IN 65281" - unknown
type (65281)
```

The workaround for this is to configure the Microsoft DNS Server to filter out the proprietary record before transferring the zone. You do this by selecting the zone in the left pane of DNS Manager, right-clicking it, and selecting **Properties**. Click on the **WINS Lookup** tab in the resulting **Zone Properties** window, which is shown in Figure 12-5.

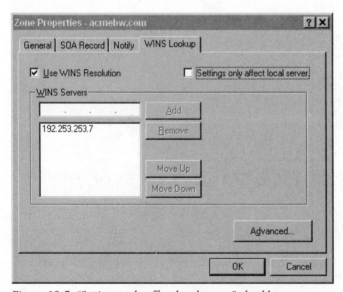

*Figure 12-5. "Settings only affect local server" checkbox*

Checking **Settings only affect local server** will filter out the WINS record for that zone. However, any Microsoft DNS Server slaves won't see the record, even though they could use it.

# Problem Symptoms

Some problems, unfortunately, aren't as easy to identify as the ones we listed. You'll experience some misbehavior but won't be able to attribute it directly to its cause, often because any of a number of problems may cause the symptoms you see. For cases like this, we'll suggest some of the common causes of these symptoms and ways to isolate them.

## Local Name Can't Be Looked Up

The first thing to do when a program like *telnet* or *ftp* can't look up a local name is to use *nslookup* to try to look up the same name. When we say "the same name," we mean *literally* the same name—don't add a domain name and a trailing dot if the user didn't type either one. Don't query a different name server than the user did.

As often as not, the user mistyped the name or doesn't understand how the search list works, and just needs direction. Occasionally, you'll turn up real host configuration errors:

- A mistake in the resolver configuration, like the wrong IP address for a name server
- An unset default domain (problem 13 in the "Potential Problem List" mentioned earlier in this chapter)

You can check for either of these using *nslookup*'s *set all* command.

If *nslookup* points to a problem with the name server, rather than with the host configuration, check for the problems associated with the type of name server. If the name server is the primary master for the zone, but it doesn't respond with data you think it should:

- Check that the zone or zone data file contains the data in question.
- Check the pertinent zone data file for syntax errors (problem 2).
- Ensure that the domain names in the records are correct (problem 9).

If the name server is a slave server, you should first check whether or not its master has the correct data. If it does, and the slave doesn't:

- Make sure you've incremented the serial number on the primary (problem 4).
- Look for a problem on the slave in updating the zone (problem 7).

If the primary *doesn't* have the correct data, of course, diagnose the problem on the primary.

If the problem server isn't authoritative for the zone that contains the data, check that your parent zone's delegation to your zone exists and is correct (problems 9 and 10). Remember that to that name server, your zone looks just like any other remote zone. Even though the host it runs on may be inside your zone, the name server must be able to locate an authoritative server for your zone from your parent zone's servers.

## Remote Names Can't Be Looked Up

If your local lookups succeed, but you can't look up names outside your local zones, there is a different set of problems to check:

- Can you *ping* the remote zone's name servers? Maybe you can't reach the remote zone's servers because of connectivity loss (problem 10).

- Is the remote zone new? Maybe its delegation hasn't yet appeared (problem 11). Or the delegation information for the remote zone may be wrong or out of date, due to neglect (problem 12).

- Does the domain name actually exist on the remote zone's servers? On all of them (problems 4, 5, and 7)?

## Wrong or Inconsistent Answer

If you get the wrong answer when looking up a local name or an inconsistent answer, depending on which name server you ask or when you ask, first check the synchronization between your name servers:

- Are they all holding the same serial number for the zone? Did you forget to increment the serial number on the primary after you made a manual change (problem 4)? If you did, the name servers may all have the same serial number, but they will answer differently out of their authoritative data.

- Did you forget to restart the primary after making a manual change (problem 5)? Then the primary will return (via *nslookup*, for example) a different serial number than the serial number in the zone data file.

- Are the slaves having trouble updating from the primary (problem 7)?

- Is the name server's round robin feature rotating the addresses of the domain name you're looking up?

If you get these results when looking up a name in a remote zone, you should check whether the remote zone's name servers have lost synchronization. You can use tools like *nslookup* to determine whether the remote zone's administrator has forgotten to increment the serial number, for example. If the name servers answer differently from their authoritative data but show the same serial number, the serial number probably wasn't incremented. If the primary's serial number is much lower than the slaves', the primary's serial number was probably accidentally reset. We usually assume a zone's primary name server is running on the host listed as the origin in the SOA record.

You probably can't determine conclusively that the primary hasn't been signaled, though. It's also difficult to pin down updating problems between remote name servers. In cases like this, if you've determined that the remote name servers are giving out incorrect data, contact the zone administrator and (gently) relay what you've found. This will help the administrator track down the problem on the remote end.

## *Lookups Take a Long Time*

Long name resolution is usually due to one of two problems:

* Connectivity loss (problem 8), which you can diagnose with tools like *ping* and *tracert*

* Incorrect delegation information (problem 12), which points to the wrong name servers or the wrong IP addresses

Usually, sending a few *ping*s will point to one or the other. Either you can't reach the name servers at all, or you can reach the hosts, but the name servers aren't responding.

Sometimes, though, the results are inconclusive. For example, the parent name servers delegate to a set of name servers that don't respond to *ping*s or queries, but connectivity to the remote network seems all right (a *tracert*, for example, will get you to the remote network's "doorstep"—the last router between you and the host). Is the delegation information so badly out of date that the name servers have long since moved to other addresses? Are the hosts simply down? Or is there really a remote network problem? Usually, finding out will require a call or a message to the administrator of the remote zone. (And remember, *whois* gives you phone numbers!)

That's about all we can think to cover. It's certainly less than a comprehensive list, but we hope it'll help you solve the more common problems you encounter with DNS and give you ideas about how to approach the rest. Boy, if we'd only had a troubleshooting guide when *we* started!

# 13

## Miscellaneous

*"The time has come," the Walrus said,*
*"To talk of many things:*
*Of shoes—and ships—and sealing-wax—*
*Of cabbages—and kings—*
*And why the sea is boiling hot—*
*And whether pigs have wings."*

It's time we tied up loose ends. We've already covered the mainstream of DNS, but we haven't explored a handful of interesting niches. Some of these may actually be useful, like instructions on how to set up DNS on a network without Internet connectivity; others may just be interesting. We can't in good conscience send you out into the world without completing your education!

## Using CNAME Records

We talked about CNAME resource records in Chapter 4, *Setting Up the Microsoft DNS Server.* We didn't tell you all about CNAME records, though; we saved that for this chapter. When you set up your first name servers, you didn't care about the subtle nuances of the magical CNAME record. Maybe you didn't realize there was more to it than we explained; maybe you didn't care. Some of this trivia is interesting, some is arcane. We'll let you decide which is which.

### CNAMEs Attached to Interior Nodes

If you've ever renamed your zone because of a company reorganization, you may have considered creating a single CNAME record that pointed from the zone's old domain name to the new domain name. For instance, if the *fx.movie.edu* zone were renamed to *magic.movie.edu*, we'd be tempted to create a single CNAME record to map all the old names to the new names:

```
fx.movie.edu.  IN  CNAME  magic.movie.edu.
```

With this in place, you'd expect a lookup of *empire.fx.movie.edu* to result in a lookup of *empire.magic.movie.edu.* Unfortunately, this doesn't work—you *can't*

246

have a CNAME record attached to an interior node like *fx.movie.edu* if it owns other records. Remember that *fx.movie.edu* has an SOA record and NS records, so attaching a CNAME record to it violates the rule that a domain name be either an alias or a canonical name, not both. So, instead of a single CNAME record to rename a complete zone, you'll have to do it the old-fashioned way—a CNAME record for each individual host within the zone:

```
empire.fx.movie.edu.        IN  CNAME  empire.magic.movie.edu.
bladerunner.fx.movie.edu.   IN  CNAME  bladerunner.magic.movie.edu.
```

If the subdomain isn't delegated, and consequently doesn't have an SOA record and NS records attached, you can create an alias for *fx.movie.edu,* but it will apply only to the domain name *fx.movie.edu,* and not to domain names in *fx.movie.edu.*

Hopefully, the tool you use to manage your DNS database files will handle creating CNAME records for you.

## CNAMEs Pointing to CNAMEs

You may have wondered whether it was possible to have an alias (CNAME record) pointing to another alias. This might be useful in situations where an alias points from a domain name outside of your zone to a domain name inside your zone. You may not have any control over the alias outside of your zone. What if you want to change the domain name it points to? Can you simply add another CNAME record?

The answer is yes: you can chain together CNAME records. The Microsoft DNS Server supports it, and the RFCs don't expressly forbid it. But, while you *can* chain CNAME records, is it a wise thing to do? The RFCs recommend against it, because of the possibility of creating a CNAME loop, and because it slows resolution. You may be able to do it in a pinch, but you probably won't find much sympathy on the Net if something breaks.

## CNAMEs in the Resource Record Data

For any other record besides a CNAME record, you must have the canonical domain name in the resource record data. Applications and name servers won't operate correctly otherwise. As we mentioned back in Chapter 5, *DNS and Electronic Mail*, for example, many mailers only recognize the canonical name of the local host on the right side of an MX record. If a mailer doesn't recognize the local host name, it won't strip out the right MX records when paring down the MX list and may deliver mail to itself or less-preferred hosts, causing mail to loop.

## Looking Up CNAMEs

At times you may want to look up a CNAME record itself, not data for the canonical name. With *nslookup*, this is easy to do. You can set the query type either to *cname* or to *any* and then look up the name.

```
% nslookup
Default Server:  wormhole
Address:  0.0.0.0

> set query=cname
> bigt
Server:  wormhole
Address:  0.0.0.0

bigt.movie.edu  canonical name = terminator.movie.edu
> set query=any
> bigt
Server:  wormhole
Address:  0.0.0.0

bigt.movie.edu  canonical name = terminator.movie.edu
```

## Finding Out a Host's Aliases

One thing you can't easily do with DNS is find out a host's aliases. With the host table, it's easy to find both the canonical name of a host and any aliases. No matter which you look up; they're all there, together, on the same line, as shown in the following excerpt from *HOSTS*:

```
192.249.249.3  terminator.movie.edu terminator bigt
```

With DNS, however, if you look up the canonical name, all you get is the canonical name. There's no easy way for the name server or the application to know whether aliases exist for that canonical name.

```
% nslookup
Default Server:  wormhole
Address:  0.0.0.0

> terminator
Server:  wormhole
Address:  0.0.0.0

Name:    terminator.movie.edu
Address:  192.249.249.3
```

If you use *nslookup* to look up an alias, you'll see that alias and the canonical name. *nslookup* reports both the alias and the canonical name in the packet. But you won't see any other aliases that might point to that canonical name.

```
% nslookup
Default Server:  wormhole
Address:  0.0.0.0

> bigt
Server:  wormhole
Address:  0.0.0.0

Name:     terminator.movie.edu
Address:  192.249.249.3
Aliases:  bigt.movie.edu
```

About the only way to find out all the CNAMEs for a host is to transfer the whole zone and pick out the CNAME records where that host is the canonical name. You can have *nslookup* filter on CNAME records:

```
% nslookup
Default Server:  wormhole
Address:  0.0.0.0

> ls -t cname movie.edu
[wormhole]
 bigt                      terminator.movie.edu
 wh                        wormhole.movie.edu
 dh                        diehard.movie.edu
```

Even this method will only show you the aliases within that zone—there could be aliases in a different zone, pointing to canonical names in this zone.

# Wildcards

Something else we haven't covered yet is DNS *wildcards*. At times you want a single resource record to cover any possible name, rather than creating zillions of resource records that are all the same except for the domain name to which they apply. DNS reserves a special character, the asterisk (*), to be used in a DNS database file as a wildcard name. It will match any number of labels in a name, as long as there isn't an exact match with a name already in the DNS database.

Most often, you'd use wildcards to forward mail to non-Internet-connected networks. Suppose your site is not connected to the Internet, but you have a host that will relay mail between the Internet and your network. You could add a wildcard MX record to the *movie.edu* zone for Internet consumption that points all your mail to the relay. Here is an example:

```
*.movie.edu.  IN  MX  10 movie-relay.nea.gov.
```

Since the wildcard matches one or more labels, this resource record would apply to names like *terminator.movie.edu*, *empire.fx.movie.edu*, or *casablanca.bogart.classics.movie.edu*. The danger with wildcards is that they clash with search lists. This wildcard also matches *cujo.movie.edu.movie.edu*, making wildcards dangerous to use in your internal zone data. Remember that some mailers apply the search list when looking up MX records:

```
% nslookup
Default Server: wormhole
Address: 0.0.0.0

> set type=mx        --Look up MX records
> cujo.movie.edu     --for cujo
Server: wormhole
Address: 0.0.0.0

cujo.movie.edu.movie.edu      --This isn't a real host's name!
        preference = 10, mail exchanger = movie-relay.nea.gov
```

What are the limitations of wildcards? Wildcards do not match names for which there is already data. Suppose you *did* use wildcards within your zone data:

```
*.movie.edu.    IN   MX   10 mail-hub.movie.edu.
et.movie.edu.   IN   MX   10 et.movie.edu.
jaws.movie.edu  IN   A    192.253.253.113
```

Mail to *terminator.movie.edu* will be sent to *mail-hub*, but mail to *et.movie.edu* will be sent directly to *et.* An MX lookup of *jaws.movie.edu* would result in a response that said there was no MX data for that name. The wildcard doesn't apply because an A record exists. Can you use wildcards safely within your zone data? Yes. We'll cover that case a little later in this chapter.

# A Limitation of MX Records

While we are on the topic of MX records, let's talk about how they can result in mail taking a longer path than necessary. The MX records are a list of data returned when a name is looked up. The list is not ordered according to which exchanger is closest to the sender. Here is an example of this problem. Your non-Internet-connected network has two hosts capable of relaying Internet mail to your network. One host is in the U.S., and one host is in France. Your network is in Greece. Most of your mail comes from the U.S., so you have someone maintain your zone and install two wildcard MX records—the highest preference to the U.S. relay, and a lower preference to the France relay. Since the U.S. relay is at a higher preference, *all* mail will go through that relay (as long as it is reachable). If someone in France sends you a letter, it will travel across the Atlantic to the U.S. and back, because there is nothing in the MX list to indicate that the French relay is closer to that sender.

# DNS and Internet Firewalls

The Domain Name System wasn't designed to work with Internet firewalls. It's a testimony to the flexibility of DNS that you can configure DNS to work with, or even through, an Internet firewall.

That said, configuring a DNS server to work in a firewalled environment, although not difficult, requires a complete understanding of DNS. Describing it also requires a large portion of this chapter, so here's a road map.

We start by describing the two major families of Internet firewall software—packet filters and application gateways. The capabilities of each family have a bearing on how you'll need to configure your DNS servers to work through the firewall. The next section details the two most common DNS architectures used with firewalls, forwarders and internal roots, and describes the advantages and disadvantages of each. Finally, we discuss shadow name spaces and the configuration of the bastion host, the host at the core of your Internet firewall system.

## Types of Firewall Software

Before you start configuring your DNS servers to work with your firewall, it's important you understand what your firewall is capable of. Your firewall's capabilities may influence your choice of DNS architecture and will determine how you implement it. If you don't know the answers to the questions in this section, track down someone in your organization who does know, and ask. Better yet, work with your firewall's administrator when designing your architecture to ensure it will coexist with the firewall.

Note that this explanation of Internet firewalls is far from complete. These few paragraphs only describe the two most common types of Internet firewalls, and only in enough detail to show how the differences in their capabilities impact name servers. For a comprehensive treatment of Internet firewalls, see Brent Chapman and Elizabeth Zwicky's *Building Internet Firewalls.*[*]

### Packet filters

The first type of firewall we'll cover is the packet-filtering firewall. Packet-filtering firewalls operate largely at the transport and network levels of the TCP/IP stack (layers three and four of the OSI reference model, if you dig that). They decide whether to route a packet based upon packet-level criteria like the transport protocol (that is, whether it's TCP or UDP), the source and destination IP address, and the destination port (see Figure 13-1).

---

[*] O'Reilly & Associates, November 1995.

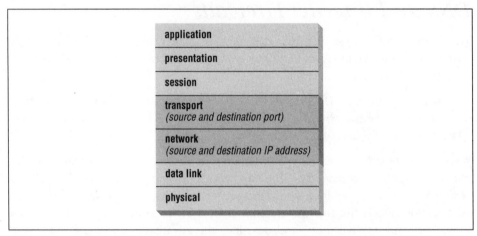

*Figure 13-1. Packet filters operate at the network and transport layers of the stack*

What's most important to us about packet-filtering firewalls is that you can typically configure them to allow DNS traffic selectively between hosts on the Internet and your internal hosts. That is, you can let an arbitrary set of internal hosts communicate with Internet name servers. Some packet-filtering firewalls can even permit your name servers to query name servers on the Internet, but not vice versa. All router-based Internet firewalls are packet-filtering firewalls. Checkpoint's Fire-Wall-1, Cisco's PIX, and Sun's SunScreen are popular commercial packet-filtering firewalls.

### Application gateways

Application gateways operate at the application protocol level, several layers higher in the OSI reference model than most packet filters (Figure 13-2). In a sense, they "understand" the application protocol in the same way a server for that particular application would. An FTP application gateway, for example, can make the decision to allow or deny a particular FTP operation, like a RETR (a *get*) or a STOR (a *put*).

The bad news, and what's important for our purposes, is that most application gateway firewalls handle only TCP-based application protocols. DNS, of course, is largely UDP-based, and we know of no application gateways for DNS. This implies that, if you run an application gateway firewall, your internal hosts will likely not be able to communicate directly with name servers on the Internet.

The popular Firewall Toolkit from Trusted Information Systems (TIS) is a suite of application gateways for common Internet protocols like Telnet, FTP, and HTTP. TIS's Gauntlet product is also based on application gateways, as is Raptor's Eagle Firewall.

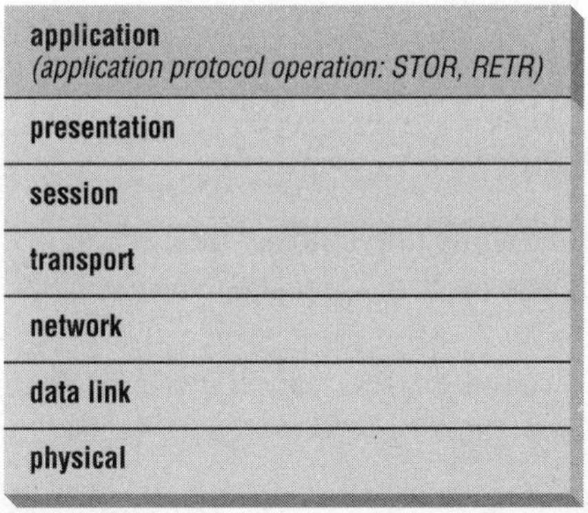

| application |
| (application protocol operation: STOR, RETR) |
| presentation |
| session |
| transport |
| network |
| data link |
| physical |

*Figure 13-2. Application gateways operate at the application layer of the stack*

Note that these two categories of firewall are really just generalizations. The state of the art in firewalls changes very quickly, and by the time you read this, you may have a firewall that includes an application gateway for DNS. Which family your firewall falls into is important only because it *suggests* what that firewall is capable of; what's more important is whether your particular firewall will let you permit DNS traffic between arbitrary internal hosts and the Internet.

## A Bad Example

The simplest configuration is to allow DNS traffic to pass freely through your firewall (assuming you can configure your firewall to do that). That way, any internal name server can query any name server on the Internet, and any Internet name server can query any of your internal name servers. You don't need any special configuration.

Unfortunately, this is a really bad idea, for a number of reasons:

*Version control*

> The developers of the Microsoft DNS Server are constantly finding and fixing security-related bugs in the code. Consequently, it's important to run the latest released version of the server, especially on name servers that are directly exposed to the Internet. If one or just a few of your name servers communicate directly with name servers on the Internet, upgrading to a new version is easy. If any of the name servers on your network can, it's another story.

*Possible vector for attack*

> Even if you're not running a name server on a particular host, a hacker might be able to take advantage of the fact that you allow DNS traffic through your firewall to attack that host. For example, a co-conspirator working on the

inside could set up a Telnet server listening on the host's DNS port, allowing the hacker to *telnet* right in.

For the rest of this chapter, we'll try to set a good example.

## Internet Forwarders

Given the dangers of allowing unrestricted bidirectional DNS traffic through the firewall, most organizations elect to limit the internal hosts that can "talk DNS" to the Internet. In an application gateway firewall, or any firewall without the ability to pass DNS traffic, the only host that can communicate with Internet name servers is the bastion host (see Figure 13-3).

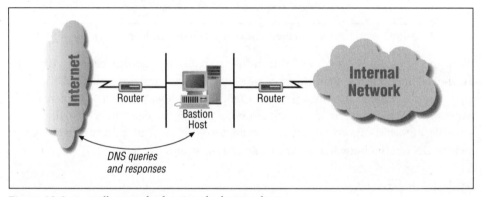

*Figure 13-3. A small network, showing the bastion host*

In a packet-filtering firewall, the firewall's administrator can configure the firewall to let any set of internal name servers communicate with Internet name servers. This is often a small set of hosts that run name servers under the direct control of the domain administrator, as depicted in Figure 13-4.

Servers that can directly query name servers on the Internet don't require any special configuration. Their root hints files contain the Internet's root name servers, which enables them to resolve Internet domain names. Internal name servers that can't query name servers on the Internet, however, need to know to forward queries they can't resolve to one of the name servers that can. This is done with the **Forwarders** tab on the server's **Properties** window, introduced in Chapter 10, *Advanced Features and Security*.

At Movie U., we put in a firewall to protect ourselves from the Big Bad Internet several years ago. Ours is a packet-filtering firewall, and we negotiated with our firewall administrator to allow DNS traffic between Internet name servers and two of our name servers, *terminator.movie.edu* and *wormhole.movie.edu*. Figure 13-5 shows how we configured the other internal name servers at the university.

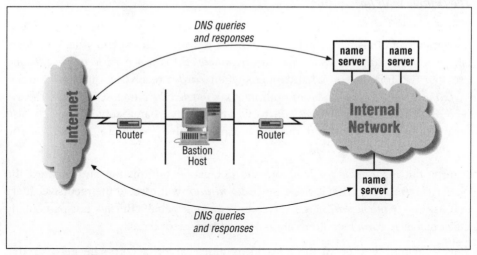

Figure 13-4. A small network, showing select internal name servers

Figure 13-5. The Forwarders tab

(We vary the order in which the forwarders appear from server to server to help spread the load between them.)

When an internal name server receives a query for a name it can't resolve locally, like an Internet domain name, it forwards that query to one of our forwarders, which can resolve the name using name servers on the Internet. Simple!

*The trouble with forwarding*

Unfortunately, it's a little too simple. Forwarding starts to get in the way once you implement subdomains or build an extensive network. To explain what we mean, take a look at *zardoz.movie.edu*. *zardoz.movie.edu* is a slave for *movie.edu* and uses our two forwarders. What happens when *zardoz* receives a query for a name in *fx.movie.edu*? *zardoz*, as an authoritative *movie.edu* name server, has the NS records that delegate *fx.movie.edu* to its authoritative name servers. But it's also been configured to forward queries it can't resolve locally to *terminator* and *wormhole*. Which will it do?

It turns out that *zardoz* will ignore the delegation information and forward the query to *terminator*. That'll work, since *terminator* will receive the recursive query and ask an *fx.movie.edu* name server on *zardoz*'s behalf. But it's not particularly efficient, since *zardoz* could easily have sent the query directly.

Now imagine the scale of the network is much larger: a corporate network that spans continents, with tens of thousands of hosts and hundreds or thousands of name servers. All of the internal name servers that don't have direct Internet connectivity—the vast majority of them—use a small set of forwarders. What are the problems with this picture?

*Single point of failure*

> If the forwarders fail, your name servers lose the ability to resolve both Internet domain names and internal domain names that they don't have cached or aren't in authoritative data.

*Concentration of load*

> The forwarders will have an enormous query load placed on them. This is both because of the large number of internal name servers that use them and because the queries are recursive and require a good deal of work to answer.

*Inefficient resolution*

> Imagine two internal name servers, authoritative for *west.acmebw.com* and *east.acmebw.com*, respectively, both on the same network segment in Boulder, Colorado. Both are configured to use the company's forwarder in Bethesda, Maryland. For the *west.acmebw.com* name server to resolve a name in *east.acmebw.com*, it sends a query to the forwarder in Bethesda. The forwarder in Bethesda then sends a query back to Boulder to the *east.acmebw.com* name server, the original querier's neighbor. The *east.acmebw.com* name server replies by sending a response back to Bethesda, which the forwarder sends back to Boulder.
>
> In a traditional configuration with root name servers, the *west.acmebw.com* name server would quickly have learned that an *east.acmebw.com* name

server was next door and would favor it (because of its low round-trip time). Using forwarders "short-circuits" the normally efficient resolution process.

Th upshot is that forwarding is fine for small networks and simple name spaces, but probably inadequate for large networks and complex name spaces. We found this out the hard way at Movie U. as our network grew, and we were forced to implement internal roots.

## Internal Roots

If you want to avoid the scalability problems of forwarding, you can set up your own root name servers. These internal roots will serve only the name servers in your organization. They'll only know about the portions of the name space relevant to your organization.

What good are they? By using an architecture based on root name servers, you gain the scalability of the Internet's name space (which should be good enough for most companies), plus redundancy, distributed load, and efficient resolution. You can have as many internal roots as the Internet has roots—13 or so—whereas having that many forwarders may be an undue security exposure and a configuration burden. Most of all, the internal roots don't get used frivolously. Name servers need to consult an internal root only when they time out the NS records for your top-level zones. Using forwarders, name servers may have to query a forwarder once *per resolution.*

The moral of our story is that if you have, or intend to have, a large name space and lots of internal name servers, internal root name servers will scale better than any other solution.

### Where to put internal root name servers

Since name servers "lock on" to the closest root name server by favoring the one with the lowest round-trip time, it pays to pepper your network with internal root name servers. If your organization's network spans the U.S., Europe, and the Pacific Rim, consider locating at least one internal root name server on each continent. If you have three major sites in Europe, give each of them an internal root.

### Forward mapping delegation

Here's how an internal root name server is configured. An internal root delegates directly to any zones you administer. For example, on the *movie.edu* network, the root zone's data file would contain:

```
movie.edu.  86400  IN  NS  terminator.movie.edu.
            86400  IN  NS  wormhole.movie.edu.
            86400  IN  NS  zardoz.movie.edu.
```

```
terminator.movie.edu.   86400   IN   A   192.249.249.3
wormhole.movie.edu.     86400   IN   A   192.249.249.1
                        86400   IN   A   192.253.253.1
zardoz.movie.edu.       86400   IN   A   192.249.249.9
                        86400   IN   A   192.253.253.9
```

On the Internet, this information would appear in the *edu* name servers' databases. On the *movie.edu* network, of course, there aren't any *edu* name servers, so you delegate directly to *movie.edu* from the root.

Notice that this doesn't contain delegation to *fx.movie.edu* or any other subdomain of *movie.edu*. The *movie.edu* name servers know which name servers are authoritative for all *movie.edu* subdomains, and all queries for information in those subdomains will pass through the *movie.edu* name servers, so there's no need to delegate them here.

### in-addr.arpa delegation

We also need to delegate from the internal roots to the *in-addr.arpa* zones that correspond to the networks *movie.edu* uses:

```
249.249.192.in-addr.arpa.   86400   IN   NS   terminator.movie.edu.
                            86400   IN   NS   wormhole.movie.edu.
                            86400   IN   NS   zardoz.movie.edu.
253.253.192.in-addr.arpa.   86400   IN   NS   terminator.movie.edu.
                            86400   IN   NS   wormhole.movie.edu.
                            86400   IN   NS   zardoz.movie.edu.
254.253.192.in-addr.arpa.   86400   IN   NS   bladerunner.fx.movie.edu.
                            86400   IN   NS   outland.fx.movie.edu.
                            86400   IN   NS   alien.fx.movie.edu.
20.254.192.in-addr.arpa.    86400   IN   NS   bladerunner.fx.movie.edu.
                            86400   IN   NS   outland.fx.movie.edu.
                            86400   IN   NS   alien.fx.movie.edu.
```

Notice that we *did* include delegation for the *254.253.192.in-addr.arpa* and *20.254.192.in-addr.arpa* zones, even though they correspond to the *fx.movie.edu* zone. We didn't need to delegate to *fx.movie.edu*, because we'd already delegated to its parent. The *movie.edu* name servers delegate to *fx.movie.edu*, so by transitivity the roots delegate to *fx.movie.edu*. Since neither of the other *in-addr.arpa* zones is a parent of *254.253.192.in-addr.arpa* or *20.254.192.in-addr.arpa*, we needed to delegate both zones from the root. As we've covered earlier, we don't need to add address records for the three Special Effects name servers, *bladerunner, outland,* and *alien,* because a remote name server can already find their addresses by following delegation from *movie.edu*.

### The root.dns file

All that's left is to add an SOA record for the root zone and NS records for this internal root name server and any others:

```
.  IN  SOA  rainman.movie.edu.  hostmaster.movie.edu.  (
            1        ; serial
            86400    ; refresh
            3600     ; retry
            608400   ; expire
            86400 )  ; minimum

   IN  NS  rainman.movie.edu.
   IN  NS  awakenings.movie.edu.

rainman.movie.edu.    86400  IN  A  192.249.249.254
awakenings.movie.edu. 86400  IN  A  192.253.253.254
```

*rainman.movie.edu* and *awakenings.movie.edu* are the hosts running internal root name servers. We shouldn't run an internal root on a bastion host, because if a name server on the Internet accidentally queries it for data it's not authoritative for, the internal root will respond with its list of roots—all internal!

So the whole *root.dns* file (by convention, we call the root zone's data file *root.dns*) looks like:

```
.  IN  SOA  rainman.movie.edu.  hostmaster.movie.edu.  (
            1        ; serial
            86400    ; refresh
            3600     ; retry
            608400   ; expire
            86400 )  ; minimum

   IN  NS  rainman.movie.edu.
   IN  NS  awakenings.movie.edu.

rainman.movie.edu.    604800  IN  A  192.249.249.254
awakenings.movie.edu. 604800  IN  A  192.253.253.254

movie.edu.  86400  IN  NS  terminator.movie.edu.
            86400  IN  NS  wormhole.movie.edu.
            86400  IN  NS  zardoz.movie.edu.

terminator.movie.edu.  86400  IN  A  192.249.249.3
wormhole.movie.edu.    86400  IN  A  192.249.249.1
                       86400  IN  A  192.253.253.1
zardoz.movie.edu.      86400  IN  A  192.249.249.9
                       86400  IN  A  192.253.253.9

249.249.192.in-addr.arpa.  86400  IN  NS  terminator.movie.edu.
                           86400  IN  NS  wormhole.movie.edu.
                           86400  IN  NS  zardoz.movie.edu.
```

```
253.253.192.in-addr.arpa.   86400   IN   NS   terminator.movie.edu.
                            86400   IN   NS   wormhole.movie.edu.
                            86400   IN   NS   zardoz.movie.edu.
254.253.192.in-addr.arpa.   86400   IN   NS   bladerunner.fx.movie.edu.
                            86400   IN   NS   outland.fx.movie.edu.
                            86400   IN   NS   alien.fx.movie.edu.
20.254.192.in-addr.arpa.    86400   IN   NS   bladerunner.fx.movie.edu.
                            86400   IN   NS   outland.fx.movie.edu.
                            86400   IN   NS   alien.fx.movie.edu.
```

Creating the root zone with DNS Manager on both of the internal root name servers, *rainman* and *awakenings,* is just like creating any primary zone: right-click on the server's IP address in the left pane, choose **New Zone**, then click the **Primary** radio button and **Next**. For the zone's domain name, choose . (a single dot). Don't use the default zone filename, *..dns*, which could cause problems with the operating system; select the field, and type **root.dns**.

Immediately after you add the root zone, DNS Manager will show both a root zone and the cache icon. This is a little confusing, because a root name server doesn't need root hints: it can find that information in *root.dns*. Don't worry: if you quit and restart DNS Manager, the Cache icon will have disappeared.

You can also create slave root zones with DNS Manager. Unfortunately, after adding the slave root zone, the server often has a funky mix of root hints information and root information. Stopping and starting the DNS server will fix this.

If you don't have a lot of idle hosts sitting around that you can turn into internal roots, don't despair! Any internal name server (that is, one that's not running on a bastion host or outside your firewall) can serve double duty as an internal root *and* as an authoritative name server for whatever other zones you need it to load. Remember, a single name server can be authoritative for many, many zones, including the root.

### Configuring other internal name servers

Once you've set up internal root name servers, configure all your name servers on hosts anywhere on your internal network to use them. Any name server running on a host without direct Internet connectivity should list the internal roots in its hints file:

```
; Internal cache.dns file, for movie.edu hosts without direct
; Internet connectivity
;
; Don't use this cache file on a host with Internet connectivity!
;

.  99999999  IN  NS  rainman.movie.edu.
   99999999  IN  NS  awakenings.movie.edu.
```

```
rainman.movie.edu.      99999999  IN  A  192.249.249.254
awakenings.movie.edu.   99999999  IN  A  192.253.253.254
```

Name servers running on hosts using this cache file will be able to resolve names in *movie.edu* and in Movie U.'s *in-addr.arpa* domains, but not outside of those domains.

### How internal name servers use internal roots

To tie together how this whole scheme works, let's go through an example of name resolution on an internal caching-only name server using these internal root name servers. First, the internal name server receives a query for a domain name in *movie.edu,* say the address of *gump.fx.movie.edu.* If the internal name server doesn't have any "better" information cached, it starts by querying an internal root name server. If it has communicated with the internal roots before, it has a round-trip time associated with each, which tells it which of the internal roots is responding to it most quickly. It sends a *nonrecursive* query to that internal root for *gump.fx.movie.edu*'s address. The internal root answers with a referral to the *movie.edu* name servers on *terminator.movie.edu, wormhole.movie.edu,* and *zardoz.movie.edu.* The caching-only name server follows up by sending another non-recursive query to one of the *movie.edu* name servers for *gump*'s address. The *movie.edu* name server responds with a referral to the *fx.movie.edu* name servers. The caching-only name server sends the same nonrecursive query for *gump*'s address to one of the *fx.movie.edu* name servers and finally receives a response.

Contrast this with the way a forwarding setup would have worked. Let's imagine that instead of using internal root name servers, our caching-only name server were configured to forward queries to first *terminator* and then *wormhole.* In that case, the caching-only name server would have checked its cache for the address of *gump.fx.movie.edu* and, not finding it, would have forwarded the query to *terminator. terminator* would have queried an *fx.movie.edu* name server on the caching-only name server's behalf and returned the answer. Should the caching-only name server need to look up another name in *fx.movie.edu,* it would still ask the forwarder, even though the forwarder's response to the query for *gump.fx.movie.edu*'s address may have contained the names and addresses of the *fx.movie.edu* name servers.

### Mail from internal hosts to the Internet

But wait! That's not all internal roots will do for you. We talked about getting mail to the Internet without changing the configuration of mailers all over the network.

Wildcard records are the key to getting mail to work—specifically, wildcard MX records. Let's say we'd like mail to the Internet to be forwarded through *postmanrings2x.movie.edu*, the Movie U. bastion host, which has direct Internet connectivity. Then adding these records to *db.root*:

```
*        IN    MX    5 postmanrings2x.movie.edu.
*.edu.   IN    MX    10 postmanrings2x.movie.edu.
```

will get the job done. We need the *.edu* MX record in addition to the * record because of the DNS wildcard production rules we described in the section "Wildcards," earlier in this chapter. Since there are explicit data for *movie.edu* in the zone, the first wildcard won't match *movie.edu* or any other subdomains of *edu*. We need another, explicit wildcard record for *edu* to match these domains.

Now mailers on our internal *movie.edu* hosts will send mail addressed to Internet domains to *postmanrings2x* for forwarding. For example, mail addressed to *nic.ddn.mil* will match the first wildcard MX record:

```
% nslookup -type=mx nic.ddn.mil.   --Matches the MX record for *
Server:  rainman.movie.edu
Address: 192.249.249.19

nic.ddn.mil
     preference = 5, mail exchanger = postmanrings2x.movie.edu
postmanrings2x.movie.edu     internet address = 192.249.249.20
```

while mail addressed to *vangogh.cs.berkeley.edu* will match the second MX record:

```
% nslookup -type=mx vangogh.cs.berkeley.edu.   --Matches the MX record for *.edu
Server:  rainman.movie.edu
Address: 192.249.249.19

vangogh.cs.berkeley.edu
     preference = 10, mail exchanger = postmanrings2x.movie.edu
postmanrings2x.movie.edu     internet address = 192.249.249.20
```

Once the mail reaches *postmanrings2x*, our bastion host, *postmanrings2x*'s mailer will look up the MX records for these addresses itself. Since *postmanrings2x* will resolve the name using the Internet's name space instead of the internal name space, it will find the real MX records for the destination domain and deliver the mail. No changes to the mailer's configuration are necessary.

### Mail to specific Internet domains

Another nice perk of this internal root scheme is that it gives you the ability to forward mail addressed to certain Internet domains through particular bastion hosts, if you have more than one. We can choose, for example, to send all mail addressed to *uk* domain recipients to our bastion host in London first and then out onto the Internet. This can be very useful if our internal network's connectivity or reliability is better than the U.K.'s section of the Internet.

Movie U. has a private network connection to our sister university in London near Pinewood Studios. As it turns out, sending mail across our private link, and then through the Pinewood host to correspondents in the U.K., is more reliable than sending it directly across the Internet. So we add the following wildcard records to *root.dns*:

```
; holygrail is at the other end of the U.K. Internet link
*.uk.   IN    MX    10 holygrail.movie.ac.uk.
holygrail.movie.ac.uk.       IN  A   192.168.76.4
```

Now mail addressed to users in subdomains of *uk* will be forwarded to the host *holygrail.movie.ac.uk* at our sister university, which presumably has facilities to forward that mail to other domains in the U.K.

### The trouble with internal roots

Unfortunately, just as forwarding has its problems, internal roots have their limitations. Chief among these is the fact that your internal hosts can't see the Internet name space. On some networks, this isn't an issue, because most internal hosts don't have any direct Internet connectivity. On others, however, the Internet firewall or other software may require that all internal hosts have the ability to resolve names in the Internet's name space. For these networks, an internal root architecture won't work.

# A Shadow Name Space

Many organizations would like to advertise different zone data to the Internet than they do internally. In most cases, much of the internal zone data is irrelevant to the Internet because of the organization's Internet firewall. The firewall may not allow direct access to most internal hosts and may also translate internal, unregistered IP addresses into a range of IP addresses registered to the organization. Therefore, the organization may need to trim out irrelevant information from the external view of the zone or change internal addresses to their external equivalents.

Unfortunately, the Microsoft DNS Server doesn't support automatic filtering and translation of zone data—no name servers do. Consequently, many organizations manually create what have become known as *split name spaces*. In a split name space, the real name space is available only internally, while a pared-down, translated version of it, called the *shadow name space*, is visible to the Internet.

The shadow name space contains the name-to-address and address-to-name mappings of only those hosts that are accessible from the Internet, through the firewall. The addresses advertised may be the translated equivalents of real internal addresses. The shadow name space may also contain one or more MX records to direct email from the Internet through the firewall to a mail server.

Since Movie U. has an Internet firewall that greatly limits access from the Internet
to the internal network, we elected to create a shadow name space. For
*movie.edu*, the only information we need to give out is about the zone (an SOA
and a few NS records), the bastion host (*postmanrings2x*), and the new external
name server, *ns.movie.edu*, which also functions as an external web server,
*www.movie.edu*. The address of the external interface on the bastion host is
200.1.4.2, while the address of the name/web server is 200.1.4.3. The shadow
*movie.edu* zone data file looks like this:

```
@    IN    SOA    ns.movie.edu.      hostmaster.movie.edu. (
                                1        ; Serial
                                86400    ; Refresh
                                3600     ; Retry
                                608400   ; Expire
                                86400 )  ; Default TTL

     IN    NS     ns.movie.edu.
     IN    NS     ns.isp.net.           ; our ISP's name server

     IN    A      200.1.4.3
     IN    MX     10 postmanrings2x.movie.edu.
     IN    MX     100 mail.isp.net.

www  IN    CNAME  movie.edu.

postmanrings2x IN    A      200.1.4.2
               IN    MX     10 postmanrings2x.movie.edu.
               IN    MX     100 mail.isp.net.

;postmanrings2x handles mail addressed to ns
ns             IN    A      200.1.4.3
               IN    MX     10 postmanrings2x.movie.edu.
               IN    MX     100 mail.isp.net.
postmanrings2x.movie.edu.
               IN    MX     100 mail.isp.net.

*              IN    MX     10 postmanrings2x.movie.edu.
               IN    MX     100 mail.isp.net.
```

Note that there's no mention of any of the subdomains of *movie.edu*, including
any delegation to the servers for those subdomains. The information simply isn't
necessary, since there's nothing in any of the subdomains that you can get to from
the Internet, and inbound mail addressed to hosts in the subdomains is caught by
the wildcard.

The *4.1.200.in-addr.arpa.dns* file, which we need to reverse-map the two Movie U.
IP addresses that hosts on the Internet might see, looks like this:

```
@    IN    SOA    ns.movie.edu.      hostmaster.movie.edu. (
                                1        ; Serial
                                86400    ; Refresh
```

```
                          3600    ; Retry
                          608400  ; Expire
                          86400 ) ; Default TTL

        IN    NS    ns.movie.edu.
        IN    NS    ns.isp.net.

    2   IN    PTR   postmanrings2x.movie.edu.
    3   IN    PTR   ns.movie.edu.
```

One precaution that we need to take is to make sure that the resolver on our bastion host isn't configured to use the server on *ns.movie.edu*. Since that server can't see the real *movie.edu*, using it would render *postmanrings2x* unable to map internal names to addresses or addresses to names.

### The bastion host

The bastion host is a special case in a split name space. The bastion host has a foot in each environment: one network interface connects it to the Internet, and another connects it to the internal network. Now that we have split our name space in two, how can our bastion host see both the Internet name space and our real internal name space? If we configure it with the Internet root name servers in its hints file, it will follow delegation from the Internet's *edu* name servers to an external *movie.edu* name server with shadow zone data. It would be blind to our internal name space, which it needs to see to log connections, deliver inbound mail, and more. On the other hand, if we configure it with our internal roots, it won't see the Internet's name space, which it clearly needs to do in order to function as a bastion host. What to do?

If we use forwarding internally, depending on the type of firewall we're running, we may need to run a name server on the bastion host itself. If the firewall won't pass DNS traffic, we'll need to run a name server, configured with the Internet roots, on the bastion host, so that our internal name servers will have somewhere to forward their unresolved queries. This name server must be configured as a slave for *movie.edu* and any *in-addr.arpa* zones in which it needs to resolve addresses. This way, if it receives a query for a name in *movie.edu*, it'll use its local authoritative data to resolve the name rather than trying to query an Internet root. If the name is in a subdomain of *movie.edu*, it'll follow NS records in the zone data to query an internal name server for the name. Therefore, it doesn't need to be configured as a slave for any *movie.edu* subdomains, such as *fx.movie.edu*, just the "top" zone (see Figure 13-6).

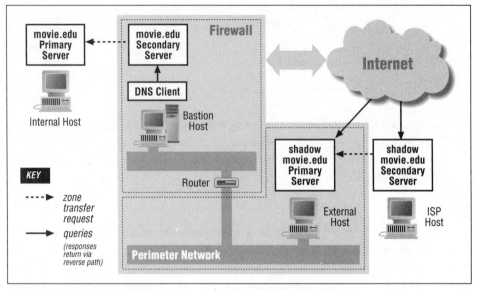

*Figure 13-6. A split DNS solution*

# Dialup Connections

Another relatively recent development in networking that presents a challenge to DNS is the dialup Internet connection. When the Internet was young and DNS was born, there was no such thing as a dialup connection. With the enormous explosion in the Internet's popularity and the propagation of Internet service providers who offer dialup Internet connectivity to the masses, a whole new breed of problems with name service has been introduced.

We'll separate dialup connections into two categories: simple dialup, by which we mean a single computer that connects to the Internet occasionally, when a user manually initiates a connection, and dial-on-demand, which means one or more computers that connect to the Internet automatically whenever they generate traffic bound for the Internet. Often, the device that makes this dial-on-demand connectivity possible is a small dialup router with an analog modem or ISDN interface, like an Ascend Pipeline 25.

## Simple Dialup

The easiest way to deal with simple dialup is to configure your dialup computer's resolver to use a name server provided by your ISP. Most ISPs run name servers for their subscribers' use. If you're not sure whether your ISP provides name servers for your use, or if you don't know what their IP addresses are, check their web site, send them email, or give them a call.

Some operating systems, like Windows 95 and NT, will let you define a set of name servers for a particular dialup provider. So, for example, you can configure one set of name servers to use when you dial up Netcom and another to use when you dial up your office. Unfortunately, defining name servers for your LAN connection under Windows 95 currently overrides all your precious dialup settings.*

This configuration is usually adequate for most casual dialup users. Name resolution will fail unless the dialup connection is up, but that's not likely to be a problem, since there's no use for Internet name service without Internet connectivity. If you have special needs that aren't addressed by this configuration, take a look at the recommendations in the dial-on-demand section.

## *Dial-on-Demand*

A more sophisticated dialup solution is dial-on-demand. Dial-on-demand Internet connections often use dedicated hardware, like a small dialup router, to provide connectivity whenever it's needed. If you initiate a connection to the Internet from the "remote" end of a dial-on-demand router, bingo, it dials up another router on the Internet and routes your packets across. If the connection is idle for more than a specified amount of time, the router drops the connection.

The challenge with DNS is to keep a local name server from continuously bringing the demand dial connection up and down like a yo-yo. This could be costly because you sometimes pay a premium for connection setup with technologies like ISDN.

The most important strategy for minimizing this off-net traffic is to configure your resolvers to use a minimal search list, or DNS Suffix Search Order, as it's called in Windows. The default Windows search list with just the **Domain** set searches the ancestors of your local domain, which can cause unnecessary remote traffic. For instance, say your local domain is *tinyoffice.majorcorp.com*, and you have a dial-on-demand connection to Majorcorp's enterprise network. On hosts configured with **Domain** set to the local domain and no explicit DNS Suffix Search Order, your default search list is

```
tinyoffice.majorcorp.com
majorcorp.com
```

---

* A handy shareware utility called *Netswitcher* allows Windows 95 users to change resolver settings easily. For more information, see *http://www.netswitcher.com/*.

A user typing *telnet foo.tinyoffice.majorcorp.com* to log in to the workstation next to him will inadvertently cause lookups of:

```
foo.tinyoffice.majorcorp.com.tinyoffice.majorcorp.com and
foo.tinyoffice.majorcorp.com.majorcorp.com
```

before the correct domain name, *foo.tinyoffice.majorcorp.com*, is looked up. Since your local name server is probably authoritative for *tinyoffice.majorcorp.com*, it can tell that the first domain name, *foo.tinyoffice.majorcorp.com.tinyoffice.major-corp.com*, is bogus. (It ends in *com.tinyoffice.majorcorp.com*, so it would require the existence of a *com* subdomain of your local domain, and there isn't one.) But it can't tell about the second domain name without talking to a *majorcorp.com* name server first. If there isn't one locally, it'll have to bring up that dial-on-demand connection.

The easiest way to prevent these unnecessary queries is to trim the parent domain out of your search list explicitly, using the DNS Suffix Search Order. In this example, the DNS Suffix Search Order *tinyoffice.majorcorp.com* (just one entry) would probably cause fewer failed, offsite lookups.

If many of the names your users look up are in your parent zone, you might also consider configuring your local name server as a slave for your parent zone. At least that way you'll bring up the link at most only once per refresh interval to resolve names in your parent zone. The same logic could be applied to nearly any zone your local name server queries often.

# Network Names and Numbers

The original DNS definitions didn't provide the ability to look up network names based on a network number—a feature that was provided by the original *HOSTS.TXT* file. More recently, a procedure for storing network names has been defined; this procedure also works for subnets and subnet masks, so it goes significantly beyond *HOSTS.TXT*. Moreover, it doesn't require any modification to the DNS server software at all; it's based entirely on the clever use of pointer and address records.

If you remember, to map an IP address to a name in DNS, you reverse the IP address, append *in-addr.arpa*, and look up PTR data. This same technique is used to map a network number to a network name; for example, to map network 15.0.0.0 to "HP Internet." To look up the network number, include the trailing zeros to make it four bytes, and look up PTR data just as you did with a host's IP address. For example, to find the network name for the old ARPANET, network 10.0.0.0, look up PTR data for *0.0.0.10.in-addr.arpa*. You'd get back an answer like *ARPANET.ARPA*.

If the ARPANET were subnetted, you'd also find an address record at *0.0.0.10.in-addr.arpa.* The address would be the subnet mask, 255.255.0.0, for instance. If you were interested in the subnet name instead of the network name, you'd apply the mask to the IP address and look up the subnet number.

This technique allows you to map the network number to a name. To provide a complete solution, there must be a way to map a network name to its network number. This, again, is accomplished with PTR records. The network name has PTR data that point to the network number (reversed with *in-addr.arpa* appended).

Let's see what the data might look like in HP's zone data files (the HP Internet has network number 15.0.0.0) and step through mapping a network number to a network name.

Here's the partial contents of file *hp.com.dns*:

```
;
; Map HP's network name to 15.0.0.0.
;
hp-net.hp.com.              IN  PTR 0.0.0.15.in-addr.arpa.
```

The following is the partial contents of file *corp.hp.com.dns*:

```
;
; Map corp's subnet name to 15.1.0.0.
;
corp-subnet.corp.hp.com.   IN  PTR 0.0.1.15.in-addr.arpa.
```

Here's the partial contents of file *15.in-addr.arpa.dns*:

```
;
; Map 15.0.0.0 to hp-net.hp.com.
; HP's subnet mask is 255.255.248.0.
;
0.0.0.15.in-addr.arpa.     IN  PTR hp-net.hp.com.
                           IN  A    255.255.248.0
```

And here's the partial contents of file *1.15.in-addr.arpa.dns*:

```
;
; Map the 15.1.0.0 back to its subnet name.
;
0.0.1.15.in-addr.arpa.     IN  PTR corp-subnet.corp.hp.com.
```

Unfortunately, you can't add these records using DNS Manager, because DNS Manager won't let you add PTR records to zones whose names don't end in *in-addr.arpa,* nor will it let you add A records to zones whose names do end in *in-addr.arpa.* However, you can create the zone data manually and import it using **New Zone.**

Here's the procedure to look up the subnet name for the IP address 15.1.0.1:

1. Apply the default network mask for the address's class. Address 15.1.0.1 is a class A address, so the mask is 255.0.0.0. Applying the mask to the IP address makes the network number 15.

2. Send a query (*type=a* or *type=any*) for *0.0.0.15.in-addr.arpa.*

3. The query response contains address data. Since address data is at *0.0.0.15.in-addr.arpa* (the subnet mask—255.255.248.0), apply the subnet mask to the IP address. This yields 15.1.0.0.

4. Send a query (*type=a* or *type=any*) for *0.0.1.15.in-addr.arpa.*

5. The query response does not contain address data, so 15.1.0.0 is not further subnetted.

6. Send a PTR query for *0.0.1.15.in-addr.arpa.*

7. The query response contains the network name for 15.1.0.1: *corp-sub-net.corp.hp.com.*

In addition to mapping between network names and numbers, you can also list all the networks for your domain with PTR records:

```
movie.edu.   IN  PTR  0.249.249.192.in-addr.arpa.
             IN  PTR  0.253.253.192.in-addr.arpa.
```

Now for the bad news: despite the fact that RFC 1101 contains everything you need to know to set this up, we know of no software (yet) that actually *uses* this type of network name encoding, and very few administrators go to the trouble of adding this information. Until software actually makes use of DNS-encoded network names, about the only reason for setting this up is to show off. But that's a good enough reason for many of us.

# Additional Resource Records

We haven't covered a couple of resource records yet in this book. The first of these has been around since the beginning, HINFO, but hasn't been widely used. The others were defined in RFC 1183 and several successive RFCs. Most are experimental, but some are on the standards track and are coming into more prevalent use. We'll describe them here to give you a little head start in getting used to them.

## Host Information

HINFO stands for Host Information. The data are a pair of strings identifying the host's hardware type and operating system. The strings should come from the MACHINE NAMES and OPERATING SYSTEM NAMES listed in the "Assigned Numbers" RFC (currently RFC 1700), but this requirement is not enforced; you can use your own abbreviations. The RFC isn't at all comprehensive, so it is quite possible you won't find your system in the list anyway. Originally, host information records were designed to let services like FTP determine how to interact with the remote system. This would have made it possible to automatically negotiate data type transformations. Unfortunately, this didn't happen—few sites supply accurate HINFO values for all their systems. Some network administrators use HINFO records to help them keep track of the machine types, instead of recording the machine types in a database or a notebook. Here are two examples of HINFO records; note that the hardware type or operating system must be surrounded with quotes if it includes any whitespace:

```
;
; These machine names and system names did not come from RFC 1700
;
wormhole  IN  HINFO  ACME-HW  ACME-GW
cujo      IN  HINFO  "Watch Dog Hardware"  "Rabid OS"
```

You'd see the window shown in Figure 13-7 if you added an HINFO record with DNS Manager.

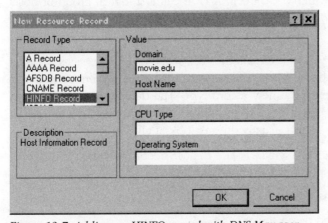

*Figure 13-7. Adding an HINFO record with DNS Manager*

If you include whitespace in the values you type in the **CPU Type** and **Operating System** fields, DNS Manager will automatically put double quotes around it, so don't use double quotes in either field—you'll get double double quotes.

As we pointed out, HINFO records are a security risk—by providing easily accessible information about a system, you are making it easier for a hacker to break in.

## *AFSDB*

AFSDB has a syntax like that of the MX record and semantics a bit like that of the NS record. An AFSDB record gives either the location of an AFS cell database server or of a DCE cell's authenticated name server. The type of server the record points to, and the name of the host running the server, are contained in the record-specific data portion of the record.

So what's an AFS cell database server? Or AFS, for that matter? AFS originally stood for the Andrew File System, designed by the good folks at Carnegie-Mellon University as part of the Andrew Project. (It's now a registered trademark of Transarc Corporation, which sells AFS as a product.) AFS is a network filesystem, like NFS, but one that handles the latency of wide area networks much better than NFS does and provides local caching of files to enhance performance. An AFS cell database server runs the process responsible for tracking the location of filesets (groups of files) on various AFS file servers within a cell (a logical group of hosts). So being able to find the AFS cell database server is the key to finding any file in the cell.

And what's an authenticated name server? It holds location information about all sorts of services available within a DCE cell. A DCE cell is a logical group of hosts that share services offered by the Open Group's Distributed Computing Environment (DCE).

And now, back to our story. To access another cell's AFS or DCE services across a network, you must first find out where that cell's cell database servers or authenticated name servers are. Hence the new record type. The domain name the record is attached to gives the name of the cell the server knows about. Cells are often named after DNS domains, so this usually doesn't look at all odd.

As we said, the AFSDB record's syntax is like the MX record's syntax. In place of the preference value, you specify the number 1 or 2:

*1*   For an AFS cell database server

*2*   For a DCE authenticated name server

In place of the mail exchanger host, you specify the name of the host running the server. Simple!

Say an *fx.movie.edu* systems administrator sets up a DCE cell (which includes AFS services) because she wants to experiment with distributed processing to speed graphics rendering. She runs both an AFS cell database server and a DCE name server on *bladerunner.fx.movie.edu*, another cell database server on *empire*, and another DCE name server on *aliens*. She should set up the AFSDB records as follows:

```
; Our DCE cell is called fx.movie.edu, same as the domain
fx.movie.edu.  IN  AFSDB  1 bladerunner.fx.movie.edu.
```

```
IN   AFSDB   2 bladerunner.fx.movie.edu.
IN   AFSDB   1 empire.fx.movie.edu.
IN   AFSDB   2 aliens.fx.movie.edu.
```

DNS Manager will also let you add AFSDB records. In Figure 13-8, we add the first AFSDB record shown in the preceding example.

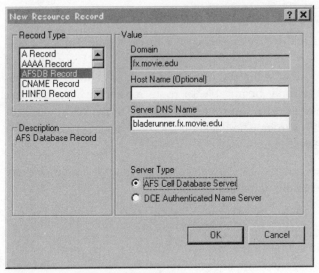

*Figure 13-8. Adding an AFSDB record*

Note that the radio buttons replace the values 1 and 2 in the raw record format.

## X25, ISDN, and RT

These three record types were created specifically in support of research on next-generation internets. Two of the records, X25 and ISDN, are simply address records specific to X.25 and ISDN networks, respectively. Both take arguments (record-specific data) appropriate to the type of network. The X25 record type uses an X.121 address (X.121 is the ITU-T recommendation that specifies the format of addresses used in X.25 networks). The ISDN record type uses an ISDN address.

ISDN stands for Integrated Services Digital Network. Telephone companies around the world have proposed using ISDN protocols to allow their telephone networks to carry both voice and data, creating an integrated network. Although ISDN's availability is spotty throughout the U.S., it has been widely adopted in some international markets. Since ISDN uses the telephone companies' networks, an ISDN address is just a phone number and in fact consists of a country code, followed by an area code or city code, and then by a local phone number. Sometimes a few extra digits, called a *subaddress*, you wouldn't see in a phone number are at the end. The subaddress is specified in a separate field in the record-specific data.

Examples of the X25 and ISDN record types are

```
relay.pink.com.  IN  X25  31105060845

delay.hp.com.    IN  ISDN  141555514539488
hep.hp.com.      IN  ISDN  141555514539488 004
```

These records are intended for use in conjunction with the Route Through (RT) record type. RT is syntactically and semantically similar to the MX record type: it specifies an intermediate host that will route *packets* (instead of mail) to a destination host. So now, instead of only being able to route mail to a host that isn't directly connected to the Internet, you can route any kind of IP packet to that host by using another host as a forwarder. The packet could be part of a Telnet or FTP session, or perhaps even a DNS query!

Like MX, RT includes a preference value, which indicates how desirable delivery to a particular host is. For example, the records:

```
housesitter.movie.edu.  IN  RT  10 relay.pink.com.
                        IN  RT  20 delay.hp.com.
```

instruct hosts to route packets bound for *housesitter* through *relay.pink.com* (the first choice) or through *delay.hp.com* (the second choice).

The way RT works with X25 and ISDN (and even A) records is like this:

1. Internet host A wants to send a packet to host B, which is not connected to the Internet.

2. Host A looks up host B's RT records. This search also returns all address records (A, X25, *and* ISDN) for each intermediate host.

3. Host A sorts the list of intermediate hosts and looks for its own domain name. If it finds it, it removes it and all intermediate hosts at higher preference values. This is analogous to a mailer's "paring down" of a list of mail exchangers.

4. Host A examines the address record(s) for the most preferred intermediate host that remains. If host A is attached to a network that corresponds to the type of address record indicated, it uses that network to send the packet to the intermediate host. For example, if host A were trying to send a packet through *relay.pink.com*, it would need connectivity to an X.25 network.

5. If host A lacks appropriate connectivity, it tries the next intermediate host specified by the RT records. For example, if host A lacked X.25 connectivity, it might fall back to delivering via ISDN to *delay.hp.com*.

This process continues until the packet is routed to the most preferred intermediate host. The most preferred intermediate host may then deliver the packet directly to the destination host's address (which may be A, X25, or ISDN).

DNS Manager gives you the ability to add ISDN, X25, and RT records using **Add Record**.

## IPv6 Addresses

If you're to believe the hype, IPv6 is coming soon to a network near you. Clearly, the existing A record won't accommodate IPv6's 128-bit addresses: DNS servers expect an A record's record-specific data to be a 32-bit address in dotted-octet format.

RFC 1886 introduces a new address record, AAAA, used to store a 128-bit IPv6 address. AAAA takes as its record-specific data the textual format of an IPv6 record described in RFC 1884. This format expresses the 128 bits of the address as eight sets of four hexadecimal digits, separated by colons (:). The first set of four digits encodes the high-order 16 bits of the address. Every set of four bits are compressed into the equivalent hexadecimal digit (for example, *1111* becomes f). You can omit leading zeroes in a set of hexadecimal digits.

So, for example, you'd see AAAA records like this:

```
ipv6        IN  AAAA    4321:0:1:2:3:4:567:89ab
```

RFC 1886 also extends the additional processing name servers do, so that name servers include AAAA records for mail exchangers and name servers that speak IPv6, for example.

Finally, RFC 1886 establishes a new reverse mapping namespace for IPv6 addresses, called *ip6.int*. Each level of subdomain under *ip6.int* represents a nibble (a 4-bit quantity) in the 128-bit address, with the low-order nibble encoded first (appearing at the far left of the domain name). Unlike the format of addresses in AAAA records, omitting leading zeroes is not allowed, so there are always 32 nibbles and 32 levels of subdomain below *ip6.int* in a domain name corresponding to a full IPv6 address. The domain name that corresponds to the address in the preceding example is

```
b.a.9.8.7.6.5.0.4.0.0.0.3.0.0.0.2.0.0.0.1.0.0.0.0.0.0.0.1.2.3.4.IP6.INT.
```

These domain names have PTR records attached, just as domain names under *in-addr.arpa* do.

# DNS versus X.500

X.500 is an ISO (International Standards Organization) standard distributed directory system that's sometimes seen as a "competitor" to DNS. X.500 does, indeed, include some of the same functionality DNS does. For example, you can use X.500 to retrieve address information for a particular host. And in some ways, the two are similar: X.500 directories store data in hierarchical name spaces and use recursion and iteration (well, ISO calls them "chaining" and "referral"). While we can hardly claim to be experts on X.500, we can make some general comparisons between DNS and X.500:

- X.500, as a directory service, supports many types of searches. Whereas DNS servers simply look up data attached to a given domain name, you can search the X.500 Directory Information Tree for soundalike matches or specify incomplete information ("I know his last name is Buttle and he works in the Ministry of Information") and still turn up data.

- X.500 is a full-blown distributed database meant to be used for a wide variety of applications. You can store the phone book in an X.500 database. You can store location data in an X.500 database. You can store information about all sorts of network devices and their attributes. DNS, on the other hand, is a relatively simple distributed database meant to solve a particular problem—an intractable *HOSTS.TXT* database.

- X.500 has security features involving credentials and the support of multiple encryption types; DNS is not secure.[*]

Anyway, you get the idea. X.500 is rich in capabilities and will be extremely useful when it is completely defined, implemented, and optimized. DNS provides a few, critical functions. It is, for the most part, fully implemented, and it will continue to evolve and improve.

Don't let this turn you off to DNS, though. The Domain Name System really is admirably good at its job, and it does it much faster than X.500 does. True, X.500 offers richer functionality, but it may never usurp DNS's position as the Internet's directory system of choice.

---

[*] Yet—the DNS Security Extensions described in RFC 2065 will allow cryptographic authentication of the source of zone data as well as data integrity checking and more.

# DNS Message Format and Resource Records

This appendix outlines the format of DNS messages and enumerates all the resource record types. The resource records are shown in their textual format, as you would specify them in a DNS database file, and in their binary format, as they appear in DNS messages. You'll find a few resource records here that we didn't cover in the book because they are experimental or obsolete.

We've included here the portions of RFC 1035, written by Paul Mockapetris, that deal with the textual format of master files (what we called *db files* or *DNS database files* in the book) or with the DNS message format (for those of you who need to parse DNS packets).

## Master File Format

*(from RFC 1035, pages 33–35)*

The format of these files is a sequence of entries. Entries are predominantly line oriented, though parentheses can be used to continue a list of items across a line boundary, and text literals can contain CRLF within the text. Any combination of tabs and spaces act as a delimiter between the separate items that make up an entry. The end of any line in the master file can end with a comment. The comment starts with a semicolon (;).

The following entries are defined:

```
<blank>[<comment>]

$ORIGIN <domain-name> [<comment>]

$INCLUDE <file-name> [<domain-name>] [<comment>]
```

```
<domain-name><rr> [<comment>]

<blank><rr> [<comment>]
```

Blank lines, with or without comments, are allowed anywhere in the file.

Two control entries are defined: $ORIGIN and $INCLUDE. $ORIGIN is followed by a domain name and resets the current origin for relative domain names to the stated name. $INCLUDE inserts the named file into the current file, and may optionally specify a domain name that sets the relative domain name origin for the included file. $INCLUDE may also have a comment. Note that a $INCLUDE entry never changes the relative origin of the parent file, regardless of changes to the relative origin made within the included file.

The last two forms represent RRs. If an entry for an RR begins with a blank, then the RR is assumed to be owned by the last stated owner. If an RR entry begins with a *<domain-name>*, then the owner name is reset.

*<rr>* contents take one of the following forms:

```
[<TTL>] [<class>] <type> <RDATA>
[<class>] [<TTL>] <type> <RDATA>
```

The RR begins with optional TTL and class fields, followed by a type and RDATA field appropriate to the type and class. Class and type use the standard mnemonics; TTL is a decimal integer. Omitted class and TTL values are defaulted to the last explicitly stated values. Since type and class mnemonics are disjoint, the parse is unique.

*<domain-name>*s make up a large share of the data in the master file. The labels in the domain name are expressed as character strings and separated by dots. Quoting conventions allow arbitrary characters to be stored in domain names. Domain names that end in a dot are called *absolute*, and are taken as complete. Domain names that do not end in a dot are called *relative*; the actual domain name is the concatenation of the relative part with an origin specified in $ORIGIN or $INCLUDE, or as an argument to the master file loading routine. A relative name is an error when no origin is available.

*<character-string>* is expressed in one of two ways: as a contiguous set of characters without interior spaces, or as a string beginning and ending with quotation marks. Inside a quotation mark (") delimited string any character can occur, except for quotation marks themselves, which must be quoted using a backslash (\).

Because these files are text files, several special encodings are necessary to allow arbitrary data to be loaded. In particular:

. *(dot)*

> Of the root

@

> A free standing at sign is used to denote the current origin

\X

> Where X is any character other than a digit (0–9) and is used to quote that character so that its special meaning does not apply. For example, "\." can be used to place a dot character in a label.*

\DDD

> Where each D is a digit in the octet corresponding to the decimal number described by DDD. The resulting octet is assumed to be text and is not checked for special meaning.†

( )

> Parentheses are used to group data that crosses a line boundary. In effect, line terminations are not recognized within parentheses.‡

;

> A semicolon is used to start a comment; the remainder of the line is ignored.

## Character Case

*(from RFC 1035, page 9)*

For all parts of the DNS that are part of the official protocol, all comparisons between character strings (for example, labels, domain names, and so on) are done in a case-insensitive manner. At present, this rule is in force throughout the domain system without exception. However, future additions beyond current usage may need to use the full binary octet capabilities in names, so attempts to store domain names in 7-bit ASCII or use of special bytes to terminate labels, and so forth, should be avoided.

## Types

Here is a complete list of resource record types. The textual representation is used in master files. The binary representation is used in DNS queries and responses. These resource records are described on pages 13–21 of RFC 1035.

---

\* Not implemented by BIND 4.8.3.

† Not implemented by BIND 4.8.3.

‡ BIND 4.8.3 allows parentheses only on SOA and WKS resource records.

## A address
*(from RFC 1035, page 20)*

*Textual Representation:*

        <owner> <class> <ttl> A <address>

*Example:*

        localhost.movie.edu.    IN A 127.0.0.1

*Binary Representation:*

    Address type code: 1
        +--+--+--+--+--+--+--+--+--+--+--+--+--+--+--+--+
        |                     ADDRESS                   |
        +--+--+--+--+--+--+--+--+--+--+--+--+--+--+--+--+
    where:
    ADDRESS         A 32 bit Internet address.

## CNAME: canonical name
*(from RFC 1035, page 14)*

*Textual Representation:*

        <owner> <class> <ttl> CNAME <canonical-dname>

*Example:*

        wh.movie.edu.   IN   CNAME   wormhole.movie.edu.

*Binary Representation:*

    CNAME type code: 5
        +--+--+--+--+--+--+--+--+--+--+--+--+--+--+--+--+
        /                      CNAME                    /
        /                                               /
        +--+--+--+--+--+--+--+--+--+--+--+--+--+--+--+--+
    where:
    CNAME           A <domain-name> which specifies the canonical
                    or primary name for the owner.  The owner name is
                    an alias.

## HINFO host information
*(from RFC 1035, page 14)*

*Textual Representation:*

        <owner> <class> <ttl> HINFO <cpu> <os>

*Example:*

        grizzly.movie.edu.  IN  HINFO  VAX-11/780 UNIX

*Binary Representation:*

    HINFO type code: 13
        +--+--+--+--+--+--+--+--+--+--+--+--+--+--+--+--+
        /                       CPU                     /
        +--+--+--+--+--+--+--+--+--+--+--+--+--+--+--+--+
        /                        OS                     /
        +--+--+--+--+--+--+--+--+--+--+--+--+--+--+--+--+

```
where:
CPU              A <character-string> which specifies the CPU type.
OS               A <character-string> which specifies the
                 operating system type.
```

## MB mailbox domain name—experimental
*(from RFC 1035, page 14)*

### Textual Representation:
```
<owner> <class> <ttl> MB <mbox-dname>
```

### Example:
```
al.movie.edu.   IN   MB   robocop.movie.edu.
```

### Binary Representation:
```
MB type code: 7
    +--+--+--+--+--+--+--+--+--+--+--+--+--+--+--+--+
    /                   MADNAME                     /
    /                                               /
    +--+--+--+--+--+--+--+--+--+--+--+--+--+--+--+--+
where:
MADNAME          A <domain-name> which specifies a host which has
                 the specified mailbox.
```

## MD mail destination—obsolete

MD has been replaced with MX.

## MF mail forwarder—obsolete

MF has been replaced with MX.

## MG mail group member—experimental
*(from RFC 1035, page 16)*

### Textual Representation:
```
<owner> <class> <ttl> MG <mgroup-dname>
```

### Example:
```
admin.movie.edu.   IN   MG   al.movie.edu.
                   IN   MG   ed.movie.edu.
                   IN   MG   jc.movie.edu.
```

### Binary Representation:
```
MG type code: 8
    +--+--+--+--+--+--+--+--+--+--+--+--+--+--+--+--+
    /                   MGMNAME                     /
    /                                               /
    +--+--+--+--+--+--+--+--+--+--+--+--+--+--+--+--+
where:
MGMNAME          A <domain-name> which specifies a mailbox which
                 is a member of the mail group specified by the
                 domain name.
```

## MINFO mailbox or mail list information—experimental
*(from RFC 1035, page 16)*

*Textual Representation:*

    <owner> <class> <ttl> MINFO <resp-mbox> <error-mbox>

*Example:*

    admin.movie.edu.  IN  MINFO  al.movie.edu. al.movie.edu.

*Binary Representation:*

    MINFO type code: 14
        +--+--+--+--+--+--+--+--+--+--+--+--+--+--+--+--+
        /                     RMAILBX                   /
        +--+--+--+--+--+--+--+--+--+--+--+--+--+--+--+--+
        /                     EMAILBX                   /
        +--+--+--+--+--+--+--+--+--+--+--+--+--+--+--+--+
    where:
    RMAILBX            A <domain-name> which specifies a mailbox which
                       is responsible for the mailing list or mailbox.
                       If this domain name names the root, the owner of
                       the MINFO RR is responsible for itself.  Note
                       that many existing mailing lists use a mailbox
                       X-request for the RMAILBX field of mailing list
                       X, e.g., Msgroup-request for Msgroup.  This field
                       provides a more general mechanism.
    EMAILBX            A <domain-name> which specifies a mailbox which is
                       to receive error messages related to the mailing
                       list or mailbox specified by the owner of the
                       MINFO RR (similar to the ERRORS-TO: field which has
                       been proposed). If this domain name names the root,
                       errors should be returned to the sender of the
                       message.

## MR mail rename—experimental
*(from RFC 1035, page 17)*

*Textual Representation:*

    <owner> <class> <ttl> MR <new-mbox>

*Example:*

    eddie.movie.edu.  IN  MR  eddie.bornagain.edu.

*Binary Representation:*

    MR type code: 9
        +--+--+--+--+--+--+--+--+--+--+--+--+--+--+--+--+
        /                     NEWNAME                   /
        /                                               /
        +--+--+--+--+--+--+--+--+--+--+--+--+--+--+--+--+
    where:
    NEWNAME            A <domain-name> which specifies a mailbox which
                       is the proper rename of the specified mailbox.

# MX mail exchanger
*(from RFC 1035, page 17)*

### Textual Representation:

    <owner> <class> <ttl> MX <preference> <exchange-dname>

### Example:

    ora.com.   IN   MX   0   ora.ora.com.
               IN   MX   10  ruby.ora.com.
               IN   MX   10  opal.ora.com.

### Binary Representation:

    MX type code: 15

    where:
    PREFERENCE        A 16 bit integer which specifies the preference
                      given to this RR among others at the same owner.
                      Lower values are preferred.
    EXCHANGE          A <domain-name> which specifies a host willing
                      to act as a mail exchange for the owner name.

# NS name server
*(from RFC 1035, page 18)*

### Textual Representation:

    <owner> <class> <ttl> NS <name-server-dname>

### Example:

    movie.edu.     IN NS terminator.movie.edu

### Binary Representation:

    NS type code: 1

    where:
    NSDNAME           A <domain-name> which specifies a host which
                      should be authoritative for the specified
                      class and domain.

# NULL null—experimental
*(from RFC 1035, page 17)*

### Binary Representation:

    NULL type code: 10

    +--+--+--+--+--+--+--+--+--+--+--+--+--+--+--+--+
    /                   <anything>                  /
    /                                               /
    +--+--+--+--+--+--+--+--+--+--+--+--+--+--+--+--+

```
Anything at all may be in the RDATA field so long as it is 65535
octets or less.
```

NULL is not implemented by BIND.

## PTR pointer
*(from RFC 1035, page 18)*

*Textual Representation:*

```
<owner> <class> <ttl> PTR <dname>
```

*Example:*

```
1.249.249.192.in-addr.arpa.  IN PTR wormhole.movie.edu.
```

*Binary Representation:*

```
PTR type code: 12
    +--+--+--+--+--+--+--+--+--+--+--+--+--+--+--+--+
    /                     PTRDNAME                  /
    +--+--+--+--+--+--+--+--+--+--+--+--+--+--+--+--+
where:
PTRDNAME        A <domain-name> which points to some location in
                the domain name space.
```

## SOA start of authority
*(from RFC 1035, pages 19–20)*

*Textual Representation:*

```
<owner> <class> <ttl> SOA <source-dname> <mbox> (
    <serial> <refresh> <retry> <expire> <minimum> )
```

*Example:*

```
movie.edu. IN SOA terminator.movie.edu. al.robocop.movie.edu. (
                1          ; Serial
                10800      ; Refresh after 3 hours
                3600       ; Retry after 1 hour
                604800     ; Expire after 1 week
                86400 )    ; Minimum TTL of 1 day
```

*Binary Representation:*

```
SOA type code: 6
    +--+--+--+--+--+--+--+--+--+--+--+--+--+--+--+--+
    /                      MNAME                    /
    /                                               /
    +--+--+--+--+--+--+--+--+--+--+--+--+--+--+--+--+
    /                      RNAME                    /
    +--+--+--+--+--+--+--+--+--+--+--+--+--+--+--+--+
    |                      SERIAL                   |
    |                                               |
    +--+--+--+--+--+--+--+--+--+--+--+--+--+--+--+--+
    |                     REFRESH                   |
    |                                               |
    +--+--+--+--+--+--+--+--+--+--+--+--+--+--+--+--+
    |                      RETRY                    |
    |                                               |
    +--+--+--+--+--+--+--+--+--+--+--+--+--+--+--+--+
    |                     EXPIRE                    |
```

```
         |                                           |
         +--+--+--+--+--+--+--+--+--+--+--+--+--+--+--+--+
         |                  MINIMUM                      |
         |                                           |
         +--+--+--+--+--+--+--+--+--+--+--+--+--+--+--+--+
```
where:

MNAME        The <domain-name> of the name server that was the
             original or primary source of data for this zone.

RNAME        A <domain-name> which specifies the mailbox of the
             person responsible for this zone.

SERIAL       The unsigned 32 bit version number of the original
             copy of the zone.  Zone transfers preserve this
             value.  This value wraps and should be compared
             using sequence space arithmetic.

REFRESH      A 32 bit time interval before the zone should be
             refreshed.

RETRY        A 32 bit time interval that should elapse before
             a failed refresh should be retried.

EXPIRE       A 32 bit time value that specifies the upper limit
             on the time interval that can elapse before the
             zone is no longer authoritative.

MINIMUM      The unsigned 32 bit minimum TTL field that should
             be exported with any RR from this zone.

## TXT text

*(from RFC 1035, page 20)*

### Textual Representation:

    <owner> <class> <ttl> TXT <txt-strings>

### Example:

    cujo.movie.edu.  IN  TXT  "Location: machine room dog house"

### Binary Representation:

    TXT type code: 16
        +--+--+--+--+--+--+--+--+--+--+--+--+--+--+--+--+
        /                    TXT-DATA                   /
        +--+--+--+--+--+--+--+--+--+--+--+--+--+--+--+--+
    where:
    TXT-DATA        One or more <character-string>s.

## WKS well-known services

*(from RFC 1035, page 21)*

### Textual Representation:

    <owner> <class> <ttl> WKS <address> <protocol> <service-list>

### Example:

    terminator.movie.edu.  IN  WKS 192.249.249.3  TCP ( telnet smtp
                                            ftp shell domain )

### Binary Representation:

    WKS type code: 11

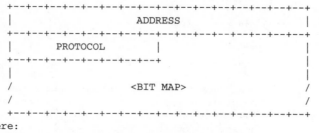

```
where:
ADDRESS          An 32 bit Internet address
PROTOCOL         An 8 bit IP protocol number
<BIT MAP>        A variable length bit map.  The bit map must
                 be a multiple of 8 bits long.
```

## New Types from RFC 1183

### AFSDB Andrew File System Data Base—experimental

*Textual Representation:*

```
<owner> <ttl> <class> AFSDB <subtype> <hostname>
```

*Example:*

```
fx.movie.edu.   IN   AFSDB   1 bladerunner.fx.movie.edu.
                IN   AFSDB   2 bladerunner.fx.movie.edu.
                IN   AFSDB   1 empire.fx.movie.edu.
                IN   AFSDB   2 aliens.fx.movie.edu.
```

*Binary Representation:*

```
AFSDB type code: 18
```

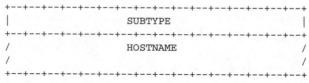

```
where:
SUBTYPE          Subtype 1 is an AFS cell database server. Subtype 2
                 is a DCE authenticated name server.
HOSTNAME         A <domain-name> which specifies a host that has a
                 server for the cell named by the owner of the RR.
```

### ISDN Integrated Services Digital Network address—experimental

*Textual Representation:*

```
<owner> <ttl> <class> ISDN <ISDN-address> <sa>
```

*Example:*

```
delay.hp.com.    IN   ISDN   141555514539488
hep.hp.com.      IN   ISDN   141555514539488 004
```

*Binary Representation:*

```
ISDN type code: 20
    +--+--+--+--+--+--+--+--+--+--+--+--+--+--+--+--+
    /                   ISDN ADDRESS                 /
    +--+--+--+--+--+--+--+--+--+--+--+--+--+--+--+--+
    /                    SUBADDRESS                  /
    +--+--+--+--+--+--+--+--+--+--+--+--+--+--+--+--+
```

where:

| | |
|---|---|
| ISDN ADDRESS | A <character-string> which identifies the ISDN number of <owner> and DDI (Direct Dial In) if any. |
| SUBADDRESS | An optional <character-string> specifying the subaddress. |

## RP Responsible Person—experimental

*Textual Representation:*

```
<owner> <ttl> <class> RP <mbox-dname> <txt-dname>
```

*Example:*

```
; The current origin is fx.movie.edu
@            IN   RP   ajs.fx.movie.edu.    ajs.fx.movie.edu.
bladerunner  IN   RP   root.fx.movie.edu.   hotline.fx.movie.edu.
             IN   RP   richard.fx.movie.edu.  rb.fx.movie.edu.
ajs          IN   TXT  "Arty Segue, (415) 555-3610"
hotline      IN   TXT  "Movie U. Network Hotline, (415) 555-4111"
rb           IN   TXT  "Richard Boisclair, (415) 555-9612"
```

*Binary Representation:*

```
RP type code: 17
    +--+--+--+--+--+--+--+--+--+--+--+--+--+--+--+--+
    /                     MAILBOX                    /
    /                                                /
    +--+--+--+--+--+--+--+--+--+--+--+--+--+--+--+--+
    /                     TXTDNAME                   /
    /                                                /
    +--+--+--+--+--+--+--+--+--+--+--+--+--+--+--+--+
```

where:

| | |
|---|---|
| MAILBOX | A <domain-name> that specifies the mailbox for the responsible person. |
| TXTDNAME | A <domain-name> for which TXT RR's exist. A subsequent query can be performed to retrieve the associated TXT resource records at <txt-dname> |

## RT Route Through—experimental

*Textual Representation:*

```
<owner> <ttl> <class> RT <preference> <intermediate-host>
```

*Example:*

```
sh.prime.com.  IN  RT   2   Relay.Prime.COM..
               IN  RT  10   NET.Prime.COM.
```

*Binary Representation:*

```
RT type code: 21
    +--+--+--+--+--+--+--+--+--+--+--+--+--+--+--+--+
    |                     PREFERENCE                |
    +--+--+--+--+--+--+--+--+--+--+--+--+--+--+--+--+
    /                    INTERMEDIATE               /
    /                                               /
    +--+--+--+--+--+--+--+--+--+--+--+--+--+--+--+--+
where:
PREFERENCE      A 16 bit integer which specifies the preference
                given to this RR among others at the same owner.
                Lower values are preferred.
EXCHANGE        A <domain-name> which specifies a host which will
                serve as an intermediate in reaching the host
                specified by <owner>.
```

## X25 X.25 address—experimental

*Textual Representation:*

```
<owner> <ttl> <class> X25 <PSDN-address>
```

*Example:*

```
relay.pink.com.  IN  X25   31105060845
```

*Binary Representation:*

```
X25 type code: 19
    +--+--+--+--+--+--+--+--+--+--+--+--+--+--+--+--+
    /                    PSDN ADDRESS               /
    +--+--+--+--+--+--+--+--+--+--+--+--+--+--+--+--+
where:
PSDN ADDRESS    A <character-string> which identifies the PSDN
                (Public Switched Data Network) address in the
                X.121 numbering plan associated with <owner>.
```

# *New Types from RFC 1664*

## PX pointer to X.400/RFC822 mapping information

*Textual Representation:*

```
<owner> <ttl> <class> PX <preference> <RFC822 address> <X.400 address>
```

*Example:*

```
ab.net2.it.  IN  PX  10   ab.net2.it.  O-ab.PRMD-net2.ADMDb.C-it.
```

*Binary Representation:*

```
PX type code: 26
    +--+--+--+--+--+--+--+--+--+--+--+--+--+--+--+--+
    |                     PREFERENCE                |
    +--+--+--+--+--+--+--+--+--+--+--+--+--+--+--+--+
    /                      MAP822                   /
    /                                               /
    +--+--+--+--+--+--+--+--+--+--+--+--+--+--+--+--+
    /                      MAPX400                  /
    /                                               /
    +--+--+--+--+--+--+--+--+--+--+--+--+--+--+--+--+
```

```
where:
PREFERENCE      A 16 bit integer which specifies the preference given to
                this RR among others at the same owner.  Lower values
                are preferred.
MAP822          A <domain-name> element containing <rfc822-domain>,
the
                RFC822 part of the RFC1327 mapping information.
MAPX400         A <domain-name> element containing the value of
                <x400-in-domain-syntax> derived from the X.400 part of
                the RFC1327 mapping information.
```

## Classes
*(from RFC 1035, page 13)*

CLASS fields appear in resource records. The following CLASS mnemonics and values are defined:

IN: 1 the Internet
CS: 2 the CSNET class (Obsolete—used only for examples in some obsolete RFCs)
CH: 3 the CHAO class
HS: 4 the Hesiod class

# DNS Message

In order to write programs that parse DNS packets, you need to understand the message format. DNS queries and responses are most often contained within UDP packets. Each message is fully contained within a UDP packet. If the query and response are sent over TCP, they are prefixed with a two-byte value indicating the length of the query or response, excluding the two-byte length. The format and content of the DNS packet are given in the following sections.

## Format
*(from RFC 1035, page 25)*

All communications inside of the domain protocol are carried in a single format called a *message*. The top-level format of the message is divided into five sections (some of which are empty in certain cases) as follows:

```
+---------------------+
|       Header        |
+---------------------+
|      Question       | the question for the name server
+---------------------+
|       Answer        | RRs answering the question
+---------------------+
|      Authority      | RRs pointing toward an authority
+---------------------+
|      Additional     | RRs holding additional information
+---------------------+
```

The Header section is always present. The header includes fields that specify which of the remaining sections are present and also specify whether the message is a query or a response, a standard query or some other opcode, and so on.

The names of the sections after the header are derived from their use in standard queries. The Question section contains fields that describe a question to a name server. These fields are a query type (QTYPE), a query class (QCLASS), and a query domain name (QNAME). The last three sections have the same format: a possibly empty list of concatenated resource records (RRs). The Answer section contains RRs that answer the question; the Authority section contains RRs that point toward an authoritative name server; the Additional records section contains RRs that relate to the query but are not strictly answers for the question.

## *Header Section Format*

*(from RFC 1035, pages 26–28)*

```
                                         1  1  1  1  1  1
     0  1  2  3  4  5  6  7  8  9  0  1  2  3  4  5
   +--+--+--+--+--+--+--+--+--+--+--+--+--+--+--+--+
   |                      ID                       |
   +--+--+--+--+--+--+--+--+--+--+--+--+--+--+--+--+
   |QR|   Opcode  |AA|TC|RD|RA|   Z    |   RCODE   |
   +--+--+--+--+--+--+--+--+--+--+--+--+--+--+--+--+
   |                    QDCOUNT                    |
   +--+--+--+--+--+--+--+--+--+--+--+--+--+--+--+--+
   |                    ANCOUNT                    |
   +--+--+--+--+--+--+--+--+--+--+--+--+--+--+--+--+
   |                    NSCOUNT                    |
   +--+--+--+--+--+--+--+--+--+--+--+--+--+--+--+--+
   |                    ARCOUNT                    |
   +--+--+--+--+--+--+--+--+--+--+--+--+--+--+--+--+
```

```
where:
ID              A 16 bit identifier assigned by the program that
                generates any kind of query.  This identifier is copied
                the corresponding reply and can be used by the requester
                to match up replies to outstanding queries.
QR              A one bit field that specifies whether this message is a
                query (0), or a response (1).
OPCODE          A four bit field that specifies kind of query in this
                message.  This value is set by the originator of a query
                and copied into the response.  The values are:
                0               a standard query (QUERY)
                1               an inverse query (IQUERY)
                2               a server status request (STATUS)
                3-15            reserved for future use
AA              Authoritative Answer - this bit is valid in responses,
                and specifies that the responding name server is an
                authority for the domain name in question section.
                Note that the contents of the answer section may have
                multiple owner names because of aliases.  The AA bit
```

corresponds to the name which matches the query name, or the first owner name in the answer section.

TC — TrunCation - specifies that this message was truncated due to length greater than that permitted on the transmission channel.

RD — Recursion Desired - this bit may be set in a query and is copied into the response. If RD is set, it directs the name server to pursue the query recursively. Recursive query support is optional.

RA — Recursion Available - this bit is set or cleared in a response, and denotes whether recursive query support is available in the name server.

Z — Reserved for future use. Must be zero in all queries and responses.

RCODE — Response code - this 4 bit field is set as part of responses. The values have the following interpretation:

0 — No error condition

1 — Format error - The name server was unable to interpret the query.

2 — Server failure - The name server was unable to process this query due to a problem with the name server.

3 — Name Error - Meaningful only for responses from an authoritative name server, this code signifies that the domain name referenced in the query does not exist.

4 — Not Implemented - The name server does not support the requested kind of query.

5 — Refused - The name server refuses to perform the specified operation for policy reasons. For example, a name server may not wish to provide the information to the particular requester, or a name server may not wish to perform a particular operation (e.g., zone transfer) for particular data.

6-15 — Reserved for future use.

QDCOUNT — an unsigned 16 bit integer specifying the number of entries in the question section.

ANCOUNT — an unsigned 16 bit integer specifying the number of resource records in the answer section.

NSCOUNT — an unsigned 16 bit integer specifying the number of name server resource records in the authority records section.

ARCOUNT — an unsigned 16 bit integer specifying the number of resource records in the additional records section.

## Question Section Format
*(from RFC 1035, pages 28–29)*

The Question section is used to carry the "question" in most queries—that is, the parameters that define what is being asked. The section contains QDCOUNT (usually one) entries, each of the following format:

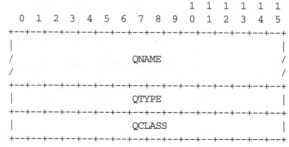

```
                                  1  1  1  1  1  1
      0  1  2  3  4  5  6  7  8  9  0  1  2  3  4  5
    +--+--+--+--+--+--+--+--+--+--+--+--+--+--+--+--+
    |                                               |
    /                     QNAME                     /
    /                                               /
    +--+--+--+--+--+--+--+--+--+--+--+--+--+--+--+--+
    |                     QTYPE                     |
    +--+--+--+--+--+--+--+--+--+--+--+--+--+--+--+--+
    |                     QCLASS                    |
    +--+--+--+--+--+--+--+--+--+--+--+--+--+--+--+--+
```

where:

| | |
|---|---|
| QNAME | a domain name represented as a sequence of labels, where each label consists of a length octet followed by that number of octets. The domain name terminates with the zero length octet for the null label of the root. Note that this field may be an odd number of octets; no padding is used. |
| QTYPE | a two octet code which specifies the type of the query. The values for this field include all codes valid for a TYPE field, together with some more general codes which can match more than one type of RR. |
| QCLASS | a two octet code that specifies the class of the query. For example, the QCLASS field is IN for the Internet. |

## QCLASS Values
*(from RFC 1035, page 13)*

QCLASS fields appear in the Question section of a query. QCLASS values are a superset of CLASS values; every CLASS is a valid QCLASS. In addition to CLASS values, the following QCLASSes are defined:

*:    255 any class

## QTYPE Values
*(from RFC 1035, pages 12–13)*

QTYPE fields appear in the question part of a query. QTYPES are a superset of TYPEs, hence all TYPEs are valid QTYPEs. In addition, the following QTYPEs are defined:

| | |
|---|---|
| AXFR: | 252 A request for a transfer of an entire zone |
| MAILB: | 253 A request for mailbox-related records (MB, MG or MR) |

MAILA:      254 A request for mail agent RRs (Obsolete—see MX)
*:          255 A request for all records

## *Answer, Authority, and Additional Section Format*
*(from RFC 1035, pages 29–30)*

The Answer, Authority, and Additional sections all share the same format: a variable number of resource records, where the number of records is specified in the corresponding count field in the header. Each resource record has the following format:

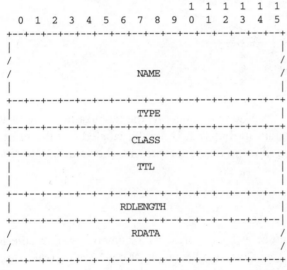

```
                                    1 1 1 1 1 1
        0 1 2 3 4 5 6 7 8 9 0 1 2 3 4 5
      +--+--+--+--+--+--+--+--+--+--+--+--+--+--+--+--+
      |                                               |
      /                                               /
      /                     NAME                      /
      |                                               |
      +--+--+--+--+--+--+--+--+--+--+--+--+--+--+--+--+
      |                     TYPE                      |
      +--+--+--+--+--+--+--+--+--+--+--+--+--+--+--+--+
      |                     CLASS                     |
      +--+--+--+--+--+--+--+--+--+--+--+--+--+--+--+--+
      |                     TTL                       |
      |                                               |
      +--+--+--+--+--+--+--+--+--+--+--+--+--+--+--+--+
      |                   RDLENGTH                    |
      +--+--+--+--+--+--+--+--+--+--+--+--+--+--+--+--|
      /                    RDATA                      /
      /                                               /
      +--+--+--+--+--+--+--+--+--+--+--+--+--+--+--+--+
```

where:
NAME        a domain name to which this resource record pertains.
TYPE        two octets containing one of the RR type codes.  This
            field specifies the meaning of the data in the RDATA
            field.
CLASS       two octets which specify the class of the data in the
            RDATA field.
TTL         a 32 bit unsigned integer that specifies the time
            interval (in seconds) that the resource record may be
            cached before it should be discarded.  Zero values are
            interpreted to mean that the RR can only be used for the
            transaction in progress, and should not be cached.
RDLENGTH    an unsigned 16 bit integer that specifies the length in
            octets of the RDATA field.
RDATA       a variable length string of octets that describes the
            resource.  The format of this information varies
            according to the TYPE and CLASS of the resource record.
            For example, if the TYPE is A and the CLASS is IN,
            the RDATA field is a 4 octet ARPA Internet address.

## Data Transmission Order
*(from RFC 1035, pages 8–9)*

The order of transmission of the header and data described in this document is resolved to the octet level. Whenever a diagram shows a group of octets, the order of transmission of those octets is the normal order in which they are read in English. For example, in the following diagram, the octets are transmitted in the order they are numbered:

```
 0                   1
 0 1 2 3 4 5 6 7 8 9 0 1 2 3 4 5
+-+-+-+-+-+-+-+-+-+-+-+-+-+-+-+-+
|       1       |       2       |
+-+-+-+-+-+-+-+-+-+-+-+-+-+-+-+-+
|       3       |       4       |
+-+-+-+-+-+-+-+-+-+-+-+-+-+-+-+-+
|       5       |       6       |
+-+-+-+-+-+-+-+-+-+-+-+-+-+-+-+-+
```

Whenever an octet represents a numeric quantity, the leftmost bit in the diagram is the high order or most significant bit. That is, the bit labeled 0 is the most significant bit. For example, the following diagram represents the value 170 (decimal):

```
 0 1 2 3 4 5 6 7
+-+-+-+-+-+-+-+-+
|1 0 1 0 1 0 1 0|
+-+-+-+-+-+-+-+-+
```

Similarly, whenever a multi-octet field represents a numeric quantity, the leftmost bit of the whole field is the most significant bit. When a multi-octet quantity is transmitted, the most significant octet is transmitted first.

# Resource Record Data

## Data Format

In addition to two- and four-octet integer values, resource record data can contain *domain names* or *character strings*.

### Domain Name
*(from RFC 1035, page 10)*

Domain names in messages are expressed in terms of a sequence of labels. Each label is represented as a one octet length field followed by that number of octets. Since every domain name ends with the null label of the root, a domain name is terminated by a length byte of zero. The high order two bits of every length octet must be zero, and the remaining six bits of the length field limit the label to 63 octets or less.

## Message Compression
*(from RFC 1035, page 30)*

In order to reduce the size of messages, the domain system utilizes a compression scheme that eliminates the repetition of domain names in a message. In this scheme, an entire domain name or a list of labels at the end of a domain name is replaced with a pointer to a prior occurrence of the same name.

The pointer takes the form of a two octet sequence:

```
+--+--+--+--+--+--+--+--+--+--+--+--+--+--+--+--+
| 1  1|                 OFFSET                   |
+--+--+--+--+--+--+--+--+--+--+--+--+--+--+--+--+
```

The first two bits are ones. This allows a pointer to be distinguished from a label, since the label must begin with two zero bits because labels are restricted to 63 octets or less. (The 10 and 01 combinations are reserved for future use.) The OFFSET field specifies an offset from the start of the message (that is, the first octet of the ID field in the domain header). A zero offset specifies the first byte of the ID field, and so on.

## Character String
*(from RFC 1035, page 13)*

A character string is a single length octet followed by that number of characters. A character string is treated as binary information and can be up to 256 characters in length (including the length octet).

# B

## *Installing the DNS Server from CD-ROM*

This brief appendix guides you through installing the DNS Server from CD-ROM.

1. Insert the Windows NT Server CD-ROM in your CD-ROM drive.

2. Open the Control Panel, and double-click the **Network** icon.

3. Click the **Services** tab.

4. Click the **Add** button.

5. Double-click **Microsoft DNS Server**.

6. You'll be prompted for the location of your CD-ROM drive. Enter it, and press Return.

7. After the installation, you'll need to reboot. Following the reboot, the DNS Server will be running, and you'll see **DNS Manager** in the **Administrative Tools (Common)** menu.

# C

# *Converting from BIND to the Microsoft DNS Server*

This appendix covers the steps necessary to convert a BIND version 4.x name server to a Microsoft DNS Server. We assume that after the conversion, you'll use DNS Manager for any future changes.

## Step 1: Stop the Microsoft DNS Server

The first step is stopping the DNS Server on the NT server, if it's running. Follow the instructions in the section "Starting and Stopping the DNS Server" in Chapter 4, *Setting Up the Microsoft DNS Server*, if you're not familiar with the process of starting and stopping an NT service.

## Step 2: Change Zone Database Filenaming Convention

This step is optional. Chances are, your BIND zone database files don't follow the same naming convention used by the Microsoft DNS Server. Recall from Chapter 4 that the Microsoft convention is the name of the zone followed by the *.dns* extension—for example, *movie.edu.dns*. You can continue to use your current naming convention, but if you add new zones with DNS Manager, they'll have the *.dns* extensions unless you go out of your way to make the names conform to your scheme. If you're not particularly attached to your naming scheme and don't want to fight DNS Manager every time you create a new zone, this Perl script will rename your zone database files in the *.dns* style and modify your *named.boot* file accordingly:

```
# name-convert.pl -- Convert zone database file naming convention in
#                    a BIND named.boot file to Microsoft *.dns format
```

```
#

die "usage: name-convert.pl path-to-named.boot\n" unless $ARGV[0];

open (BOOTIN, $ARGV[0]) || die "Can't open boot file for reading: $!\n";
open (BOOTOUT, ">boot") || die "Can't open boot file for writing: $!\n";

while (<BOOTIN>) {
    $dir="$1/" if /^directory\s+(.+).*$/;
    &changeit (1, $1, $2) if /^primary\s+(.+)\s+(.+)$/;
    &changeit (2, $1, $5, $2) if /^secondary\s+([\w\.]+)\s+(((\d{1,3}\.){3}\
    d{1,3}\s+)+)(.+)$/;
    &changeit (3, "cache", $1) if /^cache\s+\.\s+(.+)$/;
}

sub changeit {
    local ($zonetype, $zonename, $oldfilename, $mastersips) = @_;
    $newfilename="$zonename.dns";
    rename ($dir.$oldfilename, $dir.$newfilename) || print "Error renaming
    $oldfilename to $newfilename!\n";
    if ($zonetype == 1) {
        print BOOTOUT "primary $zonename $newfilename\n";
    } elsif ($zonetype == 2) {
        print BOOTOUT "secondary $zonename $mastersips $newfilename\n";
    } else {
        print BOOTOUT "cache . $newfilename\n";
    }
}
```

The script takes one argument: the name of the name server boot file, for example:

**name-convert.pl /etc/named.boot**

It outputs a file called *boot* in the current directory, which is a Microsoft DNS Server boot file with the zone database filenames changed. It's probably easiest to run the script on the UNIX host with the BIND name server, then copy over *boot* and the newly renamed *\*.dns* zone database files.

## Step 3: Copy Files

The next step is copying the necessary files from the BIND name server to the Windows NT server. You'll need to copy the name server boot file, usually */etc/named.boot*, and all the zone database files that the BIND server is a primary master for. The zone database files will be in the directory specified by the *directory* directive in the boot file. The files should be copied to the *%SystemRoot%\system32\dns* directory on the NT server. The *named.boot* file goes in that directory, too, but you need to rename it to just *boot*. One final note: only the *primary, secondary,* and *cache* directives are supported. You should delete the *directory* directive from your boot file or ignore the warning it causes in the Event Log.

# Step 4: Get a New Root Name Server Cache File

Now is a good time to make sure that you've got the latest and greatest root name server cache file. Follow the instructions in Chapter 4 to retrieve the file from *ftp.rs.internic.net.* Be sure the name matches the one in the boot file's *cache* directive. If you went through the name conversion process (step 2), the file should be called *cache.dns.*

# Step 5: Change to Booting from the Boot File

Next you need to tell the Microsoft DNS Server to obtain its configuration information—or boot from—the newly copied BIND boot file rather than the Registry. You'll need to start *Regedit* for this. Choose **Start → Run**, and enter **regedit**. Then find this key in the Registry:

*HKEY_LOCAL_MACHINE\SYSTEM\CurrentControlSet\Services\DNS\Parameters\ EnableRegistryBoot*

Double-click the *EnableRegistryBoot* key. In the edit box, change the value to 0 (zero). Don't delete the key, just change its value. And don't close *Regedit*—you'll need it again in a minute.

# Step 6: Restart the DNS Server

Now restart the DNS Server. The server will now read the BIND boot file for its configuration information and—here's the nice part—update its configuration information in the Registry to match what it read from the boot file. You can verify that the name server really did boot from the boot file: select the server in the left pane, and choose **DNS → Properties**. Then select the **Boot Method** tab. This is a read-only indication of how the server booted—from a boot file or the Registry.

If you want to the server to use the boot file permanently, then you're finished now. But you need to beware of DNS Manager. You can safely use DNS Manager to read and even change the contents of your existing zones, but if you use it to add or delete a zone, it will silently change the DNS Server to boot from the Registry. Don't say we didn't warn you!

# Step 7: Change to Booting from the Registry

Finally, you need to configure the DNS Server to boot from the Registry. Hopefully you left *Regedit* open, because remember that *EnableRegistryBoot* key you changed to 0? Now you need to change it back to 1 (one). After making the change you can exit *Regedit.*

Congratulations! You're done! The next time the DNS Server starts, it will boot from the Registry. In the meantime, you can use DNS Manager to make all the changes you want.

# D

## *Top-Level Domains*

This table lists all of the two-letter country codes and all of the top-level domains that aren't countries. Not all of the countries are registered in the Internet's name space at the time of this writing, but there aren't many missing.

| Domain | Country or Organization | Domain | Country or Organization |
|--------|-------------------------|--------|-------------------------|
| AD | Andorra | BF | Burkina Faso |
| AE | United Arab Emirates | BG | Bulgaria |
| AF | Afghanistan | BH | Bahrain |
| AG | Antigua and Barbuda | BI | Burundi |
| AI | Anguilla | BJ | Benin |
| AL | Albania | BM | Bermuda |
| AM | Armenia | BN | Brunei Darussalam |
| AN | Netherlands Antilles | BO | Bolivia |
| AO | Angola | BR | Brazil |
| AQ | Antarctica | BS | Bahamas |
| AR | Argentina | BT | Bhutan |
| ARPA | ARPA Internet | BV | Bouvet Island |
| AS | American Samoa | BW | Botswana |
| AT | Austria | BY | Belarus |
| AU | Australia | BZ | Belize |
| AW | Aruba | CA | Canada |
| AZ | Azerbaijan | CC | Cocos (Keeling) Islands |
| BA | Bosnia and Herzegowina | CD | Congo, Democratic Republic of the |
| BB | Barbados | | |
| BD | Bangladesh | CF | Central African Republic |
| BE | Belgium | CG | Congo |

| Domain | Country or Organization | Domain | Country or Organization |
|--------|------------------------|--------|------------------------|
| CH | Switzerland | FX | France, Metropolitan |
| CI | Cote d'Ivoire | GA | Gabon |
| CK | Cook Islands | GB | United Kingdom* |
| CL | Chile | GOV | government |
| CM | Cameroon | GD | Grenada |
| CN | China | GE | Georgia |
| CO | Colombia | GF | French Guiana |
| COM | commercial | GH | Ghana |
| CR | Costa Rica | GI | Gibraltar |
| CU | Cuba | GL | Greenland |
| CV | Cape Verde | GM | Gambia |
| CX | Christmas Island | GN | Guinea |
| CY | Cyprus | GP | Guadeloupe |
| CZ | Czech Republic | GQ | Equatorial Guinea |
| DE | Germany | GR | Greece |
| DJ | Djibouti | GS | South Georgia and the South Sandwich Islands |
| DK | Denmark | | |
| DM | Dominica | GT | Guatemala |
| DO | Dominican Republic | GU | Guam |
| DZ | Algeria | GW | Guinea-Bissau |
| EC | Ecuador | GY | Guyana |
| EDU | education | HK | Hong Kong |
| EE | Estonia | HM | Heard and McDonald Islands |
| EG | Egypt | HN | Honduras |
| EH | Western Sahara | HR | Croatia |
| ER | Eritrea | HT | Haiti |
| ES | Spain | HU | Hungary |
| ET | Ethiopia | ID | Indonesia |
| FI | Finland | IE | Ireland |
| FJ | Fiji | IL | Israel |
| FK | Falkland Islands (Malvinas) | IN | India |
| FM | Micronesia, Federated States of | INT | international entities |
| | | IO | British Indian Ocean Territory |
| FO | Faroe Islands | IQ | Iraq |
| FR | France | IR | Iran |

* In practice, the United Kingdom uses "UK" for its top-level domain.

| Domain | Country or Organization | Domain | Country or Organization |
|--------|-------------------------|--------|-------------------------|
| IS | Iceland | ML | Mali |
| IT | Italy | MM | Myanmar |
| JM | Jamaica | MN | Mongolia |
| JO | Jordan | MO | Macau |
| JP | Japan | MP | Northern Mariana Islands |
| KE | Kenya | MQ | Martinique |
| KG | Kyrgyzstan | MR | Mauritania |
| KH | Cambodia | MS | Montserrat |
| KI | Kiribati | MT | Malta |
| KM | Comoros | MU | Mauritius |
| KN | Saint Kitts and Nevis | MV | Maldives |
| KP | Korea, Democratic People's Republic of | MW | Malawi |
| | | MX | Mexico |
| KR | Korea, Republic of | MY | Malaysia |
| KW | Kuwait | MZ | Mozambique |
| KY | Cayman Islands | NA | Namibia |
| KZ | Kazakhstan | NATO | North Atlantic Treaty Organization |
| LA | Lao People's Democratic Republic | | |
| | | NC | New Caledonia |
| LB | Lebanon | NE | Niger |
| LC | Saint Lucia | NET | networking organizations |
| LI | Liechtenstein | NF | Norfolk Island |
| LK | Sri Lanka | NG | Nigeria |
| LR | Liberia | NI | Nicaragua |
| LS | Lesotho | NL | Netherlands |
| LT | Lithuania | NO | Norway |
| LU | Luxembourg | NP | Nepal |
| LV | Latvia | NR | Nauru |
| LY | Libyan Arab Jamahiriya | NU | Niue |
| MA | Morocco | NZ | New Zealand |
| MC | Monaco | OM | Oman |
| MD | Moldova, Republic of | ORG | organizations |
| MG | Madagascar | PA | Panama |
| MH | Marshall Islands | PE | Peru |
| MIL | military | PF | French Polynesia |
| MK | Macedonia, the Former Yugoslav Republic of | PG | Papua New Guinea |

| Domain | Country or Organization | Domain | Country or Organization |
|--------|-------------------------|--------|-------------------------|
| PH | Philippines | TG | Togo |
| PK | Pakistan | TH | Thailand |
| PL | Poland | TJ | Tajikistan |
| PM | St. Pierre and Miquelon | TK | Tokelau |
| PN | Pitcairn | TM | Turkmenistan |
| PR | Puerto Rico | TN | Tunisia |
| PT | Portugal | TO | Tonga |
| PW | Palau | TP | East Timor |
| PY | Paraguay | TR | Turkey |
| QA | Qatar | TT | Trinidad and Tobago |
| RE | Reunion | TV | Tuvalu |
| RO | Romania | TW | Taiwan, Province of China |
| RU | Russian Federation | TZ | Tanzania, United Republic of |
| RW | Rwanda | UA | Ukraine |
| SA | Saudi Arabia | UG | Uganda |
| SB | Solomon Islands | UK | United Kingdom |
| SC | Seychelles | UM | United States Minor Outlying Islands |
| SD | Sudan | | |
| SE | Sweden | US | United States |
| SG | Singapore | UY | Uruguay |
| SH | St. Helena | UZ | Uzbekistan |
| SI | Slovenia | VA | Holy See (Vatican City State) |
| SJ | Svalbard and Jan Mayen Islands | VC | Saint Vincent and the Grenadines |
| SK | Slovakia | VE | Venezuela |
| SL | Sierra Leone | VG | Virgin Islands (British) |
| SM | San Marino | VI | Virgin Islands (U.S.) |
| SN | Senegal | VN | Vietnam |
| SO | Somalia | VU | Vanuatu |
| SR | Suriname | WF | Wallis and Futuna Islands |
| ST | Sao Tome and Principe | WS | Samoa |
| SV | El Salvador | YE | Yemen |
| SY | Syrian Arab Republic | YT | Mayotte |
| SZ | Swaziland | YU | Yugoslavia |
| TC | Turks and Caicos Islands | ZA | South Africa |
| TD | Chad | ZM | Zambia |
| TF | French Southern Territories | ZW | Zimbabwe |

# E

# *Domain Registration Form*

This appendix contains the form used to register the name of your domain with the InterNIC. For the most current version of this form, or for the InterNIC's online, HTML-based interface for completing the form, see *http://www.rs.internic.net/rs-internic.html.*

```
[ URL ftp://rs.internic.net/templates/domain-template.txt ] [ 03/98 ]

******* Please DO NOT REMOVE Version Number or Sections A-Q ********

Domain Version Number: 4.0

******* Email completed agreement to hostmaster@internic.net *******

    NETWORK SOLUTIONS, INC.

    DOMAIN NAME REGISTRATION AGREEMENT


A.  Introduction. This domain name registration agreement
("Registration Agreement") is submitted to NETWORK SOLUTIONS, INC.
("NSI") for the purpose of applying for and registering a domain name
on the Internet. If this Registration Agreement is accepted by NSI,
and a domain name is registered in NSI's domain name database and
assigned to the Registrant, Registrant ("Registrant") agrees to be
bound by the terms of this Registration Agreement and the terms of
NSI's Domain Name Dispute Policy ("Dispute Policy") which is
incorporated herein by reference and made a part of this Registration
Agreement. This Registration Agreement shall be accepted at the
offices of NSI.

B. Fees and Payments.

1) Registration or renewal (re-registration) date through March 31, 1998:
Registrant agrees to pay a registration fee of One Hundred United States
```

Dollars (US$100) as consideration for the registration of each new domain
name or Fifty United States Dollars (US$50) to renew (re-register) an
existing registration.

2) Registration or renewal date on and after April 1, 1998:  Registrant
agrees to pay a registration fee of Seventy United States Dollars (US$70)
as consideration for the registration of each new domain name or the
applicable renewal (re-registration) fee (currently Thirty-Five United
States Dollars (US$35)) at the time of renewal (re-registration).

3) Period of Service:  The non-refundable fee covers a period of two (2)
years for each new registration, and one (1) year for each renewal,
and includes any permitted modification(s) to the domain name record
during the covered period.

4) Payment:  Payment is due to Network Solutions within thirty (30)
days from the date of the invoice.

C.   Dispute Policy. Registrant agrees, as a condition to
submitting this Registration Agreement, and if the Registration
Agreement is accepted by NSI, that the Registrant shall be bound by
NSI's current Dispute Policy. The current version of the Dispute
Policy may be found at the InterNIC Registration Services web site:
"http://www.netsol.com/rs/dispute-policy.html".

D.   Dispute Policy Changes or Modifications. Registrant agrees
that NSI, in its sole discretion, may change or modify the Dispute
Policy, incorporated by reference herein, at any time. Registrant
agrees that Registrant's maintaining the registration of a domain name
after changes or modifications to the Dispute Policy become effective
constitutes Registrant's continued acceptance of these changes or
modifications. Registrant agrees that if Registrant considers any such
changes or modifications to be unacceptable, Registrant may request
that the domain name be deleted from the domain name database.

E.   Disputes. Registrant agrees that, if the registration of its
domain name is challenged by any third party, the Registrant will be
subject to the provisions specified in the Dispute Policy.

F.   Agents. Registrant agrees that if this Registration Agreement
is completed by an agent for the Registrant, such as an ISP or
Administrative Contact/Agent, the Registrant is nonetheless bound as a
principal by all terms and conditions herein, including the Dispute
Policy.

G.   Limitation of Liability. Registrant agrees that NSI shall have
no liability to the Registrant for any loss Registrant may incur in
connection with NSI's processing of this Registration Agreement, in
connection with NSI's processing of any authorized modification to the
domain name's record during the covered period, as a result of the
Registrant's ISP's failure to pay either the initial registration fee
or renewal fee, or as a result of the application of the provisions of
the Dispute Policy. Registrant agrees that in no event shall the
maximum liability of NSI under this Agreement for any matter exceed
Five Hundred United States Dollars (US$500).

H.   Indemnity. Registrant agrees, in the event the Registration Agreement is accepted by NSI and a subsequent dispute arises with any third party, to indemnify and hold NSI harmless pursuant to the terms and conditions contained in the Dispute Policy.

I.   Breach. Registrant agrees that failure to abide by any provision of this Registration Agreement or the Dispute Policy may be considered by NSI to be a material breach and that NSI may provide a written notice, describing the breach, to the Registrant. If, within thirty (30) days of the date of mailing such notice, the Registrant fails to provide evidence, which is reasonably satisfactory to NSI, that it has not breached its obligations, then NSI may delete Registrant's registration of the domain name. Any such breach by a Registrant shall not be deemed to be excused simply because NSI did not act earlier in response to that, or any other, breach by the Registrant.

J.   No Guaranty. Registrant agrees that, by registration of a domain name, such registration does not confer immunity from objection to either the registration or use of the domain name.

K.   Warranty. Registrant warrants by submitting this Registration Agreement that, to the best of Registrant's knowledge and belief, the information submitted herein is true and correct, and that any future changes to this information will be provided to NSI in a timely manner according to the domain name modification procedures in place at that time. Breach of this warranty will constitute a material breach.

L.   Revocation. Registrant agrees that NSI may delete a Registrant's domain name if this Registration Agreement, or subsequent modification(s) thereto, contains false or misleading information, or conceals or omits any information NSI would likely consider material to its decision to approve this Registration Agreement.

M.   Right of Refusal. NSI, in its sole discretion, reserves the right to refuse to approve the Registration Agreement for any Registrant. Registrant agrees that the submission of this Registration Agreement does not obligate NSI to accept this Registration Agreement. Registrant agrees that NSI shall not be liable for loss or damages that may result from NSI's refusal to accept this Registration Agreement.

N.   Severability. Registrant agrees that the terms of this Registration Agreement are severable. If any term or provision is declared invalid, it shall not affect the remaining terms or provisions which shall continue to be binding.

O.   Entirety. Registrant agrees that this Registration Agreement and the Dispute Policy is the complete and exclusive agreement between Registrant and NSI regarding the registration of Registrant's domain name. This Registration Agreement and the Dispute Policy supersede all prior agreements and understandings, whether established by custom, practice, policy, or precedent.

P.   Governing Law. Registrant agrees that this Registration
Agreement shall be governed in all respects by and construed in
accordance with the laws of the Commonwealth of Virginia, United
States of America. By submitting this Registration Agreement,
Registrant consents to the exclusive jurisdiction and venue of the
United States District Court for the Eastern District of Virginia,
Alexandria Division. If there is no jurisdiction in the United States
District Court for the Eastern District of Virginia, Alexandria
Division, then jurisdiction shall be in the Circuit Court of Fairfax
County, Fairfax, Virginia.

Q.   This is Domain Name Registration Agreement Version
Number 4.0. This Registration Agreement is only for registrations
under top-level domains: COM, ORG, NET, and EDU. By completing
and submitting this Registration Agreement for consideration and
acceptance by NSI, the Registrant agrees that he/she has read and
agrees to be bound by A through P above.


```
Authorization
0a.   (N)ew (M)odify (D)elete....:
0b.   Auth Scheme...............:
0c.   Auth Info.................:

1.    Comments..................:

2.    Complete Domain Name......:

Organization Using Domain Name

3a.   Organization Name.........:
3b.   Street Address............,:
3c.   City......................:
3d.   State.....................:
3e.   Postal Code...............:
3f.   Country...................:

Administrative Contact
4a.   NIC Handle (if known).....:
4b.   (I)ndividual (R)ole.......:
4c.   Name (Last, First)........:
4d.   Organization Name.........:
4e.   Street Address............:
4f.   City......................:
4g.   State.....................:
4h.   Postal Code...............:
4i.   Country...................:
4j.   Phone Number..............:
4k.   Fax Number................:
4l.   E-Mailbox.................:

Technical Contact
5a.   NIC Handle (if known).....:
5b.   (I)ndividual (R)ole.......:
```

```
5c.   Name (Last, First).........:
5d.   Organization Name..........:
5e.   Street Address.............:
5f.   City.......................:
5g.   State......................:
5h.   Postal Code................:
5i.   Country....................:
5j.   Phone Number...............:
5k.   Fax Number.................:
5l.   E-Mailbox..................:

Billing Contact
6a.   NIC Handle (if known)......:
6b.   (I)ndividual (R)ole........:
6c.   Name (Last, First).........:
6d.   Organization Name..........:
6e.   Street Address.............:
6f.   City.......................:
6g.   State......................:
6h.   Postal Code................:
6i.   Country....................:
6j.   Phone Number...............:
6k.   Fax Number.................:
6l.   E-Mailbox..................:

Prime Name Server
7a.   Primary Server Hostname....:
7b.   Primary Server Netaddress..:

Secondary Name Server(s)
8a.   Secondary Server Hostname..:
8b.   Secondary Server Netaddress:


END OF AGREEMENT


For instructions, please refer to:
"http://rs.internic.net/help/instructions.txt"
```

# F

# *in-addr.arpa*
# *Registration Form*

This appendix contains the form used to register your *in-addr.arpa* domain with ARIN, the American Registry for Internet Numbers. For the most current version of this form, see *http://www.arin.net/templates/inaddrtemplate.txt.*

03/98

```
*************** Please DO NOT REMOVE Version Number ******************

IN-ADDR Version Number: 1.0

************* Please see attached detailed instructions **************

Registration Action Type
0.   (N)ew (M)odify (D)elete:

Network Information
1a.   Network Name.................:
1b.   Start of Network Block........:
1c.   End of Network Block..........:

2a.   Name of Organization..........:
2b.   Postal address of Organization:

Technical Contact
3a.   ARIN-Handle (if known)........:
3b.   Name (Last, First)............:
3c.   Organization..................:
3d.   Postal Address................:

3e.   Phone Number..................:
3f.   E-Mail Address................:
```

```
Primary Name Server
4a.   Primary Server Hostname.......:
4b.   Primary Server Netaddress.....:

Secondary Name Server(s)
5a.   Secondary Server Hostname.....:
5b.   Secondary Server Netaddress...:

6.    Comments.....................:
```

----------------------------- cut here -----------------------------

GENERAL INSTRUCTIONS: REGISTERING INVERSE ADDRESSING (NAME MAPPING) WITH ARIN

The Internet uses a special domain to support gateway location and Internet address to host mapping called In-ADDR.ARPA.  The intent of this domain is to provide a guaranteed method to perform host address to host name mapping, and to facilitate queries to locate all gateways on a particular network in the Internet.  Whenever an application is used that requires user identification, i.e., ftp, or remote login, the domain must be registered in the IN-ADDR.ARPA zone or the application will be unable to determine the origin of the IP.

IN-ADDR domains are represented using the network number in reverse.

> EXAMPLE: The IN-ADDR domain for network 123.45.67.0 is represented as

> 67.45.123.IN-ADDR.ARPA.

> NOTE:  Please do not list your network number in reverse on your template.

Use the above template for registering new IN-ADDR entries, making changes to existing IN-ADDR records, and removing inverse-address mapping from the ARIN database and root servers.

The IN-ADDR template should be submitted via E-mail to ARIN at:

> hostmaster@arin.net

In order to ensure prompt and accurate processing of IN-ADDR requests, follow precisely the instructions below.  Please do not modify the template nor remove the version number.  IN-ADDR templates are automatically parsed.  Errors in a template result in the template being returned for correction.

Please send only one template per message.  In the Subject of the message, use the words: NEW IN-ADDR,  MODIFY IN-ADDR, or REMOVE IN-ADDR, as appropriate.

Please do not send hardcopy registrations to ARIN.  If you do not have an E-mail connection, you should arrange for your Internet Service Provider (ISP) to send E-mail applications to ARIN on your behalf.

When you submit a template, you will receive an auto-reply from ARIN with a ticket number.  The ticket number format is:

> ARIN -<year><month><day>.<queue position>.

Use the ticket number in the Subject of any message you send regarding a
registration action.  When the registration has been completed, you will be
notified via E-mail.

All ISPs receiving from ARIN /16 CIDR blocks (Class B) which are greater than or
equal to (>= )256 Class C's) will be responsible for maintaining all IN-ADDR.ARPA
domain  records for their respective customers.  The ISP is responsible for the
maintenance of IN-ADDR.ARPA domain records of all longer prefixes that have been
delegated out of that block.


DETAILED INSTRUCTIONS FOR COMPLETING EACH IN-ADDR TEMPLATE FIELD


Section 0.   Registration Action Type

N) New (M) Modify (D) Delete:

(N)   New:
      For new IN-ADDR registration, place an N after the colon.

(M)   Modify:
      To modify/change an EXISTING record IN-ADDR registration, place an M after
      the colon. When "M" is selected, the current records will be replaced with
      the information listed in the template.  Please provide a complete list of
      name servers in the order in which they should appear on the record.

      If the modification involves first registering a person or name server(s)
      not entered in the database, the instructions for completing Sections 2, 3,
      4 and 5 apply.  Search the WHOIS database for more information if you are
      unsure of the current information for the technical POC or name server(s).

      The requested changes will be made if ARIN registry personnel determine
      that the modification request was issued by an authorized source. The
      issuing source may be a listed contact for the domain, others in the same
      organization, the current provider, or a new provider initiating network
      support.

(D)   Delete.
      To delete an existing IN-ADDR from your network record, place a D after
      the colon.  List the IN-ADDR server and IP number and it will be deleted.
      The host entry will still exist in the global host tables.


Section 1.  Network Record Information.

1a.   Network Name.
      Please supply the network name.

          NOTE:  The network name is not the domain name.

      To verify an existing Network Name, use the searchable WHOIS database.

The Network Name is used as an identifier in Internet name and address tables. To create a network name, supply a short name consisting of a combination of up to 12 numbers and letters for the network. You may use a dash (-) as part of the Network Name, but no other special characters. Please do not use periods or underscores.

1b./1c.  Start/End of Network Block.

1b.  Start of Network Block.

If the network record is for a single network, enter the IP address of the single network here. Item 1c is then left blank. If the record is a block of IP addresses, enter the IP address of the start of the network block.

1c.  End of Network Block.

If the network record is a block of IP addresses, Item 1c will be the last IP address of the network block.

If you received a block of IP addresses from your ISP, there may already be IN-ADDR servers on the parent block held by that provider. Please query your ISP before submitting an IN-ADDR request.


Section 2.  Name and Postal Address of Organization.

2a.  Name of Organization.

The network is considered to be registered to an organization, even if the "organization" is an individual. If you are an ISP submitting this request on behalf of your customer, please provide here the name and postal address of the organization that uses the IP address(es).

2b.  Postal Address of Organization.

This is the physical address of the organization. Place the city, state, and zip code together on the same line below the Street Address or Post Office Box. Use a comma to separate the city and state. Do not insert a period following the state abbreviation. To change an address, please provide the new address information in this item, and flag the change in Section 6: Comments.

   EXAMPLE:

              111 Town Center Drive
              Herndon, VA 22070

If the organization is located in a country other than the United States, please include the two-letter country code on the last line by itself.

   EXAMPLE:
          161 James Street
          Montreal, QC H2S 2C8
          CA

For the country entry, please use the two-letter country code found at:

URL: [ftp://rs.arin.net/netinfo/iso3166-countrycodes]


NOTE: If you wish to make a change to an existing registered physical
address of an organization, please note the change you want in
Section 6: Comments.

Section 3. Technical Contact

The technical point of contact (POC) is the person responsible for
the technical aspects of maintaining the network's name servers.
The POC should be able to answer any utilization questions ARIN may have.

3a. User Handle (if known)

Each person in the ARIN database is assigned a user handle, which is a
unique tag consisting of the user's initials and a serial number. This
tag is used in database records indicate a POC for a domain name, network,
name server or other entity. Each user should have only one handle.

If the user handle is known, insert the handle in Item 3a and leave the
rest of Section 3 blank. If the user's handle is unknown or the user has
never been registered, leave Item 3a blank. The user's database record
will be updated with any new information on the template.

3b. Name (Last, First)
Enter the name of the Technical Contact in the format:

Last Name, First Name.

Separate first and last names by a comma.


3c. Organization.

Provide the name of the organization with which the Technical Contact
is affiliated. Refer to the instructions for Item 2a.

3d. Postal Address.

Refer to the instructions for Item 2b.



Section 4. Primary Name Server.

Networks are required to provide at least two independent servers for translating
address to name mapping for hosts in the domain. The servers should be in
physically separate locations and on different networks, if possible. The
servers should be active and responsive to domain name server (DNS) queries prior
to submission of this application.

ARIN requires that you provide complete information on your primary and
secondary servers in order to process your registration request. Incomplete
information in sections 4 and 5, or inactive servers will result in the return of
the registration request.

NOTE:   To change the name or the number of a registered name server, submit
            a separate IN-ADDR template requesting a modification of your IN-ADDR
            registration.  Do this by placing an M after the Modify command in
Section 0:   Registration Action Type. New IN-ADDR registrations cannot
            be used to change the name or the number of a registered name server.

4a.   Primary Name Server Hostname.
      Please provide the fully-qualified name of the machine that is to be
      the name server.

         EXAMPLE:
              Use "machine.domainame.com" not just "machine" or just
"domainame.com"
              Many reverse-authentication programs will not search for the
nameserver if only the domain name is listed.

4b.   Primary Name Server Netaddress.

      It is suggested that the fourth octet of an IP address of a server
      should be neither 0 nor 255.  The remaining 254 numbers in the fourth
      octet of the IP address are valid.


Section 5.   Secondary Name Server(s)

5a./5b.   Secondary Name Server Hostname/Secondary Name Server Netaddress.

      Please refer to the instructions and examples in Items 4a./4b. above.

      Copy Section 5 as needed to include all Secondary Name Servers.
      Do not renumber or change the copied section.  A maximum of six domain
      name servers may be added to a network record.


Section 6.   Comments.

Please use Section 6 to provide ARIN with all comments and any additional
detailed updates relevant to your IN-ADDR registration not provided in Sections 0
through 5. Please provide a brief explanation for
changing an organization name or point of contact information.

# G

## Microsoft DNS Server Registry Settings

### Global Server Settings

Global variables affecting the DNS Server's operation are stored as values of this Registry key:

> *HKEY_LOCAL_MACHINE\SYSTEM\CurrentControlSet\Services\DNS\ Parameters*

A list of values recognized by the server is listed in this appendix. Note that most values do not exist in the Registry by default. If the value is missing, the default value hardcoded in the DNS Server is used. These defaults are listed, too.

*EnableRegistryBoot*

> Value Type: REG_DWORD (Boolean)
>
> Default: 0 (False)
>
> Valid Range: 0–1 (False, True)
>
> Controls whether the DNS Server reads configuration information about zones from a BIND 4.x-compatible boot file or from the Registry. Using a boot file overwrites any zone configuration information already in the Registry (for example, primary master or slave zones added via DNS Manager). See Appendix C, *Converting from BIND to the Microsoft DNS Server*, for more information about DNS Server boot methods.

*Forwarders*

> Value Type: REG_BINARY (Binary list of IP addresses)
>
> Default: None
>
> The IP address(es) of forwarder(s). This list is also accessible via DNS Manager's **Server Properties → Forwarders** window.

*ForwardingTimeout*

   Value Type: REG_DWORD (Time in seconds)

   Default: 5 seconds

   The time the server waits for a response from each forwarder.

*IsSlave*

   Value Type: REG_DWORD (Boolean)

   Default: 0 (False)

   Valid Range: 0–1 (False, True)

   Makes the DNS Server a forwarding slave server. This value is also accessible via DNS Manager's **Server Properties** → **Forwarders** window and may only be true when a list of forwarders is also set. This use of a slave has no relation to zones—that is, primary master and slave. See Chapter 10, *Advanced Features and Security*, for more information on forwarding and slave servers.

*ListenAddresses*

   Value Type: REG_BINARY (Binary list of IP addresses)

   Default: None

   A list of IP addresses the DNS Server will listen on. On a multihomed host you can configure the DNS Server to accept queries only from specific network interface IP addresses. This value is also accessible via DNS Manager's **Server Properties** → **Interfaces** window. See Chapter 4, *Setting Up the Microsoft DNS Server*, for more information on listening on specific interface addresses.

*BindSecondaries*

   Value Type: REG_DWORD (Boolean)

   Default: 1 (BIND zone transfer compatibility enabled)

   Valid Range: 0–1 (False, True)

   Disables BIND-compatible zone transfers. BIND name servers prior to version 4.9.4 send zone transfers using one resource record per DNS message and only understand this format for incoming zone transfers. To ensure compability with older BIND servers, the Microsoft DNS Server uses this zone transfer format with any non-Microsoft DNS slave server. See Chapter 10 for more information about zone transfer format.

*CleanupInterval*

   Value Type: REG_DWORD (Time in seconds)

   Default: 900 (15 minutes)

   Valid Range: 600–86,400 seconds (10 minutes–24 hours)

Specifies how often the DNS Server will examine its cache to remove expired records. The DNS Server also verifies that it can reach the root name servers at this interval. If no root name servers are reachable, the DNS Server reloads the cache file. Database cleanup is described in more detail in Chapter 10.

*DisableAutoReverseZones*

Value Type: REG_DWORD (Boolean)

Default: 0 (Zones are created)

Valid Range: 0–1 (False, True)

This value controls the automatic creation of three zones: *0.in-addr.arpa, 127.in-addr.arpa,* and *255.in-addr.arpa.* The server's default behavior is to create these zones in memory, which provide reverse mapping for the loop-back IP address 127.0.0.1 and stop other PTR queries to the root name servers. Since the zones have no database files, changing them requires enabling this value (to disable their automatic creation) and creating the zones by hand in DNS Manager. Automatic zones are discussed in Chapter 4.

*NoRecursion*

Value Type: REG_DWORD (Boolean)

Default: 0 (Recursion enabled)

Valid Range: 0–1 (False, True)

Controls whether or not the DNS Server responds to recursive lookups. More information is in Chapter 10.

*RecursionRetry*

Value Type: REG_DWORD (Time in seconds)

Default: 2 seconds

Specifies how long the DNS Server waits for a reply to a nonrecursive query to another name server.

*RecursionTimeout*

Value Type: REG_DWORD (Time in seconds)

Default: 15 seconds

Specifies how long the DNS Server waits before returning an unsuccessful answer to a recursive query. For example, let's say *RecursionTimeout* is set to 15, *RecursionRetry* is set to two, and the server receives a recursive query. To find the answer, the server will send up to eight nonrecursive queries to other name servers before giving up and responding with an error to the original recursive query.

# *Zone-specific Settings*

The DNS Server stores information about every zone for which it is a primary master or slave in the Registry. Even when using a BIND boot file, the server still updates the Registry to reflect the *primary* and *secondary* directives in the file.

Each zone has a separate key under this key:

   *HKEY_LOCAL_MACHINE\SYSTEM\CurrentControlSet\Services\DNS\Zones*

The name of the key is the fully qualified name of the zone—for example, *movie.edu* or *249.249.192.in-addr.arpa*. The root zone has a key named ".", which refers to the root name server cache file unless the server is really a root name server (that is, authoritative for the root zone).

These are the values associated with each zone key:

*DatabaseFile*
>   Value Type: REG_SZ (Zone database file name)
>
>   Default: None
>
>   The name of the zone database file in *%SystemRoot%\system32\dns*. For example, *movie.edu.dns* for the *movie.edu* zone.

*Type*
>   Value Type: REG_DWORD
>
>   Default: None
>
>   Valid Range: 0, 1, or 2 (cache zone, primary zone, or secondary zone, respectively)
>
>   The type of zone. If the server is a root name server, then *Type* under the "." key is set to one, and *DatabaseFile* points to the root zone database file, not a cache file.

*MasterServers*
>   Value Type: REG_BINARY (Binary list of IP addresses)
>
>   Default: None
>
>   Only applicable for secondary zones: the list of master servers from which the server can perform a zone transfer.

*SecondaryServers*
>   Value Type: REG_BINARY (Binary list of IP addresses)
>
>   Default: None
>
>   The list of secondary servers used for NOTIFY and limiting zone transfers to authorized secondaries. Both features are described in Chapter 10.

*SecureSecondaries*

Value Type: REG_DWORD (Boolean)

Default: 0 (False)

Valid Range: 0–1 (False, True)

Specifies if zone transfers are limited to the list of servers in *SecondaryServers*. The default is to not restrict zone transfers.

# *Index*

# About the Author

**Paul Albitz** is a software engineer at Hewlett-Packard. Paul earned a Bachelor of Science degree from the University of Wisconsin, LaCrosse, and a Master of Science degree from Purdue University.

Paul worked on BIND for the HP-UX 7.0 and 8.0 releases. During this time Paul developed the tools used to run the *hp.com* domain. More recently, he has been involved in networking HP's DesignJet plotter. Before joining HP, Paul was a system administrator in the CS Department of Purdue University. As system administrator, Paul ran versions of BIND before BIND's initial release with 4.3 BSD.

Paul and his wife Katherine live in San Diego, California.

**Matt Larson** started Acme Byte & Wire, a company specializing in DNS consulting and training, with Cricket Liu in January 1997. Previously, he worked for Hewlett-Packard, first as Cricket's successor as *hp.com* hostmaster, then as a consultant in HP's Professional Services Organization.

Matt graduated from Northwestern University in 1992 with two degrees: a Bachelor of Arts in computer science and a Bachelor of Music in church music/organ performance. He lives in Bethesda, Maryland, with his wife, Sonja Kahler, and their two pugs. In his spare time, he enjoys playing the 10-rank pipe organ in his house and flying light airplanes.

**Cricket Liu** matriculated at the University of California's Berkeley campus, that great bastion of free speech, unencumbered Unix, and cheap pizza. He went to work for Hewlett-Packard Company after graduation and stayed at HP for nine years.

Cricket began managing the *hp.com* zone after the Loma Prieta earthquake forcibly moved the zone's management from HP Labs to HP's Corporate Offices. He was *hostmaster@hp.com* for over three years, and then joined HP's Professional Services Organization to found HP's Internet consulting program. Cricket currently runs his own DNS consulting and training company, Acme Byte & Wire, with his friend Matt Larson.

Cricket, his wife Paige, and their son Walt live in Colorado with two Siberian Huskies, Annie and Dakota. On warm weekends, you'll probably find them on the flying trapeze.

# Colophon

The animal on the cover of *DNS on Windows NT* is an African white-necked raven (*Corvus albicollis*), a subspecies of raven, the largest of the crow-like birds at about 24 inches long. The sexes look alike; the female is slightly smaller. Perceived as spirited or even impudent, the raven has a distinctive, hoarse, carrying call. They are excellent flyers, hovering and gliding, and are safe in flight from predators. Ravens are scavengers and eat carrion and small live animals, as well as some plants. They sometimes hide and store excess food, and will occasionally carry food in their feet.

African raven nests, built in niches in rocks, are crafted of an underlying stick structure, covered by grass, dirt, and rocks, then smaller twigs with soft materials such as moss or rags, and finally a layer of grass or similar plant material. Ravens lay 3–6 mottled grayish-green eggs, and the young hatch after 18–20 days of incubation. Both parents (a pair mated for life) will change the nest lining materials to adjust for changes in temperature and climate.

The raven is a popular figure, both profane and sacred, in many legends. Ravens, along with their relatives jays and crows, have long been considered omens of evil in folklore, possibly due to the supposed annual tribute in feathers paid to the Devil; this legend is probably based on the molting of feathers every summer, during which the raven stays relatively well hidden—only this and nothing more. The Old Testament lists ravens among "unclean" birds; ravens also fed Elijah by the brook. Other ancient and medieval cultures considered the raven a symbol of virility or wisdom. An ancient Norse saga describes the use of ravens by ocean navigators as guides to land, and Norse mythology describes ravens as scouts for Odin. Native American folklore tells that the raven created the world and its creatures.

Because they prey on locusts, mice, and rats, the white-necked raven is generally welcomed in Africa (despite the occasional theft of domestic fowl). Like that of many other wild animals, the raven's habitat is dwindling with expansion of the human population.

Paula Carroll was production editor for this book; the copyeditor and indexer was Nancy Crumpton; the proofreader, Marleis Roberts; and the production tools specialists, Mike Sierra and Lenny Muellner.

Edie Freedman designed the cover of this book, using a 19th-century engraving from the Dover Pictorial Archive. The cover layout was produced with Quark XPress 3.32 using the ITC Garamond font. Whenever possible, our books use RepKover™, a durable and flexible lay-flat binding. If the page count exceeds RepKover's limit, perfect binding is used.

The inside layout was designed by Nancy Priest and implemented in FrameMaker 5.5 by Mike Sierra. The text and heading fonts are ITC Garamond Light and Garamond Book. The illustrations that appear in the book were created in Macromedia FreeHand 7 and Adobe Photoshop 5 by Robert Romano. This colophon was written by Nancy Kotary.

 # More Titles from O'Reilly

## Windows Software for the WWW

### WebBoard™ 3.0

By O'Reilly & Associates, Inc.
Documentation by Susan B. Peck & Jay York
1st Edition April 1998
CD-ROM & 350-page book
ISBN 1-56592-429-0

The new enterprise-class version of O'Reilly's live chat and multi-threaded web conferencing system adds a score of enhancements sure to make it the discussion server of choice for the most active corporate intranets and public chat areas. *WebBoard™ 3.0* builds on its predecessor's reputation for easy administration and customization with these new features: IRC chat, Microsoft SQL Server 6.5 database support, HTTP logging support, and mailing list support.

### Building Your Own Web Conferences™

By Susan B. Peck & Beverly Murray Scherf
1st Edition March 1997
270 pages, Includes CD-ROM
ISBN 1-56592-279-4

*Building Your Own Web Conferences* is a complete guide for Windows® 95 and Windows NT™ users on how to set up and manage dynamic virtual communities that improve workgroup collaboration and keep visitors coming back to your site. The second in O'Reilly's "Build Your Own..." series, this book comes with O'Reilly's state-of-the-art WebBoard™ 2.0 software on CD-ROM.

### PolyForm™

By O'Reilly & Associates, Inc.
Documentation by John Robert Boynton
1st Edition May 1996
Two diskettes & 146-page book
ISBN 1-56592-182-8

*PolyForm™* is a powerful 32-bit web forms tool that helps you easily build and manage interactive web pages. PolyForm's interactive forms make it easy and fun for users to respond to the contents of your web with their own feedback, ideas, or requests for more information. PolyForm lets you collect, process, and respond to each user's specific input. Best of all, forms that once required hours of complicated programming can be created in minutes because PolyForm automatically handles all of the CGI programming for processing form contents. Requires Windows NT™ 3.51 or higher or Windows® 95.

### WebSite Professional™ V2.0

By O'Reilly & Associates, Inc.
Documentation by Susan B. Peck,
Judy Helfand & Mary Jane Walsh
September 1997
970 pages (2 Vols.), Includes CD-ROM
ISBN 1-56592-327-8

While providing the latest innovations in web server technology, *WebSite Professional™ 2.0* offers more options for creating dynamic sites than any other Windows web server. From programmability and publishing power to commerce and security, it is the most open, flexible, and robust web server on the market. Requires Windows NT™ 4.0 or Windows® 95.

### Building Your Own WebSite™

By Susan B. Peck & Stephen Arrants
1st Edition July 1996
514 pages, Includes CD-ROM,
ISBN 1-56592-232-8

This is a hands-on reference for Windows® 95 and Windows NT™ users who want to host a site on the Web or on a corporate intranet. This step-by-step guide will have you creating live web pages in minutes. You'll also learn how to connect your web to information in other Windows applications, such as word processing documents and databases. The book is packed with examples and tutorials on every aspect of web management, and it includes the highly acclaimed WebSite™ 1.1 server software on CD-ROM.

## Windows NT System Administration

### Learning Perl on Win32 Systems

By Randal L. Schwartz, Erik Olson &
Tom Christiansen
1st Edition August 1997
306 pages, ISBN 1-56592-324-3

In this carefully paced course, leading Perl trainers and a Windows NT practitioner teach you to program in the language that promises to emerge as the scripting language of choice on NT. Based on the "llama" book, this book features tips for PC users and new, NT-specific examples, along with a foreword by Larry Wall, the creator of Perl, and Dick Hardt, the creator of Perl for Win32.

# Windows NT System Administration

## Windows NT in a Nutshell

By Eric Pearce
1st Edition June 1997
364 pages, ISBN 1-56592-251-4

Anyone who installs Windows NT, creates a user, or adds a printer is an NT system administrator (whether they realize it or not). This book features a new tagged callout approach to documenting the 4.0 GUI as well as real-life examples of command usage and strategies for problem solving, with an emphasis on networking. *Windows NT in a Nutshell* will be as useful to the single-system home user as it will be to the administrator of a 1,000-node corporate network.

## Windows NT User Administration

By Ashley J. Meggitt & Timothy D. Ritchey
1st Edition November 1997
218 pages, ISBN 1-56592-301-4

Many Windows NT books introduce you to a range of topics, but seldom do they give you enough information to master any one thing. This book (like other O'Reilly animal books) is different. *Windows NT User Administration* makes you an expert at creating users efficiently, controlling what they can do, limiting the damage they can cause, and monitoring their activities on your system. Don't simply react to problems; use the techniques in this book to anticipate and prevent them.

## Windows NT SNMP

By James D. Murray
1st Edition February 1998
464 pages, Includes CD-ROM
ISBN 1-56592-338-3

This book describes the implementation of SNMP (the Simple Network Management Protocol) on Windows NT 3.51 and 4.0 (with a look ahead to NT 5.0) and Windows 95 systems. It covers SNMP and network basics and detailed information on developing SNMP management applications and extension agents. The book comes with a CD-ROM containing a wealth of additional information: standards documents, sample code from the book, and many third-party, SNMP-related software tools, libraries, and demos.

## Essential Windows NT System Administration

By Æleen Frisch
1st Edition February 1998
486 pages, ISBN 1-56592-274-3

This book combines practical experience with technical expertise to help you manage Windows NT systems as productively as possible. It covers the standard utilities offered with the Windows NT operating system and from the Resource Kit, as well as important commercial and free third-party tools. By the author of O'Reilly's bestselling book, *Essential System Administration*.

## Windows NT Backup & Restore

By Jody Leber
1st Edition May 1998
320 pages, ISBN 1-56592-272-7

Beginning with the need for a workable recovery policy and ways to translate that policy into requirements, *Windows NT Backup & Restore* presents the reader with practical guidelines for setting up an effective backup system in both small and large environments. It covers the native NT utilities as well as major third-party hardware and software.

## Windows NT Server 4.0 for NetWare Administrators

By Robert Bruce Thompson
1st Edition November 1997
756 pages, ISBN 1-56592-280-8

This book provides a fast-track means for experienced NetWare administrators to build on their knowledge and master the fundamentals of using the Microsoft Windows NT Server. The broad coverage of many aspects of Windows NT Server is balanced by a tightly focused approach of comparison, contrast, and differentiation between NetWare and NT features and methodologies.

## Windows NT Desktop Reference

By Æleen Frisch
1st Edition January 1998
64 pages, ISBN 1-56592-437-1

A hip-pocket quick reference to Windows NT commands, as well as the most useful commands from the Resource Kits. Commands are arranged ingroups related to their purpose and function. Covers Windows NT 4.0.

# How to stay in touch with O'Reilly

## 1. Visit Our Award-Winning Web Site

http://www.oreilly.com/

★ "Top 100 Sites on the Web" —*PC Magazine*
★ "Top 5% Web sites" —*Point Communications*
★ "3-Star site" — *The McKinley Group*

Our web site contains a library of comprehensive product information (including book excerpts and tables of contents), downloadable software, background articles, interviews with technology leaders, links to relevant sites, book cover art, and more. File us in your Bookmarks or Hotlist!

## 2. Join Our Email Mailing Lists

### New Product Releases
To receive automatic email with brief descriptions of all new O'Reilly products as they are released, send email to:
**listproc@online.oreilly.com**
Put the following information in the first line of your message (*not* in the Subject field):
**subscribe oreilly-news**

### O'Reilly Events
If you'd also like us to send information about trade show events, special promotions, and other O'Reilly events, send email to:
**listproc@online.oreilly.com**
Put the following information in the first line of your message (*not* in the Subject field):
**subscribe oreilly-events**

## 3. Get Examples from Our Books via FTP

There are two ways to access an archive of example files from our books:

### Regular FTP
- ftp to:
  **ftp.oreilly.com**
  (login: anonymous
  password: your email address)
- Point your web browser to:
  **ftp://ftp.oreilly.com/**

### FTPMAIL
- Send an email message to:
  **ftpmail@online.oreilly.com**
  (Write "help" in the message body)

## 4. Contact Us via Email

**order@oreilly.com**
To place a book or software order online. Good for North American and international customers.

**subscriptions@oreilly.com**
To place an order for any of our newsletters or periodicals.

**books@oreilly.com**
General questions about any of our books.

**software@oreilly.com**
For general questions and product information about our software. Check out O'Reilly Software Online at **http://software.oreilly.com/** for software and technical support information. Registered O'Reilly software users send your questions to: **website-support@oreilly.com**

**cs@oreilly.com**
For answers to problems regarding your order or our products.

**booktech@oreilly.com**
For book content technical questions or corrections.

**proposals@oreilly.com**
To submit new book or software proposals to our editors and product managers.

**international@oreilly.com**
For information about our international distributors or translation queries. For a list of our distributors outside of North America check out:
**http://www.oreilly.com/www/order/country.html**

O'Reilly & Associates, Inc.
101 Morris Street, Sebastopol, CA 95472 USA
TEL     707-829-0515 or 800-998-9938
             (6am to 5pm PST)
FAX     707-829-0104

# International Distributors

## O'REILLY™

O'Reilly & Associates, Inc.
101 Morris Street
Sebastopol, CA 95472-9902
1-800-998-9938

*Visit us online at:*
**http://www.ora.com/**
**orders@ora.com**

# O'REILLY WOULD LIKE TO HEAR FROM YOU

Which book did this card come from?

_____

Where did you buy this book?
- ❏ Bookstore
- ❏ Direct from O'Reilly
- ❏ Bundled with hardware/software
- ❏ Computer Store
- ❏ Class/seminar
- ❏ Other _____

What operating system do you use?
- ❏ UNIX
- ❏ Windows NT
- ❏ Macintosh
- ❏ PC(Windows/DOS)
- ❏ Other _____

What is your job description?
- ❏ System Administrator
- ❏ Network Administrator
- ❏ Web Developer
- ❏ Programmer
- ❏ Educator/Teacher
- ❏ Other _____

❏ Please send me O'Reilly's catalog, containing a complete listing of O'Reilly books and software.

Name _____    Company/Organization _____

Address _____

City _____    State _____    Zip/Postal Code _____    Country _____

Telephone _____    Internet or other email address (specify network) _____

Nineteenth century wood engraving
of a bear from the O'Reilly &
Associates Nutshell Handbook®
*Using & Managing UUCP.*

POST CARD

# BUSINESS REPLY MAIL

FIRST CLASS MAIL   PERMIT NO. 80   SEBASTOPOL, CA

*Postage will be paid by addressee*

**O'Reilly & Associates, Inc.**
101 Morris Street
Sebastopol, CA  95472-9902